—IRISH—
TOURING GUIDE

-IRISH-
TOURING GUIDE

What to do, Where to go, What to see

Salem House
Salem, New Hampshire

Appletree Press
Ireland

Little Hills Press
Sydney

First published in Ireland by The Appletree Press Ltd
7 James Street South, Belfast BT2 8DL
1985

9 8 7 6 5 4 3 2 1

British Library Cataloguing in Publication Data
Irish touring guide: what to do, where to go,
what to see.
1. Ireland—Description and travel—1981
—Guide-books
914.15'04824   DA980
ISBN 0-86281-148-1

First published in the United States by Salem House, 1985
A member of the Merrimack Publishers' Circle,
47 Pelham Road, Salem NH 03079
ISBN 0-88162-049-1
Library of Congress Catalog Card Number 84-052304

First published in Australia and New Zealand by
Little Hills Press, Sydney
ISBN 0 949773 24 7

Gazetteer compiled by Hugh Oram
Additional text: Fergus Mulligan
Photographs: Bord Fáilte, Down District Council, Light Fingers, Media Management and Production
Ltd, John Murphy, Northern Ireland Tourist Board, Waterford Glass Ltd, Office of Public Works
(Dublin). City and town maps: Bord Fáilte, based on the Ordnance Survey of the Republic of Ireland
(Permit No. 4358). The inclusion of Belfast is reproduced from the Ordnance Survey Map with the
sanction of H.M. Stationery Office, Crown Copyright Reserved.
Printed in the U.K.
Road Atlas: printed by John Bartholomew & Son Ltd

The assistance of Bord Fáilte and the Northern Ireland Tourist Board in the preparation of this book
is gratefully acknowledged.

Contents

Introduction

This guide is a comprehensive and up-to-date compilation of facts and ideas to help you plan your holiday in Ireland. The book combines reliable, up-to-the-minute information with background sections on Ireland's history, landscape and customs.

Many visitors are perfectly content to spend their holiday simply exploring the countryside and getting to know the people, but if you have a more specific purpose in making your trip to Ireland — perhaps you're curious to trace your ancestors or eager to participate in a particular festival or musical event — it is well worth consulting our special sections on various aspects of Irish life and culture. Fifteen succinct and informative chapters covering everything from ancient monuments to contemporary theatre will tell you all you need to know and give you essential details of dates, venues, addresses and contacts. We also give you some appetising suggestions for places where you might like to eat, drink and be entertained in traditional Irish style — but the choice is yours. There's so much to see, so much to do, that we can't make all the decisions for you! We've even thought of your last-minute holiday gift and souvenir dilemma — our section on shopping is crammed with ideas, both classic and original, for items you'll treasure long after you've returned home. Our further reading list covers a wide range of topics you might like to read up on — we're sure you'll be keen to explore some new aspect of Irish culture discovered on your travels, whether it be the history of poitín or the art of traditional cookery!

Of all possible holiday destinations, Ireland lends itself especially well to touring. The roads are blissfully quiet and uncrowded, the scenery is spectacular and you'll find no shortage of welcoming guesthouses, farms and hotels. What's more, the whole island can comfortably be covered by bus, car or train in the space of a short holiday. Our self-drive touring ideas have been designed to let you travel through the country's most beautiful spots, both inland and coastal, at your own pace. The suggested routes will take you to lakes, mountains, beaches and famous cities — but feel free to stray from the main roads and thoroughfares when the notion takes you; you'll make your own discoveries and, wherever you end up, you can be sure the locals will give you a warm welcome.

At the heart of the touring guide is our attractively illustrated gazetteer, which you'll find invaluable. Its listings are based around 55 of Ireland's main towns and cities selected on the basis of their cultural, historic, geographic and commercial importance. Whatever attracts you to any of these towns, whether it is a church, art gallery or swimming pool — or even if you just want to know who hires out bicycles or boats — you'll find it here, classed by type. Places of interest and activities in the areas around each of these towns and cities then follow, listed alphabetically.

In the greater Dublin area, the scheme is slightly different: one major section is devoted to Dublin city, and the surrounding areas are

Area Map

Each entry contains several types of information:

covered in three separate sections — Dun Laoghaire (south), Naas (west) and North of Dublin.

Finally, whether you're travelling by bus, car, train or a combination of all three you'll want to see where you're going, so to make things even easier we've included an extensive all-colour map section which is clearly laid out and simple to use.

Abbreviations

Aft: afternoon

BH: Bank Holiday

By arr: visits by arrangements only

C: Roman Catholic

CI: Church of Ireland

D: wheelchair access

EC: early closing

Eve: evening

Inc: including

Opp: opposite

SO: summer only

TIO: Tourist Information Office

History

The first people who settled in Ireland were hunters, probably from Scotland, who arrived in Co. Antrim *c.* 7000 BC. By 3000 BC tribes from the Mediterranean were building megalithic tombs all over Ireland which reveal a high degree of civilisation. The most spectacular are the passage graves at Newgrange, Co. Meath, Carrowmore and Lough Crew, all of which can be visited. The National Museum in Dublin has a collection of masterpieces from this period: gold collars, torcs, dress fasteners and hair ornaments.

The Celts arrived around 300 BC bringing their distinctive culture, laws and customs. The Irish language derives from a dialect of Celtic, and *The Tain* is an epic account of Celtic life at the time.

In the 5th century St Patrick brought Christianity from Britain, establishing monasteries which became not only centres of learning but in effect small towns. Places associated with Patrick include Slane, Co. Meath, where he lit the Paschal fire in defiance of the Druids, Tara where he used the shamrock to convince the high king about the Trinity and Downpatrick where a crude slab marks his grave.

Irish monks produced a large number of beautifully illustrated manuscripts, among them the Books of Durrow, Armagh and Kells, which can be seen in Trinity College Dublin. The monasteries of Clonmacnoise, Glendalough and Kildare drew scholars from all over Europe. In turn Irish missionaries took education and religion to every corner of Europe. At the same time craftsmen were producing exquisite reliquaries, brooches, belts, and personal adornments made of gold and studded with precious stones (see the Ardagh Chalice and the Cross of Cong in the National Museum). This period is rightly known as the golden age.

The wealth of the monasteries and their towns attracted the Vikings, who swept in burning and killing. Distinctive round towers and bell towers were built as a refuge from them. Later the Vikings settled around the coast and founded towns such as Cork, Waterford, Limerick and Dublin. They were finally defeated by Brian Boru at the Battle of Clontarf in 1014.

On his death, inter-kingdom rivalry led to a century of chaos until the Normans arrived from England and brought order and prosperity. They were so well assimilated into Irish society that the English crown decided a reconquest was needed. Ulster put up fierce resistance under Hugh O'Neill and Hugh O'Donnell but they were finally defeated at the Battle of Kinsale in 1601. Their exile and that of the Gaelic aristocracy is known as the 'flight of the earls'. The systematic dispossession of the natives and settlement of migrants from England and Scotland followed. This division of Protestant settler and native Catholic has had repercussions ever since.

The campaign of Oliver Cromwell in Ireland is infamous and lives on in folk memory as the 'curse of Cromwell'. His approach to the Irish problem was drastic: the remaining lands

GPO, O'Connell Street, Dublin

were taken from their owners; those who could prove themselves loyal were exiled to Connacht, while others were put to death. The incompetent James II was deposed from the English throne (for trying to impose Catholicism on the English) by William of Orange in 1688. William then defeated him at the Battle of the Boyne on 12 July 1690. This battle is celebrated each year as Orangeman's Day, a public holiday in Northern Ireland.

James was replaced by Patrick Sarsfield, and the war dragged on until the signing of the Treaty of Limerick, which was accompanied by the imposition of harsh penal laws. This oppression, coupled with grinding poverty and recurring food shortages, set the pattern for more than a century. A series of revolts at the end of the 18th century culminated in the French invasion of Killala, Co. Mayo. Although initially successful it was

finally suppressed with great slaughter.

The Act of Union in 1800 abolished the Dublin parliament and removed power to London. Daniel O'Connell's election to Westminster (which, as a Catholic, he was forbidden to enter) led to the repeal of the more oppressive laws and to Catholic emancipation. A firm believer in non-violence, he came near to the repeal of the union but his final years were clouded by the Great Famine when nearly a million died and two million emigrated.

Parnell became leader of the Home Rule Party in 1877, and, with Gladstone's support, a home rule bill nearly succeeded. Other leaders followed: Arthur Griffith founded Sinn Féin as a non-violent movement and James Larkin and James Connolly became key people in the labour movement. In 1912 the Commons passed the home rule bill. Ireland was to have self-government after World War I.

There was no rejoicing among the Protestants in Ulster. They quickly armed themselves to fight to maintain the link with Britain. In Dublin a group of volunteers decided they could not wait for the end of the war, and began the Easter Rising of 1916. Although unsuccessful and condemned by most Irish people, the execution of its leaders changed public opinion. The Anglo-Irish war lasted from 1919 to 1921.

The Treaty of 1921 gave independence to 26 of the 32 counties; six of the Ulster counties remained under British rule with a parliament in Belfast. A sector of the Republican movement opposed this compromise and a bitter civil war followed, culminating in the death of Michael Collins, the brilliant young Corkman who masterminded the war of independence. World War II imposed great strains on the Free State (economically stagnant for many years) which stayed neutral. Seán Lemass later adopted a more vigorous, expansionist economic policy which brought new prosperity and paved the way for Ireland's entry to the European Economic Community (EEC) in 1972.

Today the Republic of Ireland is a parliamentary democracy with a president as head of state. There are two houses of parliament, the Dáil and the Seanad, and three major political parties, Fianna Fáil, Fine Gael, and the smaller Labour Party.

Northern Ireland has suffered some unrest since 1921. In 1968 the Civil Rights movement called for power sharing and equality in jobs and housing. Since then there has been an upsurge of extremist republican and loyalist paramilitary violence. However, despite its beleaguered image, it is quite safe to visit.

Geography

Ireland, an island in north-west Europe, has an area of 32,595 square miles. At its greatest it is 302 miles long and 171 miles wide and consists of a central lowland surrounded by a broken range of hills and small mountains.

The climate is mild on account of the Gulf Stream, without extremes of heat or cold. Average temperatures in January are 4-7°C and in July 14-16°C, rising occasionally as high as 25°C. May and June are often the sunniest months, and North American visitors in particular will notice that there are many more daylight hours in summer than in the US. Rainfall is heaviest in the mountainous west and lightest in the east but the weather is at all times very changeable. A day of prolonged and depressing drizzle can end with a clear sky, a spectacular sunset and the promise of a sunny day to follow. Even so it is wise to have a raincoat or umbrella to hand while touring.

There are 32 counties and four provinces: Connacht, Leinster, Munster and Ulster. Six of the 9 Ulster counties are part of the United Kingdom and the other 26 form the republic of Ireland. The population of the Republic is (1981) 3,443,405 and of Northern Ireland 1,509,892. Dublin is the capital of the former, with an urban population of about one million.

Provinces and Counties Map

The principal cities and towns are Dublin, Belfast, Cork, Derry, Limerick, Waterford and Galway. Of these only the first three have a population in excess of 100,000.

Food, drink, tobacco, engineering, textiles, chemicals and electronics are the chief manufacturing industries. The recession has caused many redundancies but exports show a steady increase in real terms. The Industrial Development Authority (IDA) conducts a vigorous campaign to attract foreign companies to the Republic with a package of financial incentives for foreign and Irish firms. Many firms from the USA, Britain, Germany, the Netherlands and France among others have located in Ireland. In the north the old reliance on linen and shipbuilding has been largely replaced now by light engineering and textiles, most of it from Britain and located in the east of the province.

Ireland does not have great mineral resources. There are some small coal deposits, cement is quarried at Limerick, Drogheda, Larne, and Cookstown, and there is a large lead and zinc mine at Navan. Natural gas has been discovered off the Cork coast but while oil exploration goes on there has not yet been a major find. Other minerals are

dolomite, gypsum, barytes and salt.

Turf is one natural fuel found in abundance. Bord na Móna, a state company, produces over 4 million tons of peat and 1 million tons of moss peat annually. Production is highly mechanised and much of the peat is used for electricity generation as well as by the domestic and industrial consumer. Other sources of electricity are oil, natural gas, hydroelectric systems and coal.

Farming is a major industry, being mainly of a mixed pastoral nature. Irish beef, lamb and pork, along with dairy products such as cheese, butter, yoghurt and cream, are famous. Output and profitability have greatly increased in recent years, largely as a result of Ireland's entry into the EEC.

The main types of sea fish landed are herring, cod, mackerel and plaice. Shellfish include lobsters, mussels, periwinkles and oysters. Much of this is exported to Europe, where pollution-free Irish seafood is greatly prized. Salmon and trout are taken in large numbers, particularly from inland waters, and are also highly valued.

About 5 per cent of Irish land is under forest. Coniferous trees grow particularly well in Irish soil. Over 350 forests are open to the public, and many are laid out with car parks, picnic areas, nature trails and walks. Among the loveliest are Glenveagh (Co. Donegal), Lough Key (Co. Roscommon), Connemara, Lough Navar (Co. Fermanagh) and the John F. Kennedy park (New Ross, Co. Wexford).

Ireland, as everyone knows, is very green. This is caused by the mild, damp climate which encourages growth. Two areas of great botanical interest may be cited. Around Glengarriff, Co. Cork, which enjoys the full benefit of the Gulf Stream, there is a luxuriant growth of tropical flora such as arbutus, fuchsia and other delightful flowering plants. A trip to Garinish Island, just offshore from Glengarriff, with its beautiful plant collection is well worth while. By contrast the Burren is an area of Co. Clare which resembles a lunar-like landscape of bare, carboniferous limestone. It is 100 square miles in size but in spring and early summer produces a host of exotic orchids, ferns and rare plants.

There are at least 380 wild birds to be seen in Ireland, for migrations goes on all year. The most common species are blackbird, thrush, goldcrest, starling and curlew. Among the indigenous animal species are the Irish hare (once seen on the old three pence coin), the Irish stoat, fox and red deer. Wild deer roam the Kerry and Wicklow mountains and are also to be seen in the Phoenix Park, Dublin.

Irish horse breeding is world famous, being centred on counties Meath and Kildare. The national stud at Tully, Co. Kildare (near the Curragh) can be visited at certain times of the year. There are seven distinct breeds of Irish dog, the best known being the giant Irish wolfhound, the Irish setter and the Irish water spaniel. There is only one reptile, the common lizard, and, thanks to St Patrick, no snakes!

Ancient Monuments

All archaeological remains in Ireland are under state care and most can be easily visited, including those on private land. Please take care to close gates, not to disturb farm animals and to respect the landowner's property. A good detailed map, a pair of stout shoes or boots and occasionally a torch will be useful, especially for the more remote examples. Once you are in the area ask the locals for directions. They will tell you exactly where to find the item — and a lot more besides.

There is a vast number of ancient monuments including dolmens, crannógs, forts, clocháns, tumuli, cairns, passage graves, stone circles, round towers and high crosses. Many of the finest examples have been beautifully photographed by Kenneth McNally for his book *Standing Stones and other monuments of early Ireland,* and it is well worth visiting at least some of these, as they reveal much about how people have lived in Ireland over the last 5,000 years.

Forts were ramparts built of clay (raths) and stone (cahers or cashels). They have given their name to many Irish towns, for example Rathdrum, Rathfriland, Cahirciveen and Cashel. Since there are said to be 40,000 forts it would be hard to miss them. The term was used for any strengthened structure including

Stone circle, Castletownbere, Co. Cork

stockades and cattle enclosures. Staigue Fort in Kerry, Garranes in Cork, Grianan of Aileach in Donegal and Navan Fort near Armagh City are among the best. Tara, once the palace of the high kings of Ireland, has a number of raths.

Dolmens are tombs dating from about 2000 BC and consist of two or more unhewn stones supporting a flat capstone. There is a huge one at Kilternan, Co. Dublin. It is 23 ft long, 17 ft wide and 6 ft thick. Others are at Proleek, Co. Louth, Knockeen, Co. Waterford and Leananny, Co. Down.

Passage Graves are set in a mound of earth or stone with a passage leading to the central chamber, and often have side chambers. Many are 4,500 years old and show a sophisticated knowledge of construction, design and astronomy. They are often decorated with geometrical motifs, spirals, concentric circles, triangles, zigzags, the human face and of course the sun. Their meaning has not been deciphered but presumably they are connected with the religion of the people who built them.

Passage graves often occur in groups and those found in the Boyne valley are superb: Newgrange, Knowth and Dowth. Newgrange is a vast earthen mound penetrated by a long narrow passage. The tumulus is surrounded by a ditch with a number of the original pillar stones in place. A kerb of 97 huge stones (many with spiral motifs) supports a dry wall. The threshold stone is carved with a triple spiral, circles and diamonds about whose meaning we can only speculate.

The passageway is narrow and low and the central chamber artificially lit. However, on one day of the year, the Winter Solstice (21 December), a shaft of light enters the

passage at dawn and for a few minutes strikes the centre of the floor illuminating the chamber. It is by all accounts an extraordinary experience.

Stone circles (cromlechs) are quite rare but can be visited at Lough Gur, Co. Limerick, whose shores have a large number of ancient monuments including forts and tiny remains of stone age dwellings.

Pillar stones or gallans can often be seen in fields alongside the road. The most interesting are indicated by a signpost. Some have traces of carving and many have inscriptions in ogham writing. The letters consist of up to five lines cut above, below or across the stem line and may record a name of event in Irish. They date from about AD 300 and are the earliest form of writing known in Ireland. While it is easy enough to transliterate ogham the meaning is often unclear because the Irish use is very obscure. Dunloe, Co. Kerry, has a number of ogham stones in good condition. One inscription reads 'Cunacena' — probably someone's name. There are many more in Kerry and Cork.

Crannógs are lake dwellings built on a small island, sometimes reached by a causeway. There are crannógs at Fair Head, Co. Antrim, and a splendid reconstruction at Quin, near Shannon Airport in Co. Clare. There the Craggaunowen Project has recreated a number of ancient dwellings and ring forts which vividly show the lifestyle of people in Ireland 3,000 years ago.

Clocháns are the distinctive beehive huts built of stone which were used as monk's cells. Many are on offshore islands such as Bishop's Island, Co. Clare, High Island, Co. Galway, Inishmurray, Co. Sligo, and the breathtakingly beautiful Skellig Michael, Co. Kerry. There are many more accessible ones on the Dingle peninsula, including the delightful Gallarus Oratory.

Round towers are spread evenly across the country, with about 65 examples to be seen. Many are still intact with the distinctive conical cap. They were used as places of refuge and as belfries, usually with the entrance high off the ground. Once the occupants were inside the ladder was drawn up. It is worth climbing at least one round tower just for the view of the surrounding countryside. Among the best are those at Glendalough, Co. Wicklow, Ardmore, Co. Waterford, Devenish, Co. Fermanagh, Clonmacnoise, Co. Offaly and that beside St Canice's Cathedral, Kilkenny.

High Crosses vary from small inscribed stones to massive free-standing sculptures with beautifully detailed carvings and a celtic circle around the head of the cross. Good examples are Muiredach's Cross at Monasterboice, Co. Louth and Clonmacnoise, where a number of inscribed crosses are individually displayed. Both sites have round towers and extensive monastic remains. Another high cross and the stump of a round tower are located at Drumcliff, Co. Sligo, burial place of the poet William Butler Yeats

Architecture

The Rock of Cashel, once the palace of the kings of Muster, dominates the surrounding plain and has a fine collection of early Irish buildings. The 13th-century cathedral, although a ruin, is a most impressive edifice. Nearby there is a round tower and the delightful 11th-century Cormac's Chapel built in Irish-Romanesque style. It is similar to Clonfert cathedral with its ornate yet delicate doorway.

Gothic architecture was brought to Ireland by the Normans and the expanding monastic orders. The ruined Mellifont Abbey which still has part of its cloister and octagonal lavabo is an early example. Boyle Abbey, also built around 1200, retains its solid arcade but St Patrick's Cathedral, Dublin, and St Canice's, Kilkenny, are perhaps the finest examples of gothic architecture intact today. Also worth a visit is Jerpoint Abbey which has a 15th-century tower and an elaborately decorated cloister. Nearby is the cleanly restored Duiske Abbey at Grainguenamanagh with its outstanding processional doorway and delightful medieval tiles (ask to see them).

Castles or fortified houses are found in great numbers in Ireland. One of the largest is Trim Castle, whose extensive ruins cover several acres. It was built in 1170 by Hugh de Lacy. Reginald's Tower in Waterford dates from the same period and is a circular building with a conical roof and walls 10 ft thick. Once used as a prison, it now houses a small museum. Blarney Castle is a large tower with a parapet 83 ft from the ground and houses the famous Blarney Stone, which promises eloquence to all who kiss it. The 15th-century Bunratty Castle near Shannon Airport has been carefully restored and holds a good collection of old Irish furniture and tapestries. In the grounds is the Folk Park, where typical thatched farmhouses, fishermen's and labourers' cottages have been reconstructed.

Kilkenny city has a number of first rate buildings. The medieval castle of the Dukes of Ormonde stands on a commanding site above the River Nore. Rothe House dates from the 16th century and is built around a cobbled courtyard. Other noteworthy buildings are the Black Abbey, the Tholsel and St Canice's Cathedral.

Among other superb castles worth visiting are Carrickfergus, Cahir, Malahide, Dunguaire, Thoor Ballylee (once home of W. B. Yeats) and Dublin Castle. An outstanding unfortified 16th-century house is that of the Ormondes at Carrick-on-Suir. Town walls have survived in part at Limerick, Dublin, Clonmel, Wexford and Kilmallock. The walls of Derry are almost complete and give an excellent view over the whole city.

Dating from the late 17th century is one of Ireland's prize buildings, the Royal Hospital, Kilmainham. Originally an old soldiers' home, it is in the form of an arcaded quadrangle with dormer windows on its two stories. It also has a spacious hall and a beautiful clock tower.

Classical architecture came to Ireland in the early 18th century when Castletown House was built for William Connolly, speaker of the Irish House of Commons. Many of the finest buildings, including Trinity College, the Bank of Ireland (old Parliament House), Leinster House, the Rotunda, the Custom House, Powerscourt House, the Four Courts, the Marino Casino, Carton House, the King's Inns and the City hall were built in the Palladian. style. They are the supreme jewels of Irish architecture. This was also the period when the gracious Georgian squares of Dublin were laid out — Merrion Square, Fitzwilliam Square, Parnell Square, Mountjoy Square and St Stephen's Green. The interiors of many of these buildings are equally beautiful. Visit Russborough House, Castletown, Powerscourt Town House, 85-86 St Stephen's Green, 20 Lr Dominick Street or 9 Henrietta Street (by appointment) and you will appreciate the exquisite plasterwork, carving and decor of these magnificent houses. Outside Dublin several towns were built along classical lines, for example Tyrellspass, Hillsborough, Birr, Armagh, Portarlington and Westport.

Cahir Castle, Co. Tipperary

The 19th century saw an upsurge in church building. Noted examples are Killarney and Enniscorthy cathedrals — both by Pugin the gothic revivalist — St Finbarr's, Cork and St Saviour's, Dublin. The railway companies have also left a valuable heritage in the large number of elegant stations. In Dublin the terminals of Heuston, Connolly, the Broadstone and Harcourt Street are gracious buildings. When travelling by train it is also worth noting the many excellent country stations, especially en route to Galway/Sligo and Kilkenny. Their structure has, for the most part, scarcely altered since the day they opened. Around the time the government built a series of sturdy coastal forts known as Martello towers to counter the threat of a French invasion. The best known is probably James Joyce's tower at Sandycove, south of Dublin.

Not all interesting buildings were designed for the wealthy. All over Ireland the traditional thatched cottage may be seen, especially in the west and in Adare. There are also elaborate, brightly painted shop fronts in every town along with neat little churches and simple public houses that have escaped 'modernisation'. The local Protestant church is usually older and or more interest than its Catholic counterpart.

Twentieth-century architecture is the subject of some controversy. Most towns have undergone ribbon housing development, and modern rural bungalows sometimes show a depressing sameness with unimaginative siting. The population of inner cities has fallen as people move to the suburbs, and a number of architectural horrors have been inflicted on Dublin — notably O'Connell Bridge House and the ESB headquarters in Fitzwilliam Street. However, some new buildings blend happily into their background, such as the Irish Life Centre in Abbey Street and the corporation housing schemes in Ringsend, the Coombe and along the south quays of the Liffey. A great addition to the Smithfield area is the attractive Irish Distillers' building, while the Central Bank, the Arts Block in Trinity College and the Abbey Theatre deserve favourable mention.

Literature and Theatre

From the 6th to the 17th century most literature was composed in Irish. Some has been lost but a good deal is still available in the original and in translation. The early monks produced a large body of poetry, much of it religious, but they also recorded a great deal of pre-Christian material. Perhaps the best known of these is the *Tain Bo Cuailnge* (the Cattle Raid of Cooley). This is the epic account of the raid by the men of Connacht led by Queen Maeve to capture the marvellous bull owned by the men of Ulster. It has been beautifully translated by Thomas Kinsella, among others. The *Navigatio Brendani* (Voyage of St Brendan) is another example of this type of writing.

Later classics include the *Book of the Dun Cow* and the *Book of Leinster* which date from the 12th century and feature the adventures of Cuchulain, Fionn McCool, Oisin, the Fianna and other legendary heroes who succumbed to Patrick's crozier. These works provided great inspiration for writers such as Yeats and James Stephens.

Also dating from this period are the *Annals of the Four Masters,* a magnificent historical record of events in Ireland from the earliest times. Much of our knowledge of Irish history comes from the work of these Donegal scholars.

In the 18th century a schoolmaster from Clare, Brian Merriman, composed *The Midnight Court* (Cúirt an Mheán Oíche), a witty satire on the reluctance of Irish men to marry. Writing later in the same century Jonathan Swift was the first Irish author to win fame for work in English. He lampooned social and political mores at the time and the English attitude to Ireland in *A Tale of a Tub, A Modest Proposal* and *Gulliver's Travels.* Contemporary with him was George Berkeley, the noted philosopher and author of *Principles of Human Knowledge.*

Grand Opera House, Belfast

Other outstanding figures of this period are Edmund Burke, the philosopher and orator whose statue stands outside Trinity College and Oliver Goldsmith, the gentle author of *The Vicar of Wakefield, The Deserted Village* and *She Stoops to Conquer.* Richard Brinsley Sheridan is remembered for his dramatic works including *The Rivals* and *The School for Scandal* while Thomas Moore gained a reputation as a poet, author and musician. The brilliant wit and bohemian lifestyle of Oscar Wilde coupled with his novel *The Picture of Dorian Gray* and comedies such as *Lady Windermere's Fan* and *The Importance of Being Earnest* have made his name immortal.

George Bernard Shaw had no doubt of his ability and compared his best works *Arms and the Man, Saint Joan* and *Candida* to those of

Shakespeare; his *Pygmalion* was the basis for *My Fair Lady.* In 1925 he won the Nobel Prize for literature. William Butler Yeats is probably Ireland's best known poet and has had an immense influence on Irish letters. He won the Noble Prize in 1923. Collections of his poetry and plays are now available in many languages. In celebration of life on the western seaboard John Millington Synge wrote his plays *Riders to the Sea* and *The Playboy of the Western World.*

The Blasket Islands off the Kerry coast were Irish-speaking and have produced three great writers: Peig Sayers *(An Old Woman's Reflections),* Tomás Ó Criomhtháin *(An t-Oileanach)* and Muiris Ó Súilleabháin *(Fiche Blian ag Fas).* They lyrically portrayed the hard but contented life of the islanders at the turn of the century. *Irish Fairy Tales* and the exquisitely written *The Crock of Gold* are the fanciful work of James Stephens while Sean O'Casey is remembered for his tragicomedies *The Shadow of a Gunman, Juno and the Paycock,* and *The Plough and the Stars.* James Joyce, the author of *Ulysses* and *Dubliners,* now has a worldwide following.

Among the leading contemporary poets are Patrick Kavanagh, Louis MacNiece, Thomas Kinsella, Seamus Heaney, John Montague, Richard Murphy and Derek Mahon. Prominent prose writers include masters of the short story such as Sean O'Faolain, Frank O'Connor, Liam O'Flaherty, Bryan McMahon, Benedict Kiely, Mary Lavin and James Plunkett. Brian Moore, Francis Stuart, Flann O'Brien and Edna O'Brien have also been widely praised. Of the major living Irish playwrights mention must be made of Samuel Beckett (another Nobel Prize winner), Brian Friel, Tom Murphy, M. J. Molloy and Hugh Leonard.

The founding of the Abbey Theatre in 1904 by Lady Gregory, Edward Martyn and W. B. Yeats marks a turning point for Irish drama. The early years of the Abbey were marked by great controversy. One of the first productions was *The Playboy of the Western World* and it caused a small riot when members of the audience disrupted the performance, saying it was an attack on rural life. This was one of the occasions when Yeats delivered his famous rebuttal of the audience's narrow-mindedness. Such protests occurred from time to time when any works considered remotely salacious or critical of the old Gaelic-Catholic way of life were performed. Indeed at one point such a disrupted performance became the guarantee of a work's success.

These events marked the growing pains of the literary movements as Irish writers fought to free themselves from the suffocating constraints of a narrow nationalist philosophy. It was a time when any foreign work of art was considered suspect and led to the vicious and absurd censorship laws which plagued Irish writing for half a century, driving many of the finest authors into exile.

Happily times have changed and there is now a diverse richness in the literary and theatrical diet which is unsurpassed. Modern farce, Shakespeare, classical pieces and modern Irish plays can now be seen happily co-existing. Every large town has its own amateur drama group which puts on at least one production a year. Ask at the tourist office for details of amateur dramatics in your area.

As the National Theatre, the Abbey is today dedicated to producing the best works of Irish and international playwrights. Michael Mac-Liammoir and Hilton Edwards set up the Gate Theatre in 1928 to produce a broad range of plays while the Project Arts Centre is an experimental theatre. In addition there are a large number of repertory groups, amateur enthusiasts, lunchtime plays and pub theatres offering a rich programme of drama throughout Ireland. Among them is Siamsa Tire, the National Folk Theatre established in Tralee, which presents authentic folk productions in the Kerry area.

Folklore

Ireland has a vast heritage of folklore going back to pre-Christian times. The sagas, epics, legends, stories, poems, proverbs, riddles, sayings, curses and prayers are all part of that tradition. Much of it comes by way of the seanachie, the storyteller who sat beside the fire and enchanted his audience with tales of times past. Often he was a nomad and moved from house to house earning his bed and board by storytelling. The characters featured in the main tales are identified by Ronan Coghlan in his *Pocket Dictionary of Irish Myth and Legend,* a comprehensive handbook which will introduce you to the best known legendary persons and events. The Department of Irish Folklore at University College, Dublin, has recorded and preserved a great part of the country's heritage, and there are many fascinating books on various aspects of the topic, such as Patrick Logan's enthusiastic guide to Ireland's 'unofficial' medicine, *Irish Country Cures.*

Fleadh Ceoil, Ballycastle, Co. Antrim

Almost every sizeable town in Ireland has a small museum where the life and history of the local community is documented in antiquities and relics of the past. A good place to start is the National Museum in Dublin which has a large collection dating from pre-history to the recent past. Also in Dublin are the Civic Museum for items relating to the capital, the Heraldic Museum where you can trace your ancestors, the Guinness Museum, dedicated to Dublin's famous brew, and the Royal Hospital, Kilmainham, recently re-opened, which has a superb array of folklore items gathered over many years. Other recommended museums are the Ulster Museum in Belfast, the Ulster Folk and Transport Museum, Co. Down, Rothe House in Kilkenny, the James Joyce Museum at Sandycove, Enniscorthy Museum, Co. Wexford, Limerick and Galway Museums, and Kinsale Museum, in Co. Cork, which displays mementoes of the ill-fated *Lusitania* sunk off Kinsale in 1915. A number of towns have developed heritage centres and folk parks where the richness of local life is displayed in a less formal setting. Fine examples are located at Damer House, Roscrea (Co. Tipperary), Glencolumbkille (Co. Donegal), Bunratty (Co. Clare), Cultra (Co. Down) and the Ulster-American Folk Park near Omagh (Co. Tyrone).

A delightful way to see a collection of old furniture, farming implements and kitchenware is to visit one of the many pubs displaying such times and imbibe a pint and some culture at the same time. Among them are the Seanachie (Dungarvan, Co. Waterford), Durty Nelly's (Bunratty, Co. Clare), the Asgard (Westport, Co. Mayo) and the Hideout (Kilcullen, Co. Kildare).

Craftworkers now produce a wide range of first class products such as pottery, ceramics, leatherwork, wood carving, jewelry, weaving,

basketry, linen, lace, crystal, tweed, pewter and other quality souvenirs. Almost everywhere you will find a shop selling the products of local craftworkers, many of whom employ techniques handed from one generation to the next. Craft centres where these skills can be seen in practice will be found at Marlay Grange and Powerscourt Town House in Dublin and at Muckross House, Killarney (see also Shopping).

Music

Like the seanachie, the music teacher of old once wandered the country, playing an instrument and teaching music and dance to his pupils. The best known is probably Turlough O'Carolan, the blind harpist and composer of the late 1600s. His beautiful lilting airs are now available on record. Two 19th-century composers are particularly outstanding: John Field, the inventor of the nocturne, and Thomas Moore, whose famous *Irish Melodies* includes the 'Last Rose of Summer' and 'The Vale of Avoca'. There is a monument to Moore at the Meeting of the Waters near Avoca, in Co. Wicklow, where he is is said to have composed this song; it is a magical spot. Notable among modern composers are A. J. Potter, Gerard Victory, Seoirse Bodley and Seán Ó Riada, who wrote the haunting *Mise Éire*.

It is easy to join in a traditional ballad session. Traditional music and dance is jealously guarded by Comhaltas Ceoltóirí Éireann which organises music festivals all over the country and has regular sessions at its Monkstown headquarters in south Dublin. Many pubs also hold impromptu ballad evenings. In Dublin they occur regularly at O'Donoghue's, the Abbey Tavern, the Chariot Inn, Slattery's, the Stag's Head, and the Old Shieling. For an idea of the kind of traditonal songs you can expect to hear have a look at *The Wind That Shakes The Barley*, a selection of popular Irish folk songs put together by Gareth James. Irish cabaret can be seen at Jury's, the Braemor Rooms, the Burlington and Clontarf Castle. There are nightly sessions also at the Granary in Limerick, McCann's and O'Connor's in Doolin, near Ennis, Co. Clare, Duchas in Tralee, Teach Beg in Cork and O'Flaherty's in Dingle, but every town has at least one pub with music. All you have to do is stroll around until you hear singing or the sound of an accordian, tin whistle or the wail of uileann pipes. You can even acquire your own personal tin whistle tutor in the form of a kit devised by Brian and Eithne Vallely. Their *Making Music: The Tin Whistle* consists of a real tin whistle, an instruction book and a cassette tape of recorded demonstration to set you on your way.

The recently opened National Concert Hall in Dublin has become the centre for music in Ireland. There is a musical event there every day of the year ranging from classical to jazz, traditional, folk music, piano recitals and pop concerts. There are two principal orchestras, the Radio Telefís Éireann Symphony Orchestra in the Republic and the Ulster Orchestra in Northern Ireland. Both can be heard throughout the year at the National Concert Hall in Dublin and the Ulster Hall in Belfast respectively, with occasional performances in other centres. The Dublin Grand Opera Society has one or two seasons in the Gaiety Theatre, Dublin, and at the Opera House, Cork. In Dublin, other concerts and recitals take place in the Royal Dublin Society, Ballsbridge, the National Stadium, the Player-Wills Theatre and the Examination Hall of Trinity College.

During the winter months musicals and light opera are performed in many provincial towns by amateur groups, culminating in the Waterford Festival of Light Opera. For those who like them discos and night clubs will be found in the major cities, sometimes attached to hotels. In Dublin the area around Leeson Street and Baggot Street has a number of such places.

Festivals

Wherever you go in Ireland you can't avoid coming across a festival. They range from the prestigious Dublin Horse Show to small celebrations of some aspect of local life which happen almost spontaneously. Many festivals centre on music, dancing, food, drink and sport and in every case the visitor is welcome to participate by joining in the fun or simply watching from the sidelines.

Some of the best known are the Rose of Tralee Festival, a week-long Irish beauty contest which draws the comely daughters of exiles from as far afield as Australia and the USA. The Galway Oyster Festival offers the chance of sampling delicious Irish shellfish in the pleasant city of Galway, washed down with Guinness, of course, while the Yeats Summer School is a gathering of the followers of Ireland's foremost poet. The Wexford Opera Festival has international status and attracts world stars but you need to book months in advance.

There are many more which take in dancing, traditional music, drama, steam traction, boating, agricultural shows and sports of all kinds. In fact there are very few you need to book beforehand so look through the following list and plan your vacation to take in those that interest you most. Dates and venues may change so check with the tourist office on arrival.

Calendar of Events

March:
Irish Motor Show, Royal Dublin Society, Ballsbridge.
St Patrick's Day, 17 March: national holiday with parades in Dublin and many other centres.
Irish International Boat Show, Dublin.

April:
Spring Season of Opera, Dublin Grand Opera Society
Galway Arts Festival.

May:
Spring Show, Royal Dublin Society, Ballsbridge: a superb display of Irish agriculture, horses, cattle and industry.
Cork Choral and Folk Dance Festival, City Hall.
Pan Celtic Week: cultural events from all the Celtic countries, Killarney.
Belfast Civic Festival.
Dublin Grand Opera Season, Dublin and Cork.
Tipperary Remembers Weekend, Tipperary Town.
International 3-day event, Punchestown Racecourse.
Dundalk Internatioanl Amateur Theatre Festival.
Fleadh Nua, traditional Irish dance, music and song, Ennis.
Sligo School of Landscape Painting.
Royal Ulster Agricultural Show, Belfast.
Listowel Writers' Week.

June:
Carling Country Music Festival, Cork.
Festival of Tipperary.
Music Festival in Great Irish Houses: recitals by world famous artists in lovely 18th-century mansions.
Glengarriff Festival.
Spancilhill Horse Fair, Ennis.
An Tostal, Drumshanbo: a festival of dance, ballads and traditional singing.
Dun Laoghaire Summer Festival.
Ballybunion Batchelor Festival.
Dublin International Organ Festival.
Discover Your Irish Family History, Galway.
West Cork Festival, Clonakilty.
Wexford Strawberry Fair, Enniscorthy.

July:
Willie Clancy Summer School, Miltown Malbay.
Drimoleague Festival.
Festival of Humour, Shannon.
Schull Festival.
Cobh International Folk Dance Festival.
Kerry Summer Painting School, Cahirciveen.
Bridge Congress, Ballina.
Glens of Antrim Feis, Glenariff: music, dancing, sports.
Queen of Connemara Festival, Oughterard.
Bandon Week.
Skibbereen Annual Show.
Orangeman's Day, 12 July: parades throughout Northern Ireland.
Mary From Dungloe Festival, Dungloe.
Sham Fight, Scarva, re-enacts Battle of the Boyne.
Ulster Steam Traction Rally, Shane's Castle.

August:
Ballyshannon International Folk Festival.
Gorey Arts Week.
O'Carolan Harp and Music Festival, Keadue.
Stradbally Steam Rally.
Claddagh Festival, Galway.
Sligo School of Landscape Painting.
Irish Antique Dealers' Fair, Dublin.
Dublin Horse Show, Royal Dublin Society.

August (cont.);

Granard Harp Festival.
Puck Fair, Killorglin.
Percy French Festival, Newcastle, Co. Down.
Oul' Lammas Fair, Ballycastle — one of the oldest and biggest fairs in Ireland.
Wild Rose Festival, Manorhamilton.
Connemara Pony Show, Clifden.
Ulster Grand Prix, motorcycling, Belfast.
Schull Regatta.
Carroll's Irish Open Golf Tournament, Royal Dublin Golf Club.
Birr Vintage Week.
Merriman Summer School, Lahinch.
Limerick Show.
Carlingford Oyster Festival.
Letterkenny International Folk Festival.
Fleadh Cheoil na hÉireann: top festival for traditional music, song, dance; location changes each year.
Kilkenny Arts Week.
Galway Races — more than just horse racing.
Rose of Tralee Festival.
Vintage Car Rally, Inistioge.
Wexford Mussel Festival.

September:

Salthill Festival.
Cork Folk Festival.
International Angling Festival, Drumconrath.
Waterford International Festival of Light Opera.
Listowell Harvest Festival and Races.
Lisdoonvarna Folk Festival.
All Ireland Hurling and Football Finals, Dublin.
Galway Oyster Festival.
Phoenix Park Motor Races.

October:

Castlebar International Song Festival.
Kinsale Gourmet Festival.
Fruits de Mer, Kenmare.
Flower Festival, St Nicholas, Galway.
Ballinasloe October Fair.
Wexford Opera Festival.
Cork Jazz Festival.
Irish National Stamp Exhibiton, Royal Dublin Society.

November:

Belfast Festival at Queen's
Dublin Indoor International Showjumping, Royal Dublin Society.

Sport

The traditional Irish games are known as gaelic games and include hurling (very old), football, handball and camogie. The Gaelic Athletic Association (GAA) organises hundreds of local clubs, and county teams compete in hurling and gaelic football at the All Ireland finals each year in Croke Park, Dublin. Hurling is a fast game played with wooden hurley sticks while gaelic foodball resembles Australian rules football.

There are over 200 golf courses in Ireland including several of championship standard. They are sited in some beautiful locations and welcome visitors. Horse racing is a national passion and race meetings go on most of the year. The Irish Grand National is run at Fairyhouse on Easter Monday and the Irish Sweeps Derby at the Curragh in June. Bloodstock sales are conducted at Kill, Co. Kildare, and at Ballsbridge. A list of stables which hire out horses can be had from the tourist board (Bord Failte and the NITB).

Ireland's waters teem with fish and offer first-class sport. Salmon and sea trout can be fished at little or no cost, depending on the location, and free coarse fishing is available everywhere. The major sea angling centres are Kinsale, Valentia, Kilmore, Rosslare, Achill and Westport. For a complete guide to every aspect of the sport, including details of licence requirements, tackle centres and angling methods, see *Fishing in Ireland* (edited by Hugh Oram). Fieldsports in general are widely followed, and expert advice and information on hunting, shooting and fishing can be found in the comprehensive *Irish Fieldsports and Angling Handbook* compiled by Albert Titterington. Yachting and windsurfing are popular in Cork, Dun Laoghaire, Howth and Bangor with a number of sailing schools in Dublin, Cork and Kerry.

Many other sports have a good following among participants and spectators including squash, rowing, tennis, swimming, scuba diving, greyhound racing, basketball, road bowling, cycling and flying, to name but a few. Soccer is widely played and rugby reaches its peak during the international season when Ireland plays against England, Scotland and Wales for the Triple Crown. Whatever sport you follow you will be able to enjoy it in Ireland.

Hurling final, Croke Park, Dublin

Food and Eating Out

Four thousand years ago the Irish cooked enormous joints of meat by filling a ditch with water and dropping in heated stones to keep the water boiling. Recent duplicate experiments proved that this method works perfectly although it seems rather troublesome! In pre-Christian times the feasts at Tara and other royal palaces were known to go on for several weeks without a break. Since then the Irish have lost little of their enthusiasm for food although appetites are now more moderate.

A unique pleasure of a stay in Ireland is enjoying the unpretencious but delicious native cooking. Fresh ingredients simply prepared and served without fuss make eating in Ireland a real pleasure. The rich pastures produce meat of the highest quality so that beef, lamb and dairy products like cream, cheese and butter are second to none. Among the tempting dishes on offer are Limerick ham, Irish stew, bacon and cabbage, Galway oysters, sirloin steak and onions, game of all sorts, smoked salmon, Dublin Bay prawns, spring lamb, grilled trout, fresh farm eggs and delicious brown soda bread. Having sampled these, you'll want to recreate the dishes at home, and there are plenty of fine cookery books to choose from — notably John Murphy's *Traditional Irish Recipes* and Mary Kinsella's *An Irish Farmhouse Cookbook*. In each case the basic ingredients are so good that elaborate sauces are unnecessary to bring out the flavour of the food.

The humble potato is appreciated in Ireland as nowhere else and a plate of steaming, floury 'spuds' with butter, salt and a glass of milk is a meal in itself. Indeed potatoes are the principal ingredients of several dishes which once formed the bulk of the country-man's diet. Colcannon is mashed potato with butter and onions. Boxty is grated potato fried in bacon fat. Potato cakes are often served with breakfast or high tea but are delicious anytime.

It is difficult to suggest food items to take home as dairy products and the like do not travel well. However no-one should leave Ireland without at least one side of smoked salmon which keeps fresh for up to ten days. Whiskey cake, brack and soda bread can also be carried easily.

An Irish breakfast is a substantial affair: fruit juice, cereals, bacon, egg, sausage and tomato, brown bread, toast, tea or coffee. Many pubs serve tasty lunches ranging from a simple sandwich to a full meal and this is a pleasant way to break up a day's sight-seeing. Visit Bewley's in Grafton St or Westmoreland St, if in Dublin, for excellent tea, coffee and cakes, or one of the tea rooms attached to many of the stately homes. For dinner eat in your hotel or choose a restaurant to suit your taste and pocket from the list provided by the tourist board or from the book-let of the Irish Country Houses and Restaurants Association. Some people prefer to go

Restaurant Na Mara, Dun Laoghaire

Irish Soda Bread

8 ozs wholemeal flour
1 teaspoon baking soda
2 teaspoons salt
1 pint buttermilk
8 ozs white flour
3 teaspoons baking powder
1 egg, beaten

Sift flour, soda, baking powder, salt. Mix buttermilk, egg and stir in. Knead all ingredients until smooth. Shape into a flat cake on greased paper. Mark a deep cross on the top and bake in preheated oven 190°C, 375°F, Mark 5 for 35-40 minutes.

out to a hotel to eat and this is quite acceptable. If you're still hungry after that you could visit a wine bar for a nightcap and a plate of smoked salmon. The next day you can start all over again!

International cooking is available in Ireland and includes Italian, French, Indian, Chinese, Greek, Russian and Japanese. There is also a wide price range from a simple one-course meal to haute cuisine. It is worth looking for restaurants which have the Bord Failte award for excellence, an independent commendation of good and reasonable value. In addition to table d'hôte and à la carte menus many restaurants also participate in the special value tourist menu scheme. This involves offering a three-course meal at a fixed price and is usually excellent value. Look for the symbol or ask Bord Failte for a list of participating restaurants. In Northern Ireland the Tourist Board publishes a useful booklet called 'Let's Eat Out' which will help you decide where to go.

Recommending restaurants is a highly risky business and the tourist is advised to use the restaurant guides available which give information on price range, opening hours and specialities. The following Dublin restaurants

have been highly praised. For a tasty lunch try the Kilkenny Shop (Nassau St), Mitchell's (Kildare St), Midday's (Abbey Theatre), the National Gallery (Merrion Square), the Municipal Gallery (Parnell Square) or any of the very pleasant Bewley's cafés in Grafton St, Westmoreland St and South Great George's St. You could also drop into one of the many pubs serving lunch such as the Stag's Head (Dame Court), Henry Grattan (Lr Baggot St), Kitty O'Shea's (Upr Grand Canal St), or Foley's (Merrion Row). For dinner try Restaurant Na Mara (Dun Laoghaire), Locks (Portobello), Kilmartin's (Upr Baggot St), Murph's (Batchelor's Walk), the Granary (Essex St), Nico's (Dame St), Trocadero (Andrews St), Digby's (Dun Laoghaire) or the Old Bray (Bray). The Powerscourt Town House Centre (South William St) also has several excellent restaurants and coffee bars.

Outside Dublin the Cork/Kerry region is said to be excellent for eating, with Kinsale as the gourmet capital of Ireland. Other recommended restaurants include Ballymaloe House, the Arbutus Lodge (both near Cork), Aherne's (Youghal), Doyle's Seafood Bar (Dingle), the Park Hotel (Kenmare), Ballylickey House (Bantry), Renvyle House Hotel (Connemara), the Galley Floating Restaurant (New Ross), Dunderry Lodge (Navan), Durty Nelly's (Bunratty), Restaurant St John's (Fahan), Eyre House Restaurant (Galway), Dunraven Arms Hotel (Adare), Armstrong's Barn (Annamoe) and the West Wing Restaurant at Castletown House. In Northern Ireland try Blade's (Comber, Co. Down), Balloo House (Killinchy, Co. Down), The Nutgrove (Downpatrick), or the Carriage (Helen's Bay). There are many, many more and part of the fun will be discovering your own eating place.

Pubs and Drink

The Irish have always had a close relationship with drink. Public houses (as bars are called) began as illicit drink shops or shebeens where people met to exchange news and drink poitín, a raw fiery spirit whose history is traced in John McGuffin's entertaining book *In Praise of Poteen*. Pubs are still very much a social centre and a convivial meeting place where you can chat to local people in informal surroundings.

Opening hours are 11 a.m. – 11 or 11.30 p.m. on weekdays and 12.30 – 2 p.m. and 4 – 10 p.m. on Sundays. In Dublin there is a convention known as the 'holy hour' when all pubs close between 2.30 and 3.30 p.m. All pubs close on Sundays in the north.

Hugh McBride's, Dunseverick, Co. Antrim

Many pubs have preserved their original decor with features such as solid mahogany bar furniture, brass lamps, lovely old mirrors and stained glass. To experience a traditional Irish pub it is best to head for one of these and avoid brash, modern places. There are over 600 pubs in Dublin alone and many are excellent. The following is just a representative sample of the best but there are lots more worth exploring.

Doheny and Nesbitt's (Merrion Row) has kept the original interior and has a delightful little snug. This is a small enclosed room with a hatch opening directly on to the bar for discreet imbibing and is found in many pubs. Toner's (Baggot St) has loads of atmosphere and traditional music and so has O'Donoghue's nearby, Neary's (Chatham St) is a pleasant watering hole with an attractive old bar while the Stag's Head (Dame Court)

is noted for its beautiful stained glass and highly ornate snug. There is a fine collection of cartoons, photographs and drawings of noted customers in the Palace Bar (Fleet St) and Mulligan's (Poolbeg St) has a low beam inscribed 'John Mulligan estd. 1782'. Ryan's (Parkgate St) is perfectly preserved and has lovely old bar furniture.

Other traditional pubs worth visiting on a pub crawl are McDaid's, Bowe's, Davy Byrne's, the Abbey Mooney, the Long Hall, the Auld Dubliner, Kitty O'Shea's, Conway's, Keogh's, Mulligan's (Stoneybatter), the Brazen Head, O'Brien's and the International.

Outside the capital you will find every Irish town is well endowed with pubs. You should have no trouble finding a welcoming hearth, a blazing turf fire and a cheering glass. But just in case you're stuck head for one of the following: Kate O'Brien's (Fermoy), the Breffni Inn (Dromod), Dan Lowry's, Teach Beag or the Vineyard in Cork, the Seanachie, Dungarvan and Kate Kearney's (Killarney), Taylor's (Moyasta), O'Shea's (Borris), The Thatch (Ballysodare), Crown Liqor Saloon and Robinson's (Belfast), Bulman Summer Cove, The Spaniard (Kinsale), Durty Nelly's (Bunratty), The Abbey Tavern (Howth), the Granary, South's and Hogan's (Limerick), O'Flaherty's (Dingle).

When someone asks for a pint they usually mean Guinness, the dark stout with a white head which is synonymous with Ireland. There is hardly a pub in the country that does not stock Guinness on draught or in bottles. Try it on its own or with some oysters. Other top quality beers are Murphy, Macardle's, Smithwick's, Bass, Harp and Beamish.

Visitors are welcome at the Guinness brewery in Dublin, Smithwick's in Kilkenny, Beamish in Cork and Harp and Macardles' in Dundalk and will be invited to taste the product. Guinness is the oldest brewery; Arthur Guinness (Uncle Arthur as he is affectionately known) began brewing at St James's Gate in 1759. Telephone in each case before you go.

Equally famous is Irish whiskey (spelt with an 'e'). The word comes from the Irish *uisce*

beatha meaning water of life and there is an old saying 'There's more friendship in a glass of spirit than in a barrel of buttermilk!' The whiskey is matured for 7 to 12 years and has a mellow distinct flavour. It is made from malted and unmalted barley, yeast and pure spring water.

The oldest (legal) distillery is at Bushmill's near the Giant's Causeway, dating from 1609, and it welcomes visitors by appointment. Most Irish whiskey is now distilled at Middleton, Co. Cork, while at Tullamore there is the Irish Mist distillery where the famous liqueur of that name is produced. At Irish Distillers' head office in Smithfield, Dublin, there is an excellent display of models, kits and tools showing the history of whiskey and how it is made. A recent development is the number of cream liqueurs which are made from a blend of whiskey and cream. These include Bailey's, Carolan and Waterford Cream.

Irish people often drink their whiskey diluted with water. So if you order 'a ball of malt' you will usually get a jug of water with it. Try it on its own first. Some of the 12-year-old whiskies are like nectar and are as good as a fine brandy.

Irish coffee is now world famous and often drunk at the end of a meal or on a cold day (see below for recipe). Another warming drink is a hot whiskey which is simply whiskey with hot water, sugar, lemon and cloves. Black Velvet is a delicious mixture of Guinness and champagne, although you can use cider.

Irish Coffee

Heat the glass, add one or more spoonfuls of sugar and strong, hot coffee to a height of one-and-half inches from the top. Stir well, add a generous measure of Irish whiskey and carefully pour on cream over a spoon so that it rests on the surface. Drink without stirring and then have another one.

Genealogy

Many people visiting Ireland would like to find out more about their family history. What makes ancestor research so fascinating is that it tells you about yourself, who you are and where you come from. You would expect to find Christian names recurring in a family but you might be surprised to see the same occupation held by members of the family over several generations or even spot similarities between your handwriting and theirs! You can engage a professional to do the research work or you can have a go yourself. There are many sources of information although some records have been lost in the various upheavals of Irish history.

It will make things much easier if you do some simple research before you leave home. Try to find out: the full name of your emigrant ancestor; where he came from in Ireland; dates of birth, marriage and death; occupation and background (rich, poor, farmer, trades-

Some Irish Family Names

man, professional, etc.); religion; date of emigration from Ireland. The more details you have the greater the chance of success. Sources are old letters and diaries, family bibles, military service records, emigrant ship lists, newspapers, local church and state records. Ask the oldest member of your family about their earliest memories too.

Armed with as much information as you can muster you can then visit the following places in Ireland:

The Registrar General in the Custom House, Dublin 1 holds the general civil registration of births, marriages and deaths from 1864. Non-catholic marriages are listed from 1845. You can make the search yourself or have it done for you. A small fee is payable.

The Public Record Office, Four Courts, Dublin 7, although badly damaged in 1922 has many vauable records including tithes dating from 1800 (the first valuation records), wills and abstracts of wills and marriage licences for some families. The returns for the extensive 1901 census may be seen here.

The Registry of Deeds, King's Inns, Dublin 7 has documents from 1708 relating to property such as leases, mortgages and settlements. You make the search yourself and a small fee is due.

The National Library, Kildare Street, Dublin 2 has an enormous collection of useful sources including historical journals, directories, topographical works, private papers and letters and local and national newspapers from the earliest times. The staff are helpful and there is no charge.

The Genealogical Office, Dublin Castle, Dublin 2 records official pedigrees, coats of arms and will abstracts of the more well-to-do families. They will conduct a search on your behalf for a fee.

A useful reference guide is Ida Grehan's *Pocket Guide to Irish Family Names,* which lists and describes the most common names and explains their origins and associations. For first names, try *Pocket Guide to Irish First Names* by Ronan Coghlan — it explains the meanings of most popular names, whether derived from Irish words or based on the names of legendary Irish figures and saints.

The Valuation Office, 6 Ely Place, Dublin 2 has the excellent and comprehensive *Griffith's Valuation.* This was a national survey of land ownership and leases made in the 1850s. There is an immense amount of detail in it.

If your ancestors came from Northern Ireland (6 counties) the Public Record Office of Northern Ireland at 66 Balmoral Avenue, Belfast BT9 6NY will help. It has tithe appointment books and other valuable sources. Linked to it is the Ulster Historical Foundation which will carry out a search for you.

The Presbyterian Historical Society at Church House, Fisherwick Place, Belfast 1 also has various records of its members.

If you know the parish where your ancestor came from start there. Every parish keeps records of the baptisms performed in it giving details of the child's parents and sometimes their date of birth and domicile. Many go back 150 years and some over 200 years. Some Church of Ireland registers go back to the

1700s. To see them apply to the parish priest or minister. Study the baptismal and marriage registers for five years before and after the date you have. Jot down each name that seems likely. Remember too that there is another useful source nearby — the graveyard. Note the details of each gravestone bearing your family name, rubbing away the moss and using a piece of chalk to bring up faint lettering.

Contact the local historical society. Their journal may well have interesting information and perhaps articles on the history of the parish. They will put you in touch with any genealogist specialising in the families of that district. If there is a parish newsletter ask the editor if he would insert an item on your search: 'Information sought about Sean Murphy, believed born in this parish about 18—, emigrated 18—. Please contact. . .' A similar letter should be sent to the local newspaper; every county has at least one. Lastly, before you leave the area ask to speak to the person who knows most about local history. Even if he or she can't shed light on your elusive ancestor you will learn a great deal about the place where your family originated and that alone should make the trip worthwhile.

If you are unsuccessful or don't want to do a search you can employ a professional to do it for you. Results cannot be guaranteed but for a modest sum they will complete an initial search and let you know the likelihood of success. Try one of the following: Irish Genealogical Office, Dublin Castle, Dublin 2; Heritage, 8 Powerscourt Town House, Dublin 2; Heraldic Artists, 3 Nassau Street, Dublin 2; Hibernian Researchers, Windsor Road, Dublin 6. For coats of arms, plaques, parchments and the full range of heraldic goods visit Mullins 36 Upr O'Connell Street, Heritage, Heraldic Artists (see above) or Historic Families, 8 Fleet Street, Dublin 2.

Shopping

General information. Shopping in Ireland is leisurely and while the choice may not be as wide as London or New York you will discover lots which cannot be found elsewhere. Opening hours are usually 9 a.m. – 5.30 p.m. Monday to Saturday. Most shops close on Sunday and in smaller towns for lunch and on one afternoon a week. Bank hours in the Republic are 10 a.m. – 12.30 p.m. and 1 – 3 p.m. Monday-Friday, 5 p.m. on one day per week. In Northern Ireland 10 a.m.–12.30 p.m. and 1.30–3.30 p.m. (M-F). The larger shops will change currency and traveller's cheques but you will get a better rate in the bank. In the north only British currency may be used. There is a value added tax (VAT) refund scheme (up to 35%) for goods taken out of the Republic. The goods must be worth over £50 (£202 for EEC residents) and you must have the invoice stamped by customs at the exit point before returning it to the shop for refund. Ask Bord Failte for a leaflet explaining how the system works.

Visitors to Ireland will want to take home some gifts or mementoes of their stay and

Grafton Street, Dublin

there is a wide choice of quality Irish-made goods available. Avoid those displaying an excessive amount of shamrocks, leprechauns, etc. — they probably come from the Far East! If it is not marked ask the assistant where the item is made and look for the 'Guaranteed Irish' symbol, an assurance that the product is quality Irish made. Many of the larger shops will pack, insure and mail goods home for you and don't forget to visit the enormous Duty Free Shop when passing through Shannon Airport where you can save a lot of money on the full price.

In Dublin the main shopping areas are all within easy walking distance: Grafton Street, Wicklow Street, O'Connell Street and Henry Street. The Powerscourt Town House in S. William Street has a large assortment of shops, boutiques, restaurants and a craft centre all within a carefully restored 18th-century mansion. There are more shopping complexes in the ILAC Centre off Henry Street, Creation Arcade, Grafton Street, and the Irish Life Centre, Talbot Street. The principal department stores are Clery's (O'Connell St), Switzer's and Brown Thomas's (Grafton St), Arnott's, Dunne's and Roche's (Henry St). Not to be missed at any cost is the Kilkenny Design Centre in Nassau Street which displays and sells only the best designed Irish goods such as clothing, pottery, jewellery, glass and furniture. It is also a pleasant spot for lunch or afternoon tea. In Belfast the principal shops are located in Donegall Place/Royal Ave and the streets nearby. Be prepared to open your bags for security checks.

Cork, the Munster capital, is pleasantly sited on the River Lee and has Patrick Street and Grand Parade as the main shopping thoroughfare. In Galway the aptly named Shop Street has a good selection of stores, especially for clothes and crafts. In fact every town, no matter how small, has its main street and in addition many shops stay open late on Friday and Saturday. Watch out for the combined grocery shop and bar where you can order your rashers and have a pint under the same roof.

What to buy. Waterford is almost synonymous with crystal and the factory just outside the town welcomes visitors by appoint-

ment. There you can see the ancient skill of moulding, blowing and cutting glass. The factory does not sell direct to the public but the glass is available in outlets everywhere. Less well known but equally beautiful crystal is made in Galway, Dublin, Cavan, Kilkenny, Cork, Sligo and Tyrone and many have shops attached where you can pick up first-rate bargains.

Tweed is a strong woollen fabric used in making suits, skirts, curtains, jackets, ties, hats and carpets. It comes in many beautiful designs, much of it from Donegal and Connemara where the rugged landscape provides the colour and texture of this versatile cloth. You can buy tweed garments made up or choose a pattern and order a length to be made up at home. A tweed hat or cap is a useful precaution against unpredictable Irish weather.

Aran sweaters have been worn by west coast fishermen for generations. The patterns are so varied and intricate that it is said a drowned man could be recognised by his pullover alone. The bainín or undyed wool came originally from the Aran Islands and makes the garment warm and rain resistant. You can buy sweaters, cardigans, dresses, caps and mitts in Aran patterns. Ask for a card explaining the meaning of the pattern. A hand-knitted Aran sweater (more expensive than hand-loomed) will last for more than 15 years if looked after.

The north-east has a long tradition of weaving linen for tablecloths, glasscloths, sheets, handkerchiefs and blouses. Irish poplin is now woven in Cork. Locally made pottery is on sale in most towns although Kilkenny is now the mecca for potters (and most other crafts). The tiny village of Belleek in Fermanagh is the home of delicate, almost transparent porcelain. Other well known potteries are Moss's (Bennetsbridge), Kilieran (Inistioge), Noritake (Arklow), Carrigaline Pottery, O'Leary's (Goresbridge), Royal Tara and Wedgewood (Galway). In these you can buy anything from an egg cup to a full dinner service.

Claddagh rings, celtic design plaques and jewellery in gold and silver are popular souvenirs and you can have a pendant engraved with your name in ogham (ancient

Irish lettering). Every record shop stocks a selection of traditional Irish music. Among the well known performers are the Chieftains, Clannad, the Dubliners, Paddy Reilly, the Furey Brothers and the Clancy Brothers. Irish publishers produce an enormous range of books on every aspect of Irish life and there are bookshops in every large town. In Dublin the main ones are Hanna's, Eason's, Paperback Centre, Hodges Figgis and Greene's. Among the many books you'll want to take home as gifts or souvenirs are *Real Ireland,* a collection of stunning colour photographs of people and landscapes by Liam Blake, *Irish Shopfronts* by John Murphy, a colourful selection of the brightest, quaintest façades in the country and *Faces of Ireland,* a particularly valuable collection of photographs and literary texts from the turn of the century which conveys a marvellously impressionistic view of Ireland during this eventful period.

Public Transport

Train and bus services in the Republic are operated by Coras Íompair Éireann (CIE), the Irish Transport Company. Fast, comfortable trains operate from Dublin to the main centres of population; namely Cork, Belfast, Sligo, Westport, Ballina, Galway, Limerick, Tralee, Waterford and Wexford. There are two mainline stations in Dublin: Connolly Station (Amiens St) runs services to Belfast, Sligo and Wexford/Rosslare. All other long distance trains depart from Heuston (Kingsbridge). The number 24 bus runs at regular intervals between the two stations.

CIE coach tour at Sneem, Co. Kerry

Train frequency varies according to the route and time of year but there are at least three or four trains in each direction daily, and double that number to Cork and Belfast. The service is sparser on Sundays and public holidays. Travel information is available at any station or bus office, at 59 Upr O'Connell St, 35 Lr Abbey St, and the Central Bus Station (Busarus), Store St — all in central Dublin — and at Dublin Airport. For all passenger enquiries in the Dublin area ring (01) 787777.

The suburban rail lines in Dublin stretch from Drogheda to Greystones and westwards to Maynooth. The three city centre stations are Connolly, Tara Street and Pearse. The recently opened DART (Dublin Area Rapid Transit) electric service is a marvellous way to get about on the 20-mile coastal line. Trains run from early morning to late at night at 5 minute intervals during peak hours and every 15 minutes at other times.

There are many kinds of tickets available for use on Dublin public transport. Weekly and monthly commuter tickets are valid on suburban rail and all city bus services. Ten-journey tickets can be bought for a specific journey and used without a time limit. Dublin buses cover the entire city and operate from different terminal stops around the centre. Buy a CIE timetable and consult the current Ordnance Survey map for stop locations. If possible avoid city buses at peak times, as they are very crowded. Reduced fares at off-peak periods apply for journeys within the city centre.

Northern Ireland Railways (NIR) operate trains north of the border and run the Belfast-Dublin service jointly with CIE. From Central Station, Belfast, trains run to Derry, Portrush, Bangor and Dublin. York Road (connecting bus from Central) is the station for the ferryport of Larne. Local trains to Bangor, Portadown, Ballymena and Larne are frequent, with fare reductions for travel at certain times. For full information contact Central Station, tel. Belfast 230310 or 230671. Citybus services in Belfast are one-man operated. On boarding the bus you pay the driver, state your destination and, when alighting, ring the bell to stop the bus. For enquiries tel. Belfast 246485/6. In Cork there is one suburban rail line to Cobh, once a stop for transatlantic liners when it was known as Queenstown. There are a number of city bus services to the suburbs, most of which pass through Patrick Street, the main thoroughfare. Further information from Cork Station, tel. (021) 504422.

When travelling by train at peak times it may be worthwhile reserving a seat for a small charge. In addition, restaurant and buffet cars are provided on the main services where you can enjoy a drink, a snack or a full meal (served at your seat in first class). The food is in the main excellent and the service courteous. It is a very pleasant way to travel. Check that the train you are aiming for has a restaurant car.

The provincial bus network in Ireland is very extensive; there is hardly a village in the country that does not have a bus passing through at some time or another. Some operate in conjunction with trains so that on arrival at the station you can continue your journey without a great delay. For example, buses to Dingle and Clifden connect with the Tralee and Galway trains respectively. Full details are available in the bus and train timetables. Expressway buses run between the major towns and cities on a number of routes not served by the railways. These include cross border routes and services to Britain. Many buses start from Busarus, the Central (Provincial) Bus Station in Store Street, Dublin. This is also the starting point for the airport coach and CIE coach tours which can be booked for a half day or up to two weeks with accommodation and guides included. Further details

from CIE Tours, 35 Lr Abbey Street, Dublin 1.

Ulsterbus has a similar itinerary of provincial routes and express buses. These normally depart from two points in Belfast, Great Victoria Street (near the Forum Hotel) and Oxford Street. For enquiries tel. Belfast 220011. Tourist excursions run during the summer to the main beauty spots of Ulster.

If you plan to use public transport a lot enquire about Rambler and Overlander tickets. These are valid for 8 or 15 days and give unlimited travel by rail or rail and bus. For a supplement you can include both Northern Ireland and the Republic in your itinerary. They are very good value indeed and cost no more than the price of two or three ordinary return tickets. Further information from CIE, NIR and the tourist boards.

While timetables are issued for all services in every case it is worth enquiring locally before setting out, especially in rural areas. Expressway buses and mainline trains are usually reliable but in remoter areas the local bus may not adhere so painstakingly to the schedule. Nevertheless you will enjoy a spin on such a vehicle. Notice how the driver will usually know all his passengers and take a personal interest in delivering their post, luggage, groceries and children safely to their destination.

Where to Stay

Before departure contact Bord Failte or the NITB in your own country for full information on the range of accommodation available in Ireland. You can stay in anything from a hostel to a luxurious castle. In tourist board approved premises the rates are fixed and if you wish you can make your booking through the tourist office (see Useful Addresses). During the summer it is advisable to book well in advance and remember that some places close for part of the winter. Tourist staff will help you choose

accommodation and advice on eating out, excursions, sightseeing, shopping, public transport, etc.

Each year Bord Failte and the NITB assess and grade hotels and guesthouses listed in their brochures, based on the overall standard of accommodation and service. Grading also establishes the maximum price which may be charged.

Hotels:
A* The top grade awarded to hotels with a particularly high standard of comfort and service with excellent cuisine; suites available and most rooms have a private bathroom.
A Hotels with a high standard of comfort and service; many bedrooms with a private bath.
B* Well furnished hotels with very comfortable accommodation and good cuisine; private bathrooms available.
B Well kept hotels with good accommodation and bathroom facilities; limited but good cuisine.
C Clean and comfortable hotels with satisfactory service; hot and cold running water with heating in all bedrooms.

Guesthouses
A Those offering a very high standard of comfort and personal service; private bathrooms available.
B Well furnished premises with very comfortable accommodation; limited food and service.
C Clean and comfortable guesthouses with hot and cold water in all bedrooms; adequate bathroom facilities.

Town and Country Homes
A large number of houses in urban and rural areas ranging from period style houses to modern bungalows; evening meals by appointment.

Farmhouses
Many farming families offer accommodation in a unique rural setting where fresh farm produce and tranquillity are guaranteed. Ideal for children; evening meals by arrangement.

Self-catering
Houses, cottages and apartments can be rented at numerous locations across the

Dromoland Castle, Shannonside, Co. Clare

country with sleeping accommodation for up to 10 people. These are very popular and should be booked well in advance. Contact the Regional Tourism Organisation in the area of your choice for a list of such places (see Useful Addresses).

Camping and Caravanning
With quiet country roads and approved sites this can be a perfect holiday for those who don't want to rush. Many sites have shops, laundry, cafés and play areas for children.

Boating
Ireland's waterways are beautiful, uncrowded and clean and you can hire a fully-equipped 2-8 berth cruiser. Cruisers are fitted with a fridge, cooker, central heating, hot water, shower, charts, dinghy, bed linen, crockery, etc. They are easy to handle and the inexperienced sailor can receive instruction before casting off. The River Shannon is the most popular cruising waterway but equally attractive are the Grand Canal, the River Barrow and the River Erne. Hire companies are located at Carrick-on-Shannon, Co. Leitrim, Whitegate, Co. Clare, Portumna, Co. Galway, Tullamore, Co. Offaly, Athlone, Co. Westmeath, Belturbet, Co. Cavan, Kesh, Lisbellaw and Bellanaleck, Co. Fermanagh.

Rates
The current brochures from Bord Failte and the NITB contain the rates for all approved accommodation in Ireland. Check that these apply when booking. Reductions are usually available for children under 12 and those under 4 are free if they share their parents' bedroom. Special rates apply for full board and a stay for a week or longer; ask for details. Generally you will pay less and have greater choice outside the high season (June to August).

Please contact the tourist boards if you are particularly pleased with your accommodation. Any complaints should be taken up with the manager in the first instance. Failing satisfaction, contact the Regional Tourism Organisation who will investigate the matter and if appropriate refer it to Bord Failte or the NITB. Every effort will be made to satisfy the complainant.

Useful Addresses and Information

Tourist Information Offices

Bord Failte – Irish Tourist Board, PO Box 1083, Dublin 8 (postal enquiries). The following offices are open all year round. Approximately 50 others open for the summer period only (details from Bord Failte).
Athlone, 17 Church Street, tel. (0902) 2866.
Belfast, 53 Castle Street, Belfast BT1 1GH, tel. 227888, telex 74560.
Cashel, Town Hall, tel. (062) 61333, telex 70237.
Cork, Tourist House, Grand Parade, tel. (021) 23251, telex 26131.
Derry, Foyle Street, tel. 269501.
Dublin City, 14 Upper O'Connell Street, Dublin

1, tel. 747733, telex 25253.
Dublin Airport, tel. 376387, 375533, telex 25395.
Dun Laoghaire, St Michael's Wharf, tel. 806984/5/6.
Ennis, Bank Place, tel. (065) 28366.
Galway City, Aras Failte, Eyre Square, tel. (091) 63081, telex 28370.
Kilkenny, Rose Inn Street, tel. (056) 21755, telex 28652.
Killarney, Town Hall, tel. (064) 31633, telex 26952.
Letterkenny, Derry Road, tel. (074) 21160, telex 33509.
Limerick City, Michael Street, tel. (061) 317522, telex 26904.
Mullingar, Dublin Road, tel. (044) 8650, telex 24772.
Nenagh, Kickham Street, tel. (067) 31610.
Rosslare Harbour, tel. (053) 33232, telex 80204.
Shannon Airport, tel. (061) 61664.
Skibbereen, 14-15 Main Street, tel. (028) 21766, telex 26067.
Sligo, Temple Street, tel. (071) 61201, telex 24301.
Tralee, 32 The Mall, tel. (066) 21288, telex 28225.
Waterford, 41 The Quay, tel (051) 75788, telex 28713.
Westport, The Mall, tel. (098) 25711, telex 26346.
Wexford, Crescent Quay, tel. (053) 23111, telex 28667.

Regional Tourism Organisations

Cork/Kerry, Tourist House, Grand Parade, Cork, tel. (021) 23251, telex 26131.
Dublin, 51 Dawson Street, Dublin 2, tel. (01) 747733.
Eastern (Dublin excluding city, Kildare, Louth, Meath, Wicklow), 1 Clarinda Park North, Dun Laoghaire, Co. Dublin, tel. (01) 808571, telex 24846.
Midland (Cavan, Laois, Longford, Monaghan, Offaly, Roscommon, Westmeath), Dublin Road, Mullingar, Co. Westmeath, tel. (044) 8761, telex 24772.
Mid-Western (Clare, Limerick, North Tipperary), 62 O'Connell St, Limerick, tel. (061) 47522, telex 26904.
Donegal/Leitrim/Sligo, Tourist Centre, Temple Street, Sligo, tel. (071) 61201, telex 24301.
South-Eastern (Carlow, Kilkenny, South Tipperary, Waterford, Wexford), 41 The Quay, Waterford, tel. (051) 75823, telex 80713.
Western (Galway, Mayo), Aras Failte, Galway, tel. (091) 63081, telex 28037.

NITB Offices *(open all year)*

Belfast Information Office, River House, 48-52 High St, tel. 246609, telex 748087.
Belfast Airport, Aldergrove, Co. Antrim, tel. Crumlin 52103.
Larne Harbour Terminal Building, Larne, Co. Antrim, tel. Larne 2270.
Armagh Library, Market St, tel. 524052.
Ballymena, 2 Ballymoney Road, tel. 46043.
Bangor, 34 Quay St, tel. 54069.
Carnlough, Post Office, Harbour Road, tel. 85201.
Cookstown, Town Hall, Burn Road, tel. 63359/63441.
Derry, Foyle St., tel. 69501.

Downpatrick, Strangford Road, tel. 2641.
Enniskillen, Lakeland Visitor Centre, Shore Road, tel. 3110.
Newry, Arts Centre, Bank Parade, tel. 2958.
A number of other offices open for the summer only; information from NITB.

Travel

Aer Lingus Ticket Offices: 41 Upr O'Connell St, Dublin; 42 Grafton St, Dublin; 12 Upr George's St, Dun Laoghaire; Terminal Dublin Airport; 46/48 Castle St, Belfast; 38 Patrick St, Cork; 136 O'Connell St, Limerick; Passenger Bookings: Dublin area (01) 377777 (Ireland & UK), 377747 (Europe, USA); Belfast, tel. 245151; Cork, tel. (021) 24331; Limerick/Shannon, tel. (061) 45556.
British Airways, 112 Grafton St, Dublin 2, tel. 686666.
B & I Line, 16 Westmoreland St, Dublin 1, tel. 724711.
Sealink, 15 Westmorland St, Dublin 1, tel. 714455.
Belfast Car Ferries, Donegall Quay, Belfast 1, tel. 226800.
Irish Continental Line, 19 Aston Quay, Dublin 2, tel. 774331.

Tourist Office, Dun Laoghaire

Airports/Stations

Dublin 379900; Belfast 229271; Cork (021) 965974; Shannon (061) 61333.
CIE (trains and buses), HQ Heuston Station, Dublin 8, tel. 771871. Passenger enquiries (all services), tel. 787777.
Northern Ireland Railways, Belfast Central Station, East Bridge St, tel. 235282; Passenger enquiries, tel. 230310/230671.

Embassies

There are 47 accredited to Ireland, 22 of which are non-residential.
Australia, 6th Floor, Fitzwilton House, Wilton Terrace, Dublin 2, tel. (01) 761517.
Belgium, 2 Shrewsbury Road, Dublin 4, tel. 692082/691588.
Canada, 65-68 St Stephen's Green, Dublin 2, tel. 781988.
Federal German Republic, 43 Ailesbury Road, Dublin 4, tel. 693011.
France, 36 Ailesbury Road, Dublin 4, tel. 694777
Italy, 12 Fitzwilliam Square, Dublin 2, tel. 760366/760367.
Netherlands, 160 Merrion Road, Dublin 4, tel. 693444/693532.
New Zealand, New Zealand House, Haymarket, London SW1, tel. 01-930 8422.

Spain, 17A Merlyn Park, Dublin 4, tel. 691640/692597.
Switzerland, 6 Ailesbury Road, Dublin 4, tel. 692515.
United Kingdom, 33 Merrion Road, Dublin 4, tel. 695211.
United States of America, 42 Elgin Road, Dublin 4, tel. 688777.

Cultural Institutes

Goethe Institute, 37 Merrion Square, Dublin 2, tel. 766451.
Alliance Française, 1 Kildare St, Dublin 2, tel. 761732.
Istituto Italiano di Cultura, 11 Fitzwilliam Square, Dublin 2, tel. 766662.
Instituto Cultural Español, 58 Northumberland Road, Dublin 4, tel. 682024.

Government Offices

Department of Foreign Affairs, 80 St Stephen's Green, Dublin 2, tel. 780822.
Government Information Services, Upr Merrion St, Dublin 2, tel. 607555.
European Commission Press & Information Office, 39 Molesworth St, Dublin 2, tel. 712244.
National Library, Kildare St, Dublin 2, tel. 765521.
National Museum, Kildare St, Dublin 2, tel. 765521.
Northern Ireland Information Office, Stormont Castle, Belfast BT4 3ST, tel. 63011.

Radio & Television

RTÉ, Donnybrook, Dublin 4, tel. 693111.
BBC, Broadcasting House, Ormeau Ave, Belfast BT2 8HQ, tel. 44400.
UTV, Havelock House, Ormeau Rd, Belfast BT7 1EB, tel. 228122.

Public Holidays

In the Republic the following are public holidays: 1 January, 17 March (Patrick's Day), Easter Monday, first Monday in June, first Monday in August, last Monday in October, 25 and 26 December
Northern Ireland: 1 January, 17 March, Easter Monday, first and last Mondays in May, 12 July, last Monday in August, 25 and 26 December.

Currency

Northern uses the pound sterling (£), while the Republic uses the punt (IR£). Until 1979 the punt had parity with sterling, but the two currencies are no longer interchangeable and, at the time of going to press, the difference between the two was quite significant.
Banking hours in the Republic are Mon-Fri, 10 a.m.–12.30 p.m.; 1.30 p.m.–3.00 p.m. In most towns there is opening until 5.00 p.m. one day a week (Thur in Dublin). In Northern Ireland banks are open Mon-Fri 9.30 a.m.–12.30 p.m.; 1.30 p.m.–3.30 p.m.

Measurements

The following is a basic guide to the most common sizes in men's and women's shoes and clothing. Shoppers should, however, bear in mind that items can vary considerably in size depending on the make, and it is always wise to try on a garment before buying.

Women's clothing

Irish	32	34	36	38	40	42
European	38	40	42	44	46	48
USA	32	34	36	38	40	42

Women's shoes

Irish	3½	4	4½	5	5½	6	6½
European	36	36½	37	37½	38	38½	39
USA	4½	5	5½	6	6½	7	7½

Men's clothing

Irish	36	38	40	42	44
European	38	42	44	46	48
USA	36	38	40	42	44

Men's shoes

Irish	8	8½	9	9½	10
European	42	43	44	45	46
USA	26	26½	27	27½	28

Electric Current

In Ireland the usual voltage is 220v, AC current. Visitors should note that 13 amp, square-pin plugs are commonly in use — adapters are readily available from shops if required.

Further Reading

History

Belfast: The Making of the City, J. C. Beckett et al., Belfast, Appletree Press, 1982.
The Course of Irish History, ed. F. X. Martin and T. W. Moody, Cork, Mercier Press, 1984.
Dublin 1660-1860, Maurice Craig, Dublin, Figgis, 1980.
The Emergent Years, George Morrison, Dublin, Gill and MacMillan, 1984.
Faces of Ireland, Brian Walker, Art O'Broin, Sean McMahon, Belfast, Appletree Press, 1984.
The Gill History of Ireland, James Lydon and Margaret McCurtain gen. eds, 11 vols, Dublin, Gill and MacMillan, 1974-5.
The Irish Civil War, George Morrison, Dublin, Gill and MacMillan, 1981.
Medical Dublin, Liam Martin and Patrick Logan, Belfast, Appletree Press, 1984.
Northern Ireland: The Background to the Conflict, ed. John Darby, Belfast, Appletree Press, 1983.
One Hundred and Fifty Years of Irish Railways, Fergus Mulligan, Belfast, Appletree Press, 1983.
Ulster's Uncertain Defenders, Sarah Nelson, Belfast, Appletree Press, 1984.

Archaeology and Architecture

Architecture in Ireland, Maurice Craig, Dublin, Department of Foreign Affairs, 1979.
The Buildings of Irish Towns, Patrick Shaffrey, Dublin, O'Brien Press, 1983.
Irish Houses, K. M. Olbricht and H. M. Wegener, Dublin, Gill and MacMillan, 1984.
Irish Shopfronts, John Murphy, Belfast Appletree Press, 1982.
Round Towers of Ireland, George L. Barrow, Dublin, Academy Press, 1979.
Standing Stones and other monuments of early Ireland, Kenneth McNally, Belfast, Appletree Press, 1984.

Travel and Guidebooks

Atlas of Ireland, Dublin, Royal Irish Academy, 1979.

Blue Guide to Ireland, Ian Robertson, London, Benn, 1979.
Facts about Ireland, Dublin, Department of Foreign Affairs, 1981.
Guide to Historic Dublin, Adrian McLoughlin, Dublin, Gill and MacMillan, 1979.
Guide to the National Monuments of Ireland, Peter Harbison, Dublin, Gill and MacMillan, 1975.
On Foot in Ulster, Alan Warner, Belfast, Appletree Press, 1983.
Pocket Guide to Irish Place Names, P. W. Joyce, Belfast, Appletree Press, 1984.
The Way That I Went, R. L. Praeger, Dublin, Figgis, 1980.

Food and Drink

The Ballymaloe Cookbook, Myrtle Allen, Dublin, Gill and MacMillan, 1984.
In Praise of Poteen, John McGuffin, Belfast, Appletree Press, 1978.
An Irish Farmhouse Cookbook, Mary Kinsella, Belfast, Appletree Press, 1982.
Traditional Irish Recipes, John Murphy, Belfast, Appletree Press, 1982.

Culture, Folklore and Sport

Fishing in Ireland, ed. Hugh Oram, Belfast, Appletree Press, 1980.
A Guide to the Birds of Ireland, Gordon D'Arcy, Dublin, Irish Wildlife Association, 1981.
Haunted Ireland, John Dunne, Belfast, Appletree Press, 1980.
The Holy Wells of Ireland, Patrick Logan, Gerrards Cross, Colin Smythe, 1981.
Irish Country Cures, Patrick Logan, Belfast, Appletree Press, 1982.
Irish Family Names, Brian de Breffny, Dublin, Gill and MacMillan, 1982.
The Midnight Court, Brian Merriman, Dublin, Dolmen Press, 1979.
The Old Gods, Patrick Logan, Belfast, Appletree Press, 1981.
Pocket Dictionary of Irish Myth and Legend, Ronan Coghlan, Belfast, Appletree Press, 1985.
Pocket Guide to Irish Family Names, Ida Grehan, Belfast, Appletree Press, 1985.
Pocket Guide to Irish First Names, Ronan Coghlan, Belfast, Appletree Press, 1985.
Pocket Irish Phrase Book, Paul Dorris, Belfast, Appletree Press, 1983.
Real Ireland, Liam Blake and Brendan Kennelly, Belfast, Appletree Press, 1984.
The Tain, trans. Thomas Kinsella, Dublin, Dolmen Press, 1980.
The Wind That Shakes The Barley, Gareth James, Belfast, Appletree Press, 1983.

Bord Failte Publications

For a full list write to: Bord Failte, PO Box 1083, Dublin 8.
Dining in Ireland.
Farmhouses in Ireland.
Hotels and Guesthouses.
Ireland Guide.
Irish Country Houses and Restaurants.
Tourist Guides (26 guides, one for each county).
Town and Country Homes.

Northern Ireland Tourist Board Publications

All the Places to Stay.
Coastal Resorts.
Discover Northern Ireland.
Farm and Country Holidays.
Let's Eat Out.

Motoring in IRELAND

Moll's Gap, Co. Kerry

If you plan a motoring holiday it is worth contacting your local automobile association and the tourist board beforehand. They will supply you with full details of the rules of the road, insurance, breakdown services, petrol, road signs, etc. Most of this information can be had in Ireland but it is better to find out before you arrive. Bring your driving licence and insurance certificate, and display a nationality plate if bringing your car into Ireland.

There are lots of sea routes to choose from. B&I Line operate car ferries from Holyhead-Dublin, Liverpool-Dublin, Pembroke-Rosslare; Sealink: Holyhead-Dun Laoghaire, Fishguard-Rosslare, Stranraer-Larne; Belfast Car Ferries: Liverpool-Belfast; Townsend Thoresen: Cairnryan-Larne; Irish Continental Line: Le Havre-Rosslare, Le Havre-Cork, Cherbourg-Rosslare; Brittany Ferries: Roscoff-Cork. There are also regular summer sailings from the Isle of Man to Belfast and Dublin.

Cars can be hired from a number of companies in Ireland. Bord Failte and the NITB will supply you with a list of authorised car hire firms and you can pick up your chauffeured or self-drive car at the port or airport. If you plan to cross the border check with the hire company that your insurance is valid north and south. Rates vary according to the model, time of year and hire period. Weekend rates are good value especially in the off-season. Make sure you know whether the rate is for limited or unlimited mileage. You can also save money by transferring your own insurance to the hire car. In Ireland, petrol is bought in Imperial gallons: one Imperial gallon is approximately 4½ litres, while one U.S.

Average Driving Times at cruising speed, rest not included				
From	To	Km	Miles	Hours
Belfast	Derry	117	73	2¼
Belfast	Dublin	167	104	3
Cork	Dublin	257	160	4½
Cork	Limerick	105	65	2
Derry	Belfast	117	73	2¼
Dublin	Athlone	126	78	2¼
Dublin	Belfast	167	104	3
Dublin	Cork	257	160	4½
Dublin	Donegal	222	138	4
Dublin	Galway	219	136	4
Dublin	Killarney	309	192	5½
Dublin	Limerick	198	123	3½
Dublin	Rosslare Har.	163	101	3
Dublin	Shannon	222	138	4¾
Dublin	Sligo	217	135	4
Dublin	Waterford	158	98	3
Dublin	Westport	261	162	4¾
Larne	Donegal	214	133	4¼
Rosslare Har.	Dublin	163	101	3
Rosslare Har.	Killarney	275	171	5¼
Shannon	Dublin	222	138	4¾

gallon is about 3¾ litres.

You can avail of numerous packages involving travel by sea or air and a self-drive car for the duration of your holiday. Hotel or farmhouse accommodation can be included. If you choose to stay in one area you can arrange your holiday through CIE, travelling by train to Galway or Killarney, for example, and picking up a car at the station. For full details of all these combinations and special offers contact your local tourist board, Aer Lingus, B&I or CIE (see *Useful Addresses*).

Ireland has the lowest population density in Europe so there is lots of room on the roads, which makes driving a pleasure. The speed limit is 60 mph and 30 mph in towns. In the Republic roads are classed as motorway (M7),

national primary (N5), secondary (N71) and regional (R691). In the north you will find motorways, class A and class B roads numbered M1, A5 and B52 respectively. However, when seeking directions it is more common to refer to 'the Longford road' than 'the N4'. The road network is very extensive and while the principal highways are good those in more remote areas will vary. In the country watch out for cows, sheep and other animals being herded along the road.

You will find most routes well signposted although there may not be much advance warning. It's hard to get really lost and in any case it is a pleasure to wander along a country road admiring the countryside. Ask someone along the road or stop at a country pub or shop and you'll get all the directions you need and a great deal more besides. Place names are written in Irish and English in the Republic and many signposts are being converted to kilometres. Look for 'km' after the figures. (To convert kilometres to miles divide by 5 and multiply by 3 as a rough guide.) Motorists should take care when reading roadsigns since at present some distances are given in miles and some in kilometres.

In Ireland drive on the left and yield to traffic from the right. All drivers and front-seat passengers must wear a seat belt at all times; the gardaí are likely to stop you for not wearing one. Children under twelve are not allowed on front seats. While in Dublin you would be advised to park your car in an attended car park, place all valuables in the boot and lock the car securely. Parking is unrestricted in

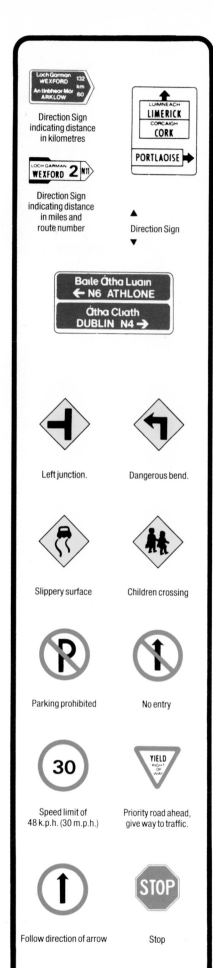

Direction Sign indicating distance in kilometres

Direction Sign indicating distance in miles and route number

Direction Sign

Left junction.

Dangerous bend.

Slippery surface

Children crossing

Parking prohibited

No entry

Speed limit of 48 k.p.h. (30 m.p.h.)

Priority road ahead, give way to traffic.

Follow direction of arrow

Stop

country towns and there are many lay-bys, picnic sites and beauty spots where you can pull in to take a break from driving. You must not park in town centres in Northern Ireland. For security reasons these are classed as control zones and unattended cars will be removed. Watch out also for ramps and be prepared to stop for security checks.

Roadsigns of various kinds are in operation. Hazards are indicated by black and yellow symbols on a diamond shaped board. Speed limits and parking restrictions are shown by black lettering inside a red circle. Watch out for accident black spots which are clearly marked. These often indicate dangerous junctions or very sharp bends and can be deceptive, especially at night. An unbroken white line in the centre of the road indicates that overtaking is forbidden.

Parking meters are common in cities although you can park at one after 6 p.m. without charge. The meter works by clocking up one or two hours according to the number of coins inserted. A single yellow line next to the kerb allows parking for a short period only. A double yellow line forbids parking at any time. In Cork you must display a parking disc inside the car indicating the time of day. These may be bought from newsagents and tobacconists. Bus lanes operate in cities and are reserved for buses and cyclists at certain times of the day. Watch out for the signs. Although some leniency is extended to visitors it is worth while observing the traffic regulations otherwise you may be fined or have your car towed away!

TEN SELF~DRIVE TOURING —IDEAS—

These ten scenic tours are designed to help you get the most from your motoring holiday in Ireland — to show you the most beautiful scenery, and to introduce you to Ireland's many interesting cities and towns. As all ten tours are circular you can commence at any point of the given routes. The daily distance covered is shown with each tour, in miles and kilometres (in italics). Included are maps of the ten tours, with alternative routes indicated by broken lines.

1. TOUR OF IRELAND

A ten-day tour over 1,000 miles *(1,610 kilometres)*, suggested starting point — Dublin.

DAY 1:
Dublin—Tramore. 118 mls *190 km.*
Having seen Dublin's historic buildings and

Georgian squares and having sampled its lively cosmopolitan atmosphere, you're on your way to Enniskerry, a pretty hillside village just twelve miles south of the city. Nearby you can visit the splendid Powerscourt Estate, with its gardens, deer herd and waterfall. Continue on through Roundwood to Glendalough and see the ruins of an early-Christian settlement in a beautiful wild setting of mountains and lakes. Your next stop, via Rathdrum is Avoca, made famous by Thomas Moore's song 'The meeting of the waters'. Southwards is the prominent holiday resort of Arklow, overlooking the sea. Onwards to Enniscorthy, with its old-world charm—just thirty three miles from the car ferry port of Rosslare Harbour—and then by New Ross, with its twisting lanes and Dutch-type houses to Waterford. Or visit Wexford and on to Waterford by the Ballyhack/Passage East car ferry. Spend your first night at Tramore, a family resort with three miles of sandy beaches.

DAY 2:
Tramore—Cork. 73 mls *117 km.*
After lunch leave for Cork, via Dungarvan into Youghal, a popular holiday resort. Continue through the market town of Midleton to Cork. Enjoy the friendly atmosphere of Cork, built on the banks of the River Lee. Visit St. Mary's Shandon, where the famous Shandon Bells are played on request, and admire the many fine public buildings.

DAY 3:
Cork—Killarney. 94 mls *151 km.*
Leaving Cork on the third day your first stop is Blarney Castle with its famous stone, said to impart the gift of eloquence to all who kiss it! Continue through Macroom, Ballingeary, Pass of Keimaneigh (two miles from Gougane Barra Forest Park), Ballylickey, and into the beautiful holiday resort of Glengarriff. Then in a northerly direction you drive through Kenmare into Killarney, enjoying one of the finest scenic drives on the way. You'll find plenty to do in Killarney—pony riding, boating and visiting islands and ancient abbeys. Drive around the 'Ring of Kerry', a brilliant 109-mile scenic drive bringing you to Killorglin, Cahirciveen, Waterville, Sneem, Parnasilla, Kenmare and back to Killarney.

DAY 4:
Killarney—
It's worth spending a day in Killarney, setting out the next day for Galway.

DAY 5:
Killarney—Galway. 156 mls *251 km.*
On the fifth day your drive takes you through Abbeyfeale, Newcastle West, the lovely village of Adare, and into Limerick, sixteen miles from Shannon Airport on the River Shannon, a graceful and historic city, featuring King John's Castle, the Treaty Stone and St. Mary's Cathedral. Traditional mediaeval banquets can be enjoyed at Bunratty Castle (eight miles from Limerick) and Knappogue Castle (eight miles from Ennis). Continuing on you reach Ennis with its old abbey and the seaside resort of Lahinch, featuring excellent golf courses. You should make your next stop by the breathtaking Cliffs of Moher, before driving to Lisdoonvarna, Ireland's premier spa. Drive through the bare limestone hills of the Burren

Tour of Ireland.

Bloody Foreland, Co. Donegal

Country to Ballyvaughan, to Kinvara (mediaeval banquets at Dunguaire Castle), Clarinbridge and into Galway. Galway is the capital of the 'Western World' with its famous Spanish Arch and Church of St. Nicholas, where, tradition holds, Columbus prayed before sailing to America.

DAY 6:
Galway—Westport. 86 mls *138 km.*
The next day your route through Connemara takes you to Moycullen, Oughterard, Recess, Clifden (capital of Connemara), Leenane and Westport—on Clew Bay, with over 100 islands.

DAY 7:
Westport-Bundoran. 96 mls *154 km.*
Head north next day to Castlebar, Pontoon, Ballina and the family resort of Inniscrone. Enjoy a swim before driving on to Sligo, where you can look around the thirteen-century Franciscan Friary and the museum, situated in the county library. Head on to Drumcliffe (burial place of W. B. Yeats) to complete your day's driving at Bundoran.

DAY 8:
Bundoran—Dunfanaghy. 120 miles *193 km.*
On the following day head further up the Atlantic Coast through Ballyshannon to Donegal town, visiting the Franciscan Friary and castle. Drive through Dunkineely, Ardara, Glenties, Maas and Kinscasslagh — noted for their cottage industries and Donegal tweed. Then by Annagry, Crolly, Bunbeg, Bloody Foreland, Gortahork into Dunfanaghy, nestling in a cosy inlet of Sheephaven Bay.

DAY 9:
Dunfanaghy—Carrick-on-Shannon. 110 mls *177 km.*
Next day your tour takes you south via Portnablagh to Letterkenny — Donegal's chief town. This is an excellent point from which to extend your drive, by taking the 'Inishowen 100' — an extremely scenic trip around the Inishowen Peninsula, to Buncrana, Malin Head and Moville. Return to Letterkenny by Manorcunningham. Total mileage for the trip is 120 miles. Continue south through the picturesque Finn Valley to the twin towns of Stranorlar and Ballybofey, completing your round trip of County Donegal in Donegal town. The next stage takes you to Ballyshannon and Bundoran in a southerly direction to Manorhamilton. Overlooking the town you'll see the picturesque ruin of Sir Frederick Hamilton's castle — built in 1638. Continue south through Drumkeeran along the beautiful shores of Lough Allen into Drumshanbo. Drive on through Leitrim into Carrick-on-Shannon,

an important cruising and angling centre.

DAY 10:
Carrick-on-Shannon—Dublin. 150 mls *241 km.*
On the final day head for Cavan, travelling by Mohill, Carrigallen, Killeshandra and Crossdoney enjoying the lake scenery on the way. Continue to Bailieborough (nine miles from the important angling centre of Virginia) and into the attractive town of Carrickmacross. The last stage of your trip takes you to Drogheda — a historic town in County Louth. From Drogheda visit the prehistoric tombs at Newgrange, Knowth and Dowth. Drive on by Slane into Navan. Six miles from here see the Hill of Tara, a former residence of Irish High Kings. Complete your tour of the Boyne Valley in Trim, rich in historical associations and ancient monuments, before returning to Dublin, via Black Bull, Clonee, Blanchardstown and the Phoenix Park.

Alternative two-day route from Dunfanaghy to Dublin taking in the Antrim Coast and the Mourne Mountains.

DAY 9:
Dunfanaghy—Belfast. 150 mls *240 km.*
Take the road from Dunfanaghy to Letterkenny, travelling north-east from here to Londonderry (you will cross the border into Northern Ireland at Bridgend). Stop to explore this historic city on the banks of the River Foyle, whose walls (the only remaining unbroken fortifications in either Britain or Ireland) afford superb views of the surrounding countryside and of the city itself. Continue north-east to Limavady, Downhill, Castlerock and Coleraine and on to the bracing seaside resort of Portrush. Then follow the coastal road eastwards

24

Giant's Causeway

to see the famous Giant's Causeway, the beautiful beaches at White Park Bay and Murlough Bay and the Carrick-a-Rede Rope Bridge (not for the faint-hearted!). The steep,

Carrick-a-Rede, Co. Antrim

winding road around Torr Head and down to the picturesque Cushendun is worth the slight detour — views are breathtaking. From Cushendun head for Larne, departure point for ferries to Scotland. The final stage of your journey takes you to Belfast via Carrickfergus, where you can visit the country's best-preserved Norman castle.

DAY 10:
Belfast—Dublin. 120 mls *192 km.*

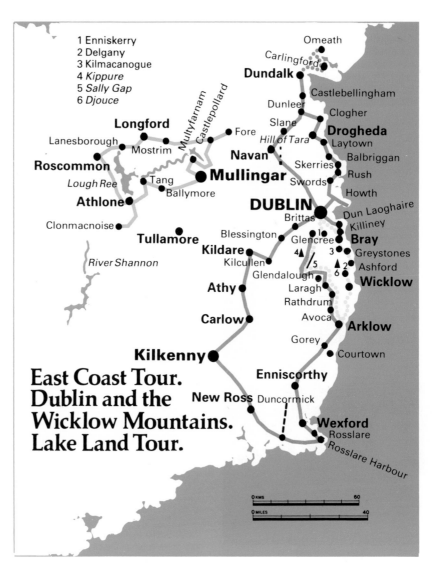

1 Enniskerry
2 Delgany
3 Kilmacanogue
4 *Kippure*
5 *Sally Gap*
6 *Djouce*

East Coast Tour. Dublin and the Wicklow Mountains. Lake Land Tour.

The last day of your tour takes you south out of Belfast through the heart of County Down towards the spectacular Mourne Mountains. Stop at Downpatrick *en route* to see Down Cathedral, in whose churchyard you will find St Patrick's grave marked by a crude slab. Continue towards Newcastle, County Down's most popular holiday resort, where, in the words of the song, 'the Mountains of Mourne sweep down to the sea'. Stroll along the beach at Dundrum or, if you're feeling energetic, make an assault on Slieve Donard (the Mournes' highest peak), which can be reached either through Donard Park or from Bloody Bridge (just outside Newcastle). Follow the road from Newcastle via Kilkeel and Warrenpoint to Newry, cross the border into the Republic, then continue to Dundalk (Cuchulainn's country), whose surrounding hills and forests are full of history and charm. Then make your way south to Drogheda (stopping at Monasterboice on the way to admire one of the most magnificent High Crosses in the country). From Drogheda, the mysterious passage tomb of Newgrange is easily accessible, and well worth a visit. The last stretch of road takes you south into Dublin city.

2. EAST COAST TOUR

Two circular tours — one north, the other south of Dublin.

DAY 1:
Northern tour. 190 mls *306 km.*
Take the Navan road out of Dublin for Tara — site of a former royal acropolis, situated in an area rich in ancient monuments and historical associations.
Continue north to Navan, Donaghmore and Slane. Visit the Bronze Age cemeteries at Brugh na Boinne, King William's Glen, Mellifont Abbey and Monasterboice, before heading for Dunleer, Castlebellingham and Dundalk — an ideal base for exploring the surrounding countryside. If you wish you can travel further north to see the delightfully rugged little Carlingford Peninsula, taking you through Ballymascanlon, Carlingford, Omeath and back into Dundalk.
Heading south you reach Castlebellingham, Clogher, Termonfeckin, Baltray, with its fine beach and golf course and on into Drogheda, on the River Boyne. In Bettystown, further south, there's a long sandy beach linking up with Laytown, while further on is Julianstown. Following the coast enjoy a pleasant drive through Balbriggan, Skerries, Rush, Lusk, Swords and Howth, stopping to admire the magnificent views from the rocky Hill of Howth. Return to Dublin via Sutton.

DAY 2:
Southern Tour. 290 mls *467 km.*
Next day the southern tour takes you through

Dun Laoghaire, Dalkey and Killiney — with its magnificent view over the bay from the Vico Road — into Bray, one of Ireland's premier seaside resorts. Continuing you reach Enniskerry, a pretty village beneath the Sugarloaf Mountain and near the beautiful Powerscourt Estate. The scenic mountain drive

Glendalough, Co. Wicklow

takes you to Glendalough, with its ancient ruins and picturesque lakes, passing through Glencree, Glenmacnass and Laragh. If you wish you can return to Dublin by Blessington, making a short but enjoyable trip — or keep south to Rathdrum, Avoca and Woodenbridge into Arklow, where you can enjoy a swim or go sea fishing. Driving on through County Wexford takes you to Gorey, Courtown Harbour (seaside resort), Ferns, Enniscorthy and Wexford, which is thirteen and a half miles from Rosslare Harbour. These charming old towns are well worth a visit. Follow the coast through Rosslare, Duncormick, Arthurstown and into New Ross.

From here take the road to Killkenny, a cheerful city steeped in history. Visit the Kilkenny Design Workshops, Rothe House and Kilkenny Castle. Return to Dublin through Carlow and County Kildare towns of Athy, Kildare, Kilcullen, and Ballymore Eustace, taking in the lake drive near Blessington and reaching the city via Brittas.

3. LAKELAND TOUR

This is a two-day circular drive of about 150 miles *(241 kilometres)*. This tour of Ireland's quiet heart offers a charm of a different kind from the coastal tours.

DAY 1:
Athlone—**Mullingar 84 mls** *135 km.*

The starting point is Athlone — 'Capital' of the midlands. From here drive to Roscommon visiting Hodson Bay and Rinndown Castle en route. Have a look around Roscommon Abbey. North-east of Roscommon is Lanesborough a popular angling centre at the head of Lough Ree. Then visit the busy market town of Longford with its nineteenth-century cathedral. Move on to Edgeworthstown, which gets its name from the remarkable literary family. Visit the Maria Edgeworth Museum. Continue to Castlepollard, a good angling centre near Lough Derravaragh — featured in a tragic legendary romance — *'Children of Lir'*. See nearby Tullynally Castle. Drive to Fore, with its ancient crosses and Benedictine Abbey, returning to Castlepollard and south via Multyfarnham to Mullingar — an important town and noted angling centre. Spend the night there.

DAY 2:
Mullingar—**Athlone 65 mls** 105 km.
Next day a westward drive takes you to Ballymore and to the Goldsmith country via Tang. Visit Lissoy and The Pigeons on the road to the pretty village of Glasson, passing the tower-like structure marking the geographical centre of Ireland. Return to Athlone.
From Athlone make an excursion to Coosan Point for a good view of Lough Ree, one of the largest Shannon lakes. Going downriver it's worth a visit to Clonmacnois, one of the country's most celebrated holy places, completing your tour in Athlone.

4. DUBLIN AND WICKLOW MOUNTAINS

This is a one-day scenic tour of about 110 miles *(177 kilometres)*.

Leave Dublin by the suburb of Rathfarnham, four miles south of the city. The ruined building known as 'The Hell Fire Club' forms a prominent landmark to the summit of Mount Pelier, four miles south of Rathfarnham. Drive via Glencullen, Kilternan and the Scalp into Enniskerry — one of the prettiest villages in Ireland. From here you can visit the Powerscourt Estate and Gardens, which include the highest waterfall in these islands.
Continue to Sally Gap, a notable crossroads situated between Kippure Mountain and the Djouce Mountain, where the road leads to Glendalough, by Glenmacnass and Laragh. Have a look around Glendalough — one of the most picturesque glens of County Wicklow with extensive ruins of the six-century Irish monastery of St. Kevin. Drive on through Laragh by the Military Road to Rathdrum. Head south by the Vale of Avoca into Arklow, a popular holiday centre. From Arklow drive north to Wicklow where you can admire the view over the bay.
Ashford is the next village on your route — close by the beautiful Mount Usher Gardens with countless varieties of trees, plants and shrubs. These gardens are open from March to September. Move on through the rugged Devil's Glen to Newtownmountkennedy, Delgany and into the attractive resort of Greystones, which retains the atmosphere of the former quiet fishing village.
Head back through Delgany to the Glen of the Downs, Kilmacanogue (from where you can climb the great Sugar Loaf) into Bray. From

this fine resort at the base of Bray Head take the route to Killiney and the Vico Road to Dalkey enjoying the superb views of Killiney Bay. Follow the coast road to Dun Laoghaire into Dublin.

5. SOUTH WEST TOUR

This is a two-day circular tour of about 430 miles *(692 kilometres)* on main route.

DAY 1:
Cork—**Killarney. 223 mls** *359 km.*
The suggested starting point is Cork — a charming city on the River Lee, excellent for shopping and offering first-class pubs and restaurants with entertainment for every member of the family. Blarney Castle, with its famous Stone of Eloquence is five miles away. Visit there to kiss the stone, before continuing to the old-world town of Kinsale. Drive on to Timoleague — where you'll see the remains of the once largest friary in Ireland — to Clonakilty, Rosscarbery, Glandore, Union Hall and Skibbereen. Continue this exceptionally beautiful drive through Ballydehob, Schull, Toormore, Durrus and Bantry into Glengarriff — visiting the Forest Park and Garinish Island, with its ornate gardens. Afterwards take the 'Tunnel Road' to Kenmare or head west over the Healy Pass.
Some of the finest sea and mountain scenery in Ireland can be enjoyed on the next stage of the tour, around the 'Ring of Kerry' — through Sneem, Castlegrove, Derrynane, Waterville, Cahirciveen, Glenbeigh and Killorglin into Killarney. There are some lovely quiet beaches in this region — for example Rossbeigh near Glenbeigh. Spend the night in Killarney.

DAY 2:
Killarney—**Cork. 220 mls** *322 km.*
From Killarney drive direct to Tralee or alternatively explore the Dingle Peninsula, the heart of the *'Ryans Daughter'* country. Places along the route are: Inch, Annascaul, Dingle, Ventry, Slea Head, Dunquin, Ballyferriter, Murreagh, back to Dingle and on through Stradbally and Camp to Tralee. An unforgettable drive of breathtaking beauty. Follow the coast from Tralee to Ardfert, Ballyheigue, Causeway, Ballyduff, Lisselton Cross Roads, Ballylongford, and Tarbert, where a car ferry operates to Killimer, County Clare. Drive through Foynes along the Shannon Estuary via Askeaton to Limerick — an old and historic city, not far from Bunratty Castle, with its mediaeval style banquets.
Having spent some time looking around Limerick head back to Cork through Tipperary and Cashel, visiting the magnificent ruins of the Rock of Cashel — including a cathedral, castle, chapel and round tower. Enjoy the mountain views on the way to historic Cahir town and into Cork by Clogheen, Lismore and Fermoy, providing a splendid trip through the Knockmealdown Mountains.

6. CORK AND 'RING OF KERRY'

A one-day tour about 220 miles *(354 kilometres)*.

Travel west from Cork via Ovens to Macroom. Turn off for Toon Bridge and Inchigeelagh through the wild mountain scenery of the Pass

Blarney Castle, Co. Cork

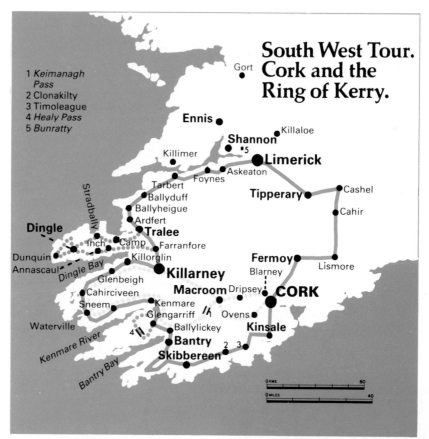

South West Tour. Cork and the Ring of Kerry.

Map labels:
1 *Keimanagh Pass*
2 *Clonakilty*
3 *Timoleague*
4 *Healy Pass*
5 *Bunratty*

Gort · Ennis · Killaloe · Shannon · Killimer · Limerick · Askeaton · Foynes · Tarbert · Ballyduff · Ballyheigue · Ardfert · Tralee · Farranfore · Cashel · Tipperary · Cahir · Stradbally · Dingle · Inch · Camp · Killorglin · Dunquin · Annascaul · Dingle Bay · Glenbeigh · Killarney · Blarney · Fermoy · Lismore · Cahirciveen · Macroom · Dripsey · CORK · Sneem · Kenmare · Ovens · Waterville · Glengarriff · Ballylickey · Kinsale · Kenmare River · Bantry · Skibbereen · Bantry Bay

of Keimaneigh into Ballylickey. Along the way you could visit Gougane Barra Forest Park which is just north of your route.

From Ballylickey enjoy the superb views of Bantry Bay en route to Glengarriff, from where you can visit the beautiful Italian gardens of Garinish Island. Head north to Kenmare through rugged mountains. Here your trip around the 'Ring of Kerry' begins — encircling the Iveragh Peninsula, which features Ireland's highest mountains, the Macgillycuddy's Reeks. Excellent views are provided over Dingle Bay to the north and the estuary of the Kenmare River to the south. Travel south-west through Parknasilla and Sneem, into Caherdaniel, where you'll find excellent swimming and diving along the fine beach. Go north to the well-known resort of Waterville, continuing your tour by Cahirciveen, Glenbeigh and Killorglin, completing this exceptionally scenic trip in Killarney.

Your route back to Cork takes you through the Derrynasaggart Mountains to Macroom, turning off the main road for Dripsey and Blarney Castle, where you can stop to kiss the famous Blarney Stone.

7. WEST COAST TOUR

This is a four-day circular tour of about 523 miles *(842 kilometres)* on main route.

DAY 1:
Athlone—Limerick. 94 mls *151 km.*
Athlone is the suggested starting point for a tour of this richly varied region. From this impressive town south of Lough Ree you pass the early-Christian site of Clonmacnois to the south and on to Birr, where the gardens of Birr Castle are open to visitors. Driving in a southerly direction you come to Nenagh with its fine castle, built about 1200. Continue via Portroe with fine views over Lough Derg into Killaloe, a popular water-skiing centre. From here drive to O'Brien's Bridge, Ardnacrusha and on to Limerick for the night.

DAY 2:
Limerick—Galway. 144 mls *232 km.*

Having seen the sights of Limerick head for Bunratty Castle where mediaeval banquets are held, and visit the Bunratty Folk Park. Drive south-west from Ennis to the resorts of Kilrush and Kilkee, going north to Lahinch and around Liscannor Bay to the magnificent ruggedness of the Cliffs of Moher, reaching up to 700 feet. Move on to Ireland's premier spa, Lisdoonvarna, enjoying the remarkable 'Burren Country', consisting of a desert of bare limestone hills which are a botanist's paradise in spring. Take the road from Lisdoonvarna through Black Head, Ballyvaughan, Kinvara and Clarinbridge into Galway. Discover Galway for yourself — its Church of St. Nicholas, The Spanish Arch and the gathering of salmon (in season) under the Salmon Weir Bridge. Salthill, Galway's fashionable seaside suburb offers you top-class restaurants and hotels, pubs, discos and many other forms of entertainment, including the amenities of the Leisureland complex.

DAY 3:
Galway—Westport. 122 mls *196 km.*
Next day start your tour of Connemara by Spiddal, Costelloe, Screeb, Gortmore, Carna, Toombeola, Ballynahinch and Glendalough. From Clifden you head northwards to Tullycross and on to Leenane, on the corner of picturesque Killary Harbour. Drive northwards through the mountains to Louisburgh, in the shadow of Croagh Patrick. Stop in Westport, an important sea angling centre. Alternatively you can get from Leenane to Westport through the Joyce Country, taking you to Maam, Cong, Ballinrobe, Parry, Ballintubber with its famous abbey and into Westport.

DAY 4:
Westport—Athlone. 163 mls *262 km.*

Magillycuddy's Reeks, near Killarney

The following day explore the beauties of Achill Island, taking the road to Newport, Mulrany, through Curraun Peninsula, Achill Sound and on to Keel and Dooagh.

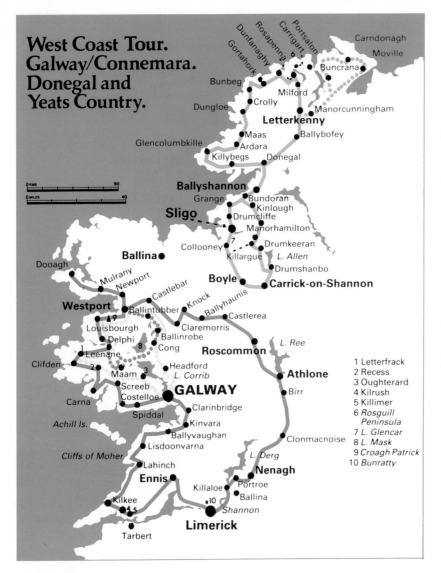

West Coast Tour. Galway/Connemara. Donegal and Yeats Country.

1 Letterfrack
2 Recess
3 Oughterard
4 Kilrush
5 Killimer
6 *Rosguill Peninsula*
7 *L. Glencar*
8 *L. Mask*
9 *Croagh Patrick*
10 *Bunratty*

Kylemore Lough, Co. Galway

Return via Newport to Castlebar, visiting Clonalis House. Then on to Claremorris, Ballyhaunis, Castlerea, Roscommon and back to Athlone.

8. GALWAY AND CONNEMARA

This is a one-day tour of about 160 miles *(257 kilometres).*

Travel north-west of Galway to the pretty village of Oughterard, with views of Lough Corrib along the way. Continue through the rugged countryside of Connemara, dominated by the craggy peaks of the Twelve Bens, via Maam Cross and Recess into Clifden — the capital of Connemara.
From Clifden drive to Letterfrack and on to Leenane, at the head of picturesque Killary Harbour. Along the way you'll see the magnificent Kylemore Abbey.
Having left Leenane turn off the main road for Louisburgh and Westport, passing Doo Lough and the lofty Croagh Patrick. The town of Westport was designed by James Wyatt — an architect of the Georgian period. Castlebar, principal town of County Mayo, is the next on your route — offering you a charming old-world atmosphere. Of particular note is the pleasant tree-lined Mall. Return to Galway by Ballintubber, with its impressive abbey,

Ballinrobe and Headford.

9. DONEGAL AND YEATS COUNTRY

This is a two-day circular tour, over 320 miles *(515 kilometres)* on main route.

DAY 1:
Carrick-on-Shannon—Carrigart. 200 mls *322 km.*
The popular centre of Carrick-on-Shannon — well known for cruising and coarse fishing — is the starting point for this tour. The first town on this route is Boyle — two miles from Lough Key Forest Park, with its numerous facilities, from boating to nature trails. Your drive will continue to Collooney, entering the magical country of Yeats. Share his experiences as you drive through Ballisodare, Kilmacowen and Strandhill on your way to Sligo, a beautifully situated town, surrounded by mountains. Pay a visit to Sligo Abbey and the museum, situated in the county library. Follow the road through Drumcliffe (Yeat's burial place) to Grange and Cliffoney into Bundoran — a resort where you'll find enjoyment for all the family. Begin your tour of Donegal from Ballyshannon, leading north to Donegal town and on to Killybegs by way of Mountcharles, Inver and Dunkineely. Following the coast to Glencolumbkille, a popular holiday centre, you are

now in a part of Ireland's 'Gaeltacht' or Irish speaking region. This area of Donegal is noted for its excellent crafts and the production of handmade Donegal tweed. From Glencolumbkille head east to Ardara, Maas and Dungloe — a remarkable tract of rocky lakeland. Drive north from Crolly to the lovely fishing village of Bunbeg, along the coast to Gortahork and Dunfanaghy, with its lovely beaches and superb cliff scenery. Turn off at Creeslough for Carrigart — beautifully situated on Mulroy Bay. Spend the night here.

DAY 2:
Carrigart—Carrick-on-Shannon. 120 mls *193 km.*
From Carrigart there is a charming twelve-mile trip around the little Rosguill Peninsula, taking in Tranarossan Bay and Rosapenna. Continue south to Letterkenny via Milford.
Before driving south for Donegal town again you could take a trip around the Inishowen Peninsula, an extra 129 miles in all, giving unrivalled views, a top-class resort at Buncrana and some very interesting antiquities, such as the cross of Carndonagh. Complete your tour from Donegal by Ballyshannon, Bundoran, Kinlough, Manorhamilton, Killarga, Drumkeeran and along the shores of Lough Allen by Drumshanbo into Carrick-on-Shannon.

10. NORTH EAST TOUR

Two circular tours – one north, the other south of Belfast.

DAY 1
Northern tour. 180 mls *288 km.*

Travel north out of Belfast through Carrick-fergus to the car ferry port of Larne. Continue along the scenic route to Cushendall and Ballycastle, enjoying the gently scooped-out contours of the Antrim Glens to your left. (You can turn inland to visit Glenariff Forest Park, where wooded paths lead to superb view-points.) Continue to the popular town of Bally-castle — famous for its annual Ould Lammas Fair — before following the road to Portrush via the Giant's Causeway. (Bushmills, home of the world's oldest distillery, is only 3 miles away, and can be visited.) Pass through Por-trush and Coleraine towards Downhill and Limavady, taking in the view from the Binevenagh plateau on the way. Then head for Derry, whose historic features deserve to be explored. When you are ready to leave, turn south-east towards Dungiven and cross the Glenshane Pass into Castledawson. From here you can go on to Antrim town and back to Belfast.

DAY 2:
Southern tour. 104 mls *166 km.*
Leave Belfast on the south side and drive via Lisburn to Hillsborough, a remarkably pretty small town with adjacent fort, park and lake — ideal for a quiet stroll. Continue through Dromore and Banbridge to Newry, where you can turn eastwards along the shores of Car-lingford Lough to the picturesque fishing port of Kilkeel. Take a walk down by the harbour to admire the fleet — and perhaps buy some freshly-landed fish — before heading north and inland towards the Silent Valley, in the heart of the beautiful Mourne Mountains (fol-

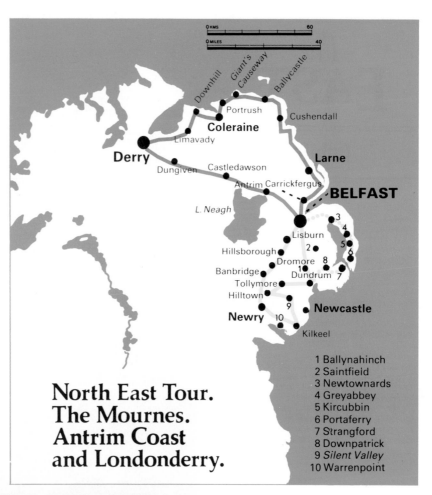

North East Tour.
The Mournes.
Antrim Coast
and Londonderry.

1 Ballynahinch
2 Saintfield
3 Newtownards
4 Greyabbey
5 Kircubbin
6 Portaferry
7 Strangford
8 Downpatrick
9 *Silent Valley*
10 Warrenpoint

Glenariff Glen, Co. Antrim

low Hilltown direction). It is worth stopping the car for a breath of the clear mountain air and the chance to enjoy the wonderful views. Then proceed via Tollymore (with its forest park) to Dundrum, whose long, unspoilt beach is always inviting. From here you can head straight back to Belfast through Ballynahinch, or travel to Downpatrick and Strangford, visiting Castleward before taking the ferry across Strangford Lough to Portaferry. Drive up the Ards Peninsula via Kircubbin and Greyabbey (interesting ruins) to Newtow-

Greyabbey, Co. Down

nards, overlooked by Scrabo Tower. From here, it's only a short drive back to your Belfast base.

The EAST

Dublin

Pop. 750,000, 103 m (165 km) S of Belfast, 161 m (262 km) NE of Cork and 123 m (198 m) NNE of Limerick. Bus and train services: most bus routes cross the city centre. Buses for W Dublin start at Aston Quay, Batchelor's Walk, Middle Abbey Street. N city buses start at Lower Abbey Street, Talbot Street. S city start at Fleet Street (off D'Olier Street), Hawkins Street (off Burgh Quay). Trains to N, NW, SE go from Connolly Station, Amiens Street. Trains to W, S and SW leave from Heuston Station, Kingsbridge. Bus and train enquiries: CIE, (01)787777, Mon–Sat, 9a.m.–9p.m. Sun: 10a.m.–7p.m. Coach tours leaving Busaras: details: CIE, 59 Upper O'Connell Street. (01)746301 or CIE, Busaras, (01)742941.

Taxis: Aston Quay (778053); Angle Ranelagh (972753); Crescent, Malahide Road (336507); Eden Quay (777054): Lansdowne Road, by Jurys hotel (684222); Upper O'Connell Street, opposite Gresham hotel (744599); Lower O'Connell Street, opposite Easons (786150); Upper Rathmines Road (973276). Taxis may be hired fairly easily at most times of day. Youth Hostels: 39 Mountjoy Square, 40, 41 bus, tel: (01)745734; Morehampton House, 78 Morehampton Road, 10 bus, tel: (01)680325. TIO: Upper O'Connell, Street. tel:(01) 747733.

Nearly 2,000 years old, in turn, a Viking, a Norman and an English city, and since 1922 the capital of an independent state.

During the early 1900's, the city enjoyed a revival of Irish culture, including literature. Today, however, it is falling to a new 'invader'—a brash Anglo-American 'pop' culture. Some parts of the city are being devastated by developers, but despite the ravages of the last 20 years, many areas of Dublin such as the Liberties, retain much of their individual character. Not far S of the traffic-clogged central streets, the mountains form a breath-taking backdrop, and a reminder that rural Ireland is not far away.

Major festivals: St Patrick's Week festivities *(Mar)*; Feis Ceoil–Irish Music Festival *(Mar)*; Dublin Grand Opera Society spring season *(Apr)*; RDS Spring Show *(May)*; Dublin Liberties' Festival *(May)*; Dublin Horse Show *(Aug)*; Irish Antique Dealers' Fair *(Aug)*; Dublin Grand Opera Society winter season *(Dec)*; Festival of Music in Great Irish Houses: feast of classical music in Dublin area Georgian mansions *(June)*. *Details: TIO, (01)747733.*

CATHEDRALS & CHURCHES

Christ Church Cathedral (CI), *Lord Edward Street, 21, 21A, 50, 50A, 50B, 54, 54A bus.* Founded 1038, rebuilt by the Normans following their invasion in 1169. Magnificent stonework on nave and aisles. Have a look at alleged tomb of Strongbow. Crypt dates from Norman times.**D St Patrick's Cathedral** (CI), *Patrick Street, 50, 50A, 50B, 54, 54A, 56 bus.* Founded 1190, restored about 1860. Jonathan Swift was Dean from 1713 to 1745, tomb in South aisle, 'where savage indignation can no longer rend his heart'. Also see monument to Turlough O'Carolan, last of the Irish bards.**D**
St Mary's Pro-Cathedral (C), *Marlboro Street, behind O'Connell Street, Dublin 1:* built in early 19th c. Its famous Palestrina choir sings Mass in Latin on Sun. **St Werburgh's Church** (CI), *Werburgh Street off Christ Church Place, 21, 21A, 50, 50B, 54, 54A bus.* Built 12th c, repaired and enlarged, 18th c. Ask to see adjacent church hall, where a

O'Connell Street and River Liffey

magnificent 100 yr old fire engine is stored. *By app. only, tel: (01)756058.*
St Michan's Church (CI), *Church Street, near Four Courts, 34, 34A, 38A bus.* 17th c church famous for the bodies in its vaults, where the dry atmosphere has prevented decomposition. Handel is said to have played the organ. *Tours of church and vaults Mon–Fri.* **St Mary's Church** (CI),

Mary Street: dates from 1627. Wolfe Tone and Sean O'Casey were baptised here. Houses death mask of Tone, a copy of the Book of Kells and an exhibition of Biblical models. *By app. only, tel: (01)724154.* **St Audoen's Church** (C), *High Street, 21, 21A, 50, 50A, 50B, 54, 54A bus.* Oldest parish church in the city. dating from late 12th c. Although partially ruined, a portion is still used.

NOTABLE BUILDINGS

Custom House, *Custom House Quay:* not open to visitors, but the fine façade may be admired while strolling along by the river.
Dublin Castle, *Dame Street:* once seat of British administration in Ireland. See State Apartments, including vast St. Patrick's Hall with lofty panelled ceiling; once residence of English Viceroys, today, used for State occasions. Church of the Most Holy Trinity: formerly Chapel Royal. Magnificent interior decorations. Exchange Court: where three men were put to death in 1920, during War of Independence. Heraldic Museum: founded in 1911, houses a wide variety of objects, from coins to glassware, all bearing coats of arms. *Check with TIO if open. Details (01)747733.*
Trinity College, *College Green:* Ireland's oldest university. Behind the magnificent 18th c façade is Library Square and the extraordinary library, which has over a million volumes. Its most distinguished possession, the Book of Kells, is on display. *Mon–Fri, 10a.m.–5 p.m.; Sat. 10a.m.–1p.m. Closed Sun and Bank Holidays.* Also Engineering Museum, Faculty of Engineering. **Bank of Ireland.** *College Green:* conducted tours of 18th c Parliament House during banking hours.

St Patrick's Cathedral

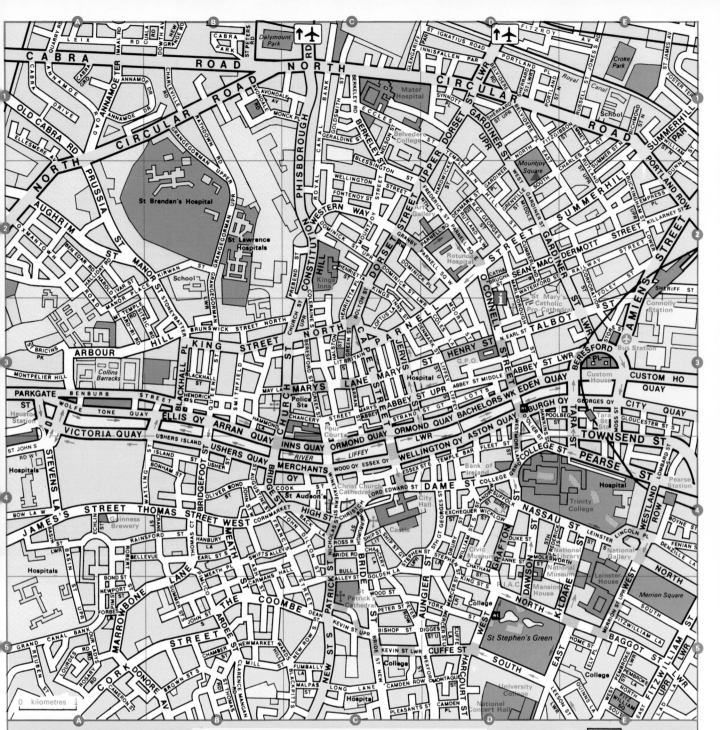

Dublin city centre

 Tourist Information Office and Accommodation Reservations Service, 14 Upr. O'Connell Street (D3) Tel: (01) 747733

Automobile Association,
23 Suffolk St., (D4).
Tel: (01) 779481.

Aer Lingus ticket offices,
41 Upr. O'Connell St., (D3)
and 42 Grafton St., (D4).

B+I Line,
16 Westmoreland St., (D3).
Tel: (01) 778271.

British Rail (Sealink),
15 Westmoreland St., (D3).
Tel: (01) 714455.

Coach and bus station,
city tours starting point and
airport buses, Store St., (E3).
Bus and train information
Tel: (01) 787777.

Irish Youth Hostel ▲
Association,
39 Mountjoy Square, (D2).
Tel: (01) 745734.

Railway stations:
Connolly, Amiens St., (E2).
Tel: (01) 742941.

Heuston, Kingsbridge, (A3).
Tel: (01) 771871.

Taxis (01) 507777, (01) 683333,
(01) 761320, (01) 766666,
(01) 783333.

Royal Irish Automobile Club,
34 Dawson St., (D4).
Tel: (01) 775141.

Dublin Tourist Trail
The 'Tourist Trail'
is a specially
selected signposted
walking tour
through the city.
An illustrated booklet is
available from Dublin tourist
information offices.

 TOURIST TRAIL

Dublin Airport ✈
Signposted routes.

PLACES OF INTEREST

Bank of Ireland
(Old Parliament House),
College Green, (D4).

Catholic Pro-Cathedral,
Marlborough St., (D3).

Christ Church Cathedral,
Christchurch Place, (C4).

City Hall,
Dame St., (D4).

Civic Museum,
Sth. William St., (C4).

Custom House,
Custom House Quay, (E3).

Dublin Castle,
off Lord Edward St., (C4).

Four Courts,
Inns Quay, (C4).

General Post Office,
O'Connell St., (D3).

Guinness' Brewery,
James's St., (A4).

Leinster House,
Kildare St., (E5).

Mansion House,
Dawson St., (D4).

Marsh's Library,
adjoins St. Patrick's Cathedral, (C5).

Municipal Art Gallery,
Parnell Square, (D2).

National Art Gallery,
Merrion Square West, (E4).

National Concert Hall,
Earlsfort Terrace, (D5).

National Museum of Natural History,
Upr. Merrion St., (E5).

National Library and Museum,
Kildare St., (E4).

St. Michan's Church,
Church St., (B3).

St. Patrick's Cathedral,
Patrick St., (C5).

Trinity College and Library,
College Green, (D4).

Leinster House, *Kildare Street:* seat of Dáil (Chamber of Deputies) and Seanad. Members of public only admitted to Dáil visitors' gallery with introduction from a T.D. *Details: (01) 789911.* **City Hall**, *Dame Street:* see Dublin Corporation Assembly Rolls, mace and sword of City of Dublin and 102 royal charters. *Details: (01)776811.* **General Post Office**, *O'Connell Street:* the 1916 Easter Rising started here. The present building is a reconstruction. See statue of the Dying Cuchulainn, a figure from Celtic mythology. **D**

MUSEUMS

National Museum, *6, 7A, 8, 10, 11, 13 bus.* Many fascinating exhibits dating from prehistoric times. Kildare Street: vast and diverse collection of antiquities including Bronze Age gold ornaments, Tara Brooch, Ardagh Chalice, Cross of Cong, 6th c ecclesiastical bells and 12th c church door, a good overview of prehistoric, early-Christian and mediaeval Ireland, plus range of 18th and 19th c dress, silverware, coins and porcelain. Ask to see section of rare stamps. The section devoted to the 1916 Rising and War of Independence has many interesting items, such as Pearse's barrister gown, the flag flown over the GPO, old photographs, captured weapons, uniforms. Natural History section, near National Gallery: fine collection of indigenous animals and birds. The third most modern section of the museum, Merrion Row, is used for exhibitions. *Tues-Sat, 10 a.m.-5 p.m. Sun, 2p.m.-5p.m. Closed Mon. Details: (01)765521.*

Museum of Broadcasting, *RTE Portobello Studios, 27 Lower Rathmines Road. 14, 14A, 15A, 15B, 83 bus.* Comprehensive collection illustrating progress of Irish radio and TV over nearly 60 years, including early TV newscast studio. Best to check in advance, (01)905798. **Egestorff Collection**, *25 Wellington Place. 4, 10, 46A buses to Morehampton Road.* Pre-1900 scientific instruments. *First Wed, every month, 7 p.m.-9 p.m. tel: (01)689325.* **Irish Theatre Archive**, *City Hall, Dame Street:* playbills, programmes, set designs, photographs, prompt books, cuttings, relating the story of Irish theatre. *Mon-Fri. Details: (01)776811.*

St Patrick's Hospital, *off James's Street, near the Guinness brewery. 21, 21A, 78, 78A, 78B bus.* Built with a legacy from Dean Swift in the 18th c. The boardroom is veritable treasure trove of Swiftiana, including the desk at which he is reputed to have written Gulliver's Travels. *To view, tel: (01)775423.*

Pearse Museum, *St. Enda's Park, Rathfarnham. 16 bus (terminus near park entrance).* Patrick Pearse, leader of the Easter Rising was headmaster at St. Enda's school in this 18th c house. 50 acre park includes beautifully situated lake and nature trail. *Mon-Sun, 10 a.m.-12.30 p.m.; 2 p.m.- 4.30 p.m. all year, except June-Sept, closes 6 p.m.; Dec, Jan. closes 3.30 p.m. Details: (01)905208.* **Sam Melbourne GAA Museum**, *Villa Park Gardens, off Navan Road:* vast assembly of GAA material. *To view, tel: (01) 743111.*

Museum of Childhood, *20 Palmerston Park, 12 bus.* Wonderful collection of dolls dating from early 18th c. Also toys, prams, rocking horses and miniature furniture. *May 1-Sept 30, Tues-Sun, 2 p.m.-5.30 p.m. Nov 1-Apr 30, Wed, Sat and Sun, 2 p.m.-5.30 p.m. Tel: (01)973223.* **Peter Matthews**, *1 Lorcan Park, Santry. 16, 41, 41A, 41B bus.* Over 100 old bicycles. Not on permanent display, although Mr Matthews hopes to set up museum. Cycling enthusiasts can see the machines. *By prior arr.* **Irish Railway Records Society**, *Heuston Station, 23, 24, 25, 26, 51, 79 bus.* Relive bygone days of the Irish railways. *Wed, 8 p.m.- 10 p.m.*

Garda Síochána Museum, *Garda depot, Phoenix Park. 10, 14, 14A buses to North Circular Road gate of Phoenix Park.* Fine collection of material: uniforms, photographs and medals depicting Irish police history. *By app. (01)771156.* **Dublin Civic Museum**, *South William Street (behind Grafton Street):* fascinating collection of items relating to social history of the city. Stone Age flint axes, coins from Dublin's Viking mint, old maps and prints, and Nelson's head, from the pillar blown up in 1966. Regular exhibitions on particular themes. *Tues-Sat, 10 a.m.-6 p.m., Sun, 11 a.m.- 2 p.m. tel: (01)771642.* **Classical Museum**, *University College, Belfield, 10 bus.* Archaeological items from ancient Greece and Rome. *By app. tel: (01)693244.*

LIBRARIES

National Library, *Kildare Street* repository of information about Ireland, very useful if you're ancestor tracing. Vast collection of Irish newspapers and magazines—virtually every issue of every title ever published. More recent newspapers are on microfilm, not the easiest to read. *Mon-Fri, 10 a.m.-9 p.m. 5 p.m. mid-July-mid-August. Sats, 10 a.m.-1 p.m. Closed Sun and Bank Holidays. Details: (01)765521.* **Marsh's Library**, *St Patrick's Close (behind St Patrick's Cathedral). 50, 50A, 50B, 54, 54A, 56 bus.* 1701 library with some 25,000 volumes. Interior, where readers are locked into wired alcoves with rare books, has great atmosphere. Librarian Mrs Muriel McCarthy is mine of information. *Mon. 2 p.m.-4 p.m.; Wed, Thurs and Fri, 10.30 a.m.-12.30 p.m.; 2 p.m.-4 p.m.; Sat, 10.30 a.m.-12.30 p.m.*
Royal Irish Academy, *Dawson Street:* one of largest collections of ancient Irish manuscripts in the country. *Closed last three weeks Aug. by app. Tel: (01)764222.*

Chester Beatty Library and Gallery of Oriental Art, *20 Shrewsbury Road. 5, 6, 7A and 8 buses to Merrion Road.* Outstanding collection of books, paintings, papyri, clay tablets, bindings, wall hangings, costumes, carvings and drawings illustrate the history of mankind from 2700 BC (Babylonian clay tablets) to present day. Vast array of Japanese prints, outstanding collection of Islamic material. *Tues-Fri, 10 a.m.-5 p.m. Sat, 2 p.m.-5 p.m. Closed Tues after Bank Holidays. Conducted tours Sat 2.30 p.m. Tel: (01)692386.* **King's Inns**, *Henrietta Street:* library founded in 1787, over 100,000 printed volumes, including all the Dublin directories except one and nearly 10,000 pamphlets. *Normally, only members of the Inns are admitted. Tel: (01)747134.*

Central Catholic Library, *74 Merrion Square:* 80,000 volumes of religious and general interest. Large Irish section. *Lending, reference department open to non-members on payment of small fee. Reading Room. Mon-Fri, 11 a.m.-7.30 p.m. Tel: (01)761264.* **Pearse Street Library**, *1, 2, 3 bus.* Impressive collection of Irish interest material including items to do with local printing and book binding. *Tel: (01)777662.* **Goethe-Institute Library**, *37 Merrion Square: Mon-Tues and Thurs, 4 p.m.-8 p.m., Wed and Fri. 10 a.m.-6 p.m., Sat, 10 a.m.-1 p.m. Tel: (01)766451.*

Commerce Library, *Capel Street. 23 bus.* Impressive reference section where you can check out almost everything under the sun. *Tel: (01)741940.* **Dublin Diocesan Library**, *Clonliffe Road:* extensive reference facilities. *Details, tel: (01)741680.* **D** Trace your ancestors at **Genealogical Office**, *65A Earl Court, Adelaide Road, Dublin 2, tel: (01)608899, Extn. 59.*

GALLERIES

National Gallery, *Merrion Square West:* some 2,000 paintings from all major European schools, exhibits include world-famous Poussins, Goyas and Gainsboroughs. In Irish rooms, outstanding works by Jack and John B. Yeats, Hone, Osborne, Lavery and Orpen. Bar and restaurant. Frequent visiting exhibitions. *Mon-Sat, 10 a.m.-6 p.m. Sun, 2 p.m.-5 p.m. Late opening, Thurs, 9 p.m. Art reference library, Mon-Fri, 10 a.m.-5.15 p.m. Public lectures Sun, 3.15 p.m., Wed, 1.15 p.m. (except summer) and Thurs, 7 p.m. June, July, Aug and Sept, free conducted tours, Sat 3 p.m. Tel: (01)767571.* **D**

Municipal Gallery, *Parnell Square:* impressive collection of works by 19th and 20th c Irish and European artists. Also Lane collection of paintings, stained glass by Harry Clarke and Evie Hone and sculptures. Restaurant. *Tues-Sat, 10 a.m.-6 p.m.; Sun, 11 a.m.-5 p.m. Tel: (01)741903.* **Solomon Gallery**, *Powerscourt Centre;* impressive array of contemporary art in equally impressive surroundings, *Mon-Sat, 10 a.m.-5.30 p.m. Tel: (01)719596.* **D** **Douglas Hyde Gallery**, *Trinity College:* about 12 exhibitions a year of Irish and international fine and applied art. *Mon-Sat, 11 a.m.- 5.30 p.m. Details: (01)772941, ext 1116.* **D** **Patrick Brown Gallery**, *15 South William Street: daily, tel: (01)719012.*

Grace Pym Gallery, *15 Duke Street:* mostly Irish paintings of 18th and 19th c. *Mon-Fri, 10 a.m.-5.30 p.m. Tel: (01) 770416.*
Wellesley Ashe Gallery, *25 South Frederick Street:* Irish paintings, including watercolours, from 18th-20th c; also bronzes. *Mon-Fri, 10 a.m.-6 p.m. Tel: (01)767425.* **Godolphin Gallery**, *20 Clare Street:* oils and watercolours by European and Irish artists of 18th, 19th and earlier 20th c. *Mon-Fri, 10 a.m.-6 p.m. Sat by app., tel: (01)763663/762135,*

Cynthia O'Connor Gallery, *35A Kildare Street:* mainly Irish oils and watercolours, 18th-early 20th c. Mon—Fri 9.45 a.m.—5.30 p.m. Tel: (01)762096. **Neptune Gallery**, *42 South William Street:* engravings, oils, prints and watercolours of 18th and 19th c. *Mon- Fri 10 a.m.-6 p.m. Sat, a.m. Tel: (01)715021.* **European Fine Arts Gallery**, *7 Lower Merrion Street:* Dutch and Flemish old masters, also Irish and English paintings and prints from 18th and 19th c *Mon-Fri, 12 noon-5 p.m. Sat, by app. Tel: (01)762506.*

Oriel Gallery, *17 Clare Street:* regular exhibitions of mainly 20th c Irish paintings in attractive two level gallery. *Mon-Fri 10 a.m.-5.30 p.m. Sat, 10 a.m.-1 p.m. Tel: (01)763410.* **Oisin Arts Gallery**, *187 Mount Prospect Avenue, Clontarf. 30, 44A bus.* Oils, prints and watercolours by Irish and European artists. *Mon-Fri, 9 a.m.-6 p.m.; Sat, 10 a.m.-6 p.m. Sun, 3 p.m.-6 p.m. Tel: (01)331895.* **Ballsbridge Gallery**, *10 Baggot Lane, Dublin 4. Mon-Sat. Tel:(01) 600363.*

Pepper Canister Gallery, *47 Percy Lane. 4, 10 bus to Baggot Street bridge.* Art exhibitions. *Tues-Sat, 11 a.m.-5.30 p.m. Tel: (01) 681179.* **Grattan Gallery**, *58 Capel Street: Mon-Fri, 10 a.m.-5 p.m., Sat, 10 a.m.-12.30 p.m. Tel: (01)749067.* **Davis Gallery**, *11 Capel Street, Dublin 1. Tel: (01)748169.*

Setanta Gallery, *Blackrock, Co. Dublin,* original work, including prints and etchings, by Irish and international artists. *Mon-Fri, 10 a.m.-6 p.m. Sat, 11 a.m.-2 p.m. By arr. Tel. (01) 887403.* **Mezzanine Gallery**, *Kilkenny Shop, Nassau Street:* regular art exhibitions. *Mon-Sat, 9 a.m.-6 p.m. Tel: (01)777066.*
David Hendriks Gallery, *119 St. Stephen's Green:* modern works by Irish and sometimes continental artists. Paintings, some sculpture. *Mon-Fri, 11 a.m.-5.30 p.m. Sat, 11 a.m.-1 p.m. Tel: (01)756062.* **D**

Robinson Gallery, *15A Fitzwilliam Lane:* work by contemporary Irish artists, including landscapes; also some abstract work. *Mon-Fri, 10.30 a.m.-5.30 p.m. Sat, 10 a.m.-1 p.m. Tel: (01)603090.* **Taylor Galleries**, *6 Dawson Street:* mainly contemporary works, including paintings, lithographs and sculptures. *Mon.-Fri, 10 a.m.-5.30 p.m. Sat, 11 a.m.-1 p.m. Tel: (01)776089.* **Lincoln Gallery**, *4 Lincoln Place:* contemporary Irish painters and sculptors. *Tues-Sat, 10 a.m.-6 p.m. Closed Mon. Open lunchtime Tel: (01)680665.* **D** **Richard Kingston**, *19 Wellington Road, Ballsbridge:* house was once occupied by Sarah Purser, celebrated Irish artist. Her studio rooms now form gallery for Richard Kingston's own paintings. *By app. Tel: (01)684803.*

Third Policeman Gallery, *24 Essex Quay:* intriguing modern art. *Mon-Sat, 10 a.m.-4 p.m. daily.* **Kenilworth Gallery**, *22 Kenilworth Lane, Dublin 6. tel: (01)964848.* **Cruagh Wood Gallery**, *Rathfarnham.* Contemporary artists. **Oliver Dowling Gallery**, *19 Kildare Street:* mainly paintings by contemporary Irish artists. *Mon-Fri, 10 a.m.-5.30 p.m. Sat, a.m. Tel: (01)766573.* **Tom Caldwell Gallery**, *31 Upper Fitzwilliam Street. 10 bus to Lower Baggot Street.* Figurative and abstract works by contemporary artists, mostly Irish. *Tues-Fri, 10 a.m.-5.30 p.m. Sat, 10 a.m.-2 p.m. Tel: (01)688629.* **D** **Cecil King Studios**, *13 Upper Pembroke Street:* contemporary paintings, sculptures, *daily. Tel: (01)603201.*

Alliance Française, *1 Kildare Street:* regular exhibitions on French themes. *Details: (01)761732.* **Original Print Gallery,** *5 Arran Quay:* old maps and prints of Ireland. *Mon–Sun, 9 a.m.–5.30 p.m. Tel: (01)727277.* **Gallery of Photography,** *37/39 Wellington Quay:* exhibitions of photographic prints. *Mon–Sat, 11 a.m.–6 p.m. Sun, 12 noon–6 p.m. Tel: (01)714654.* **D**

United Arts Club, *3 Upper Fitzwilliam Street. 4, 10 bus to Lower Baggot Street.* Regular exhibitions of members' work. *Details: (01)762965.* **Ranelagh Gallery,** *100–102 Ranelagh. 11, 11A, 13 bus.* Paintings by local artists, *Wed, Thurs, 5.30 p.m.–7.30 p.m. Sat, 11 a.m.–6 p.m.* **Gorry Gallery,** *20 Molesworth Street:* occasional exhibitions of paintings. *Mon–Fri, 10.30 a.m.–5.30 p.m. Tel: (01) 762448.* **Bective Art Gallery,** *above Kiely's pub, 22 Donnybrook Road:* occasional art shows. For once in Dublin, art is above drinking. *Details: (01)693461.*

THEATRES

Abbey and Peacock theatres, *Lower Abbey Street:* regular performances of Irish and international plays at Abbey; Peacock stages Irish language and experimental work. Occ. art exhibitions in Abbey foyer. *Details: (01)744505.* **D Focus Theatre,** *Pembroke Place, Pembroke Street. 11, 11A, 11B, 13, 46A buses.* Irish and international drama. *Details: (01)763071.* **Gate Theatre,** *Cavendish Row, Parnell Square:* Irish and international plays by its own and visiting companies. *Details: (01)744045.*

Olympia Theatre, *Dame Street:* drama, pantomime, revue and variety, also worth seeing for ornate 19th c interior. *Details: (01)778962.*
Gaiety Theatre, *South King Street:* 19th c theatre with fabulous plush interior. Due to reopen in summer after renovations. *Details: (01)771717.*
Oscar Theatre, *Serpentine Avenue, Ballsbridge. 5, 6, 7A, 8, 45 bus to Merrion Road.* Drama and revue. *Details: (01)683752.*
Tailor's Hall, *Back Lane:* exhibitions, theatre, evening cabaret. *Details: (01)780797/751459.*

Projects Arts Centre, *39 East Essex Street (between quays and Dame Street);* often forward-looking drama, exhibitions, gallery. *Mon–Fri, 10 a.m.–6 p.m., Sat, 12 noon–6 p.m. Details: (01)713327/712321.* **Grapevine Arts Centre,** *31 North Frederick Street. 3, 10, 11, 13, 16, 19, 22 buses.* Exhibitions and theatrical performances. *Details: (01)728721.* **Eblana Theatre,** *Busaras:* sited in the basement of the bus station, more congenial than it sounds, stages plays; restaurant and bar (first floor), all year, details: (01)746767.* **Players' Theatre,** *No. 3 Trinity College:* excellent performances of student drama. *Details: (01)774673.*
Pintsize Puppet Theatre, *37 Parnell Square:* regular performances, *Sat, Sun, 3 p.m.* **An Damer Theatre,** *St Stephen's Green West:* Irish language drama, *tel: (01)782535.* **Irish Film Theatre,** *Earlsfort Terrace:* temporary membership for visitors. *Details: (01)764207.* **D Player Wills Theatre,** *South Circular Road. 19, 19A, 20, 22 bus.* Regular performances, including films, music and theatre. *Details: (01)758445/ 757901.*
Beaver Theatre, *Ballinteer Avenue, 48A bus.* Regular pub theatre. *Details: (01)951183.*
Embankment, *Tallaght, Co. Dublin:* pub theatre. *Details: (01)511116.*

ROUND & ABOUT

Royal Dublin Society, *Ballsbridge, 5, 6, 7A, 8, 45 bus.* Regular trade and art exhibitions, concerts and lectures. *Details: (01) 680645.* **National Concert Hall,** *Earlsfort Terrace:* stimulating variety of musical events. Lunch, pre-show suppers. *Bookings: Mon–Sat, 12 noon–7 p.m. Credit card bookings, (01)711533. Details: (01)711888.* **D Bank of Ireland Exhibition Hall,** *Lower Baggot Street:* frequent art exhibitions. *Mon–Fri, 10 a.m.–5 p.m. Details: (01)785744.*
Powerscourt House, *South William Street (off Grafton Street):* 1771 Georgian town house with outstanding plasterwork and wood carvings, meticulously restored. Covered market in court-yard, restaurants. *Mon–Sun, 9.30 a.m.–5.30 p.m.*
Casino, *Malahide Road, 20, 20A, 27, 27A, 27B,*

42, 42A, 42B buses from city centre. 18th c structure with fine views from top. *Check opening with TIO.* **20 Lower Dominick Street,** magnificent 18th c town house, now Dominican Boys' Home. *Visitors, 10 a.m.–9 p.m. daily. Large groups should tel. in advance, (01)744149.* **9 Henrietta Street,** *off Bolton Street:* inspect fine Georgian architecture. House now run by Sisters of Charity, St Vincent de Paul. *By arr. with Sister in Charge. Tel: (01)744837.* **Quaker Friends' Meeting House,** *Eustace Street, off Dame Street:* plain but imposing interior. Library has much material relating to Irish Quakers. *Daily, 9.30 a.m.–5.30 p.m. Meetings on Sun. Details: (01)778088.*
Wood Quay, *by Christ Church Cathedral:* most of this Viking site is being covered by new offices for Dublin Corporation. Museum planned. On opp. side of river, see impressive façade of **Four Courts.** **Clondalkin Round Tower** (NM),*51, 68, 69 bus.* Only remaining relic of a 7th c monastery. **Kilmainham Jail,** *Inchicore, 21, 21A, 23, 78, 78A, 78B, 79 buses.* Received its first political prisoners in 1796. The last was Éamon de Valera in 1924. 1916 Rising leaders executed here. Fascinating museum. *Conducted tours: Sun, 3 p.m.–5 p.m. Details: (01)755990.* **D Arbour Hill,** *(rear of Collins Barracks), 72 bus to Stoneybatter.* See impressive graveyard where main leaders of Easter Rising are buried. *Mon–Sat, 8 a.m.–7 p.m. Sun, 8 a.m.–5 p.m.*
Wax Museum, *Granby Row, Parnell Square.* 81 wax replicas; tableaux and scenes portray well-known personalities. *Mon–Sat, 10 a.m.–6 p.m. Sun, 2 p.m.–6 p.m. Details: (01)746416.* **Dublin Ice Rink,** *Dolphin's Barn, 19, 20, 22 buses. Mon–Sun, 2.30 p.m.–5 p.m., 8 p.m.–11 p.m. Sat, Sun, 10 a.m.–1 p.m. Details: (01)752170.* **Stock Car Racing Stadium,** *Airport Road:* stock car racing, *mid Apr–end Sept, Sun 3 p.m. Details: (01) 318448.* Ballooning: contact Eleanor Dunleavy, Dublin Ballooning Club, *'Knockrath', Herbert Road, Bray, tel: (01) 863620.* Parachuting: Niamh O'Regan, Irish Sport Parachute Association, *5 Ashdale Road, Terenure. Tel: (01)976013..* Pleasure flights: Iona National Airways, *Dublin Airport. Tel: (01)378323.* Horse drawn cabs: touristy perhaps, but an ideal way to tour city. Paddy Sarsfield, *5 Lower Kevin Street, tel: (01) 755995.*
Guinness brewery, *21, 21A, 78, 78A, 78B buses to James's Street.* Visitors welcome at visitor centre, Crane Street, alongside the brewery. Includes the ever popular 'product sampling', *Mon–Fri, 10 a.m.–3 p.m.* Guinness museum: 2,000 exhibits relating to Guinness worldwide, and brewing industry in Ireland and Britain. *By app. only. Tel: (01)756701.*
Bewley's Dublin city centre restaurants: the city's most famous eating places, where you can see and be seen. Frequented by most Dublin celebrities. South Great George's Street cafés worth seeing for genuine late Victorian/Edwardian decor. Grafton Street for Harry Clarke stained glass windows.**D**
Stock Exchange, *28 Anglesea Street:* small public gallery, open for 30 mins at 10 a.m. and 2.15 p.m., *Mon–Fri. Details: (01) 778808.* **Irish Hospitals' Sweepstakes,** *Ballsbridge (opposite RDS), 5, 6, 7A, 8, 18, 45 buses: conducted tours, Mon–Fri, 9.30 a.m.–12 noon; 2 p.m.–4 p.m. Details: (01) 687611.* **Gallery Workshop,** 1 Adam Court and 7 Grafton Street: batik and jewellery made in its own workshop, also lines made by outside artists. *Mon–Sat, 10 a.m.–6 p.m. Tel: (01)714922.* **Antiquarian Bookcrafts,** *Marlay Park Craft Centre, Dublin 16.* Leather bookbinding. *Mon–Fri, by arr. tel (01) 942834.*
Walks: College Park: entrance at Lincoln Place, through Trinity College grounds to College Green. Dodder river bank, *11 and 62 buses to Clonskeagh bridge:* upstream from Clonskeagh bridge, taking in Rathfarnham linear park. Georgian area: Merrion Square, Upper Mount Street, Fitzwilliam Street and Fitzwilliam Square. Ideal time–Sun, no traffic. Grand Canal tow-paths and canalside footpaths: start at Lower Mount Street and go as far as Portobello. Best stretch from Baggot Street bridge to Leeson Street bridge. See seat by Baggot Street bridge in

Casino, Marino

memory of poet Patrick Kavanagh. Ringsend, *1, 2 and 3 buses to Ringsend:* walk past ESB station along breakwater as far as Poolbeg lighthouse. Sandymount Strand, *3 bus to Sandymount Tower:* can be walked safely if tide out. However, it sweeps in again at great speed. North Bull Island *Clontarf, 30 bus.* Fine outdoor recreational area connected to Clontarf Road by causeway. Good walk along adjacent Bull Wall.

Iveagh Market, *Francis Street:* old clothes and furniture. *Tues–Sat, 9 a.m.–6 p.m. Details: (01)751343.* **Liberty Market,** *Meath Street:* clothes, drapery and household goods. *Fri and Sat, all day.* **Moore Street Market,** *off Henry Street:* fruit, vegetables and classic Dublin wit. *Mon–Sat, 9 a.m.–6 p.m.* **Vegetable Market,** *St Michan's Street:* fruit, vegetables, fish and flowers. *Mon–Fri, 8 a.m.–5 p.m. Tues, closes at 4 p.m. Sat, 8 a.m.–11 a.m. Details: (01)742255.*

Ryans, *Parkgate Street (near Heuston railway station):* superb traditional bar, complete with snugs and old-fashioned lamps. Remodelled in 1896 and little changed since. **Stag's Head,** *Dame Court, off Dame Street:* one of the city's oldest pubs, founded in 1770, largely remodelled in 1895. Plenty of atmosphere. **Palace Bar,** *Fleet Street:* genuine, old-time Dublin pub. Tiled floor, dark panelling, mirrors and leaded glass in en-trance doors. Upstairs lounge has character. Much favoured by journalists from nearby Irish Times, as is **Bowes'** pub, also Fleet Street.
Mulligans, *Poolbeg Street, behind George's Quay:* authentic Dublin pub, with plenty of dark character, Dubliners and good Guinness. **Long Hall,** *51 South Great George's Street:* Dublin's most ornate traditional pub. Richly carved interior wood work, chandeliers and ceiling-high mirrors date back to 19th c.
Humphreys', *Ranelagh:* traditional establish-ment little changed by the passing years. Still has 'grocery' sign over front door, a relic from days when most Irish pubs sold both drink and groceries. The Grafton Street area has several well-known pubs. **McDaid's,** *Harry Street,* has

noted literary connections. **The Bailey,** *Duke Street,* extensively renovated, has literary and political connections going back many years. Also door of No. 7 Eccles Street, immortalised by Joyce as home of Leopold Bloom. **Davy Byrne's,** *Creation Arcade;* famous meeting place. Merrion Row/Lower Baggot Street area: **O'Donoghue's,** *Merrion Row,* **Toner's** *Lower Baggot Street,* both noted for folk music. Also see **Doheny and Nesbitt's,** *Lower Baggot Street:* dark wood and dark Guinness.

PARKS

Phoenix Park, *10, 14, 14A bus to North Circular Road gate. 23, 24, 25, 26, 51 bus to Main Gate.* Largest park in Europe (1752 acres). Numerous tree-lined roads, several lakes, herds of deer. Furry Glen nature trail in NW of park has many trees and plants. From the Fifteen acres, you will see many of Dublin's landmarks. **Herbert Park,** Ballsbridge, oasis near city centre. **Dublin Zoo,** *Phoenix Park:* one of finest in Europe, with many species of animals and reptiles to be seen in modern houses and outdoor enclosures. *Mon–Sat, 9.30 a.m.–sunset; Sun, 11 a.m.–sunset, all year. Details: (01)771425.* **D** Racecourse, tel:

Grand Canal

(01)300837.
National Botanic Gardens, *Botanic Road, Glasnevin. 13, 19, 34 and 34A buses.* Extensive selection of trees, flowering shrubs and tropical plants. In large conservatories, often glorious displays of rare and exotic species. Fine walks in gardens and along adjacent bank of River Tolka. *Summer, Mon–Sat, 9 a.m.–6 p.m. Sun, 11 a.m.–6 p.m. Otherwise, Mon–Sat, 10 a.m.–4.30 p.m. Sun, 11 a.m.–4.30 p.m. Suns: greenhouses open 2 p.m. Details: (01)377596.*
St Stephen's Green: an oasis of lawns and lakes in heart of Dublin. Ideal for walking, relaxing or observing the antics of one's fellow creatures. *Summer, concerts. Mon–Sat, all year, from 8 a.m. to dusk. Sun from 10 a.m. Details: (01)747733.* **D** St **Anne's Park Rose Garden.** *Mount Prospect Avenue, Clontarf, 30, 44A bus from Marlboro Street.* Magnificent collection of roses. *Daily, all year.* **Marley Park,** *Rathfarnham, 16, 48A bus.* Extensive park with woodlands and large pond. Nature trail. Start of Wicklow Way walk. Model steam

railway. Fine house, rebuilt in 19th c, restored. Stable courtyard has remarkable collection of craft workshops. *Mon–Fri, 9.30 a.m.–5.30 p.m. Sat, Sun, 2 p.m.–6 p.m.*

SPORT

Croke Park: main Dublin venue for Gaelic Athletic Association games. *Details: (01)743111.* **Lansdowne Road:** international rugby stadium. *Details: (01)689292/684601.* **Dalymount Park:** the national football arena. *Details: (01)300923.*
Ballyfermot Leisure Centre, roller skating, other sports. *daily. Details: (01)264648.* Star Roller Rink, Crumlin. *Tel: (01) 501438.* Swimming pools: indoor, heated. Ballyfermot. *Le Fanu Park;* Ballymun, *Seven Towers Shopping Centre;* Coolock, *Northside Shopping Centre;* Crumlin, *Windmill Road;* Finglas, *Mellowes Road;* Iveagh Baths, *Bride St;* Rathmines, *Williams Park;* Seán McDermott Street, *city centre.* Open air: Clontarf. *Details, all pools: (01)776811, extn. 189/190.*
Riding: Ashtown Equestrian Centre, *Castleknock, (01) 301046/307611/741351;* Callaighstown Riding Centre, *Callaighstown, Rathcoole, (01)589236;* Castleknock College Riding Centre, *Castleknock, (01)213958;* Penderosa, *Coolmine,*

Saggart, *(01)589310.* Bicycles: Joe Daly, *Lower Main Street, Dundrum, tel: (01)981485;* Essex Cycles, *30 Bachelor's Walk, tel: (01)740311;* Gem Cycle Service, *47/48 Chelmsford Road, Ranelagh, tel: (01)978438;* Little Sport, *Merville Avenue, Fairview, tel: (01)332405;* A. McDonald, *38 Wexford Street, tel: (01)752586;* P. J. Power, *124 Emmet Road, Inchicore, tel: (01)752647;* Rathgar Cycles, *99A Rathgar Road, tel: (01)970268;* Rent a Bike, *58 Lr. Gardiner Street, tel: (01)724779,* bicycles can be rented in Dublin and left in Rosslare or vice versa.
Golf Clubs: Royal Dublin, *Dollymount, 18 holes, tel: (01) 337153;* Newlands, *Clondalkin, 18 holes, tel: (01) 592903;* Grange, *Rathfarnham, 18 holes, tel: (01)905832;* Edmondstown, *Rathfarnham, 18 holes, tel: (01)904207;* Castle, Rathfarnham, *18 holes, tel: (01)904207;* Clontarf, *18 holes, tel: (01)332669;* (Setting for Carrolls Irish Open Championship, Aug. *Details: (01) 604311).* Elm Park, *Donnybrook, 18 holes, tel: (01)693438.*

North of Dublin

Aeronautical Museum, *Dublin Airport. Airport bus also 41A bus from Lr. Abbey St., Dublin. TIO: tel: (01)376387/375533, all year.* Fascinating collection of models, photographs, pieces of equipment showing history of Irish aviation with replica of first-ever Aer Lingus plane. *Mon–Sun all year, 10 a.m.–5 p.m. Details: (01)379900, extn. 4323.* **D** The airport has no viewing terraces, but see aircraft arrivals and departures from lounge bar on first floor.

Baily Lighthouse, *SE Howth Head:* write for pass three weeks in advance to Commissioners of Irish Lights, 16 Lower Pembroke Street, Dublin 2.

Balbriggan, *20 m (32 km) N of Dublin on NI Dublin–Belfast road. 33 bus from Lr. Abbey St., Dublin, also train.* Pleasant seaside town, with enjoyable walk from main street to beach and harbour. **Balrothery Inn,** supper theatre for most of year, *details: (01)412252/411022.* Gormanstown Riding Centre, *Knockagin Road, tel: (01) 412508.*

Baldongan Castle, *3 m (5 km) S of Skerries:* 13th c fortress now in ruins, but fine views from top of tower.

Donabate, *between Dublin and Balbriggan,* small town with a profusion of golf clubs. Dublin and County Golf Club, *Corballis, 18 holes, tel: (01) 452127;* Donabate Golf Club, *18 holes, tel: (01)450335;* Island Golf Club, *18 holes, tel: (01)450595.*

Dunsink Observatory, *between Finglas and Blanchardstown. 40C bus from Parnell Street, Dublin, to Dunsink Lane, then walk 0.5 m (0.8 km).* Founded in 1783, one of oldest in world. *Sept–Mar, first and third Sat of each month, 8 p.m.–10 p.m. Send SAE for admission tickets. Details: (01)307911/307959.*

Dunsoghly Castle, *4 m (6 km) NW of Finglas, E of N2 Dublin–Ashbourne road:* from parapets of 15th c castle, fine views of N Co. Dublin, including airport. *Key from nearby cottage. All reasonable times.*

Fairyhouse Races, *14 m (22 km) NW of Dublin, E of N3 Dublin–Navan road:* main meeting: three day Easter event. Also air show, Aug, details: (01)256167.

Howth, *31 bus from Lr. Abbey St., Dublin, also train from Connolly Station, Dublin.* Pleasant residential district and popular summertime seaside resort. **Howth Castle:** rhododendron gardens. *Daily all year, 8 a.m.–sunset. Flowering season Apr. May. June. Castle closed.* **Howth Art Gallery,** *Church Street, opp. Garda station:* regular shows by local artists. *Wed, Fri, Sat, Sun, 3 p.m.–5.30 p.m. June, July, Aug, daily, 3 p.m.–5.30 p.m. Details: (01)323529.* **Studio Gallery,** *Abbey Street:* local art, *daily, Mon–Sun.*

Abbey Tavern: traditional music, *details: (01)322006.* Howth harbour's two piers provide good walks. Howth Head: take cliff walk from Howth village. Path dangerous in places, fine views. Howth Head to Sutton: in case of weariness, 88 bus runs from Howth village to Sutton via Howth Head. Boat trips from Howth pier to Ireland's Eye, *May–Sept, daily, departures as required. Details: C. Doyle (01)322865 or F. Doyle (01)314200.* Howth Golf Club, *18 holes, tel: (01)323055.*

Kilsallaghan Church (C), *3 m (5 km) NW of Finglas:* see 1917 Michael Healy window depicting Christ the King.**D**

Lambay Island, *3 m (5 km) offshore from Rush, daily boat from Rush, depending on tides:* to visit island, write to the Steward, Lambay Island, Rush Co. Dublin.

Malahide, *9m (14 km) N of Dublin, 42 bus to Malahide from Talbot St., Dublin. Train from Connolly station.* Small coastal town, **Malahide Castle,** many features worth seeing, including

Great Hall, Front Hall, Oak Room, Library and Drawing Room. Fine furniture, panelling and National Portrait Collection. Concerts; craft, antique shop, guided tours. Extensive parkland, with sporting facilities, picnic areas, nature trails, Botanic Gardens. *All year, Mon-Fri, 10 a.m.-5 p.m. Apr-Oct, Sat, 11 a.m.-6 p.m. Sun, BH, 2 p.m.-6 p.m. Nov-Mar, Sat, Sun, BH, 2 p.m.-6 p.m. Details: (01) 452337.*

Tattan Gallery, *New Street:* originals and signed limited edition prints by contemporary artists, *Tues-Sat, 10 a.m.-1 p.m., otherwise by arr. tel:* (01)453767. Enjoyable walk through the town, past Grand Hotel, along coast road to Portmarnock. Penguin Water Ski Club, *The Strand, tel:* (01)451365/310964; Dublin Balscadden Power Boat and Water Ski Club, *The Strand, tel:* (01)450970/301170.

Portmarnock, *32 bus from Lr. Abbey St., Dublin, train from Connolly Station, Dublin.* Good beach and coastal walks. 18 hole golf course, *tel:* (01)324674. Portmarnock Raceway: regular trotting races, *details: (01)462834.*

Rush/Lusk: *18 m (29 km) N of Dublin. 33 bus from Lr. Abbey St., Dublin, train from Connolly Station, Dublin.* Twin villages: Rush is fine fishing village with two sandy beaches. In Lusk, see round tower and nearby parish church. Key to tower of latter is in shop 50 yards from entrance to churchyard. **Good Old Days Exhibition,** *Channel Road:* museum of rural life over past century. Traction engines, carriages, old mill wheels. *June-Aug, Mon-Sun, 2.30 p.m.-5.30 p.m. Details:* (01)437512/437638.**D** Rush Leisure Centre: *Channel Road, daily, tel: (01)437512.* Bicycles: A. Leonard, Millview Garage, tel: (01)437297.

Skerries, *19 m (30 km) N of Dublin. 33 bus, also train from Connolly Station, Dublin.* Pleasant holiday resort and fishing town, good walks along the front, taking in pier. Shenick's Island, offshore, can be reached on foot at low tide. **Black Raven bar:** interesting painting of Black Raven pipe band founded by Thomas Ashe, a 1916 leader. Bicycles: Fergus Cullen, *Dublin Street, tel:* (01)491845. Golf Club, 18 holes, tel: (01)491204.

St Doulagh's Church, *2 m (3 km) W of Portmarnock:* parts date back to 12th c, also subterranean chamber called St Catherine's Well, *Sat, Sun aft. SO.*

Swords, *33 bus from Dublin:* CI church, square tower in grounds, dating from 6th c monastery founded by St Colmcille. *June-Sept, 2.30 p.m.-5 p.m. daily. Other times, by arr., Mrs Thorpe, 46 Main Street, Swords.* **Swords Castle,** *Main Street:* built in 1200 undergoing renovation at time of going to press, *check with Dublin Airport TIO.*

Velvet Strand, *Portmarnock. 32 bus from Lr. Abbey St., Dublin.* Fine expanse of beach.

Drogheda

Pop. 23,000, 30 m (48 km) N of Dublin. EC. Thurs. TIO: Boyne Shopping Centre. Tel: (041)37070 July-Aug. Bus enquiries: CIE bus station, (041)38583. Train enquiries: CIE, MacBride Station, (041)38583. 1 bus from Dublin, also train. Taxis: Lawrence Street, near Tholsel; railway station.

Hilly town, over 2,000 years old. The Danes settled here in 911 and later, under Anglo-Norman rule, two separate towns developed, one on each side of the Boyne river. In 1649, after a bitter siege, Cromwell took Drogheda and killed most of its inhabitants. Today, though a busy industrial town, the wharfsides and the historic back lanes are extremely atmospheric.

St Peter's Church (C), *West Street:* Drogheda's parish church houses shrine of St Oliver Plunkett, Primate of All-Ireland martyred at Tyburn, London, in 1681. The jewelled casket containing his head is a centre of pilgrimage.**D St Mary's**

Newgrange

(CI), *top of Peter Street:* commanding views from churchyard, where Henry Ussher, Archbishop of Armagh, is buried. Church built in 1807; earlier building damaged during Cromwellian siege.**D Augustinian abbey,** *Abbey Lane, behind West Street Shopping Centre:* only the fine 13th c tower remains. If you are lucky, a stroll along the lane will evoke the 'feel' of old Drogheda. **Siena Convent** (C), *Chord Road:* built in 1796, peaceful private chapel, *open daily.***D**

Museum, *Millmount:* one of finest town museums in Ireland. All kinds of material reflecting life in Drogheda over past three centuries. *Summer, 3 p.m.-6 p.m. daily. Nov 1-Apr 1, Wed and Sun, 3 p.m.-6 p.m. Otherwise by arr. Mrs Moira Corcoran, tel: (041)36391.* **Millmount Tower,** *next to museum:* said to have been built on site of 11th c BC burial mound. View from top is magnificent, taking in whole town and much of Boyne valley. Gate normally locked, but ask for key at museum.

Courthouse, *Fair Street:* houses sword and mace presented to Drogheda Corporation by William III after Battle of the Boyne, 17th c charters and assorted municipal regalia. *By arr., Town Clerk's Office, Mon-Fri.* Library, *Fair Street:* extensive selection of local material and information. *Tues-Sat. Details: (041) 36649.*

Callan Design Centre, *Narrow West Street:* locally produced arts and crafts, including jewellery, paintings, pottery. Local interest books. Licensed restaurant. *Mon-Sat, all year, 10 a.m.-6 p.m. Details: (041)37869.* **Harvest Gallery,** *3 St. Mary's Terrace, Dublin Road.* Local Artists. *All year, daily.* **Railway Arms,** *Dublin Road:* opens at 7.30 a.m., one of few early licences granted, for workers on nearby quays.

St. Laurence Gate, *top of Laurence Street:* only survivor of ten 13th c town gates, interesting walk from here down to riverside, taking in 19th c warehouses. Riverside walk: upstream for 3m (5km) on S bank, beyond second road bridge. Kiltallaght Riding School, *Kiltallaght House, Grangebellew, tel: (041)22233.* Bicycles: P. J. Carolan, 77 Trinity Street, tel: (041)38242.

AROUND DROGHEDA

Baltray, *5m (8km) E of Drogheda, 12 bus from Drogheda.* Small village with fine golf links on N shore of Boyne estuary. Beyond links one of E Ireland's finest beaches. Baltray Golf Club, 18 holes, tel: (041)22329.

Bellewstown, *4m (6km) S of Drogheda:* races, *June, July. Details: TIO, Drogheda, June-Aug, tel:* (041)37070.

Bettystown, *5m (8km) E of Drogheda, 20 bus from Drogheda. Also train from Drogheda to 'twin' village of Laytown.* Popular holiday resort on S side of Boyne estuary. One of longest strands in Ireland—6m (9km)—ideal for walking at all states of tide. Horse racing along the strand for one day in July. *Details: Joseph Collins, 27 Fair Street, Drogheda.* Bettystown Golf Club, *18 holes, tel: (041)27563.* Laytown and Bettystown Golf Club, *18 holes, tel: (041) 27534.*

Brugh na Boinne (Palace of the Boyne), *7m (11km) W of Drogheda, immediately S of N51 to Slane. TIO: Newgrange, tel: (041)24274. May-Sept.* Within this 3m (5km) by 2m (3km) area there are at least 15 passage graves, Newgrange, Knowth and Dowth being the most striking. **Newgrange,** probably dating from 2,500 BC, is one of finest and most sophisticated passage graves in W Europe, construction required an estimated 180,000 tons of stone, which was originally finished with a dazzling coat of pebbles. *June-Sept 10 a.m.-7 p.m. daily, guide service. Otherwise, Tues-Sat, 10 a.m.-1 p.m.; 2 p.m.-5 p.m. Sun, 2 p.m.-5 p.m. Details: (041)24274.*

Knowth, closed to public until excavations completed. **Dowth,** only recommended to enthusiasts in good physical condition. Some crawling is needed to reach first of the two tombs. Directions for borrowing key posted at site entrance.

Clogher, *9m (14km) NE of Drogheda, 12 bus from Drogheda.* Walk from village to nearby fishing harbour of Port Oriel, about 1m (1.6km). From headland above harbour, excellent views of entire Co. Louth coast and Mountains of Mourne. Port Oriel Youth Hostel, *Clogher Head, tel:* (041)22247.

High Cross, Monasterboice

Dunleer, *7m (11km) N of Drogheda on N1.* Rathgory Transport Museum: superb collection of vintage cars and motorcycles, Ireland's first motor-driven fire engine. *Mar 17–Oct 31, weekends and Bank Holidays, 10.30 a.m.–6 p.m. Details: (041)51389.* **D**

Monasterboice, *5m (8km) NW of Drogheda, just off N1:* remains of ancient monastic settlement. Main interest today is High Cross, 17'8" (5.4 metres), one of best-preserved in Ireland; surface almost entirely ornamented. Nearby, explore ruins of 110 ft. (33 metres) high round tower. Key held by Patrick Crilly, house at gate. Mellifont Youth Hostel, *tel: (041)26127.*

Mornington, *4m (6.5km) E of Drogheda on L125 road to Bettystown, 20 bus from Drogheda.* Maiden Tower can be climbed, but it's dangerous. Visit Moran's pub, one of finest traditional pubs in Ireland, complete with snugs and mahogany shelves for groceries.

Mosney Holiday Centre, *Mosney, 5m (8km) S of Drogheda, train from Drogheda.* Facilities include indoor and outdoor swimming, amusement park, horse-riding. *Open to day visitors, SO.* **D**

Slane, *9m (14km) W of Drogheda, 23 bus from Drogheda.* Climb Slane Hill, where St. Patrick lit his Paschal fire in AD 433, proclaiming Christianity in Ireland, also remains of 16th c church and monastic school. From the top of the hill, see whole of Boyne valley from Trim to Drogheda.

Townley Hall, *4m (6.5km) W of Drogheda on N51 to Slane:* forest walks, nature trail, picnic area and car park. One of points on nature trail overlooks the site of the Battle of the Boyne, fought on July 12, 1690. A Boyne Museum is planned. Towards the end of the trail, good views of the Obelisk bridge across the river Boyne. Worth taking the detour off the trail to explore King William's Glen.

Dundalk

Pop. 23,000, 52 m (84 km) N of Dublin and the same distance S of Belfast on main N1 road. E.C. Thurs. TIO: Dromad lay-by on N1. Tel: (042)71221. July–Aug. Bus enquiries: CIE, Dundalk. (042)34075. Train enquiries: CIE Dundalk station. (042)35521. 1 bus from Dublin and Newry. Train from Dublin and Belfast. Taxis: Market Square.

Closely associated with the legendary early-

Christian hero Cuchulainn. In 1177, though fortified, the town fell to the Anglo-Normans, and for the next 300 years was repeatedly attacked as a frontier town of the English Pale. Most of its fortifications were removed during the 18th c and little of Dundalk's historic past is to be seen today, nevertheless parts of the town are interesting, particularly the area around the Courthouse. Maytime Festival: wide variety of entertainment, social and sporting events, *late May. Details: (042)32276.*

Seatown Castle, *junction of Castle Road and Mill Street:* see tower of 13th c Franciscan monastery. Library: *Tues–Sat, 10 a.m.–1 p.m.; 2 p.m.–5 p.m. Tues and Thurs, 6 p.m.–8 p.m. Details: (042)35457* Theatre: amateur and professional performances at the Town Hall. Occasional visits by touring companies. *Details: (042)32276.* Factory visits: Carroll's cigarette factory, *2 m (3 km) S of Dundalk on Dublin road. 2 hour tours weekdays a.m. and p.m. all year. Details: (042)34747* Harp lager brewery, *near railway station: tours all year. Details: (042)34793.*

Racecourse: regular meetings. *Details: (042)34419.* Greyhound racing: *Mon, Fri, Sat eve, all year. Occasional extra meetings for charity. Details: (042)35019.* Riding: Ballymascanlon House Hotel, *near Dundalk. Tel: (042)71124.* Bicycles: George Elliott, *Dublin Street, tel: (042)32224.*

AROUND DUNDALK

Annagassan, *near Castlebellingham, 5 bus from Dundalk.* Founded by the Danes. Good walk along seashore to nearby small bathing resort of Salterstown.

Ardee, *13 m (20 km) SW of Dundalk, 10 bus from Dundalk, 11 bus from Drogheda.* See St Mary's (CI), Main Street. Incorporates part of 13th c Carmelite church. Key from Mrs McKenney opposite or Rev Francis Jennings, *Jervis Street, tel: (041)43320.* **D** Ardee Golf Club, *Townparks, 9 holes, tel: (041)53227.*

Ballymascanlon, *4 m (7 km) NE of Dundalk on Carlingford road:* Proleek Dolmen, with 46 ton capstone resting on two 3 ft (1 metre) support stones. Pathway from nearby Ballymascanlon Hotel.

Bellurgan, *5 m (8 km) N.of Dundalk, turn N of Ballymackellett off Ravensdale–Carlingford road:* forest walks, picnic sites, car park, scenic views of Dundalk Bay.

Blackrock, *4 m (6 km) SE of Dundalk. Violet private bus from Dundalk.* Popular seaside resort. Good walk along promenade, open air swimming pool, *June–Sep, daily.* Golf Club, *18 holes, tel: (042)35379.*

Carlingford, *4 bus from Dundalk.* 13th c King John's Castle stands on rock overlooking harbour, although not completely restored, in good state of preservation. *All reasonable times. Apply: B. Fretwell, Castlehill.* Carlingford Lough Oyster Festival—*Aug. Details: Dundalk TIO.* **The Mint,** *just off Square:* well preserved 15th c three storey tower house with remarkable mullion windows. Sometimes open; *check with P. J. O'Hare, tel: (042)73128.*

Castlebellingham, *8 m (13 km) S of Dundalk, 1 bus from Dundalk.* Attractive village that once had thriving brewery. 3 m (5 km) walk from square to tiny seaside village of Annagassan very pleasant in fine weather. Bellingham Stables, *Station Road. Tel: (042)72175.*

Castletown, *2 m (3 km) W of town:* ancient Dun Dealgan, mound over 60 ft (18 metres) high and said to have been birthplace of Cuchulainn. On summit is ruin of 1780 house. Nearby, well-preserved ruin of mediaeval Castletown Castle.

Castle Roche, *5 m (8 km) NW of Dundalk:* fine views from this early 13th c castle (NM).

Cooley Peninsula, *4 bus to Greenore, Gyles Quay from Dundalk.* If you drive round the peninsula, starting in Dundalk, going via Gyles Quay (small fishing village, good bathing and sailing facilities), through Greenore, Carlingford and

Omeath back to Dundalk, you will be rewarded with some spectacular views. To S, views of Dundalk Bay and Co. Louth coast. To N, magnificent backdrop of Mountains of Mourne, just across Carlingford Lough.

Faughart, *4 m (6 km) N of Dundalk:* reputed to be birthplace of St Brigid, patroness of Ireland. From Faughart cemetery, burial place of Robert the Bruce's brother, tremendous views of area. Adjacent car park.

Greenore: Golf Club, *18 holes, tel: (042)73212.*

Kildemock, *2 m (3 km) SE of Ardee:* Jumping Church, the gable, only remaining wall, stands 3 ft (1 metre) inside its foundations. Tradition says that the wall 'jumped' inwards to exclude grave of excommunicated person. This explanation's main rival is almost as improbable: during a severe storm in 1715 the wall is held to have been lifted and deposited where it now stands.

Omeath, *19 m (30 km) NE of Dundalk, 4 bus from Dundalk.* Popular seaside resort. Jaunting cars from strand to Calvary Shrine. Daily ferry trips to Warrenpoint on N shore of Carlingford Lough, *Easter–Sept.* Youth Hostel, *tel: (042)75142.*

Ravensdale, *4 m (6 km) N of Dundalk, turn E off N1:* car park, forest walks, nature trail, standing stones.

Slieve Foye, *2 m (3 km) NW of Carlingford on T62 towards Omeath:* scenic drive to car park overlooking Carlingford Lough. Nature trail gives good climb through woods. Midway viewing point has excellent views of Rostrevor Forest, Co. Down.

Dun Laoghaire

Pop. 100,000, 7 m (11 km) S of Dublin. TIO: tel, (01)806984/ 805760/806547/807048/804321. All year. Bus and train enquiries: (01)787777. Dun Laoghaire railway station: (01)808537. Taxis: Marine Road, opp. Post Office. (01) 805263. Frequent bus and train services from Dublin. Coach tours: SO. Details TIO.

Many people's first glimpse of Ireland. Until early 19th c, this major ferry port was small fishing village, but after the opening of the railway from Dublin in 1834, the expansion of Kingstown, as it was then known, was rapid. Today, the town is a pleasant holiday and shopping centre, with a profusion of gourmet restaurants, including what is probably the dearest restaurant in Ireland, the Mirabeau. Dun Laoghaire summer festival: concerts, cultural activities and exhibitions, *June. Details: TIO.*

Dominican Convent (C), *Lower George's Street:* ask to see oratory in grounds. Built in 1919 in thanksgiving for end of World War I, Sister Mary Concepta Lynch spent from 1920 until her death in 1939 decorating every part of interior with fabulous Celtic designs. **St Michael's** (C), *corner Marine Road and George's Street:* original 19th c church burned down in 1965. Striking modern building effectively grafted onto the surviving bell tower.

National Maritime Museum, *Haigh Terrace, SE corner of Moran Park:* highlight is great working optic from Baily lighthouse at Howth. Many models of ships, including Great Eastern, also 11 metre French longboat captured at Bantry Bay in 1796, reckoned to be oldest surviving ship's boat in world. *Summer, Tues–Sun, 2.30 p.m.–5.30 p.m. Otherwise, Sun aft.*

Sir Thomas Brown Gallery, *86 Lower George's Street:* occasional shows by Irish artists. *Mon–Sat, 10 a.m.–5 p.m. Details: (01)801080.*
Kimberley Gallery, *64 Monkstown Road:* works by local artists. Daily, 10 a.m.–5 p.m. **Pavilion Theatre,** *Marine Road:* year-round entertainment ranging from drama to pop and rock concerts. *Details: (01)801808/808203.*

The piers: east pier, nearly 1 m (2 km) long, and seemingly never-ending, is the more popular for walks. *July, Aug, Sun aft*, concerts on band-stand. If you prefer solitude, try during week or early Sat or Sun. West pier can be walked, but the going is much rougher. Also Marine Parade: as far as tiny beach at Sandycove and James Joyce Tower. Return by main Sandycove Road. Squares: elegant walking N of George's Street, particularly those at Clarinda Park and Royal Terrace E and W. People's Park; concerts, *July, Aug, Sun aft*. Dun Laoghaire Sailing School, *115 Lower George's Street, tel: (01)806654.* Swimming pool, indoor, heated, Windsor Terrace, *daily*. Also seafront. *June, July and Aug, Mon–Sun. Details: (01) 806967.* Bicyles 95 Lower George's Street, *tel: (01) 803984.* Dun Laoghaire Golf Club, *18 holes, tel: (01)801055.*

AROUND DUN LAOGHAIRE

Ballinascorney, *Lower and Upper: 8 m (13 km) from Rathfarnham on L199, keep right at first junction beyond Ballinascorney Gap:* layby, picnic places, forest walks, access to Seechon Mountain.

Barnaslingan: *on Barnaslingan Lane E off T43 near Kilternan.* Car park, picnic place, forest walks, scenic view overlooking the Scalp Mountain.

Blackrock: swimming pool, open air, seafront, *SO, daily, details: (01)888306.*

Bray: *seaside town 8 m (12 km) S of Dun Laoghaire. TIO: Superquinn Shopping Centre: tel: (01)867128/9. July–Aug.* Train enquiries: Bray Station, *(01)862007. 45 bus from Hawkins St, Dublin to Bray, also train.* Coach tours: *SO details: TIO.* Splendid esplanade ideal for strolling, both in summer and equally during the dramatic winter storms. Nearby amusement arcades. *SO.* Laneways and attractive terraced streets between Main Street and seafront. Also walks alongside Dargle river in harbour area, and there is a fine cliff walk from S end of esplanade to Greystones, about 5 m (8 km). Sometimes path blocked by rock falls, check with Bray TIO. **Art Gallery,** *38 Main Street, daily.* Swimming pool: indoor, heated, Presentation College, *Putland Road. Daily by arr. Details (01)867517/862189.* Woodbrook Golf Club. *18 holes, tel: (01)821838.*

Cruagh, *5 m (8 km) S of Rathfarnham, E off L94 or W off L201.* Car park, picnic place, forest walks, nature trail, wilderness trek via Featherbed Mountain to Military Road car park.

Dalkey, *near Dun Laoghaire. 8 bus from Eden Quay, Dublin. Also train.* Popular resort town, recently immortalised by Flann O'Brien and Hugh Leonard; a prominent port during the Middle Ages. **Archibold's Castle,** *Castle Street,* is one of few reminders of mediaeval walled town. Key can be borrowed, *Mr McDonald, 59 Castle Street.* **Bullock Castle,** 12th c, extensively renovated by Carmelite sisters as an historic monument, cultural and arts centre. *By arr. (01)886993.* Magnificent coastal walk from Dalkey village up Coliemore Road to Vico Road. Continue into Killiney, with its fine beach. There is also a fine walk around Bullock Harbour and up Harbour Road to Dalkey village, Scuba diving: Scubadive, Coliemore Harbour. *Tel: (01)807872.*

Dalkey Island: ideal place for picnic, even if long grass makes walking hard. See ruins of military barracks and church, also Martello Tower in good condition. Boat trips from Coliemore harbour (next to Dalkey Island Hotel) on summer weekends.

Enniskerry: Glencree Youth Hostel: *tel: (01)867290.* Knockree Youth Hostel, *tel: (01)867196.* **Powerscourt,** estate and gardens, magnificent 18th c mansion on site of Anglo–Norman castle. 34,000 acre estate with Italian and Japanese gardens, dramatically backed by the Wicklow mountains. *Easter–Oct 31, daily 10 a.m.–5.30 p.m. Waterfall all year, daily, details: (01)863557.*

Glencree, *5 m (8 km) W of Enniskerry:* cemetery where German servicemen who died in and around Ireland in World War II are buried.

Glencullen, *Co. Dublin, 44B bus from Hawkins St, Dublin.* Frauchan (type of berry) festival, good

Fields near Glencree, Co. Wicklow

excuse for all kinds of merriment, *early July.*

Great Sugar Loaf mountain, *4 m (6 km) SW of Bray:* fine views from summit. Road to near mountain top.

Greystones, *Co. Wicklow, 84 bus from College St, Dublin, also train.* Train enquiries: Greystones Station, *tel: (01)874160.* Excellent walk around harbour and along seafront. You can follow the track between railway line and beach for about 3 m (5 km) S. Greystones Golf Club, *18 holes, tel: (01)874614.*

Hell Fire Club, *4 m (6 km) S of Rathfarnham on L201:* car park, picnic place, forest walks, access to ruins of 18th c Hell Fire Club, panoramic views.

James Joyce Tower, *Sandycove:* good collection of Joyceana. *May 1–Sept 30, Mon–Sat, 10 a.m.–1 p.m.; 2 p.m.–5.15 p.m. Sun, 2.30 p.m.–6 p.m. Otherwise by app., tel: (01)808571.*

Killakee, *Dublin mountains.* Take L94 road from Rathfarnham to Killakee, good views of city, hill walking to Glendhu, Pine Forest and Glenasmole beauty spots.

Killiney Hill, *59 bus from Dun Laoghaire.* Public park, thickly wooded in places, rising above coast road between Dalkey and Killiney. Fine views from summit.

Kilmashogue: *on cul de sac off L93 Rockbrook-Sandyford road, 1 m (2 km) E of Rockbrook,* car park, picnic place, forest walk to Three Rock Mountain, Bronze Age tomb.

Kilruddery House and Gardens. *Bray:* attractively set at foot of Little Sugar Loaf mountain, only 17th c garden in Ireland. *By app. for groups of ten or more. Details: (01)863405.*

Leopardstown: frequent horse racing, *details: (01)893607.* Squash: *Leopardstown Racecourse details of this and other Dublin area squash facilities, Anglesea House, Church Road, Dalkey, tel: (01)808426.*

Monkstown, *Co. Dublin, 7A, 8 bus from Dublin, Dun Laoghaire.* Comhaltas Ceoltóirí Éireann *32 Belgrave Square,* cultural Institute and Irish music museum. Basement converted into traditional Irish country kitchen, with open fire and flagstone floor. Regular Irish music, great fun. *Details: (01)800295.***D Lambert Puppet Theatre,**

Clifton Lane: highly entertaining shows. *Every Sat, 3 p.m. Details: (01)800974.* **Powerscourt Paddock:** *on E slopes of Djouce Mountain, 4 m (6 km) S of Enniskerry.* Delightful walks around the Paddock Pond.

Rathfarnham: Pine Forest Riding School, *Cruagh, Rockbrook, tel: (01)942246.* Andrea's Riding Stables, *Rockbrook, tel: (01) 981250/988079.*

Sallynoggin, *Co. Dublin:* Kapp and Peterson, Peterson House, Pearse Street, make pipes (the smoking variety). *Mon–Fri, 8.30 a.m.–5 p.m. Closed last week July, first two weeks Aug, details: (01)851011.*

Sandycove, *Co. Dublin, 8 bus from Dun Laoghaire.* Forty foot near James Joyce Tower is used for male-only bathing—in spite of Women's Lib protests. **Tudor Galleries,** *30 Sandycove Road. Tel: (01)803427.*

Sandyford, *Co. Dublin:* Fernhill Gardens, on slopes of Three Rock Mountain, specimen trees, rhododendrons, rock and water gardens. *All year, Tues, Sat, 10 a.m.–5 p.m. Otherwise, by arr. Tel: (01)983000/989158.*

Source of the Liffey: *just past Lough Bray, near E of Liffey Head bridge on L94,* see where the river rises.

Stepaside, *turn right off main Dublin–Enniskerry road:* mountain road towards Pine Forest and Glencullen for about 4 m (6 km). Excellent views over Dublin and Killiney bays.

Stillorgan Bowl, *46A bus from College St, Dublin or Dun Laoghaire.* Tenpin bowling, seven days a week, *details: (01) 881566.*

Three Rock Mountain: car, picnic place, panoramic views, access to summits of Three Rock and Two Rock Mountains and Kilmashogue car park.

Tibradden, *5 m (8 km) S of Rathfarnham on L201:* car park, picnic place, forest walks, nature trail.

Wicklow Way: fully marked trail that starts at Marley Park, Rathfarnham and runs S of 19 m (30 km), past Fairy Castle, Tibradden mountain, Glencullen, across the Glencree and Dargle rivers

as far as Luggala. The recently opened second stage continues from Luggala to Moyne.

Wicklow

Pop. 4,000, 16 m (26 km) N of Arklow, 32 m (51 km) S of Dublin, 60 m (96 km) N of Wexford. EC: Thur. TIO: (0404)2904, June–Sept. Bus and train enquiries: CIE, Wicklow, tel: (0404)2329. 59 bus from Dublin, Wexford, train from Dublin, Wexford.

A seaside resort and county town, with a pleasant harbour area. In centuries past, Wicklow was repeatedly attacked in squabbles between O'Byrnes, O'Tooles and the English. Today, though much modernised, the old town retains a certain historical flavour.

Fitzwilliam Square: see granite obelisk commemorating Wicklow-born captain of Brunel's 'Great Eastern', which laid the first cable across the Atlantic. Memorial, *Market Square:* commemorates Wicklow men who fought in 1798. **An Ros Duin,** *Market Square:* has kept much of 19th c atmosphere, see century-old tea caddies at back of bar. **Painters' Gallery,** *Bachelors Walk:* work by local artists. *Mon–Sat, 10 a.m.–9 p.m. Closed lunch and tea. SO.*

Black Castle, *on rocky promontory at E end of town:* begun by Maurice Fitzgerald in 1176 and frequently attacked over the following five centuries, now in ruins. Also remains of 13th c Franciscan friary in grounds of presbytery; Norman doorway in S porch of C of I. The Murrough: take a turn round the harbour area, then N towards this fine stretch of sward, now public promenade. Rowing boats for hire. Ballinteskin Indoor Riding School, *tel: (0404)2543.* Bicycles: Brian W. Harris, *1 Main Street and Church Street, tel: (0404)2247.* Blainroe Gold Club, *18 holes, tel: (0404)3168;* Wicklow Golf Club, *9 holes, tel: (0404)2379.*

Wicklow Mountains near Glendalough

AROUND WICKLOW

Arklow, *9 m (14 km) S of Wicklow, bus, train, from Wicklow.* bustling resort town with access to two excellent beaches. **Maritime Museum,** *St Mary's Road:* about 1,000 items relating to the town's nautical history. *June–Sept, 10 a.m.–5 p.m. daily. Closed 1 p.m.–2 p.m.*

Tyrell's, *South Dock:* fine tradition of ship and yacht building, *details: (0402)2403.* **Pottery:** *guided tours, mid-June-Aug 31, at 9.30 a.m., 12 noon, 1.30 p.m., 3.45 p.m. Closed last week July, first two Aug, details: (0402)2134.*

Arklow Rock, *along S Strand, past golf course, about 2 m (3 km) from town:* 415 ft (126 metres), fine view of coast; Our Lady's Well is on the Rock. 6 m (9 km) walk along minor coast road NE to ruined tower on Mizen Head. Amusement centre: pitch and putt, games room, outdoor swimming pool, *daily, 10 a.m.–7 p.m.* Golf Club, *18 holes, tel: (0402)2492.*

Ashford, *5 m (8 km) NW of Wicklow. 59 bus from Dublin, Wicklow to Ashford.* **Devil's Glen,** *2 m (3 km) NW village:* here the Vartry River falls nearly 100 ft (30 metres) into the Devil's Punchbowl, a deep· basin in the rock. Walks, nature trail, vantage points with good views of coastline to E. **Tiglin Adventure Centre,** sports such as orienteering, caving and hang gliding, *details: (0404)4169.* Bel-Air Riding School, *tel: (0404)4109;* Aughatore Equitation Centre, *tel: (01)819332.* Tiglin Youth Hostel: *tel: (0404)4259.*

Aughavannagh: *by Aughavannagh bridge, on Rathdangan–Glenmalure road:* fine forest walk to foot of Lugnaquilla mountain, 3,039 ft (926 metres).

Aughrim, *9 m (14 km) NW of Arklow on L19:* forest walks, viewing point at Mucklagh, on Aughrim—Greenane road; forest walks on both sides of Aughrim— Aghavannagh road. Aghvannagh Youth Hostel: *tel: (0402)6102.*

Avoca, *16 m (26 km) S of Wicklow, 59 bus from Wicklow*. Beautifully set village. See Tom Moore's tree, near Meeting of the Waters; where the poet is said to have spent many nours in contemplation. Forest walks: *1 m (1.5 km) S of Avoca, off N11*: picnic area, car park. Avoca Valley Riding School, *Clash, near Rathdrum, tel: (0404)6208*.

Avondale Estate, *1.5 m (2.5 km) S of Rathdrum*: Charles Stewart Parnell, great 19th c Irish leader, lived in 1779 house, now finely restored. Estate run by Forest and Wildlife Service: picnic site, carpark, planned walks, nature trail, *all year*. House *May 1–June 30, Fri–Mon, 2 p.m.–6 p.m., July, Aug, daily, 2 p.m.–6 p.m. Sept, Fri–Mon, 2 p.m.–6 p.m. Details: (0404)6111.* **D**

Ballinamona, *1 m (1.5 km) NW of Woodenbridge on L19:* forest walks, picnic area, car park.

Ballyboy, *near Drumgoff Cross on Glenmalure-Glendalough road:* forest walks, viewing points.

Ballymoyle Hill, *4 m (6 km) N of Arklow.* Take L29 to *2 m (3 km) S of Jack White's Cross*, turn right at Scratenagh crossroads, continue for *1 m NW:* forest walks, scenic views, picnic area, car park.

Ballynastragh, *just W off N11 Arklow-Gorey road at Tinnock Bridge:* picnic area, forest walks, car park.

Brittas Bay, *8 m (13 km) S of Wicklow Head:* popular 3 m (5 km) stretch of sandy beach backed by dunes. Ideal for bathing, picnicking, large car park.

Carrigeenduff, *3 m (5 km) S of Sally Gap:* forest walk, picnic area, parking.

Clonkeen, *2 m (3 km) NW of former Glenmalure Hotel on Glenmalure-Barravore road:* forest and riverside walks, viewing points.

Derrybawn, *2 m (3 km) S of Laragh on T61:* forest walk, access to River Avonmore, picnic area, car park.

Glendalough, *7 m (11 km) E of Wicklow, T7 via Rathdrum; twice daily bus trips, all year, between College of Surgeons, St Stephen's Green, Dublin and Glendalough. Details: (01)818119.* One of Ireland's most attractive monastic sites. The principal ruins, just E of Lower Lake, are the cathedral, consisting of 11th c nave, chancel and St Kevin's Church, commonly called St Kevin's Kitchen, a fine example of early Irish barrel-vaulted oratory, with a 1,000 year old, almost perfect round tower. Less accessible, on the S shore of Upper Lake, are Teampall na Skellig (Church of the Rock) and St Kevin's Bed, cut into the cliff face. Boats available. *For hire between 10.30 a.m.–6.30 p.m. daily, SO.* Refreshments, meals, Glendalough Royal Hotel, *tel: (0404)5122.*

Craft centre: weaving and jewellery, with details from local churches; gallery and tearooms. *Mon–Fri, 10 a.m.–6 p.m., by app. Shop Mon–Sun, 10 a.m.–6 p.m. Details: (0404)5156.* Glendalough Woods, *1 m (1.5 km) W of Laragh on L107:* 1 m nature trail, forest walks, picnic area, car park. Riding Stables, *Laragh, tel: (0404)5122.* Youth Hostel: *tel: (0404)5143.*

Glenealy Agricultural Museum, *5 m (8 km) SW of Wicklow:* far machinery dating from early 19th c, veteran cars. Working hours or by arr., (0404)5608.

Greenane, *2 m (3 km) SW of Rathdrum:* Glenmalure Youth Hostel.

Jack's Hole, *6 m (9 km) S of Wicklow Head:* secluded stretch of sand.

Killaveny, *3 m (5 km) NE of Tinahely on L19:* forest walks, picnic area, car park.

Kilmurray, *2 m (3 km) W of Newtownmountkennedy on L162:* forest walks.

Kilnamanagh, *turn off N11 2 m (3 km) SW of Glenealy, onto Brittas Bay road:* viewing points, forest walks.

Laragh Trout Farm, *Rathdrum road, Laragh*, equipment supplied free, pay for your catch. *June-mid-Sept, Mon–Sat, 9 a.m.–6 p.m. Sun, 2 p.m.–7 p.m. Also Easter. Details: (0404)6161.*

Loughs Tay and **Dan:** *3 m (5 km) W of Roundwood:* adjacent countryside most desolate in E Ireland.

Motte Stone, *2 m (3 km) W of Avoca:* glacial stone perched on hill overlooking village, extensive views.

Mount Usher Demesne, *Ashford, 4 m (6 km) NW of Wicklow on N11. 59 bus from Dublin, Wicklow:* delightful gardens with many sub-tropical species. Vartry River forms centrepiece; woodland walks. Souvenir shop, tea-room. *Mar 17–Sept 30, Mon–Sat, 10 a.m.–5.30 p.m. Sun, 2 p.m.–5.30 p.m. Details: (0404)4116.*

Mucklagh, *5 m (8 km) NW of Aughrim on Aughrim-Aughvannagh road, taking by-road to river:* forest walks, scenic view, picnic area, car park.

Rathdrum, *10 m (16 km) SW of Wicklow, 59 bus from Wicklow. Also train.* Attractive small town set high on W side of Avonmore valley, Vale of Clara to N and Vale of Avoca to S. Forest walks at Croneybyrne, Ballinastraw, plus picnic area, car park at Ballygannon.

Clara-Lara Funpark and Trout Farm, *Vale of Clara, Rathdrum.* Fishing, boating, adventure playground, picnic areas, café. *Daily, tel: (0404)6161.*

Redcross, *just N of Barranisky on the Barranisky-Redcross road 4 m (6 km) N of Arklow:* forest walk, scenic views, picnic area, car park.

Roundwood, *12 m (19 km) SW of Bray, St Kevin's Bus Service from Dublin, details: (01)818119.* Highest village in Ireland, 780 ft (238 metres) above sea level. A walk along Main Street, takes in almost the entire village. Boat hire (nearby reservoir): Lake View House.

Tinahely, *8 m (13 km) SW of Aughrim:* Horse Fair and Agricultural Show, *early Aug.*

Trooperstown, *1 m (1.5 km) NE of Laragh on T61:* forest walks, picnic area, car park.

Turlough Hill, *approach from Glendalough on L107, about 5 m (8 km) NW:* the ESB generating station pumps water between two reservoirs to produce electricity. *Guided tours twice daily, all year, 11 a.m., 3.30 p.m. Write in advance, details: (0404)5113.*

Shelton Abbey, *2 m (3 km) NW of Arklow:* fine rhododendrons in demesne of state forestry school.

Shillelagh, *5 m (8 km) S of Tinahely:* good hill walks.

Silver Strand, *immediately S of Wicklow Head:* popular sandy beach backed by cliffs.

Woodenbridge, *5 m (8 km) NW of Arklow, 59 bus from Arklow.* One of the most beautifully situated villages in Ireland, where Avoca, Arklow 'and Aughrim valleys meet. **Glenart** *just E of Woodenbridge on N11:* forest walks, rhododendrons, picnic area, car park. Trout Farm, catch your own fish, equipment supplied free, pay for the fish you land. *Summer daily, 10 a.m.–5 p.m. Visitors welcome in and out of seasaon.* Golf Club, 9 holes, *tel: (0402)5202.*

The SOUTH

Bantry

Pop. 3,000, 28 m (45 km) S of Kenmare, 57 m (92 km) W of Cork, 218 m (350 km) SW of Dublin. EC. Wed. TIO, tel: (027) 50229, July-Aug. Bus enquiries: (021) 504422. 102 bus from Cork, Killarney (SO), 164 bus from Cork, Glengarriff, Skibbereen.

A delightfully situated town nestling beneath hills at the head of Bantry Bay. Despite the proximity of the Whiddy Island oil terminal, change has been so slight you can almost imagine this century has passed Bantry by. With some good hotels for exploring the largely natural wonders of W Cork and adjacent SW Kerry.

Bantry House, Georgian mansion filled with treasures, many from Lord Bantry's tours abroad in the early 19th c. Chippendale, Sheraton furniture, Waterford chandeliers, Aubusson tapestries, Pompeii masaics. Italian garden terraces with superb views across the bay to the Caha Mountains in Co Kerry. *Daily, except Christmas Day, 9 a.m.–6 p.m. Open till 8 p.m. most spring and summer evenings.* Tea room, craft shop. *Details: (027) 50047.* **Kilnaurane Inscribed Stone**, *Rope Walk Road, near West Lodge Hotel:* early 7th c carving unique in Co Cork.

Gortycloona Theatre, occasional community theatre, *details: TIO.* Bantry Bay Horse and Pony Mountain Trekking Centre, *Rooska, tel: (027) 50221.* Bantry Bay cruises: *early Apr–end Sept, daily,* Michael Carroll, *tel: (027) 50275.* Bicycles: O'Mahonys, *New Street, tel: (027) 50240.*

AROUND BANTRY

Abbeystrewery, *1 m (2 km) W of Skibereen:* abbey set on the banks of the River Ilen, dates from 14th c, mass famine graves.

Adrigole, *road N to Lauragh taking in Healy Pass.* Started during the famine, but only completed in 1931. Crucifixion Shrine at top. Difficult drive but tremendous views. Riding: Mrs T. O'Sullivan, Bayview House, *Faha, tel: (027) 60026.*

Allihies, *6 m (9 km) W of Castletownbere:* 19th c copper workings, explore with care. **Black Bull Tower**, *near Lickbarran*, 18th c structure, impressive views of coast and mountains. Ballydonegan Strand, bathing, surfing. Youth Hostel.

Ballingeary, *18 m (29 km) NE of Bantry on T64, 173 bus from Cork, Killarney, Macroom.* Stronghold of the Irish language, good views of nearby Lough Allua. Scenic drive through hills to N, via Reananerree village, to N22, back through Macroom and Inchigeelagh. About 30 m (48 km). Youth Hostel: Bridge House, *tel: Ballingeary 77.*

Ballycrovane ogham stone, *just N of Eyeries, near Ballycrovane harbour:* tallest ogham stone in Ireland, 18 feet (6 metres).

Ballydehob, *10 m (16 km) S of Bantry on N71, 103 bus from Cork, Killarney (SO), 164 from Skibbereen.* Quaint harbour, a veritable warren of craft workshops. The tramway viaduct offers panoramic views of Roaring Water Bay, Carbery's hundred isles, Mount Gabriel. **Cush Strand**, *2 m (3 km) W of village:* bathing. Yachts (daily, weekly, monthly): Andrew Scott, *Rossbrin Cove, tel: (028) 37165.* Coughlan Rent-a-bike, *Main Street, tel: (028) 37110.*

Ballylickey, *3 m (5 km) N of Bantry:* beautiful stretches of coastal scenery at the head of Bantry Bay. Waterfalls, wooded glens just off N71 to

Bantry House

Glengarriff. The nearby road to Priest's Leap climbs nearly 2,000 ft (600 metres). Boats: Sea View hotel, *tel: (027) 50073;* Hugo du Plessis (weekly, monthly yacht-charters, family cruising yachts), *tel: (027) 50352.*

Ballynacarriga Castle, *4 m (6 km) SE of Dunmanway:* 16th c ruins overlooking lake, scenic views.

Baltimore, *8 m (13 km) SW of Skibbereen, 165 bus from Skibbereen.* Centuries old fishing village, full of atmosphere. The tall, whitewashed 'Beacon' offers fine views of the harbour and Sherkin Island across the bay. Regular passenger sailings to Clear Island, details: Comhar Chuman Chléire Teo, *tel: Cape Clear 219.* Baltimore Boat Hire, *The Pier, tel: (028) 20141.* Also boats to Hare Island and Long Island, also in Roaring Water Bay.

Barley Cove, magnificent sandy beach. Barley Cove Hotel swimming pool: indoor, heated. Weekly, monthly tickets, *tel: (028) 35234.*

Barnageehy, *3 m (5 km) S of Bantry on N71:* viewing point, lay-by, picnic area.

Beara Peninsula, Milleens, *nr Eyeries:* wonderful to see cheese being made in a traditional way on a full-time commercial basis. *Preferably by arr.*

Bawntemple Pillar Stone, *3 m (4 km) NW of Ballingeary:* nearly 20 ft (6 metres) high, permission from farm.

Bere Island, *ferry from Castletownbere. July/Aug, Mon–Sun; Rest of year, Tues, Fri, Sat. Details, tel:* (027) 50009. Glenans Sailing Centre, *tel: (027)* 75012; *weekly, fortnightly sailing courses; John Harrington, West End, tel: (027) 50009;* Brendan Murphy, *the Village, tel: (027) 50004.*

Brow Head, *2 m (3 km) SW of Crookhaven:* ruins of the radio station from which Marconi sent early transmissions to America.

Cahermore Strand, *W tip of Beara Peninsula:* good bathing.

Carriganass Castle, *5 m (8 km) NE of Bantry, near Kealkil:* noted landmark, built 1540.

Castletown bere: sheltered by Slieve Miskish mountains on SW side of Beara peninsula. Once an anchorage for the British Atlantic fleet, now a major deep sea angling centre, with beaches on both sides of the town. Nightly fish auction on quayside, 9 p.m. Prehistoric stone circles at Harbour View and the Rock, West End. Boats: Jack Downey, *tel: 37;* Pearse Lyon, *Main Street, tel: 81;* Dan O'Driscoll, *East End, tel: 77;* Mrs Greeff, *Waterfall, tel: 21/91,* dinghies. Surf sailing: Cametringane House Hotel, *tel: Castletownbere 27/83.* Riding: James Harrington, The Stables, *North Road;* Cametringane House Hotel, *tel: Castletownbere 27/83.* Bicycles: Dermot Murphy, Bridge House, *tel: Castletownbere 20.* Youth Hostel, *Glanmore Lake.*

Castletownshend, *5 m (8 km) SE of Skibbereen:* very beautiful single street village on W shore of Castlehaven. Edith Somerville and Violet Martin, co-authors of *The Irish R.M. and His Experiences,* are buried in graveyard of St Barrahane C of I, above village street.

Clashnacrona, *3 m (5 km) W of Dunmanway on T65:* lay-by, forest walks, picnic area.

Clear Island, Iarsmalaan Chléire (Clear Island Museum), near a church at the centre of the island. Old photographs, newspaper cuttings

Barley Cove

about area, farm implements. *Aug, daily, aft.* Bird observatory, SO, book in advance, *details:* Colin Rhind. **Dunamore Castle,** ruins on NW of island. The old lighthouse, nearby, was built in 1848, and closed only six years later. From South Harbour, see the famous **Fastnet Lighthouse,** *4 m (6 km) out to sea* on Fastnet Rock, Ireland's most southerly point. Youth Hostel on Clear Island.

Creagh Gardens, *4 m (6 km) SW of Skibbereen on L59 to Baltimore:* privately owned gardens covering some 5 acres (2 hectares) with variety of trees and shrubs. Nearby estuary of River Ilen. *Easter-Sept 30, daily, 10 a.m.-6 p.m. Details, tel:* (028) 21267.

Crookhaven: the Pilchard Palace, to the W of the charming harbour, originally used for storing fish until destroyed in 1641. During the Great Famine, there was a meal house on the site. Boats: Tom O'Driscoll, Billy O'Sullivan, *tel:* (028) 35319; James E. Pyburn, *tel:* (028) 28338.

Cullenagh, *7 m (10 km) NE of Drimoleague:* four standing stones, fifth nearby.

Derreen Woodland Garden, *1 m (1 km) from Lauragh on Castletownbere Road:* established over 100

years ago on the S shores of Kenmare River. Internationally known for splendid setting and many specimen trees and shrubs. *Apr 1-Sept 30, Sun, Tues, Thurs, 2 p.m.-6 p.m. Details: Lauragh 3.*

Diarmuid and Grainne's Bed. *W of Cullenagh Lake, near Drimoleague:* prehistoric chamber tomb.

Dinish Island, *in Castletownbere inner harbour:* connected to mainland by bridge.

Drimoleague, *9 m (14 km) N of Skibbereen on L59, 164 bus from Bantry, 165 bus from Skibbereen.* Box-shaped church, designed by Cork architect Frank Murphy.

Dunboy Castle, *2 m (3 km) W of Castletownbere on L61 on Garnish:* 16th c building set amid woodlands and spacious grounds above inlet facing Bere Island. Scenically striking. *Easter-Oct Mon-Sun, 10 a.m.-7 p.m.*

Dunmanway: St Mary's Cemetery, grave of Sam Maguire after whom the All Ireland senior football championship cup is named. Swimming pool: indoor, heated, *Tues-Sun, details:* (023) 43328.

Durrus, *7 m (11 km) SW of Bantry:* ruins of early 17th c Durrus Court at start of Sheep's Head peninsula. Pony trekking: D. Donovan, *Kealties, tel:* (027) 61006.

Dursey Sound, *cable car to Dursey Island: all year, Mon-Sat, 9 a.m.-11 a.m.; 2.30 p.m.-5 p.m. July, Aug, also 7 p.m.-8 p.m. Details, inc. Sun times: James Sheehan, Ballagh Bay, Garinish, tel:* (027) 73016.

Eyeries, *on L62 from Castletownbere:* from here on to Ardgroom and Lauragh, fine views of the Kenmare River estuary.

Falls of Donemarc, *2 m (3 km) N of Bantry on N71 to Glengarriff:* path through woods runs very close to cascade on River Mealagh.

Garinish Island, *just offshore from Glengarriff:* marvellous Italian island gardens, with rare subtropical plants. Also shrubberies, miniature Japanese and rock gardens. From Grecian temple and old Martello Tower, splendid views. Boats to Garnish Island from The Pier, Blue Pool and Ellen's Rock on Castletownbere road. *Mar 1-Oct 31, Mon-Sat, every 10 minutes from 10 a.m.-5.30 p.m., Sun, church holy days, 1 p.m.-6 p.m., public holidays 10 a.m.-6 p.m. Times subject to alteration. otherwise by arr. tel:* (01) 764071.

Garnish Strand, *W tip of Beara peninsula:* good bathing.

Glengarriff, *11 km (18 km) NW of Bantry on N71. TIO: Tel, (027) 63084. July-Aug. 103, 164, from Bantry.* Small village delightfully set in a glen.

Harbour is an inlet at NW head of Bantry Bay. Glengarrif and Garinish Boat Service, The Pier, *tel:* (027) 63116.

Glengarriff Woods, *just N of village:* nature trail. After completing this walk, cross the Carnarooska River by stepping stones of footbridge to continue along the far bank. For Carrigour Hill, take the second road branching E of Glengarriff, turn L again at dolmen, to emerge on Kenmare road. Cromwell's Bridge: short walk from village on Castletownbere road, attractive stroll among trees overhanging Glengarriff River. Lady Bantry's Lookout: 2 m (3 km) from village on Castletownbere road, return by magnificent Shrone Hill viewpoint. Alternatively, walk beyond lookout to Eagle's Nest and return to seashore by Biddy's Cove, good bathing spot. Leary's Point by Bantry Road, about 5 m (8 km). Poulgorm, take pathway to W of Post Office, a two minute walk giving very good views. O'Donoghue's Riding Stables, *3 m (5 km) from village on Bantry road, tel:* (027) 63069. *June-Sept.* Bicycles: Paddy Moriarty, Paddy O'Sullivan, *tel.* (027) 63005.

Gortnacarriga, *3 m (4 km) SW of Inchigeelagh:* forest walks, scenic views.

Gougane Barra lake, *15 m (24 km) NE of Bantry off T64:* surrounded on three sides by mountains, source of the River Lee. Forest park in nearby valley (turn off T64 at Pass Keimaneigh). Walks, nature trail, St Finbarr's Oratory on island reached by causeway. Monument at Gougane Barra crossroads to poetess Máire Bhuí Ní Laoghaire, and grave of Tailor and Ansty (from Eric Cross's famous book, *The Tailor and the Ansty*) at Gougane Barra shore cemetery.

Gour Gap, *4 m (6 km) W of Castletownbere:* forest walks, good view of Bere Haven harbour.

Hungry Hill, *3 m (5 km) W of Adrigole:* waterfall on hill tumbles 770 ft (230 metres). From mountain top, extensive view over most of Beara peninsula.

Inchigeelagh, *at E of Lough Allua:* good walks alongside River Lee and over adjoining hills. Riding: T. McCarthy, *Tír na Spideoga.* The T64 to Macroom has fine views of the Shehy Mountains. **Inchiquin Lough,** *8 m (13 km) SW of Kenmare, turn S off L62.* Forest walks amid striking scenery, good views of surrounding lakes and waterfall, car park, picnic area. **Inchiquin Waterfall,** *near Inchiquin Lough:* worth seeing, particularly in full flood. Best approached by minor road that leads off L62 near Cloonee Loughs.

Keamcorravoly, *2 m (3 km) N of Ballingeary:* megalithic tomb off Ballyvourney Road. Permission: Michael Creed, farmer.

Kilmakillogue Harbour, *near Lauragh:* boats for hire from local publican for use in an almost totally enclosed harbour.

Garinish Island

Kilmichael, *8 m (13 km) NE of Dunmanway on L58:* memorial to War of Independence ambush. On Nov 28, 1920, Tom Barry and his West Cork Flying Column of 36 riflemen ambushed British Auxiliaries, killing 18; smaller stones mark main ambush positions.

Knockdrum Hill, *1 m (2 km) NW of Castletownshend:* fine views over Castlehaven. Nearby ring fort.

Lough Hyne, *4 m (6 km) S of Skibbereen,* turn S beyond golf course on Skibbereen–Baltimore L59. Land-locked sea inlet. Viewing points, scenic walks, lay-by, picnic area.

Mizen Head, *reached by minor road off L56 at Goleen:* fine walk across headland summit. striking cliffscapes.

Mount Gabriel, *2 m (3 km) N of Schull:* good climb to top, passing futuristic satellite tracking station near summit. Wonderful views over Roaring Water and Dunmanus Bays. Bronze Age copper workings (NM).

Nowen Hill, *near Drimoleague:* good climb 1,763 ft (537 metres).

Pass of Keimaneigh, *near Gougane Barra:* wild mountain scenery.

Rathgaskig, *on Ballingeary–Kilgarvan road 2 m (3 km) from Ballingeary:* forest walks, lay-by, picnic area.

Rossbrin Castle, *2 m (3 km) SW of Ballydehob:* 14th c ruins of O'Mahony stronghold. Nearby disused copper mines, explore with care.

Schull, *4 m (6 km) SW of Ballydehob on L57, 164 bus from Bantry, Skibbereen.* Delightfully set around an almost totally enclosed harbour. Popular sea angling venue. Excellent bookshop. Passenger ferry to Clear Island. *June–Aug, daily, 2.30 p.m., returning 5.30 p.m. 6 m (10 km) trip takes about an hour. Details:* Kieran Molloy, *Pier Road, Schull, tel: (028) 28138.* Also boats to Hare Island and Long Island, also in Roaring Water

Bay. **O'Mahony's White Castle,** *1 m (2 km) from village off Ballydehob road:* 14th c ruins. Disused water mills.

There is an interesting drive SW to Goleen and Crookhaven. From Goleen, with its secluded sandy beach, a choice of two routes to Mizen Head, through Crookhaven or directly across mountains. Riding: Mr Hughes, Colla House, *tel: (028) 28185.*

Sheep's Head Peninsula: *extends for some 15 m (24 km) SW of Bantry.* Minor road goes to Sheep's Head heights at end of peninsula. Beaches, near Kilcrohane and Ahakista villages on SE side. Walks: Goat's Path along NW coast.

Sherkin Island: *regular passenger boat from Baltimore at 12 noon, 2 p.m., 4 p.m., 6 p.m., 8 p.m. daily, June 1–Sept 30. Otherwise, 12 noon, 3 p.m. daily.* Boat returns shortly after arrival. O'Driscoll castle ruins, near landing place, and the ruins of 15th c Franciscan friary. Outdoor Pursuits Centre: wide variety of outdoor sports, *tel: (028) 20187.* Bathing: beyond church, Silver Strand, Tragowenmore. **Skibbereen,** *21 m (34 km) SW of Bantry.* TIO: *tel: (028) 21766, all year.* 164 bus from Bantry. Pro-Cathedral dates from 1826. Bicycles: Roycroft's Stores, Ilen Street. *Tel: (028) 21235 (21810 after hours).* LissArd Riding and Driving Club, *tel: (028) 21109.*

South Lake Drive, *3 m (5 km) SW of Inchigeelagh:* forest walks to Memorial Cross, extensive views over Lee valley, car park, picnic area.

Togher Castle, *4 m (6 km) NW of Dunmanway:* interesting ruins on N bank of River Bandon.

Cork

Pop. 136,000, 54 m (87 km) SE of Killarney, 129 m (207 km) W of Rosslare, 161 m (259 km) SW of Dublin. TIO: Grand Parade, tel: (021) 23251, all year. Buses from Dublin, Killarney, Limerick.

Plane from Dublin, Shannon. Bus and train enquiries: CIE, Kent Station, tel: Plane from Dublin, Shannon. Train from Dublin, Limerick. Bus and train enquiries: CIE, Kent Station, tel: (021) 504422. Taxis: Patrick Street railway station. City tours, coach tours, SO, details TIO. Harbour cruises: city quays, SO, details TIO Youth Hostel: Western Road, tel: (021) 43289.

The second city of the Republic is notoriously aware of its individuality, indeed few of the locals doubt that it is in fact Ireland's leading town. After a varied and chaotic history Cork emerged in the 19th c as a centre of the Fenian Movement, earning the title 'Rebel Cork', and suffering badly in the War of Independence, when two Lord Mayors died and a large portion of the centre was burned down. Today, it is a prosperous, lively city with a keen sense of its own cultural identity. There is much of interest to see around the city centre and in the adjoining hilly districts. Cork Film Festival: *usually Oct. Details: (021) 502221 or TIO.* Jazz Festival: *Oct. Details: (021) 508122.* Choral and Folk Dance Festival: *May. Details: (021) 502221.*

St Finbarre's Cathedral (CI), *near South Mall:* built in early French Gothic style just over 100 years ago. Fine carvings, mosaics. In S transept, see cannon ball fired in 1690 seige, found embedded in tower of site's previous church.

Christ Church, *South Main Street:* built 1702. Some of foundations date from Norman church, built about 1270 and badly mangled in 1690 seige.

Church of Christ the King (C), *Turner's Cross, NW Cork:* one of most striking modern churches in Ireland. Stunning view of city from front. **Red Abbey,** *between George's Quay and Douglas Street:* only square tower left of mediaeval abbey, the oldest piece of architecture Cork. **St. Annes:** where would-be Quasimodos can peal the merry Shandon bells, *daily, all year.* **Honan Chapel,** *University College, 5 bus from Patrick Street.* Built in 1915/16, with superb Harry Clarke and Sarah Purser stained glass windows. *Usually closed during vacations.*

Public Museum, *Fitzgerald's Park, 3, 7, 7A bus from Patrick Street, 10 from Grand Parade.*

42

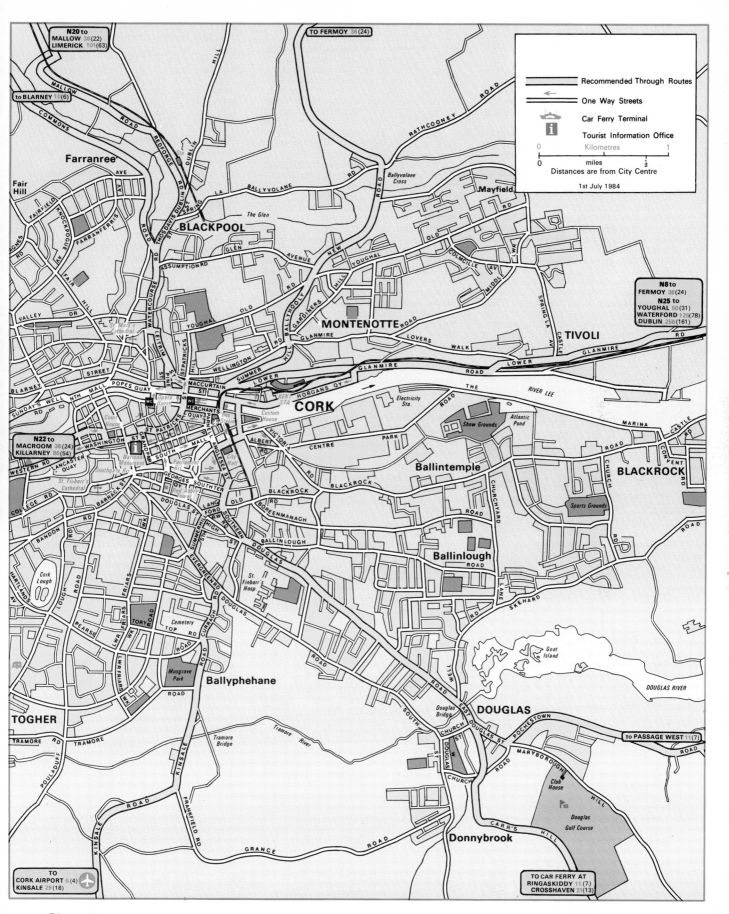

Cork

Natural history, old photographs, notably of 1916–1922 period, old documents, silver, small reference library. *All year, Mon–Fri, 11 a.m.–1 p.m.; 2.15 p.m.–5 p.m. Sun, 3 p.m.–5 p.m. June–Sept, Mon–Fri until 6 p.m. Closed Bank Hol weekends, inc Sun, all public holidays.* **University College.** *5 bus from Patrick Street.* Botany Department: herbarium, with some 3,000 dried plants from Europe, America, Australia. *By app. Tel: (021) 26871.*
Triskel Arts Centre: due to move into new centre next to Christchurch on *South Main Street, opp. TIO.* Will include exhibition area for paintings and sculptures, book shop, auditorium, coffee lounge. Adjacent public park. **Crawford Municipal School of Art,** *Emmet Place:* many local scenes in oils and watercolours, sculptures, collection of classical casts from Vatican galleries. *Mon–Fri, 10 a.m.–5 p.m; Sat, 10 a.m.–1 p.m.* **Cork Arts Society Gallery,** *16 Lavitts Quay: Tues–Sat 11 a.m.–6 p.m. Closed 2 p.m.–3 p.m. Details: (021) 505749.* **The Gallery,** *Grand Parade:* etchings, oil paintings. *Mon–Sat, closed lunch.*
Opera House, *Emmet Place:* regular theatrical performances. Details: (021) 20022/23680. **Everyman Playhouse,** *Fr. Mathew Street, off South Mall:* regular theatre. *Details: (021) 26287.* **Granary Theatre,** *University College:* regular term-time performances. *Details: (021) 26871.* **Cork School of Music,** *Union Quay:* lunchtime concerts May, June. Otherwise, except June, Aug, Sept, regular evening concerts, *Wed, Fri, eve. Details: (021) 965583* **Entertainment Centre,** *Grand Parade:* traditional and other entertainment during summer. *Details: TIO.*

Fitzgerald Park

Daly's Suspension Bridge, *Sunday's Well:* dates from early part of century, good river views. **South Gate Bridge,** *South Main Street:* atmospheric views of old quays. **Tanto Footbridge,** *adjoining Church of Annunciation, Blackpool:* rebuilt 1946, origins of name obscure. Good views. **Christ Church Lane,** *off Grand Parade:* one of oldest passageways in Cork, dating back 1,000 years. Heart of the medieval city. **Ned Ring's Smithy,** *John Street, near city centre:* Cork's last smithy. As well as shoeing horses, Ned Ring makes gates and general ironwork. **St Patrick's Hill,** *Patrick Street, far side of River Lee:* a steep climb rewarded by superb city views. The splendidly restored **Kent Station:** 1848 steam engine built for Great Southern Railway. Withdrawn in 1874 after nearly half a million miles service.
Prince's street markets in the city centre are well worth seeing, also **Coal Quay open air market,** *Cornmarket Street.*
Le Chateau, *Patrick Street:* founded in 1793, often used by performers from nearby Opera House. **Teach Beag,** *Oliver Plunket Street:* atmospheric inn noted for its traditional Irish music. **Dan Lowrey's** *MacCurtain Street:* old world atmosphere. Stained glass, period furniture. **The Vineyard,** *Market Lane, near Patrick Street:* unofficial home of Cork rugby. Other interesting Cork pubs: **Henchy's,** *St. Luke's;* **McCauliffes,** *Merchant's St;* **Old Reliable,** *Shandon St;* **Russell Inn,** *Marlboro' St;* **Swan and Cygnet,** *Patrick St.* Also try **Oyster Restaurant,** *Market*

Lane—lots of old-fashioned atmosphere.
Lee Walk Fields: riverside walk opp. County Hall, beginning at Carrigrohane Road, immediately after outdoor baths. Quayside walks: good strolls upstream from city centre. University College: charming riverside walks in the lower grounds, access from Western Road. Marina Park: pleasant riverside walks on way to Blackrock, 2 m (3 km) from city centre. **Fitzgerald Park,** *3, 7, 7A bus from Patrick Street, 10 bus from Grand Parade.* Two marvellous sculptures by Cork artist Seamus Murphy: Madonna of the Twilight and Michael Collins. The Lough, *off Lough Road, SW Cork, 14 bus from Patrick Street,* fishing, wildlife habitat. Clover Hill, *Blackrock, E Cork:* public park, arboretum.
Swimming pools: indoor, heated: Gus Healy Pool, *Douglas, 7 bus from Patrick Street, all year;* Matt Talbot Pool, *Churchfield, 2 bus from Patrick Street, all year;* Lee Outdoor Pool, Carrigrohane Road, 8 bus from Patrick Street, June–August, all daily. Bicycles: DMD Cycles, *18 Grafton Street, tel: (021) 21529;* Kilgrews, *North Main Street, tel: (021) 23458.* Pine Grove Riding Centre, *Whites Cross, tel: (021) 503857.* Skevanish Riding Centre, *Innishannon, tel: (021) 75476.* Ballymaloe Riding Stables, *tel: (021) 652531.* Lee Rowing Club, *tel: (021) 966093* Cork Boat Club, *tel: (021) 291258* Douglas Golf Club, *18 holes, tel: (021) 291086.* Monkstown Golf Club, *18 holes, tel: (021) 841225.* Cork Golf Club, *18 holes, tel: (021) 821263.*

AROUND CORK

Ahenesk Castle, *3 m (5 km) SW of Midleton:* mediaeval ruins overlooking Cork Harbour inlet.
Ardarou, *by Glenville, 10 m (16 km) N of Cork:* forest walks by Bride River, car park, picnic area.
Ballincollig: good 2 m (3 km) walk from Powder Mills, along banks of River Lee, past weir to Inishcarra Castle. White Horse Inn: tudor style pub, with woodn beam ceilings, open fires.
Ballymakeera/Ballyvourney, *8 m (13 km) NW of Macroom on N22:* Irish language and culture continues to florish in the area of the twin villages.
Barryscourt Castle, *0.5 m (0.8 km) S of Carrigtwohill on N25:* strategically sited within Cork Harbour, extensive late medieval ruins.
Blackrock Castle, *3 m (5 km) E of Cork:* from vicinity of 1830 building, good views of shipping going in and out of Cork harbour.
Blarney Castle and Stone, *5 m (8 km) NW of Cork on L69, 154 bus from Cork.* Climb 120 steps to battlements to kiss the stone and win the gift of the gab. If you're the strong, silent type, admire views of lush countryside. Good walks in castle grounds, including Rock Close, grove of ancient trees said to have been centre of Druid worship. *May, Mon–Sat, 9 a.m.–7 p.m.; June, July, Mon–Sat, 9 a.m.–8.30 p.m.; Aug, Mon–Sat, 9 a.m.–7.30 p.m.; Sept, Mon–Sat, 9 a.m.–6.30 p.m.; Oct–Apr, Mon–Sat, 9 a.m.–sundown. Summer Sun, 9.30 a.m.–5.30 p.m. Winter Sun, 9.30 a.m.–sundown. Details: (021) 85252.*
Carrigrohane Castle, *2 m (3 km) E of Ballincollig:* 14th/15th c ruins.
Cloyne, *18 m (29 km) SE of Cork:* once an ancient royal seat, now a sleepy village nestling amid E Cork hills.
Cloyne Cathedral (CI): restored 14th c building has monument to one time bishop of Cloyne and famous philosopher, George Berkeley.
Cloyne Round Tower, *opp. cathedral:* built around 900, still in good condition. Key from house in corner of cathedral grounds.
Coachford, *14 m (22 km) W of Cork on T29:* fine view of River Lee valley.
Cobh, *5 m E of Cork on Great Island, Trains from Cork:* St Colman's Cathedral (C). Impressive 19th c Gothic revival style. Regular carillon recitals in summer, fine views over harbour from entrance. **Cobh Museum:** housed in former Presbyterian 'Scots' church. Many items relating to district: maritime relics. *May–Oct, Wed, Sun, 3 p.m.–6 p.m. Otherwise, Sun, 3 p.m.–6 p.m.*

Details: Mrs O'Brien, tel: (021) 811562.
Lusitania Memorial, *quayside.* Hundreds of 'Lusitania' victims are buried in Cobh's Old Church cemetery. Cork Harbour trips: Marine Transport, *Cobh, tel: (021) 811485.* Ballywilliam Riding Centre, *tel: (021) 811908/811932.* Swimming pool: indoor, heated, Carrignafoy, *daily, details: (021) 811786.*
Coolea, *near Ballymakeera:* Seán Ó Riada, composer and musician, d. 1971, lived here the last few years of his life.
Cork Airport, *on L42 to Kinsale, 4 m (6 km) S of Cork city. TIO: Cork Airport, (021) 964347. July–Aug.* Two internal viewing terraces, *daily, all year.*
Crosshaven, *17 m (27 km) SE of Cork, 161 bus from Cork.* Favourite seaside resort for Cork holiday-makers. Royal Cork Yacht Club, oldest in the world.
Dún Uí Mheachair, fort, built 1798 on headland overlooking vast sweep of Cork Harbour. Bathing: Church Bay, Grall Bay, Myrtleville Bay, Robert's Cove (sandy beach near Carrigaline), Weaver's Point. Bicycle, boat hire: Barry Twomey, *Whispering Pines, tel: (021) 831448.*
Currabinny, *across Owenboy River from Crosshaven, entrance 4 m (6 km) E of Carrigaline, turn L off L66 at Carrigaline Catholic church:* nature trail, scenic views, Giant's Grave Bronze Age burial cairn, car park, picnic area.
Curragh, *3 m (5 km) N of Midleton on L35:* ring fort, forest walks, picnic area, car park.
Dripsey Woollen Mills, *10 m (16 km) W of Cork on T29:* handweaving mills and shop. *Mon–Fri, 8.30 a.m.–12.30 p.m.; 1.30 p.m.–5.30 p.m. Details: Coachford 5.*
Farran, *6 m (10 km) W of Ballincollig:* forest park, lakeside walks, wildlife displays, scenic views, car park, picnic area.
Fort Camden, *2 m (3 km) NE of Crosshaven:* great fortifications built at end of 18th c on S side of Ram's Head. Fine harbour views.
Fota Island, *6 m (10 km) E of Cork, Cork–Cobh train stops at estate.* Part of island. Wildlife park and arboretum. Also Regency-style Fota House with splendid collection of Irish landscape paintings. Estate grounds open *first weekend Apr–Sept 30; weekdays 10 a.m.–6 p.m., Sun 11 a.m.–6 p.m.* House open *early Mar–Sept 30; weekdays 11 a.m.–5.30 p.m., Sun 1 p.m.–5.30 p.m. Rest of year Sat, Sun 2 p.m.–6 p.m.* Arboretum also open *2 p.m.–6 p.m. during Oct. Details: (021) 812555.* Wildlife Park: *(021) 812678/812736.*
Glanmire, *4 m (6 km) E of Cork on N8:* **Dunkathel House,** attractive late 18th c building full of antiques and paintings. *May–Sept, Wed, Thurs, Sat, Sun, 2 p.m.–6 p.m. Details: (021) 821014.* **Riverstown House,** built 1602, rebuilt 1745, fine plasterwork, art gallery. *May–Sept, Thurs–Sun, 2 p.m.–6 p.m. Tours. Details: (021) 821205.* Brooklodge House Riding School, *tel: (021) 821169, 3 p.m.–6 p.m. only.*
Glenday, *6 m (9 km) N of Macroom on L41, then 2 m (3 km) W of Carriganimmy on unclassified road:* extensive forest walks amid impressive scenery.
Gortnatubbrid, *near Ballyvourney:* site of 6th c monastery, access to St Gobnet's Shrine, forest walk, view of River Sullane, car park, picnic area.
Inniscarra, *7 m (11 km) W of Cork on T29:* Sean O'Riordain, one of Ireland's greatest modern poets, commemorated by plaque on family house at Garravagh.
Kilcrea Abbey, *5 m (8 km) SW of Ballincollig:* with grave of Noble Art O'Leary, murdered in 1773 because he wouldn't sell his mare for £5. At that time, Catholics were prevented from owning a horse worth more. *Opp. abbey,* Kilcrea Castle ruins.
Kilmurry, *17 m (27 km) W of Cork and just S of N22 at Lissarda:* Mac Swiney Memorial Museum: about 1,000 items of local archaeology, folklike, history. *SO, Sun, 3 p.m.–6 p.m.*

Macroom, *24 m (37 km) W of Cork, 117(SO), 173 bus from Cork.* Lively mid-Cork town once property of Admiral Sir William Penn, whose son founded the American state of Pennsylvania. Penn Castle mostly demolished, entrance stands at one side of town square. Boat hire: Cork Boating Centre, *Coachford 140/(021) 41992;* Mr O'Leary, Coolcower Bridge, 5 m (8 km) from Macroom on S road to Cork.

Marloge Forest, *turn R just before East Ferry on Cobh–East Ferry road:* viewing points over Cork Harbour, walks, car park, picnic area.

Midleton: Irish Distillers' complex where all the famous Irish whiskies are produced, with the notable exception of Bushmills. *Details: tel: (021) 631821.*

Moanbawn, *7 m (11 km) NE of Cork, off Watergrasshill–Midleton road:* forest walks.

Mullaghanish Mountain, *N of Ballyvourney:* from top, near RTE transmitting mast, superb views of surrounding countryside. Easily accessible by road.

Musheramore, *10 m (16 km) N of Macroom, E of L41:* forest, mountain walks, holy well, car park, picnic area.

Ovens Caves, *3 m (5 km) of Ballincollig:* experts only.

Rostellan, *3 m (5 km) W of Cloyne at E edge of Cork Harbour:* old stone bridge with three ancient milestones telling distance to almost every place in Ireland. **Rostellan Forest,** *turn W off Midleton–Whitegate road at Farsid:* forest, seashore walks, car park, picnic area.

St Anne's Hydro, *2 m (3 km) W of Blarney:* 18th c ruins similar to Mallow Spa.

Trabolgan Holiday Centre, Midleton, Co. Cork. *Tel: (021) 661579.*

Tracton, *3 m (6 km) S of Carrigaline on L67:* enter by 'Overdraft' pub for extensive forest walks.

Ummera, *3 m (5 km) E of Macroom on N22:* forest walks, picnic area, car park.

Walshtown, *7 m (11 km) N of Midleton on Castlelyons road:* forest walks.

Warrenscourt, *turn S off N22 to Poulanairgid:* forest, lakeside walks, car park, picnic area.

Watergrasshill, *8 m (13 km) NE of Cork on N8:* Fir Tree Inn, with old-time tub trap perched on roof.

Killarney

Pop. 8,000, 20 m (32 km) SE of Tralee, 54 m (87 km) NW of Cork, 68 m (109 km) SW of Limerick, 190 m (305 km) SW of Dublin. EC Mon. In summer, most shops ignore it. *TIO: Town Hall, all year, tel: (064) 31633. Bus and train enquiries: (064) 31067. 106(50), 117(50), 173, 182, 195 bus from Tralee. Train from Cork, Dublin, Tralee. Taxis: College Square. Coach tours: SO, daily.*

At first glance a rather undistinguished town, very touristy in summer, Killarney is nevertheless a busy and likeable place, with plenty happening at most levels of cultural interest. It owes its fame almost entirely to its situation in the heart of Ireland's beautiful lake district, for which it's the perfect touring centre. Killarney regatta: *July.* Kerry Boating Carnival: *Sept.* Pan-Celtic Week: much after-hours jollity culminates in Celtavision Song Contest for Ireland, Scotland, Wales, Cornwall, Isle of Man and Brittany, *May.*

Cathedral of St Mary of the Assumption (C), *New Street:* designed by Pugin, great 19th c architect and recently renovated. DW **St Mary's parish church** (CI), *Main Street:* richly decorated Victorian interior. **Prince of Peace Church,** *Fossa:* modern church designed and built by men and women from the four provinces of Ireland. Main door has delightful dove and ark motifs by Helen

Moloney. **Franciscan friary,** *Fair Hill, College Street:* dates from 1860. Fine Harry Clarke stained glass window over main entrance.

Artists' Gallery, *5 Plunkett Street:* Irish scenes, oils and watercolours. *Daily, 9.30 a.m.–5.30 p.m.* **Celtic Twilight Gallery,** *Brewery Lane:* drawings, paintings, Celtic screen prints. *Daily, tel: (064) 32273.* **The Studio,** *Town Hall:* paintings of Ireland, *daily, 9.30 a.m.–5.30 p.m., tel: (064)31255.*

Ross Castle, on peninsula jutting into Lough Leane, *2 m (3 km) SW of town, off N71:* remains of magnificent 15th c keep.

Spéir Bhan, *College Street:* the foot of Seamus Murphy's statue is inscribed with the names of the great 17th and 18th c Kerry poets. Old Market Lane, Barry's Lane, Green Lane, Bóithrín Caol (Narrow Lane), and Brewery Lane (off Kenmare Place), are very atmospheric. The Knockreer Estate, off Cathedral Place, ahs pleasant walks, excellent views of Lough Leane. Bridle and cycle paths. *Open at all times.*

Jaunting car: time-honoured way of seeing the area's sights. *Check prices at TIO.* C Fair Green fun fair, amusement park: *nightly, July, Aug.* Kerry Glass, *Fair Hill:* glass blowing and moulding. *Mon–Fri, 8 am.m–1 p.m.; 2 p.m.–4 p.m.* Adjacent shop. *Tel: (064) 32587.* Kerry Woollen Mills, *Beaufort: Mon–Fri, 8.30 a.m.–1 p.m.; 2 p.m.–5 p.m. Sat by app., tel: Beaufort 9.* Racecourse, *Ross Road. May, July, Oct. Details: (064) 31860/31125.* Boat hire: Ross Castle, *details: H. Clifton, tel: (064) 32252.* Swimming pool: indoor, heated, for non-residents at Hotel Europa, *tel: (064) 31900,* Torc Great Southern Hotel, *Cork Road, tel: (064) 31611.* Killarney Riding School, *Ballydowney, tel: (064) 31686;* The Arch Farm, *Tralee Road, tel: (064) 33149.*

Bicycles: O'Callaghans, *College Street, tel: (064) 31465.* D. O'Neill, *Plunkett Street, tel: (064) 31970.* Killarney Golf Club, *Mahony's Point, 18 holes, tel: (064) 31034.* Youth Hostel: *tel: (064) 31240.*

AROUND KILLARNEY

Abbey Island, *Derrynane Bay:* remains of early Christian monastery. A short walk across at low tide.

Aghadoe Hill, *3 m (5 km) N of Killarney:* ruins of 7th c church and castle, superb views of Killarney lakes and mountains.

Ballaghisheen/Derreenageeha, *13 m (21 km) NE of Waterville, W of Ballaghhisheen Pass:* forest walks, car park, picnic area.

Ballinskelligs: *facing Waterville across Ballinskelligs Bay.* Irish-speaking resort. Miles of golden beaches, ideal for surfing.

Ballycarbery Castle, *3 m (5 km) NW of Chircirveen, off N70:* 15th c, destroyed by Cromwellian forces in 1652. Nearby, anent Cahergal stone fort.

Baslicon Dolmen, *2 m (3 km) S of Watervlle, off N70:* nearby, fine standing stone.

Beenbane Fort, *W shore of Lough Currane:* horseshoe-shaped prehistoric structure. Before you reach fort, beehive huts with 7 ft (2 metre) thick walls.

Black Valley, *4 m (6 km) SW of Lough Leane:* Youth Hostel.

Caherdaniel: *10 m (16 km) SE of Cahirciveen,* attractively set village. O'Connel Gallery: exhibits oils, water-colours, batiks, prints. *Summer, daily, 11.30 a.m.–2.30 p.m.; 4.30 p.m.–7.30 p.m. Details: Caherdaniel 35.* Walk: NW of Eagle Hill as far as Lamb's Head for excellent views of Kenmare River estuary.

Cahirciveen, *25 m (40 km) E of Killarney, 179 bus from Killarney. TIO: tel: Cahirciveen 113, July–Aug. Cahirciveen–Valentia ferry: summer, 9 a.m.–9 p.m. daily. Details: Cahirciveen 12.* O'Connell Memorial Church (C), *Main Street,* built in 1888 to honour the memory of Daniel O'Connell. **Carhan House,** *1 m (1.5 km) NE of Cahirciveen, o 70:* ruins of house where O'Connell, 'The Liberator', was born in 1775. **Kerry Studios,** *West*

End, local artists' work. *Sumr, daily, 11 a.m.–6 p.m.* Bicycles: Patrick Casey, *New Street, tel: Cahirciveen 164.*

Castlecove, *3 m (5 km) NE of Caherdaniel:* fine sandy beaches.

Coomanaspig Pass, *3 m (5 km) S of Portmgee:* one of highest places in Ireland acessible by car, spectacular views. If you continue SW, a narrow road winds down to magnificent S facing St Finan's Beach.

Coomshane, *near Kells:* forest walks.

Cromane Strand, *5 m (8 km) W of Killorglin:* good bathing.

Cross Strand, *4 m (6 km) W of Kenmare:* good bathing.

Derrynane House and National Park, *1 m (1.5 km) W of Caherdaniel on N70:* home of Daniel O'Connell restored as museum, with period furnishings and personal relics. Park covers 320 acres, exceptional coastal scenery, nature trail, sea bathing. *Park open all year, house, mid June–Sept 30, daily. 10 a.m.–1 p.m.; 2 p.m.–7 p.m. Rest of year, Tues–Sat, 10 a.m.–1 p.m.; Sun, 2 p.m.–5 p.m., details: Caherdaniel 13.*

Derrynane Ogham Stone, *1 m (1.5 km) SW of Caherdaniel on Derrynane road:* transferred here from below the waterline. this does not mean, however, that the country is capsizing! Walk, along 'Smuggler's Path' from Derrynane to Bunavalla pier.

Dooneen, *2 m (3 km) N of Castleisland on N21:* forest walks, car park, picnic area.

Dromore, *6 m (10 km) W of Kenmare on N70:* forest walks overlooking Kenmare Bay, seashore walk, car park, picnic area.

Druid's Circle, *1 m (1.5 km) SW of Kenmare, off Market Street:* 15 prehistoric standing stones.

Dunkerron castle, *2 m (3 km) W of Kenmare off Sneem road:* ruins date from 1596.

Dunloe Castle, *6 m (10 km) W of Killarney off T67, 185 bus from Killarney.* 13th c ruins in hotel grounds, nearby ogham stones.

Farranfore, *10 m (16 km) N of Killarney:* Kerry Airport, flying, parachuting lessons. Charter a plane for unusual views of Kerry. *Details: (066) 64350.*

Foileye Bay, *near Kells:* good bathing.

Gap of Dunloe: *start at Kate Kearney's cottage, 1 m (1.5 km) S of Dunloe Castle Hotel.* Magnificent 7 m (11 km) trip by pony or pony and trap. The passage is bordered by a string of dark tarns, with something interesting at almost every turn of the track. Bar at Kate Kearney's cottage. Nearby café. Pony trekking: *tel: (064) 44116/44146.*

If you can afford to take it in style, hire a jaunting car at Killarney, as far as Kate Kearney's cottage. Then go through the Gap of Dunloe by pony or trap and pony, by the Logan Stone, as far as the Upper Lake. From here, the Gap boats take you through the Long Range of the Meeting of the Waters, where you shoot the rapids and go across Lough Leane to Ross Castle. From the castle, a jaunting car will take you back to Killarney. About 25 m (40 km).

Gleensk, *Ring of Kerry, 8 m (13 km) W of Glenbeigh:* forest walk to seashore on S side of Dingle Bay. Lay-by, picnic area.

Glenbeigh, *5 m (8 km) SE of Killorglin:* small fishing village. Flapper (horse) races, *last week July.* Good bathing on the strand. Forest walks off nearby Rossbeigh road. Hill climbing paths on Seefin Mountain to SE. Panoramic views of Dingle Bay and peninsula. Good climbs on nearby Curra Mountain. Enjoyable walk following glen of River Beigh to tarn that is source of river. Splendid views of 'Glenbeigh Horseshoe' amphitheatre of mountains. Coomacarea, 2,541 ft (774 metres) is an excellent viewpoint. Boat hire: John O'Sullivan, *Rossbeigh;* Michael Rahilly, *Caragh Lake.* Bicycles: John O'Sullivan, the Garage, *tel: (066) 68207.* Dooks Golf Club, *18 holes, tel: (066) 68205.*

Gap of Dunloe

Glenflesk, *8 m (13 km) SE of Killarney on N22:* robber's cave on N slopes of Carrigawaddra. Here Owen MacCarthy, a 16th c thief with an educational bent, trained his apprentices (mostly children) in cattle stealing and highway robbery.

Gortboy, Corran Tuathail Youth Hostel: *tel: Beaufort (064) 44187.*

Inishfallen Island, *1 m (1.5 km) from Ross Castle:* near landing stage are ruins of abbey, dating from about 600. Annals of Innisfallen, chronicle of Irish and world history, written in Irish and Latin here between 950 and 1320. Now in Bodleian Library, Oxford.

Kells, *midway between Glenbeigh and Cahirciveen, off N70, 180 bus from Cahirciveen, Glenbeigh.* Panoramic views of Dingle Bay, Blasket Islands, Kells Bay. Abandoned railway tunnels at Drung Hill and Gleensk Viaduct, relics of old GSR railway that ran from Cahirciveen to Farranfore Junction. Kells Bay: good bathing.

Kenmare, *21 m (34 km) S of Killarney on N71. EC Thurs. TIO: tel: (064) 41233. 102, 180 bus from Killarney.* Delightfully set where River Roughty opens into Kenmare River estuary. Town is backed by fearsome mountains. Kenmare Fruits de Mer seafood festival: street entertainments, arts and crafts shows. *Sept/early Oct.* Kenmare Regatta: *late Aug.*

   Convent of the Poor Clares, lace-making. *Daily, 10 a.m.–12 noon; 2 p.m.–4 p.m.; 7 p.m.–9 p.m. Details: (064) 41385.*   Boat trips: Harry Rook, Tubrid, *tel: (064) 41170;* C. Keenan, *Killaha, tel: (064) 41024;* Bernard O'Connor, *tel: (064) 41300.* Bathing from pier, also off Glengariff road on outskirts of town. Surfing equipment at pier. Drumquinna Riding Stables, *tel: (064) 41043.* Bicycles: John P. Finnegan, *Henry Street, tel: (064) 41083;* Tuohy Bicycle Hire, *Main Street.* Kenmare Golf Club, *9 holes, tel: (064) 41291.* Bonane Youth Hostel.

Kilderry, *1 m (1.5 km) SW of Milltown on N70:* forest walks, picnic area.

Kilgarvan, *8 m (13 km) E of Kenmare on L62:* Ardtully Castle, 13th c ruins. The grave of local clan chief MacCarthaigh, killed here in battle in 1261 is 1 m (1.5 km) S of village on Bantry road. **Kilgarvan Eagle,** *4 m (6 km) S of village on Bantry road:* said to have been carved into mountainside in 1626.

Killabonia, *S side of Knocknaskerrig Mountain, 6 m (10 km) SW of Cahirciveen:* ruins of oratory and beehive huts, dating from early monastic settlement.

Killaha Castle, *6 m (10 km) SE of Killarney, W of N22:* 17th c ruins. Nearby, minor road leads to wild, solitary splendour of Lough Guitane, climb of about 2 m (3 km).

Killarney National Park, *3 m (5 km) S of Killarney on N71:* wonderful walks amid 20,000 acres, also ideal for driving through. Keep a lookout for deer and a fine herd of pedigree Kerry cattle. *Open at all times.*

Killeenagh Strand, *5 m (8 km) W of Kenmare:* good bathing.

Killorglin, *13 m (21 km) NW of Killarney on T67. EC Wed. 179 bus from Killarney, Tralee.* Hilly town overlooking River Laune. Rather desolate looking, but full of warm, quixotic Kerry character. Puck Fair: three days and nights of drink and revelry as tens of thousands of people crowd in to see a mountain goat crowned 'King' of the fair and enjoy the free-flow of Guinness, *Aug.* Nearby Caragh Lake area has forest walks, viewing points.

Conway castle: 12th c ruins. Also see ogham stones, caves and forts in vicinity.

Kilreilrig, *near Ballinskelligs, far W of Iveragh peninsula:* village abandoned some 20 years ago, cottages built with their backs to the westerly winds, without doors or windows on that side, to keep out ocean spray. Local barracks once used by Royal Irish Constabulary; design is Moorish Kilreilrig stone fort: *on road from Ballinskelligs to Bolus Head.*

Kimego, *3 m (6 km) N of Cahiriciveen via Castlequin village:* forest walks, sea views, ruins of 18th c turf drying plant.

Ladies' View, *12 m (19 km) SW of Killarney on N71, 182 bus from Killarney (SO), also 186 bus.* Over a century ago, Queen Victoria and her ladies-in-waiting were enchanted by the view, hence the name. Nearby tearoom.

Leacanabuaile Fort, *3 m (5 km) NW of Cahircirveen, access by minor road to Cooncrome Harbour:* massive fort of uncertain date, excellent interior. Fine coastal views from ramparts.

Lickeen Forest, *S end of Lough Caragh on lakeside road to Killorglin to Ballaghbeama:* scenic walks, lay-by, picnic area.

Loo Bridge, *4 m (6 km) SE of Lough Guitane,* Youth Hostel, *tel: Clonkeen 2.*

Lough Acoose/Cloon Lake, boat hire: Glencar Hotel, *tel: (066) 60102.*

Lough Caragh, *near Glenbeigh:* 6 m (10 km) walk round W and N shores and lake.

Lough Currane: near S shore, by road to Tooreens, (cul-de-sac), you can see part of intriguing submerged castle. If walking, you can continue from Tooreens over mountain path to Sneem, *7 m (11 km).*

Macgillicuddy's Reeks: excellent climbing, including Carrantuohill, Ireland's highest mountain. *Details:* Sean O'Sullivan, Killarney Mountaineering Club, *Langford Street, Killorglin, tel: (066) 61127.*

Mangerton, *5 m (8 km) S of Killarney on N71, turn L at Muckross Hotel:* mountain walks, panoramic lake views, car park, picnic area.

Meeting of the Waters, *6 m (10 km) SW of Killarney on Kenmare road:* picturesque spot, where luxuriant plants and shrubs flourish in the particularly mild Kerry climate.

Milltown, *4 m (6 km) NE of Killorglin:* ruins of 13th c Kilcoman Abbey. Also large prehistoric circular fort.

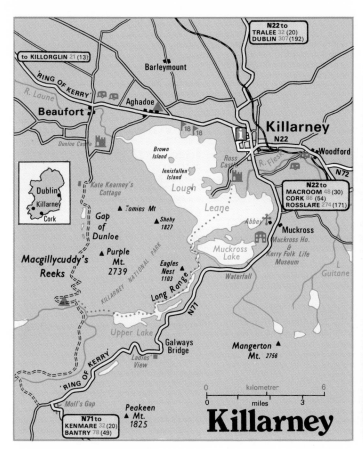

Killarney

Muckross House and folk museum, *4 m (7 km) S of Killarney, off N71:* built in Elizabethan style in 1843. Many of its rooms retain Victorian furnishings. Museum of Kerry folklife has locally carved period furniture, maps, tools of trades and crafts (some how extinct), old printing presses, coins and natural history section. In basement craft centre, you can see weaver, blacksmith and potter at work. Magnificent gardens, with nature trails and exquisite rock garden. Excellent views of surrounding lakes, mountains and woodlands. Allow at least half day to tour house and gardens. *Mar 17–June 30, 10 a.m.–7 p.m. daily, July, Aug, 9 a.m.–9 p.m. daily, Sept 1–Oct 31, 10 a.m.–7 p.m. daily. Rest of year, Tues–Sun, 11 a.m.–5 p.m. Café. Details: (064) 31440.*

Muckross Abbey, *just N of park off N71:* mid-15th c ruins in good repair. Old Kenmare Road, *starts near House:* good walk across mountains to Kenmare just E of present road. Mangerton Track: *starts near House,* climbs for about 3 m (5 km) to near Devil's Punch Bowl.

Our Lady's Holy Well, *of Killarney road, 1 m (1.5 km) N of Kenmare:* waters reputed to have healing powers.

Parknasilla, *2 m (3 km) S of Sneem, entrance 1 m (1.5 km) E of Great Southern Hotel, off N70:* pleasant walks through woods, good views of surrounding bay, safe bathing in nearby coves, picnic area. Parknasilla Golf Club, *9 holes.*

Pass of Coomakista, *between Caherdaniel and Waterville:* fine views of Ballinskelligs Bay and Skelligs rocks.

Peter and Paul's Holy Well, *2 m (3 km) N of Kilgarvan on Mangerton road.* On June 29, local people circle well reciting prayers.

Pike Wood, *1 m (1.5 km) SE of town on N22:* forest walks, access to Crooked Tree, lay-by, picnic area.

Reenagross Park, *1 m (1.5 km) from Kenmare on Glengarriff road:* woodland walks.

Rossacrue, *12 m (19 km) E of Kenmare on L62:* forest walks, picnic area.

Rossdohan Island, *3 m (5 km) SE of Sneem, S of N70:*

delightful gardens, wonderful trees, including cypresses. Many botanical wonders. *By arr., tel: (064) 45114.*

The Seven Sisters, *Lissivigeen, 2 m (3 km) E of Killarney, just off N22:* ancient stone circle within a rath.

The Skelligs: *two rock islets 8 m (13 km) out to sea, off Bolus Head. Make arrangements with a boatman in either Cahirciveen or Knightstown Harbour on Valentia Island.* Little Skellig is uninhabited: landing is rarely possible. Landing on Great Skellig is very difficult and only possible in calm weather. Cliff pathway rise to a 7th c monastic settlement: church, two oratories, six beehive cells. If you are an experienced climber, you can go as far as cross carved in the 'summit', a hazardous ascent indeed. A visit to Great Skellig is probably the most memorable experience to be had in Co Kerry.

The Skelligs

Staigue Fort, *2 m (3 km) NE of Castlecove:* probably finest Iron Age fort in Ireland, N side in perfect condition; stairways run inside the walls. *By arr., landowner.*

Sheen Falls, *2 m (3 km) from Kenmare on Glengarriff road:* 'must' for visitors to area.

Sneem, *11 m (17 km) E of Kenmare:* charmingly situated where estuary of Ardsheelaun River flows into Kenmare River, noted angling centre. Safe sandy beaches. **St Michael's** (C) has grave of Fr Michael Walsh, the Father O'Flynn of the famous song.

Church of the Transfiguration (CI), dates from Elizabethan times. Bicycles: Michael Burns, *North Square, tel: Sneem 16.*

Knightstown, Valentia Island

47

Torc Waterfall, *5 m (8 km) S of Killarney, just S of main Killarney–Kenmare road:* one of finest in Ireland. Climb up footpath that wends upwards alongside waterfall. Magnificent lake views. Signposted.

Valentia Island, *7 m (11 km) long, 2 m (3 km) wide:* connected to mainland by bridge at Portmagee. Car or bike essential, no public transport. Magnificent cliffs and seascapes and profusion of bustropical flowers and shrubs. Valentia Regatta: highlight is traditional seine (fishing) boat race, *Aug.* **Knightstown,** the island's main settlement, has an attractive harbour, and lots of atmosphere. Site of now-disused Western Union Cable Station, where the first trans-Atlantic cable was joined in 1866. Knightstown slate quarry, now disused, fine views of harbour and Dingle peninsula.
  Bray Head, *SW tip of island, 792 ft (241 metres), excellent views.* **Geokaun Mountain,** *on N, 880 ft (268 metres)* excellent vantage point. Beginish Island, off Valentia and half covered by sand is good for bathing. Adjacent Church Island has ruins of early monastic settlement. Valentia Gallery: sculpture by the owner. *Tel: Valentia 5.* Youth Hostel, *tel: Valentia Island 54.* Bicycles from hostel.

Waterville, *W edge of Iveragh peninsula:* popular resort town, and noted angling centre. Fine sandy beaches. Salmon and trout festival and regatta, *late July, early Aug.* Boat hire: D. O'Connell, *Portmagee, tel: Portmagee 1;* Vincent O'Sullivan, 'Southview'; P. Donnelly, *Lake Road;* Jim Quinlan, *tel: (0667) 4232.* Car tours: G. Cronin, *tel: (0667) 4294;* A. McGillycuddy, *tel: (0667) 4252.* Bicycles: Jim Quinlan, *the village, tel: (0667) 4232.* Waterville Golf Club, *18 holes, tel: (0667) 4261.*

White Strand, *3 m (5 km) SW of Cahirciveen:* good bathing and surfing.

Kinsale

Pop. 1,700, 18 m (29 km) S of Cork, 22 m (35 km) NE of Clonakilty, 179 m (288 km) SW of Dublin. EC Thurs. TIO: (021) 72234. July–Aug. Bus enquiries: CIE, Cork. (021) 504422. 162 bus from Cork.
Extravagantly beautiful town overlooking the Bandon estuary. Kinsale has a strong Spanish flavour, its narrow, winding streets have been compared to those of Toledo and in 1601–2 a Spanish force took the town and held it against English armies.
  Recaptured, and anglicised, Kinsale became one of the chief ports of the British navy. In recent years it has happily enjoyed a more peaceful prosperity; it now boasts a number of gourmet restaurants and is one of Ireland's major sea angling centres. Gourmet Festival: feast of good eating and drinking in Kinsale's many bistros and restaurants, *Oct.*
  St Multose Church (CI): built 1190, subsequently enlarged. In fine interior, see old town stocks and flags carried at Battle of Waterloo. Three victims of the 'Lusitania', torpedoed off Old Head of Kinsale in May, 1915, are buried in graveyard. *Daily, details: Rev. O. A. P. Peare, (021) 72220.* **St John the Baptist Church** (C), *Friar's Street:* ornate, T-shaped 19th c church with interesting slate memorials. **Carmelite Friary,** *Carmel Avenue:* excellent views from front of friary.
  Kinsale Museum, *Old Town Hall:* among exhibits in 17th c building, model of HMS Kinsale, local lace and silver, photographs, maps and several of the famous all-enveloping Kinsale cloaks. Also charters granted to the town by Elizabeth I in 1590 and James I in 1610. The 'giant' Patrick Cotter O'Brien (1760–1806), who found fame and fortune on the English stage, was born here: see his slippers, outsize boots, gigantic knife and fork. *daily, all year, 10 a.m.–5 p.m. Closed for lunch.*
  Bowling Green: small, tree-lined public park on flat ground half-way up the hill overlooking the harbour. Walks: Compas Hill: start on S heights of Kinsale above the Trident Hotel. The road follows semi-circular route for about 2 m (3 km), giving excellent views of harbour and estuary before bringing you back to the town. Scilly: walk along harbour, past new marina, for about 1 m (1.5 km) to tiny 'suburb' of Scilly. Stop off at old-world 'Spaniard' pub, with attractive interior decor, including súgán (Irish-style rope) chairs, wooden beam ceilings and mahogany fittings.
  Kinsale Angling Centre. *Lower O'Connell Street:* fishing tackle, boats, *tel: (021) 72611, or 75241 after hours.* For small boats for use in harbour only: (021) 72242/72301. Bicycles: Mylie Murphy, *Pearse Street, tel: (021) 72122;* Sea View, *Pier Road, tel: (021) 72248.* Coolcorrow Equestrian Centre, *tel: (021) 71353.* Golf Club, *9 holes, tel: (021) 72197.*

AROUND KINSALE

Aultagh Wood, *9 m (14 km) NW of Ballineen:* forest walks, car park, picnic area.

Ballinascarthy, *5 m (8 km) N of Clonakilty on N71:* birthplace of Henry Ford, founder of American motor industry. Ardnavaha Riding Centre, *tel: (023) 49135.*

Ballycatteen ring fort, *4 m (6 km) SW of Kinsale:* remains of circular prehistoric fort covering some 3 acres. From top, good views of nearby Ballinspittle village.

Bandon, *13 m (21 km) NW of Kinsale EC Thurs. Bus enquiries: (021) 504422. 103 bus (SO), 139, 164 from Cork.* Good salmon and sea trout angling centre. Agricultural Show, *late May.* Kilbrigan Church (CI), built 1610, has old town stocks. R. & J. Forrester craft shop and gallery, *83 North Main Street:* pottery made in workshop. *All year, Mon–Sat, 10 a.m.–6 p.m. Details: (023) 41360.* W Bicycle hire: Jerry O'Donovan, *4 South Main Street, tel: (023) 41227.*

Beal-na-mBlath, *2 m (3 km) SW of Crookstown on L41:* memorial to Generar Michael Collins, killed here in 1922.

Castle Bernard, *1 m (1.5 km) W of Bandon:* imposing ruins of 16th c castle burned down in 1921. Bandon Golf Club, *18 holes, tel: (023) 41711.*

Castlefreke, *6 m (9 km) SW of Clonakilty:* forest walks, picnic area, car park. Castlefreke Castle: built over 100 years ago, now ruins. From views of Owenhincha Bay. Near castle, Rathbarry church ruins, large Celtic cross on hill erected in memory of ninth Lord Carberry.

Charles Fort, *near Summer Cove on E shore of Kinsale harbour:* magnificent ruin of 1677 sea fort, occupied until British left in 1922. Dungeons, armouries, arches and buildings, most atmospheric. *Mid June–mid Sept, daily, 10 a.m.–6.30 p.m. otherwise, Mon–Fri, 8 a.m.–4.30 p.m., except public holidays. Conducted tours. Details: TIO, Kinsale.*

Clonakilty, *22 m (35 km) SW of Kinsale. EC Wed. TIO: Tel: (023) 43226. 102, 164 buses from Bandon, Cork. SO.* Good sea angling centre at head of Clonakilty Bay. West Cork Festival, *end June, beginning July. Details: TIO.* 100 year old pure Gothic Catholic church, stained glass and statuary worth seeing. **West Cork regional museum,** *Western Road, opposite Vocational School:* archaeological relics from the area, historical records and maps. *June–Sept. Mon–Sat, 10.30 a.m.–12.30 p.m.; 3 p.m.–5 p.m. Closed Sun.* Georgian houses, *Emmet Square.* Nearby Kennedy Gardens, a mass of flowers.
  Riding: Ardnavaha House Hotel, *tel: (023) 49135;* West Cork Travel Agency, *Rossa Street, tel: (023) 43220.* Bicycles: J. E. Spiller and Co., *41 Pearse Street, tel: (023) 43321.*

Coppinger's Court, *2 m (3 km) SW of Rosscarbery:* ruin of 1610 mansion burned down 30 years later. According to legend, it had a chimney for every month, a door for every week and a window for every day of the year.

Courtmacsherry, *just W of Courtmacsherry Bay:* attractive seaside village backed by woods. Sea angling centre.

Drombeg Stone Circle, *2 m (3 km) E of Glandore:* one of finest West Cork circles, dating from 150 BC. Layout, information signs on site.

Dromilihy, *4 m (6 km) NW of Rosscarbery on N71:* forest walks, picnic area, car park.

Dromkeen Wood, *between Inishannon and Ballinadee:* walks, scenic view over Bandon river, picnic area, lay-by.

Dukes Wood, *3 m (5 km) N of Bandon on L41:* forest walks, walks alongside Sall River, lay-by, picnic area.

Garretstown, *162 bus from Kinsale:* good beaches on shores of Courtmacsherry Bay. *1 m (1.5 km) W of O'Neill's Hotel on unclassified road to Kilbrittain:* woodland walks, picnic place, car park. See remains of 'Big House', including orangery.

Glandore, *4 m (6 km) W of Rosscarbery, 102 bus (SO), 164 bus from Cork, Skibbereen to Leap.* Beautifully set village looking over Glandore harbour.

Inchadoney Island, *2 m (3 km) S of Clonakilty, 102 bus (SO) and 164 bus from Cork, Skibbereen to Clonakilty.* Despite its name, part of mainland. Noted for long, golden sands, ideal for bathing and surfing. Strand divided by grass-topped hill called Virgin Mary's Bank.

Inishannon, *8 m (13 km) NW of Kinsale on L41, 103 bus (SO), 164 from Bandon.* Ruined Dundaniel Castle, built in 1476 on banks of river Bandon, amid luxuriant foliage and woodlands.

Jagoes Mill, *3 m (5 km) from Kinsale on back road to Cork:* Kinsale Pottery, see pottery being made. Adjacent coffee shop. *Pottery Mon–Fri, 10 a.m.–5 p.m.*

James's Fort, *opp. Charles Fort, first bridge over Bandon River from Kinsale, turn E for 2 m (3 km):* built about 1601/2 ruins include well-preserved remains of blockhouse at water level, explore with care.

Kilbrittain, *7 m (11 km) NW of Clonakilty:* pleasantly situated village, forest walks. Home of Minta Winn, Ireland's only female harness maker. Impressive working of an ancient craft, *by app.* Riding: Jerry Desmond, Bay View House, *tel: (023) 49731/49626.* Ocean Breeze Bicycle Hire, *tel: (023) 49626;* Hickeys, *tel: (023) 49669.*

Kilfinnan Castle, *1 m (1.5 km) SE of Glandore:* from ruins, excellent view of Glandore harbour.

Kinneigh, *4 m (6 km) N of Enniskean:* round tower built in 1015, 68 ft (21 metres) high, next to St Bartholomew's church.

Knockdrum, *1 m (1.5 km) NE of Castletownshend:* two forts, a prehistoric fort, and Bryan's Fort, built about 1650.

Leap, *2 m (3 km) upriver from Glandore, 103 bus (SO), 164 from Cork, Skibbereen.* From hill above village, excellent views of harbour.

Lougherea Wood, *just outside Union Hall:* forest walks, picnic site.

Old Head of Kinsale, *8 m (13 km) S of Kinsale:* good walks and seascapes. Ruins of 15th c de Courcey castle. Fair walk from Kinsale if you haven't car or bicycle, but you could well be offered a lift.

Owenchincha, *7 m (11 km) SW of Clonakilty:* sandy beach, some 2 m (3 km) long. Trotting races, St Patrick's Day, *Mar 17.*

Palace Anne, *on T65 2 m (3 km) E of Enniskean:* ruins of 17th c house.

Rinneen, *on Castletownshend–Leap road:* forest walks, picnic area and lay-by.

Rosscarbery, *head of Rosscarbery Bay, 164 bus from Bantry, Skibbereen:* safe, sandy beaches in vicinity. Ancient Protestant cathedral, built 1612, nearby remains of 6th c St Fachnan's monastery. Pony trekking: J. Anthony Collins, *Barley Hill, tel: (023) 48189.* Boat hire: M. Sweeney, *Strand Road.*

Sam's Crossroads, *5 m (8 km) SW of Clonakilty:* Seamus Murphy memorial to Michael Collins, born at nearby Woodfield.

Shippool, *2 m (3 km) S of Inishannon on L41 from Kinsale:* forest walks to river Bandon, viewing points, picnic place, lay-by. Ruins of Shippool Castle, built 1543.

Summer Cove, *2 m (3 km) SE of Kinsale:* from Rincurran churchyard the view S over Kinsale harbour is breathtaking. Just before the steep descent into the village, turn left for about 300 yds (90 metres). Bulman pub faces harbour: pine panelled walls lined with fascinating photographs of old fishing and hurling triumphs. Youth Hostel, *tel: (021) 72309.*

Timoleague, *10 m (16 km) SW of Kinsale, 164 bus from Cork, Bandon.* Small village on estuary of Argideen River. **Timoleague Abbey:** one of 13 best-preserved Franciscan friaries of pre-Reformation Ireland, built around 1240, much of present building dates from early 16th c, sacked in 1642 by British forces under Lord Forbes. At entrance commemorative plaque by Oisin Kelly, Dublin sculptor. *Conducted tours on Thurs eve. SO.* Contact Con Harrington, Abbey Street, Timoleague, *tel: (023) 46160.* The village's early 20th c Catholic church has one of last stained glass windows produced by Harry Clarke. CI church has Italian mosaic work.   **Castle Gardens,** laid out and maintained by Travers family for past 150 years. Palm trees thrive in mild W Cork climate. Car park, picnic sites, childrens' playground. *Daily, June, July, Aug, 12 p.m.-6 p.m. Details: (023) 46116.*

Union Hall, *103 bus (SO), 164 from Cork, Skibbereen to Leap:* quaint little village just across harbour from Glandore, surrounded by extensive woodlands.

Mallow

Pop. 6,000, 22 m (35 km) NW of Cork 42 m (67 km) E of Killarney, 149 m (240 km) SW of Dublin. EC Wed. TIO: Cork, tel: (021) 23251. Bus and train enquiries, tel: (022) 21120. 121, 153 bus from Cork. Train from Cork, Dublin, Killarney.

Now a quiet, prosperous market town noted for its fishing, Mallow was once a much livelier proposition: up to a century ago, the now-defunct Spa drew thousands of visitors who would sup the water and conversely indulge in riotous living, if the song 'The Rakes of Mallow' is anything to go by. Today the area has interesting historical remains, good walking and sport, all very sedate. Fishing controlled by local hotels.

Old Mallow Castle: built late 16th c, SE end of town, *daily, all year.* **Museum,** *New Castle:* many interesting local items, including photographs, paintings and items from the Spa House at the peak of its popularity. *May–Sept, aft, preferably by arr. (022) 21469.*   **Clock House:** picturesque half-timbered building, *all year, Mon–Fri, 9.30 a.m.-5.30 p.m.* Spa Well: the source of Mallow's former glory, *daily, all year.*

Race meetings: occasional, *details: (022) 21338.* Swimming pool: indoor heated, daily, details (022) 21863. Riding: Mallow Riding Centre, *tel: (022) 21240.* Banteer House, *tel: Banteer 8.* Golf Club, 18 holes, *tel: (022) 21145.*

AROUND MALLOW

Annes Grove Gardens, *1 m (1.5 km) SE of Castletownroche on N72, 79 bus from Mallow.* Famous gardens sloping down to River Awbeg, a Blackwater tributary. Formal walled garden, woodland garden, water garden, exotic plants, delightful riverside walks. A must for every true gardener: *Easter-Sept 30, Mon-Fri, 10 a.m.-5 p.m., Sun, 1 p.m.-6 p.m. Other times by arr. Details: (022) 26145.*

Ballinaboola, *turn E for 1 m (2 km) off N20 at Ballyhea Church 4 m (6 km) S of Rath Luirc:* forest walks, views over Golden Vale, car park, picnic.

Ballintlea/Glenanaar, *10 m (16 km) NE of Mallow on N73:* forest walks in Canon Sheehan country. Car park, picnic place.

Ballygiblin, *6 m (10 km) E of Kanturk:* forest walks.

Ballyporeen, *8 m (13 km) E of Mitchelstown on L28, 100, 146 bus from Cahir, Mitchelstown.* Reagan homestead ruins. Great grandfather of Ronald Reagan, US president, lived here 150 years ago. Also Ronald Reagan pub, parish church with Reagan family records

Blackwater valley: good walks in vicinity of Mallow.

Bottle Hill, *on Mallow-Killavullen road:* forest walks, scenic views, car park, picnic place.

Bridgetown Abbey, *10 m (16 km) NE of Mallow, off N72:* ruins of Augustinian priory founded 1314, now being restored.

Burncourt House, *8 m (13 km) NE of Mitchelstown:* 17th c building said to have been burned to prevent occupation by Cromwell. Shell has 26 gables, several tall chimneys. Ask at nearby farm for permission.

Buttevant: *ruins just S on Mallow road.* Ruins of 13th c Augustinian abbey, dovecot in near perfect condition.

Castlyons, *4 m (6 km) SE of Fermoy:* Barrymore Castle ruins, just S of village, once home of noted 16th, 17th c landowners.

Cloghvolla, *3 m (4 km) SE of Killavullen:* forest walks, scenic views.

Coolfree/Glenanaar, *10 m (16 km) NE of Mallow off N73:* forest walks, hill climbs.

Cooper's Wood, *off N8 at Skeheenarinky between Cahir and Mitchelstown:* riverside forest walk, car park, picnic place.

Corrin Hill, *1 m (2 km) S of Fermoy on N8, turning R to golf course:* forest walks, access to Carntiarna, an Iron Age fort.

Doneraile, *6 m (10 km) NE of Mallow, 153 bus from Mallow.* Canon Sheehan memorial, the author was parish priest here from 1895–1913. **Doneraile Court Forest Park,** includes forest walks, deer herds.

Fanningstown/Greenwood, *3 m (5 km) W of Kilfinnane:* forest walks, hill climbing, car park, picnic area.

Fermoy, *19 m (30 km) E of Mallow. All day closing: Wed. TIO: tel: (025) 31110, July/Aug. 86, 100, 145, 146 bus from Cork.* Delightfully set on banks of River Blackwater, a noted fishing spot. Old, stately trees line both riverbanks—ideal for scenic walks. **Kate O'Brien's Tavern** gets name from first owner, who was aunt of novelist Kate O'Brien, a frequent guest here. Over a century old, turf fire. **Fermoy Museum,** Bishop Murphy Memorial School. *SO, Sat, Sun, 11 a.m.–9 p.m.* W Swimming pool: *Tues–Sun, details: (025) 31949.* Bicycles: Cavanagh's *McCurtain Street, SO, tel: (025) 31339.* Fermoy Golf Club, 18 holes, *tel: (025) 31472.*

Annes Grove Gardens

Galtee Castle, *5 m (8 km) NE of Mitchelstown on N8:* forest walk, car park, picnic area. **Galtee Mountains:** S slopes provided many easy routes to peaks, most notably Galtymore Mountain 3,018 ft (920 metres), from which there are fine views.

Glenagear, *1 m (2 km) S of Killavullen on Cork road:* forest walks, lay-by, picnic area.

Glenboe, *1 m (2 km) W of Fermoy:* forest walks.

Glengarra Wood, *8 m (13 km) NE of Mitchelstown in N8:* well laid out nature trail near Burncourt River. Many exotic trees of Indian origin along main avenue. Car park.

Glennaharee East, *2 m (3 km) W of Bweeng off L40:* forest walks.

Glensheskin, *1 m (2 km) NE of Kilworth:* forest walks.

Gortmore caves, *10 m (16 km) W of Mallow, near Banteer:* experts only. *Details:* Pat Barry, *tel: (058) 59171.*

Gortroche, *Ballyhooley, on Carrignavar road, 6 m (10 km) W of Fermoy:* forest, mountain walks, car park, picnic area.

Gurteen, *1 m (2 km) S of Ballyhooley on Fermoy–Killavullen road:* forest walks.

Island Wood, *1 m (2 km) S of Newmarket on byroad:* forest, riverside walks, viewing point, car park, picnic area.

Kanturk, *10 m (16 km) NW of Mallow, 153 bus from Mallow to Kanturk.* Pleasant market town. **Kanturk Castle,** *1 m (2 km) S of Kanturk:* ruins of four storey building started early 17th c, never completed. *All year, Mon-Fri, except public holidays. Details: tel: (029) 50194.* Attractive town park. Riding: Assolas Country House, *tel: (029) 76015;* Collins Riding School, *Meelehera, tel: (029) 50152.* Bicycles: F. J. Jones, *Strand Street, tel: (029) 76118;* Nolan's, *Main Street.* Kanturk Golf Club, 9 holes.

Kilcoman Bog: bird observatory. various species, including Greenland white-fronted goose. *Details:* Kilcoman Wildfowl refuse, Buttevant, *tel: (022) 24200.*

Kilcoman Castle, *3 m (5 km) NW of Doneraile:* ruins of building where English poet Edmund Spenser once lived for eight years; he may have written the *Faerie queen* here.

Kildorrey, *8 m (13 km) W of Mitchelstown on N73, 146 bus from Mitchelstown.* Site of Bowen's Court, where distinguished novelist Elizabeth Bowen once lived. House had to be sold as financial embarrassment in 1959, then pulled down. She said: 'It was a clean end.' Bowen's Court never lived to be a ruin.' Old C of I church being converted into Bowen Museum.

Killavullen, *6 m (10 km) E of Mallow, 145 bus from Castletownroche, Fermoy.* 250 year old house of ancestor of Hennessy, original distillers of brandy. Picturesque setting on cliff overhanging River Blackwater. Ballymacroy House now a bed and breakfast establishment.

Knockawoddra/Bween Mountain, *near Bweeng village:* forest walks.

Lyradane, *8 m (13 km) S of Mallow off N20:* forest walks.

Mitchelstown, *21 m (34 km) NE of Mallow on N73, 85, 86, 100, 147 bus from Cork, Fermoy.* Centre of great butter and cheese producing area. **New Square:** monument to John Manderville, and three local men shot by police at Land League meeting here in 1887. On pavement at S end of square, three crosses mark where they fell. **St. Fanahan's Holy Well.** The saint died over 1,500 years ago. Waters said to have curative powers. Feast day: Nov 25. Swimming pool, *turn R at Dublin end of town, SO, Mon-Sun.* Bicycles: O'Sullivans, *Main Street, tel: (025) 24316.*

Mitchelstown Caves, *10 m (16 km) NE of Mitchelstown off N8, 101, 144, 146 bus from Mitchelstown.* Two groups of caves, signposted. Old or Desmond cave must be entered by rope or ladder. New cave easier access. Local guide will take you through 2 m (3 km) of passages and chambers at any reasonable time. *All year, daily, 10 a.m.–6 p.m.* Contact: John English, *tel: (052) 67246.*

Moorestown, *2 m (3 km) NE of Kilfinnane in S Co. Limerick:* forest walks.

Mount Hillary, *2 m (3 km) SE of Banteer, off L9:* forest walks, good views of Blackwater valley from top after energetic climb.

Mourne Abbey, *6 m (10 km) S of Mallow:* ruins of preceptory of Knights Templar founded in 13th c.

Nagles Mountains, *from N72, 7 m (11 km) E of Mallow:* several minor roads leads into mountains; fine walks.

Newmarket graveyard, *20 m (32 km) NW of Mallow:* Sarah Curran, Robert Emmet's beloved, buried here.

Quitrent, *12 m (19 km) NE of Mallow turn L off N73:* forest walks.

Rowls, *8 m (13 km) W of Drumcolliher, on by-road off L71:* forest walks.

Shanbally Castle, *4 m (6 km) NW of Clogheen:* ruins of 18th c John Nash design.

Streamhill, *3 m (5 km) N of Doneraile:* forest walks.

Waterford

Pop. 35,000, *39 m (63 km) W of Wexford, 103 m (166 km) SW of Dublin. EC Thurs. TIO: 41 The Quay, tel: (051) 75788, all year. Bus and train enquiries: tel: (051) 73401. 104, 135 bus from Cork, 77, 103 from Wexford. Train from Dublin, Kilkenny. Air Service to Dublin & Cork.*

Busy port set on the S bank of the broad River Suir, dour looking, but riddled with interesting little laneways and graced by some notable Georgian buildings. Waterford Light Opera Festival: the hills come alive with the sound of song, *every Sept, details: TIO.*

French Church, *Greyfriars Street:* built 1240 as Franciscan foundation. Once housed Huguenot refugees, now in ruins. Key: Mrs N. White, *5 Greyfriars Street, opp. Any reasonable time.* **Holy Trinity Church,** (CI) *Barronstrand Street:* fine edifice, completed 1796. **Blackfriars Dominican Priory,** *Arundel Square:* founded 1226 and used as court until end of 18th c; square tower only major

remnant. Key: City Hall, *The Mall.*

Library. *Lady Lane. Mon–Sat.* Waterford Arts Centre, *O'Connell St.* Permanent collection, occasional exhibitions and other events. *Open daily. Colbeck Street:* Birthplace of composer **William Vincent Wallace. Municipal Theatre, Theatre Royal,** *The Mall,* two lovely old buildings, used mainly for variety shows, amateur dramatics.

Reginald's Tower, *corner Parade Quay, The Mall:* mighty stone fortress built in 1003 by the Vikings. Houses Civic Museum, with fine collection of Corporation archive material and regalia; Maritime Museum. *May-Sept, Mon-Fri, 10 a.m.-12.30 p.m.; 2 p.m.-5 p.m., Sat, 10 a.m.-12.30 p.m. Also holidays. Otherwise: on request to City Hall, tel: (051) 73501, extn 408.*

Chamber of Commerce, *George's Street:* Georgian house, built 1795 with beautiful staircase and fine carvings. *All year, Mon–Fri, 9.30 a.m.–5 p.m.* Waterford Trade Centre, *The Mall:* products of locality. Traces of the Danish walls can be seen near railway station, Mayor's Walk, Castle Street. Try Downes' Pub, *Thomas St,* **Downes' No 9 whiskey,** unique to the area. **Walsh's pub,** Ballybricken Hill, is good for local "characters". **Garter Lane Arts Centre,** *5 O'Connell Street:* regular events, inc. exhibitions. *Daily.* Airport Museum, *Waterford Airport, Killowen, tel: (051) 75589. Daily, 2.30 p.m.-5.30 p.m.*

Waterford Glass, *Cork Road:* factory tour takes in all stages of production, from blowing molten glass to polishing. No children under 12, no photographs, no glass on sale—try Knox's famous shop, 3 Barronstrand Street. Tours all year, Mon–Fri, six times daily. Closed most of Aug. Details: TIO or (051) 73311.* Waterford Craft Centre, *28 Michael Street:* demonstrations, *Mon–Sat, 9 a.m.–5.30 p.m.*

River cruises: depart from quayside opp. TIO, summer, 3 p.m. daily, details: TIO or (051) 21723, 75017. Greyhound racing: Kilcohan Park, details: (051) 74531. Riding: Joan O'Mahoney, Killotteran Equestrian Centre, tel: (051) 84158. Bicycles: Wright's Cycle Depot, Henrietta Street, tel: (051) 74411. Golf Club, 18 holes, tel: (051) 76748.*

AROUND WATERFORD

Ahenny, *4.5 m (7 km) N of Carrick-on-Suir, on L26:*

a graveyard with two 8th c High Crosses.

Annestown, *6 m (20 km) W of Tramore:* small resort with good sandy beach. Nearby secluded beach at Kilfarrasy.

Ardfinnan, *9 m (14 km) SW of Clonmel:* ruins of 12th c castle, one square tower partly restored.

Arthurstown, *E bank of Waterford Harbour:* bicycles, King's Bay Inn, *tel: (051) 89173.* Youth Hostel. Car and passenger ferry.

Ballyhack, *E side of Waterford Harbour.* Ferry to Passage East, Waterford side, *all year. details TIO.* Picturesque fishing village with ruined castle. Further down the road is the attractive fishing village of Arthurstown.

Ballymacarberry, *6 m (10 km) S of Tramel:* pony trekking, Melody's *tel: (052) 36147;* Slievenamon Centre.

Ballyscanlan, *2 m (3 km) W of Tramore:* forest walks in hills around Ballyscanlon lake, car park, picnic area.

Bannow, *on S Wexford coast opp. Fethard-on-Sea:* first town in Ireland founded by the Normans, it disappeared under sand during the 17th c. Only the ruins of St Mary's church remain. Miles of beach below low cliffs.

Big Wood, *7 m (11 km) N of New Ross on L18:* forest walks.

Bohadoon, *on Comeragh drive near Kilrossanty village, W Waterford:* forest walks, viewing point.

Brownstown Head, *E of Tramore:* fine walks.

Bunmahon, *11 m (18 km) W of Tramore, 79 bus from Waterford.* Tiny fishing village with fine sandy beaches, surrounded by cliffs. Bracing 4 m (6 km) cliff walk to Stradbally.

Carrick-on-Suir, *17 m (27 km) NW of Waterford. EC Thurs, 109, 213 bus, train from Waterford: enquiries: (051) 40044.* One of Munster's most picturesque town, scenically set on banks of River Suir. Carrick Castle: Elizabeth fortified mansion, only one of its kind in Ireland. N Gallery has fine stucco work. Resident caretaker. *Mid-*

Passage East

Crystal Jug, Waterford Crystal

June-mid-Sept, daily, 10.00 a.m.-7.30 p.m. Rest of year key with caretaker. Details: (051) 40787. Whitechurch Riding Centre, tel: (051) 40289.

Cheekpoint, 8 m (13 km) E of Waterford: Suirway Inn has lots of atmosphere, many curios. Cheekpoint Hill, excellent views of Waterford city and harbour.

Clonea, 3 m (5 km) E of Dungarvan: fine, andy beach.

Cloneen, near Fethard: pony trekking, Anr House Farm, tel: (052) 31201.

Clonmel, 30 m (48 km) NW of Waterford. EC Thurs. TIO: (052) 22960. July, Aug. Otherwise Waterford TIO. Bus and train enquiries: (052) 21599. 109, 213, bus, train from Waterford. Tipperary's main town, most attractively set in River Suir valley, includes a number of interesting old buildings. Excellent base for exploring Comeragh and Knockmealdown Mountains.
　　Franciscan church, Abbey Street: 19th c restoration on site of 13th c foundation. **St Mary's** (C), near Franciscan church: also dates from 19th c, magnificent ceiling, elaborate high altar.
　　Museum and Art Gallery, Parnell Street: large collection of local material, paintings and photographs. Undergone extensive renovation, likely to re-open early 1985. Details: Patrick Holland, (052) 21308. Town Hall, Corporation regalia. By arr. tel: (052) 22100.
　　Old Town Wall, best-preserved section partly encloses 19th c St Mary's C of I, Mary Street; **Hearn's Hotel,** Parnell Street: Bianconi horse-drawn car service started here in 1815. Clock which timed the system in hotel. **Regal Theatre,** occasional performances, details: TIO.
　　Gladstone Street offers superb views across river to mountains: attractive old shopfronts. Mitchel Street, off Gladstone Street: narrow, shop-lined, interesting. Pleasant riverside walks.
　　Racing: regular meetings at Powerstown, details: (052) 22852/22971. Greyhound racing: twice weekly races at Davis Road track, details: (052) 21118. Swimming pool: indoor, heated, Emmet Street, daily, tel: (052) 21972. Powers 'o' the Pot, pony trekking centre, Harneys Cross. Bicycles: Hackett, West Gate, tel: (052) 21869; Michael McDermott, Foodmarket, Irishtown, tel: (052) 22272; Bill Purcell, The Mall, tel: (052) 21831. Clonmel Golf Club, 18 holes, tel: (052) 21118.

Clonmines: head of Bannow Bay: mediaeval town falling into decay: all you can see today are parts of four castles and three churches, overlooking a pleasant estuary.

Coolfin, just beyond Portlaw C church: forest walks, rhododendrons.

Coolnamuck, 3 m (5 km) W of Carrick-on-Suir, off L27: forest walks, viewing points.

Crehanagh North, 1 m (1.5 km) E of Carrick-on-Suir: forest walks.

Curraghmore House, Portlaw, 10 m (16 km) W of Waterford: gardens in beautiful setting, fine bronze statues, only shell of house remains; Apr 1-Sept 30, Thurs and BH, 1.30 p.m.-4.30 p.m. NE of demesne, Mother Brown's Hill.

Davwood, 3 m (5 km) W of Mahonbridge (near Kilmacthomas) on N25: forest and riverside walks, viewing points, scenic drive.

Dunbrody Abbey, near Campile: great roofless church dating from 12th c. Fine views to confluence of Nore and Suir rivers.

Dunmore East, 9 m (14 km) SE of Waterford: Suir Valley private bus from Waterford. Breton-style fishing village, neat, thatched cottages. Tiers of houses rise steeply from harbour. Sea angling centre. Walks around harbour area and to nearby Creadon Head and black Knob promontory. Coves also worth exploring. Sailing: June Bullock, tel: (051) 83350.

Geneva Barracks, 2 m (3 km) S of Passage East: settlement founded in 1785 by gold and silversmiths from Geneva. Later used as military barracks and prison, now ruins, in process of restoration.

Glenarey, 2 m (3 km) S of Clonmel off T27: forest walks, strolls alongside Glenarey River. Castle ruins, car park, picnic area.

Gurteen, near Kilsheelan on L27: walks by river Suir, riverside picnic area, lay-by.

Hook Peninsula, 20 m (32 km) SE of Waterford: craggy 'finger' of land pointing into the Atlantic. Whatever the wind direction, one side of the Hook is always calm. **Lighthouse:** one of the oldest in the world. Tower over 700 years old, but a light has been burning here for over twice as long. Visiting pass: write in advance to Commissioners of Irish Lights, 16 Lower Pembroke Street, Dublin 2. The peninsula has many undisturbed beaches and coves. Dollar Bay, on W side reputedly hides an 18th c Spanish treasure.

John F. Kennedy Park, 5 m (8 km) S of New Ross: 410 acre park, opened 1968, overlooks Kennedy ancestral home at Dunganstown, 1 m (1.5 km) away. 270 acres devoted to arboretum, with world-wide selection of trees and shrubs. Forest garden, tremendous views, many varied walks. Picnic area, visitor centre, café, shelters. May–Aug, 10 a.m.–8 p.m. daily; Apr, Sept, 10 a.m.–6.30 p.m. daily; Oct–Mar, 10 a.m.–5 p.m. daily. Details: (051) 88171.

Kilcash, 4 m (6 km) N of Kilsheelan, between Carrick-on-Suir and Waterford: forest walks, viewing points. Kilcash Castle: ruins, overshadowed by Slievenamon Mountain, well worth the climb.

Kilclooney, on Carrick-on-Suir–Dungarvan T56: forest walks, access to Crotty's Rock and Comeragh Mountain lakes. Car park, picnic area.

Kilmacthomas, 15 m (25 km) SW of Waterford on N25: good views, good climbing country.

Kilnamack, 1 m (1.5 km) N of Clonmel: forest walks, viewing point, lay-by.

Kilsheelan, near Clonmel: forest, riverside walks, scenic walks, 1 m (1.5 km) S of village and bordering old Clonmel—Kilsheelan road W of River Suir.

Knockadirragh Hill, 2 m (3 km) N of Dunmore East: fine views.

Knockatourney/Croaghaun Hill, 12 m (19 km) NE of Dungarvan, off N25: forest walks, viewing points.

Knockballinery, on Clogheen–Newcastle road: riverside walks, woodland drive, car park, picnic area.

Knockeen, 1 m (1.5 km) SW of Waterford on N25 to Dungarvan: picnic site, access to Sugar Loaf Rock.

Knockeen Dolmen, 3 m (5 km) N of Tramore: excellently preserved.

Lady's Abbey, 1.5 m (2 km) S of Ardfinnan: ruins of ancient Carmelite foundation.

Lough Coumshingaum, 10 m (16 km) SW of Carrick, off T56: rock climbing centre.

Lyreanearla, 5 m (8 km) S of Clonmel on Nire valley road: walks with extensive views, car park, picnic area.

Marlfied, near Clonmel: riverside walk just E of Knocklofty Bridge.

Mount Congreve Demesne, 5 m (8 km) W of Waterford, just N of N25: attractive gardens, woodlands.

New Ross, 21 m (34 km) NE of Waterford: one of Co. Wexford's oldest towns, on banks of the River Barrow. Narrow streets have mediaeval air. Very fetching tall, Dutch-style houses on quays.
　　St Mary's (NM) Church Lane: ruins of early 13th c parish church. **Tholsel,** civic insignia and documents, including James II Charter, tel: (051) 21284. River cruises along Barrow and Nore rivers, Tues–Sat, dep. 7 p.m. Three hour cruise, dinner served aboard, details: (051) 21723. Kennedy Memorial pool: indoor, heated, daily, details: (051) 21169. Golf Club, 9 holes, tel: (051) 21433.

Nire Valley, 4 m (6 km) E of Ballymacarbery on T27: walks, car park, picnic area.

Oaklands, 1m (1.5 km) S of New Ross on Campile road: forest walks, picnic place, lay-by.

Passage East, 7 m (11 km) E of Waterford: charming, old world riverside villageGood views from hill behind village. Ferry to Ballyhack. Regular daily service. Also forest walks to N.

River Suir: two roads, one each side, run E from Clonmel. Many fine views of river and Comeragh Mountains.

Rocket's Castle, 2 m (3 km) N of Portlaw on L26: forest walks, car park, picnic area.

St Patrick's Well, 1 m (1.5 km) W of Clonmel: still a place of pilgrimage. One of Tipperary's most attractive glen.

Slade: E side of Hook Head, near lighthose: tiny fishing village, ruins of 14th c castle and later fortified house overlook mole encircling harbour.

Stradbally, 6 m (10 km) NE of Dungarvan: interesting coves, fine cliff walks.

Tintern Abbey, 3.5 m (6 km) N of Fethard: Cistercian, built about 1200, ruins hidden among trees. Approached by long drive, signpost at gate.

Tory Hill, 8 m (13 km) N of Waterford, off N9: superb views of surrounding plain, Waterford city and harbour.

Tower Hill, ½ m (3 km) NW of Portlaw: forest walk, viewing points.

Tramore, 8 m (13 km) S of Waterford. TIO: (051) 81572. July–Aug. 76, 80 bus from Waterford. Enquiries: (051) 73401. Top holiday resort, with 3 m (5 km) of sandy beach. Attractions include 50 acre amusement park, miniature railway, marina. Tramore races: Feb, June, Aug (four day event), Sept, Nov.
　　Walks: SW, along the Doneraile cliffs—tremendous natural views, plus three white pillars, 18th c navigational aids topped by 'The Metal Man'. Also along the promenade to a range of sandhills known as The Burrows. Garrarus Strand and Kilfarrasy Strand, W of town. Bicycles: Pickardstown Service Station, tel: (051) 81094. Tramore Golf Club, 18 holes, tel: (051) 81247.

Woodstown Strand, 3 m (5 km) S of Passage East: pleasant, secluded beach. Ballyglan Riding Centre, tel: (051) 82133.

Wexford

Pop. 15,000, 16 m (26 km) NW of Rosslare, 90 m (144 km) S of Dublin. EC Thur. TIO: The Quays. (053) 23111, all year. Bus and train enquiries: (053) 22522. 59, 104, 118 bus from Rosslare Harbour, 77, 104 bus from Waterford. Trains from Dublin, Rosslare Harbour. Taxis: Redmond Road.
　　An ancient town with a tangy sea air and a refreshing, individual character. The narrow main streets and innumerable little laneways are full of atmosphere, and during the summer, choked with cars and people.
　　Wexford Opera Festival: attracts the cosmopolitan black-tie crowd to the tiny and charming Theatre Royal. Many fringe events, such as art exhibitions. Late Oct. Details: (053) 22144/22240. Wexford Mussel Festival: mussel-tasting contests, seafood banquets, surf-gliding, lectures and exhibitions. Early Sept. Details: TIO.
　　Selskar Abbey, Westgate: 12th c ruins, Henry II spent entire season of Lent here in 1172 as penance for murder of Thomas à Beckett. Key: P. Murphy, 9 Abbey Street. **St Francis'** (C), School Street: L-shaped Franciscan friary church founded 1230, plundered in Cromwell's time. Remodelled 1784.**D Twin Sisters:** Church of Immaculate Conception (C), Rowe Street, Church of Assumption (C), Bride Street, 19th c, of almost identical appearance.**D**
　　Maritime Museum, The Quays: former lightship, now a floating museum with items from town's

seafaring past, inc. special section on Irish Navy. *June, July, Aug, daily, 10 a.m.–9 p.m. Also during Opera Festival.* **Arts Centre,** *Cornmarket:* something for everyone all year, concerts, dance drama, art and historical exhibitions. Coffee bar in basement. *All year, Mon–Fri, 10 a.m.–6 p.m. Also some eves. Details: (053) 23764.* Summer theatre: Talbot and White's Hotels, *details: TIO.*

Main Street: narrow, shopfronts and shops worth exploring. Also atmospheric narrow alleyways running to quays. Walking tours: conducted by members of Old Wexford Society, starting Talbot and White's Hotels, *Every summer eve.* **Crown Bar,** *Skeffington Street:* relics of old Wexford, including old military items. **Kinsella's** *Main Street:* engraved window advertises splendid interior, complete with panelling and draws in the old-fashioned Irish pub style.

Wildfowl Reserve, *N shore of Wexford harbour, 3 m (5 km) from town:* observation tower, lecture hall, laboratory, library, car park, picnic area. *All year, daily.* **D** Racing: Bettyville, details: (053) 22307. Swimming pool: indoor, heated. *Ferrybank, all year, daily, tel: (053) 23274.* Roche's Cycle Service, *Spawell Road, tel: (053) 23348.* Golf Club, 9 holes, tel: (053) 22238.

AROUND WEXFORD

Ballintemple, *3 m (5 km) NW of Clonegal:* forest walk, car park, picnic area between Bunclody and Tullow.

Bargy Castle, *10 m (16 km) S of Wexford:* Norman castle, now hotel. Dinner served in baronial banqueting hall. *Tel: (053) 35203.*

Borodale, *just S of Enniscorthy:* riverside beauty spot with excellent views.

Bree Hill, *5 m (8 km) SW of Enniscorthy:* forest walks.

Bunclody, *14 m (21 km) N of Enniscorthy. 58, 98 bus from Enniscorthy.* Large square, elegant mall. Ideal base for climbing the Blackstairs Mountains.

Camolin Park, *10 m (16 km) E of Enniscorthy on Gorey road:* forest walks, car park, picnic area. **Trout Farm,** *7 m (11 km) SE of Gorey on N11:* catch your own dinner. *Mon–Sun, all year. Details: (054) 83214.*

Carley's Bridge Pottery, *near Enniscorthy:* probably oldest in Ireland, founded 1659 by two brothers from Cornwall. Makes flower pots and gardenware. *All year, Mon–Fri, 8.30 a.m.–5.30 p.m. Lunch break. By arr., (054) 2512.*

Carne, *E side of Carnsore Point:* attractive fishing village, safe, sandy beach.

Carrickbyrne Hill, *7 m (11 km) E of New Ross on N25:* forest walks, car park, picnic area.

Clonegall, *4 m (7 km) N of Bunclody:* 15th c. Huntingdon Castle, owned by the Robertson family. *Tours by arr.*

Courtown, *3.5 m (6 km) SE of Gorey. 68 bus from Gorey, Wexford.* Popular seaside resort, beach. Harbour: 19th c Bar, front bar little changed over 160 years. Gorey Little Theatre group play Tara Hall twice weekly, *July, Aug.* Walks: Boro Road, small harbour area and immediate environs. Forest walks W of village on L31; car park, picnic area. Golf Club, 18 holes, tel: (055)25166.

Cullenstown: good beach near Kilmore Quay, at W edge of Ballyteige Bay. Best approached from Wellingtonbridge.

Dunandre, *3 m (5 km) S of Enniscorthy on W bank of River Slaney:* riverside and forest walks, viewing points, car park, picnic area.

Enniscorthy, *15 m (24 km) N of Wexford. TIO: (054) 33341. July, Aug. Bus and train enquiries: (054) 2488. 59 bus from Wexford. Also train.* Delightful town set on steeply sloping ground on banks of River Slaney. Lots of historical atmosphere and interest. Worth exploring quaysides and narrow streets.

Strawberry Fair, plenty of outdoor amusements and an abundance of locally-grown strawberries, *late June, early July.* Wexford

Agricultural Show, *July.*

St Aidan's Cathedral (C), fine Gothic building designed by Pugin in 1840s. **D Castle,** rebuilt around 1586, perfectly preserved, houses county museum with interesting folk section. Relics of 1798 and of the town's industrial history *June–Sept, Mon–Fri, 10 a.m.–6 p.m. Sat, Sun, 2 p.m.–6 p.m. Oct–May, Mon–Fri, 2 p.m.–5.30 p.m. Sat, Sun, 2 p.m.–5 p.m.* **Antique Tavern,** *Slaney Street:* full of interesting curios. Customers are advised not to carry muskets inside! Breen's Carriage Works, *next to Friend's Meeting House, quayside:* makes horse-drawn carriages, a fascinating process. Visitors welcomed, *preferably Sat a.m. (054) 2391.* Slaneyside Park, *due S of town:* pleasant walks.

Greyhound racing, *Show Grounds,* regular meetings, *details: (054) 2174.* Slaney View Riding School, *Brownswood, tel: (054) 3102.* Bicycles: P. J. Kenny, *Slaney Street, tel: (054) 2255.* Golf Club, 9 holes, tel: (054) 2191.

Ferns, *21 m (34 km) N of Wexford. 59 bus from Arklow, Enniscorthy.* Once capital of Leinster. Imposing ruins, include 13th c castle, 12th c Augustinian abbey, cathedral. On high ground just outside town, ruins of 16th c St Peter's Church.

Ferrycarrig, *2.5 m (4 km) NW of Wexford:* fine river views from vicinity of Crimean War Memorial.

Forth Mountain, *4 m (6 km) SW of Wexford:* forest walks, magnificent panoramas of Wexford coast from Kilmore Quay to Hook Head.

Gorey, *TIO: Gorey, tel: (055) 21248. July, Aug. 59, 68 bus, train from Wexford.* St. Michael's (C), 19th c. designed by Pugin, has massive square tower. The Church of Ardamine (CI) was designed by George Edmund Street, who restored Dublin's Christ Church Cathedral. **D** Funge Arts Centre. *Rafter Street:* hosts major arts festival with many internationally known names, *July, Aug, details: (055) 21470.* **D Gorey Theatre.** *Details, TIO.*

Johnstown Castle, *near Murntown, 4 m (6 km) S of Wexford:* fine landscaped grounds of State agricultural college, extensive lakes. *Daily, 9 a.m.–5 p.m. all year.* Museum: many items of now vanished rural life, such as harness ware, butter churns. *May 1–Oct 31, Mon–Fri, 9 a.m.–12.30 p.m., 1.30 p.m.–5 p.m. Sun, 2 p.m.–5 a.m., otherwise by arr. tel: (053)22888.*

Kilbranish North, *adjoining Bunclody–Mount Leinster road:* forest walks in scenic setting, car park, picnic area.

Kilmore Quay, *10 m (16 km) S of Wexford, 70 bus from Wexford, Wed, Sat only.* Fishing village full of thatched cottages, plenty of atmosphere. Beach extending 6 m (10 km) NW.

Lady's Island, *just W of Carnsore Point:* place of pilgrimage in sea inlet. Interesting ruins, including tower of Norman castle that leans at greater angle than Pisa. Causeway joins island to mainland.

Mayglass, *7 m (11 km) S of Wexford on L29:* ruins of church built in 1798. Plaque on N wall marks grave of Bagenal Harvey, leader of 1798 rising.

Mount Leinster, *6 m (10 km) SW of Bunclody:* best views in the whole SE. Road runs to summit.

Raheenkyle, *6 m (10 km) W of Bunclody on Mount Leinster road:* forest walks, picnic area. lay-by.

Rathmackee Castle, *5 m (8 km) SW of Wexford:* 15th c well-preserved ruins, when closed, key from caretaker.

Raven Point, *opp. Wexford:* fine strand running some 25 m (40 km) to near Arklow Head. Minor road N from Blackwater, near Curracloe follows coastline. Laneways lead to beach.

Rosslare Harbour, *16 m (26 km) SE of Wexford. TIO: Rosslare harbour. Tel: (053) 33232. All year. 59, 104, 118 bus, train from Wexford, train from Dublin.* Terminal of car ferries from Wales and N France. **Rosslare,** *11 m (18 km) SE of Wexford,* fine arc of beach, stretching for some 6 m (10 km). St Helen's Pony Trekking Centre. Golf Club, 18 holes, tel: (053) 32113.

Saltee Islands: *3 m (5 km) S of Kilmore Quay. Boats from quay in suitable weather. Details:* Bill Bates, *(053) 29644.* Two main islands, each about 0.5 m (0.8 km) long, form Ireland's largest bird sanctuary. A leader of the 1798 Rising, Bagenal Harvey, was captured here after fleeing from the Battle of Vinegar Hill near Enniscorthy.

Tacumshin Windmill, *just W of Lady's Island:* 19th c, in perfect condition. *All year, by arr. caretaker.*

Tara Hill, *3 m (5 km) N of Courtown:* 833 ft (254 metres), forest walks, viewing points.

Vinegar Hill, *just E of Enniscorthy:* scene of the decisive battle of the 1798 Rising, when Wexford men were defeated by General Lake. Fine views from summit over River Slaney and surrounding countryside, car park.

Youghal

Pop. 6,000, 30 m (48 km) E of Cork, 46 m (74 km) SW of Waterford and 149 m (240 km) SW of Dublin. TIO: (024) 2390 July–Aug. Bus enquiries: (021) 504422. 104, 135 bus from Cork, Dungarvan, Waterford.

An historic seaport and market town set most attractively between steep hillsides and the broad expanse of the Blackwater River. Founded by the Anglo-Normans in 13th c, and an important base during the succeeding centuries, the town acquired magnificent walls which, in their prime had 13 towers. The surviving sections are considered the best preserved in Ireland.

St Mary's: built about 1250, considerably renovated, see 14th c font and beautiful E window. **North Abbey,** *N end of North Main Street:* founded 1286, W gable and part of central aisle remain. The doorway of the Old Benedictine priory in Main Street is all that remains of the 14th c foundation used as Cromwell's headquarters during 1649 Munster campaign.

Walls, *grounds of St Mary's:* plus old town guns, excellent view of town and Blackwater estuary. **Tynte's Castle,** *North Main Street:* built 1602, well preserved. To view: Dan McCarthy, grocer, *12 North Main Street, tel: (024) 2440.* **Clock Gate:** built 1771m once a notorious jail, now an art gallery, museum, TIO. Gallery shows local work, museum has charters granted to town, Youghal silver, lace, paintings and maps related to Sir Walter Raleigh, who lived here. *June–Sept, Mon–Sat, 11 a.m.–1 p.m.; 2 p.m.–7 p.m. Details: (024) 2390/2926.*

Walks: Green's Dock, Market Dock, Mall Dock and Market Square; also S of town, as far as old lighthouse on Cork road. 5 m (8 km) of sandy beaches in vicinity. River Blackwater scenic drive: start Youghal, continue along minor roads to W to Lismore, Cappoquin. Youghal Pottery, *Quarry Road: All year, Mon–Fri, 9 a.m.–5 p.m. July, Aug, also Sat, 10 a.m.–5 p.m.; Sun, 3 p.m.–5 p.m.* Craft shop. *Details: (024) 2339.* Perks Indoor Amusements. *Dodgems, ghost trains, etc. All year.* Boat trips: Bernard O'Keeffe, *126 North Main Street, tel: (024) 2320;* Stonebridge Cottage, *tel: (024) 2313.* Greyhound racing: *Tues, Fri eve, details: (024) 2305.* Riding: Monatrea Hotel, *Ferry Point, tel: (024) 4293.* Bicycles: Fergus McClean, *tel: (024) 2733.* Bob Troy, *tel: (024) 2509.* Golf Club, 18 holes, tel: (024) 2787.

AROUND YOUGHAL

Ardmore, *8 m (13 km) E of Youghal, 135 bus from Dungarvan, Youghal.* Pleasant seaside resort, long, sandy beach. **St Declan's:** 7th c monastic settlement, includes round tower, oratory and cathedral. Ardmore amusement park: dodgems, amusement arcade, *Easter– Sept 30.* St Declan's Stone: glacial boulder on beach.

Ballycotton, *20 m (32 km) SW of Youghal, 137 bus from Cork.* Fishing village on hill overlooking bay. In season, harbour crammed with fishing boats. Sandy beaches. Cliff walk, good views.

Ballynagaul, *1 m (1.5 km) E of Ring:* old-world village with small harbour.

Ballylemon, *5 m (8 km) NW of Dungarvan on T75:* forest walks, strolls along banks of Colligan River, car park, picnic area.

Ballynoe, *8 m (13 km) S of Tallow on L34:* forest walks, car park, picnic area.

Bohernagore, *on L34 at Vee hairpin bend:* Knockmealdown mountains viewing point, forest walks, picnic area.

Cappoquin, *19 m (30 km) N of Youghal, 105 bus from Cork, Dungarvan.* Noted coarse fishing spot at head of tidal section of River Blackwater, near slopes of Knockmealdown Mountain walks: excellent exercise and views, best route along T27, N through Ballymacarberry to Clonmel.

Cappoquin House, *Apr-Sept, Mon, 11 a.m.-1 p.m.; 2.30 p.m.-4 p.m.*

Carnglass, *11 m (18 km) N of Youghal on Hill Route to Cappoquin:* forest walks, lay-by, picnic area.

Castlemartyr: *1m (1.5 km) W of village, off N25:* lakeside walks, car park, picnic area.

Clogheen, *12 m (19 km) E of Mitchelstown:* splendid views, road zig-zags up to Knockmealdown Gap, thence to Lismore and Cappoquin.

Coolatoor, *6 m (10 km) W of Dungarvan:* forest walks, viewing points over Drum hills.

Cooleydoody, *2 m (3 km) W of Tallowbridge on N72:* forest walks, lay-by, picnic area.

Cunnigar Peninsula, *near Dungarvan:* safe, sandy beaches.

Dromana, *between Villierstown and Cappoquin, 10 m (16 km) N of Youghal:* forest walks, strolls along banks of River Blackwater, Hindu-Gothic arch, lay-by, picnic area.

Dungarvan, *19 m (30 km) NE of Youghal. EC Thur. TIO: tel, (058) 41741. July-Aug. 104, 135 bus from Waterford, Youghal. Ferry to Cunnigar Peninsula, June, July, check with TIO.* Attractive town set on lovely stretch of coast where River Colligan broadens into Dungarvan Harbour. Good beach NE of town.

Augustinian Priory, *Abbeyside:* square tower of 13th c building used as belfry by church next-door. **Dungarvan Castle:** built 1185, huge circular keep surrounded by fortified walls, remains of barracks. Abbeyside Castle: only W wall of 12th/13th c building remains.

Seanachie Inn, *Cork Road:* fine traditional atmosphere, rebuilt interior, old furniture, kitchen tools. Shell Cottage, *Abbeyside:* walls covered by thousands of shells. *Walks* round docks, harbour area full of character. Kilrush Riding Centre: pony trekking. Seawater swimming pool: *esplanade, by park.* Bicycles: F. Murphy, *Main Street, tel: (058) 41376.*

Gairha, *3 m (5 km) W of Lismor on T30 to Fermoy:* forest walks.

Garryvoe Strand, *4 m (6 km) N of Ballycotton:* cotton bathing beach.

Glenbower, *8 m (13 km) W of Youghal, entrance at Thatch Inn, Killeagh village, on N25:* forest, lakeside walks, nature trail, car park, picnic area.

Glendalligan North, *1 m (1.5 km) off N25 on scenic Comeragh Drive:* forest walks, viewing point.
Glendalligan South, *2 m (3 km) NE of Dungarvan on N25:* forest walks, viewing point, picnic area, lay-by.

Glenshelane, *2 m (3 km) N of Cappoquin, turn right at Grotto on Mount Melleray road:* forest walks, strolls by Glenshelane River, car park, picnic area.

Grubb's Grave, *2 m (3 km) SE of Glogheen on Vee Road, on N slope of Sugar Loaf hill:* where Quaker Samuel Grubb was buried in a large cairn overlooking his estates.

Helvick Head: tremendous ocean views from promontory.

Kilmore Rath, *3 m (5 km) S of Aglish on T27:* great kidney-shaped prehistoric earthwork.

Killahaley, *3 m (5 km) S of Cappoquin:* walks, scenic views of River Blackwater, lay-by, picnic

area.

Knockaun, *4 m (6 km) S of Tallow on L36:* forest walks, lay-by, picnic area.

Knocknasheega, *3 m (5 km) of Mount Mellerary Abbey:* forest walks, viewing points.

Lacken, *2 m (3 km) NE of Dungarvan on N25:* forest walks, viewing point.

Lismore, *4 m (6 km) W of Cappoquin, 104 bus from Cork, Dungarvan.* Beautifully set village on banks of River Blackwater. **St Carthach's Cathedral,** (CI): one of the country's most striking mediaeval churches, with Gothic vaulting and elegant memorials, in striking contrast to modern C cathedral nearby. **Lismore Castle gardens:** magnificent setting overlooking river, many rare shrubs. *Mid-May-mid-Sept, Mon-Fri, 1.45 p.m.-4.45 p.m. Also July, Aug, Sun, 1.45 p.m.-4.45 p.m. Details: (058) 54424. Castle closed.* St Carthach's Holy Well, in private grounds near castle, open on Pattern Day, *May 14.* Forest walks beside Vee Road to Clogheen. Ballyrafter Indoor Riding School. *Apr-Sept, tel: (058) 54002.* Golf Club, *9 holes, tel: (058) 54026.* Youth Hostel.

Macallop Glen, *2 m (3 km) W of Ballyduff on N72 to Fermoy:* delightful rhododendron paths, excellent in early summer, lay-by.
Master McGrath monument, *junction of Clonmel-Cappoquin road, 2 m (3 km) NW of Dungarvan:* commemorates the dog that was only beaten once in 37 races.

Mine Head, *6 m (10 km) S of Helvick Head:* good vantage point.

Monameen, *Drum Hills:* walks, lay-bys, picnic area

Monatrea, *just across Blackwater from Youghal:* picturesque bathing spot.

Mount Mellerary Abbey: *on slopes of Knockmealdown Mountains above Cappoquin:* peaceful Cistercian Foundation, monks undertake various crafts, including baking. *Tel first: (058) 54404.*

Rhincrew Abbey, *2 m (3 km) N of Youghal, on hill overlooking Rhincrew Bridge:* founded by Knights Templar in 1183, now ruined.

Ring, *Waterford Gaeltacht, 135 bus from Dungarvan.* Good, small beaches in Irish-speaking area. Fine coastal drive to Ring from Dungarvan along L177.

Shanagarry, *2 m (3 km) NW of Ballycotton:* ruins of home of 17th c Quaker William Penn who founded American state of Pennsylvania.

Strancally, *10 m (16 km) E of Tallow:* forest walks on W bank of River Blackwater, viewing points.

Tallow Hill, *12 m (19 km) N of Youghal:* fine views of Bride and Blackwater valleys.

Youghal Bay: sandy beaches.

The WEST

Achill Island

20m (32 km) NW of Westport. TIO: (098) 45384 July-Aug. 125 bus from Westport (from Belfast, SO), 255 from Ballina. Joined to mainland by a swivel-bridge at Achill Sound, this is the largest island off the Irish coast, 15 m (24 km) × 12 m (19 km) at widest point. The scenery on this largely heather-covered island is truly superb, with great mountains on the N side and magnificent cliffs and strands, it is a popular get-away-from-it-all spot.

Achill Sound: all island roads radiate from here. Good fishing, boat hire centre. Atlantic Drive: Achill Sound, round coast to Dooega, superb views. Bicycles: Kilbane Stores, *tel: (098) 45245.*

Bullsmouth, *NE Achill:* near Dooniver strand; Achill Island Crafts Centre: candles, pottery, craft shop. *Mon-Fri, 10 a.m.-7.30 p.m. Shop, Mon-Sun, 10 a.m.-9 p.m. Tel: Bunnacurry 107.*

Corrymore House, *near Dooagh village:* once home of Captain Boycott, whose ostracism during the 19th c Land League campaign gave the English language a new word.

Croghaun Mountain, *near Keem:* 2,192 ft (668 metres), magnificent views. On seaward side, cliff falls nearly 2,000 ft (600 metres) to ocean. Don't go too near the edge, as cliff face curves inwards at some points.

Dugort, *at the foot of Slievemore:* popular resort, with good bathing strand at Poulavaddy. Dugort boatman will take you on fascinating trip to Seal Caves, which extend far into the cliffs under Slievemore, 2 m (3 km) NW of Dugort. Bicycles: Strand Hotel, *tel: Dugort 6/Keel 56.*

Giant's Grave, *2 m (3 km) SW of Dugort:* ruined cairn, also chamber tomb, the Cromlech Tumulus, and the Keel West Giant's Grave.

Keel, *9 m (15 km) NW of Achill Sound:* charming village set in curving, S facing bay. Sheltered to N by Slievemore. Walk a short distance up the road going due N from Keel towards Slievemore; stupendous views. Achill Island Pottery, coffeeshop, *Apr-Sept, Mon-Sun, 10 a.m.-6 p.m. Tel: Keel 45.*

Keem Strand, *1.5 m (2 km) past Corrymore:* popular bathing spot enlivened by the occasional basking shark.

Kildavnet Castle, *near S tip of Achill Island:* fine structure, once a stronghold of Gráinne Uí Mhaille (Grace O'Malley), a 16th c warrior queen. Nearby 12th c Kildavnet Church.

Minaun Heights, *N of Dooega:* one of the best hang gliding areas in Ireland.

Saddle Head, *N of Croghaun:* old signal tower, from here, coastline turns E towards Slievemore.

Slievemore village, *1.5 m (2.5 km) N of Keel:* once a thriving village, populace driven out by 1840s Famine. Deserted ever since.

Trawmore Strand, *near Keel:* 3 m (5 km) of Ireland's finest golden sand. SE are the striking Minaun Cliffs. From Holy Well, during low tide, see Cathedral Rocks.

Valley, *between Lough Doa and Lough Sruhill:* tiny village with two beaches to W. Local boatman will arrange trip to Inishbiggle and Annagh islands, between Achill and mainland.

Aran Islands

25 m (40 km) off coast in Galway Bay. Ferry: CIE regular sailings from Galway Docks to each island. June-Sept, daily. Otherwise, sailings less regular and sometimes disrupted by bad weather. Details, CIE, Galway, (091) 62141/TIO, Galway, (091) 63081. Summer sailings from Doolin (Clare) to Inis Oirr and Inis Meáin. Details: Sea Árainn Ltd, Lickeen, Kilfenora. Tel: Lisdoonvarna 103. Daily summer sailings from Rossaveal, 26 m (42 km) W of Galway off L100. Details: Comharchumann Inis Meáin, (091) 62163/4 or Galway TIO. Aer Arran: daily flights from Galway Airport to each of the islands. Details: (091) 84348/84235.

The three islands, where Irish is the everyday language, are renowned for a way of life that has changed little for generations. The cultural tradition is oral and the islanders have a rich fund of stories and legends. Many spin and weave their own clothes, such as the *bainín* (white coat), the *crios* (coloured woollen belt) and make *pampooties* (hide shoes without a heel). **Árainn** (Inishmore) is by far the largest island. The smaller islands are **Inish Meáin** (Inishmaan) and **Inish Oirr** (inisheer) and each has a wide variety of accommodation. A visit can be an unforgettable experience.

ÁRAINN (Inishmore)

Cill Éinne: long, sandy beach. **Teampall Bheanain,** *immediately S of village:* primitive church measuring 11×7 ft (3.3×2.1 metres), reckoned to be one of smallest in world.

Cill Mhuirbhigh: two cottages by pier built by Robert Flaherty when making his film *Man of Aran.* He and his family stayed in adjacent large house. Film processing was done in old fish-curing shed by pier. Boats: Bairtle Óhlarnáin, *in village;* Stiophán ÓConghaile, *Sruthán.* Long, sandy beach.

Cill Rónáin, village 'capital' of the islands. Between lifeboat slip and pier, a monument to Ridgeway and Blythe, who rowed Atlantic in 1966. Harbour boasts 150 yd (140 metre) pier. Small beaches to E and S. Folk museum: shows history of Aran Islands, including photographs, old clothes and utensils. Kitchen and bedroom furnished in old style. Reading room features letters from Pearse, Casement. *All year, daily, 10 a.m.–7 p.m. Details: (099) 61115.*

  Church of Ss. Brigid and Oliver Plunkett, recently restored, fine Stations of the Cross.**D** Teampall Breachain, the 9th c Church of St Brecan, also Teampall a Cheathrair Álainn (Church of the Heavenly Four). Dún Eoghanacht, fort on a ridge overlooking Teampall Breachain. Aran Bicycle Hire, or Liam ÓCoistealbha, *by quay.*

Achill Island

Islanders

Creig an Chéirín, *near W of island:* remains of 19th c still-house where illegal poitín was surreptitiously distilled. The 'Éire' identification sign, used by aircraft during World War II, is also on the extreme W. Halla Rónáin, céilís, film shows.

Dún Aonghus, fort covering eleven acres on the edge of a cliff. Half the site, consisting of three 'concentric' enclosures, defended by vast walls of dry masonry, has fallen into the sea, nonetheless it is one of Europe's finest prehistoric sites. Superb views of mainland coast.

Dún Óghil, *near Eochail and Dubhchathair, on S cliffs, 2 m (3 km) W of Cill Éinne,* may be oldest fort on island.

Teampall Chiaran (St Ciaran's Monastery) *halfway between Eochail and Cill Rónáin.*

INIS MEÁIN (Inishmann)

Baile an Dúna, Synge's cottage. The writer stayed here every summer from 1898 to 1902, visitors included Eoin MacNeill and Patrick Pearse. **Inis Meáin Museum:** a must for Synge devotees, housing his typewriter, camera, photographs, manuscripts. *Usually June–Sept, Mon–Fri, 11.30 a.m.–12.30 p.m.; 2 p.m.–4 p.m.* 1 m (1.5 km) away, on cliff edge, see seat where Synge sat.

Cill Ceann Fhionnaigh (Church of the Fair-Headed One), *near slip, mid E coast:* once-splendid primitive church now in ruins.

Dún Chonchuir, *near village of Baile an Dúna:* magnificent fort, though the three outer rings have gone (but for remnants of the inner curtain) the massive fortress wall is almost intact. Most impressive.

INIS ÓIRR (Inisheer)

O'Brien's Castle, *S of landing point:* 15th c , set on rocky hill, one of the island's most striking features.

Teampall Chaomhain, *between airstrip and Baile an Chaisleáin:* church ruins now largely buried in sand, pilgrimage to it on June 14.

Trá Caorach, *E of island:* twenty years ago, a freighter was wrecked offshore, sucessive storms have left her beached upright. An island of magnificent beaches.

Ballina

Pop. 7,000, 31 m (50 km) NE of Westport, 37 m (59 km) SW of Sligo, 153 m (246 km) NW of Dublin. EC Thur. TIO: (096)21544, Bus and train enquiries: (096)21011. 125 from Belfast (SO) June–Aug 120, 122, 125, 255, 259 bus from Castlebar; 120, 121, 122, 259 bus from Galway; 125, 267 bus from Sligo. Train from Claremorris, Dublin, Westport.

  Ballina may not be the most architecturally impressive town in Ireland, with a dour, straggling Main Street, but it's one of the best angling centres in the country, noted for high quality salmon fishing. At the foot of the Main Street, the broad vistas of the River Moy's banks make up for the cramped town centre. Summer, fishing, sporting events, *details, TIO.*

  Dolmen of the Four Maols, *SW of town, across level crossing at railway station, up narrow road for 1 m (2 km) Signposted.* Walks, downstream, on both banks of River Moy, from bridge. Boat hire: John Walkin, *Tone Street, tel: (096) 22442.* Bicycles: W. J. Kearney, *Abbey Street, tel: (096)21249.* Attymass Trekking Centre, *Tel: Bonniconlon 32.*

AROUND BALLINA

Abbeytown, *1 m (2 km) N of Crossmolina:* 10th c abbey.

Ardnaree Hill, *E bank of River Moy overlooking Ballina on L133:* ruins of 14th c Augustinian church.

Ballycastle, *16 m (26 km) NW of Ballìna on L133, 261 bus from Ballina.* Interesting prehistoric remains. Attractive N Mayo coast scenery. Bicycles: Barrett's Stores, *Tel: Ballycastle 6.*

Barony of Erris, *S of Belderg, L133 crosses it to Glenamoy.* One of most desolate areas of Ireland.

Bartragh Island: 377 acres at mouth of Moy, ideal

Downpatrick Head

for picnics. Boats, Ballina.

Behy, *4 m (6 km) NW of Ballycastle:* neolithic stone court cairn.

Bellacorick, *11 m (17 km) W of Crossmolina on N59 to Belmullet, 262 bus from Ballina (infrequent service).*Musical Bridge—play a tune by rubbing stone along N parapet. Local legend says that the bridge will never be completed; beware, a sudden end awaits anyone who tries.

Belleek, *0.5 m (1 km) N of Ballina on W bank of River Moy:* car park, picnic area, forest walks.

Belmullet, *39 m (63 km) W of Ballina, 262 bus from Ballina (infrequent service).* Entrance to Mullet Peninsula, nine sandy beaches within easy driving distance. Belmullet Golf Club, 9 holes.

Benwee Head, *10 m (16 km) W of Belderg:* outstanding cliffscapes. Off-shore Stags of Broadhaven rocks rise dramatically out of the sea.

Bunatrahir Bay, *2 m (3 km) N of Ballycastle:* two fine court cairns, two dolmens.

Cashlaunicrobin/Port Conaghra, *3 m (5 km) NW of Ballycastle:* large promontory forts.

Castle Firbis, *3 m (5 km) NE of Enniscrone:* ruined 12th c stronghold of MacFirbis clan, noted Gaelic poets.

Cliffs of Ceide, *near Belderg, 261 bus from Ballina to Belderg (infrequent service).* Awe-inspiring coastal scenery.

Coryosla/Coryosla Bridge, *1 m (2 km) from Pontoon on L140 in Crossmolina direction:* car park, picnic area, forest walks.

Crossmolina, *8 m (13 km) W of Ballina on N59, 262 bus from Ballina (infrequent service).* Beautifully set on River Deel under shadows of Nephin Mountains, less than 1 m (2 km) from Lough Conn, in heart of fabulous salmon and brown trout fishing country. Deel Riding Centre, *Moylaw, tel: (096) 31197.*

Danish Cellar, *5 m (8 km) N of Belmullet:* beautiful bay fringed with cliffs. *Doonamo Point, 5 m (7 km)*

NW of Belmullet. Ruined prehistoric fort on cliff edge. Tremendous views of offshore Eagle Island with lighthouse. Elly Bay, on E side, has magnificent strand. **Fallmore,** *S end of peninsula:* remains of St Derival's Church. Also ruins of St Derival's Vat, a holy well believed to have great restorative powers.

Doonbristy, *Downpatrick Head:* striking ancient fort on isolated cliff.

Doonfeeney Upper, *2 m (3 km) NW of Ballycastle:* two ancient graveyards, one with ruined early church, other with 18 ft (6 metre) pillar stone. To NW, 'Fairy Fort', large ring fort.

Easkey, *16 m (26 km) NE of Ballina, 125, 268 bus from Ballina.* Pleasant little seaside village guarded at either end by a Martello Tower. Nearby, dolmen held up by four pillars. Rare fossils at back of pier. **Split Rock,** Ice Age boulder: *2 m (3 km) on Ballina side of village.* Children's playground. *Mar 17–June 1, weekends. June 2–Oct 31, daily.* Crazy golf, good surfing, golf, pitch and putt, tennis. Indoor amusements, Improvement Society Pavilion, *June 1–Sept 1.* Youth Hostel. The Atlantic Drive skirts O'Donnell Castle, pier, natural swimming pool.

Enniscrone, *9 m (14 km) NE of Ballina on E side of Killala Bay, 125, 269, 268 bus from Ballina.* 3 m (5 km) beach. Medicinal baths. Many pleasant walks. Bicycles. G. Helly, *tel: Enniscrone 101.* Enniscrone Golf Club, 18 holes, tel: (096)36392.

Errew Abbey, *6 m (10 km) S of Crossmolina,* on peninsula jutting into Conn, ruins of Augustinian foundation.

Foxford, *10 m (16 km) S of Ballina, 87, 120, 255, 259, 265, 266 bus from Ballina. Also train.* Bust of birthplace of Admiral Brown, founder of the Argentinian Navy. Providence Woollen Mills: fabulous tweeds. *Tours Apr–Sept, Mon–Thurs, 11 a.m. & 2.15 p.m. Fri, 11 a.m.* Factory shop, *Apr–Sept, Mon–Sat, 9 a.m.–5.30 p.m. Winter, Mon–Fri, 9 a.m.–5.30 p.m. Details: (094) 56104.*

Giant Rocking Stone, *Pontoon Bridge, just W of Pontoon Bridge Hotel:* huge chunk of granite that looks as if you can set it rocking with a gentle push. Trying is a great anticlimax.

Kilcummin Strand, *4 m (6 km) N of Killala:* well signposted beach where French forces under General Humbert landed in August, 1798 to aid the '98 Rising. Since publication of Thomas Flanagan's book, *The Year of the French,* and filming of the subsequent TV series, this part of Mayo has become popular hunting ground for visitors with literary and historical leanings. Nearby, St Cummin's monastery ruins.

Killala, *7 m (11 km) NW of Ballina on W shores of Killala Bay, 261 bus from Ballina.* CI cathedral, fine paintings, many historical records. If closed, contact Very Rev. Malcolm Graham, Dean of Killala, Crossmolina. In churchyard, elaborate souterrain. Nearby round tower.**D**

Kilmoremoy, *2 m (3 km) NW of Ballina on L133 to Killala, 261 bus from Ballina.* Ancient church with rampart, founded by disciple of St Patrick. Beside church, cross-inscribed rock said to have been blessed by St Patrick.

Laughil, *on shores of Lough Conn between Pontoon and Coryosla Bridges:* forest walks.

Lough Cullin, *2 m (3 km) W of Foxford on L22:* car park, picnic area, fishing, forest walks. Excellent views over lough and nearby Lough Conn.

Moista Sound, *W of Belderg:* narrow chasm enclosed by vertical cliffs.

Moyne Friary, *2 m (3 km) SE of Killala:* stream runs through ruins. Most attractive. Etchings of 16th c ships on nave wall plaster. From top of nearby friary tower, magnificent views of Bartragh Island, Killala Bay.

Mullet Peninsula, Blind Harbour, *4 m (6 km) NW of Belmullet,* remarkable silted inlet. **Cliffs of Erris,** *on W of Peninsula.* These run N from Bingham Lodge for 14 m (22 km), wonderful views.

Pollatomish, *5 m (8 km) NW of Glenamoy:* Youth Hostel.

Pontoon, *9 m (14 km) N of Castlebar on L134, on W shore of Lough Cullin:* Terrybaun Pottery, Bofeenaun. *By app., Mon–Fri, 9 a.m.–6 p.m., Sat, 9 a.m.–12 noon.*

Porturlin, *4 m (6 km) E of Benwee Head:* excellent 3 m (5 km) clifftop walk to tiny Portacloy harbour. Fine cliff scenery.

Poulnachantinny Puffing Holes, *Downpatrick Head:* magnificent natural display as caverns fill with sea.

Rosserk Friary, *3 m (5 km) N of Ballina:* founded in 15th c, one of finest Franciscan friaries in Ireland. Well-preserved. Access at all times.

Clifden

Pop. 1,400, 49 m (79 km) W of Galway, 184 m (296 km) W of Dublin. EC Thurs. TIO: Clifden 103, June–Sept. Bus enquiries: Clifden 11. 116(SO), 242 bus from Galway.

'Capital' of Connemara, this wild, desolate-looking town with splendidly wide main street is the ideal base for exploring the great natural beauties of the West. The two hour bus journey from Galway provides a truly memorable approach. Situated between the Atlantic and the peaks of the Twelve Bens, Clifden has an almost Alpine air, most refreshing. Connemara Pony Show: *Aug.*

Two buildings dominate the town: the Protestant church built in 1820, just eight years after Clifden was founded has a silver copy of the Cross of Cong. The C church, built 1830, stands on site of ancient 'clochán' or beehive-shaped monastic stone hut from which Clifden takes its name. Also see old railway station; the line to Galway closed over 50 years ago.

Clifden Castle, *1 m (2 km) W of town:* ruined mansion of John D'Arcy of Killtulla, who founded Clifden in early 19th c. Continue walk up sky road for exhilerating views of coastline, as far as

Eyrephort beaches. **Owenglin Cascade,** *just below town:* where the Owenglin River falls steeply over boulders, most attractive. Walk: start at Quay Road, continue past beach and tiny harbour through castle grounds, returning by Cloghavard. Connemara Pottery: *all year except Dec. Mon–Sat, tel: Clifden 59.* See tweed being woven at Millars, *Main St. Tel: Clifden 32.* Errislannan Riding Centre, *tel: Clifden 27.* Connemara Golf Club, *18 holes, tel: Ballyconneely 5.*

The Twelve Bens

AROUND CLIFDEN

Ballynahinch Lake, *on N59 from Clifden to Recess:* route skirts Twelve Bens and runs along N shore of lake, most attractive.

Carna/Killieran: sandy beaches at Callowfeanish, Mweenish, Moyrus, Ardmore.

Cashel, *14 m (22 km) SE of Clifden, 242, 243 bus from Clifden, Galway:* angling, shooting centre at head of Cashel Bay. Takes its name from circular stone fort, remains of which lie on mountain slope 1 km NE of village.

Cleggan, *242 bus from Clifden.* Six safe, sandy beaches nearby, two within walking distance.

Connemara National Park, *near Letterfrack, 242 bus from Clifden, Galway.* 3,800 acres, short distance walks, paddock with pedigree Connemara ponies, visitor centre with lounge, rest room, permanent exhibition of park features. *Daily, all year.***D**

Coral Strand, *4 m (6 km) SW of Clifden:* one of many fine bathing strands in Mannin Bay.

Cnoc Athy, *near Clifden:* spectacular views of lake, moor, sea from 400 ft (120 metre) hill.

Derreen, *4 m (6 km) SE of Leenane on L100 to Maam:* interesting forest walks.

Derryclare Lough: breathtaking drive from Ballynahinch Lake, E of Twelve Bens, continue past Lough Inagh and Kylemore Lough, on both sides of valley, mountains rise over 2,000 ft (609 metres). Good fishing country.

Derrygimlagh Bog, *4 m (6 km) S of Clifden, 2 m (3*

km) NE of Ballyconneely: foundations and some masts of Marconi company's first transatlantic wireless station, destroyed during Civil War. Nearby is spot where Alcock and Brown landed after first non-stop transatlantic flight in June, 1919. Cairn. On higher ground, 2 m (3 km) away, 14 ft (4 metre) stone monument in shape of plane.

Diamond Hill, *just E of Letterfrack:* 1,460 ft (445 metres), marvellous views of N Connemara coast.

Dog's Bay/Gurteen Bay, *2 m (3 km) SW of Roundstone off L102:* fine, sandy beaches. Nearby strands include Murvey, Dolin, Aillebrack and Dunloughan.

Doon Hill, *2 m (3 km) SW of Ballyconneely on L102 to Clifden:* derelict coast watching post built during World War II. Hill 215 ft (65 metres) an easy climb, fine beach at nearby Bunowen Bay.

Errisbeg Mountain, *W of Roundstone:* 987 ft (300 metres). Worth easy climb for fine views of lake-dotted countryside to N and NW and seascapes to S and W.

Errislannan, walk: leave Clifden by Ardbear road. Cross Weir Bridge (salmon congregate beneath it during spawning season), keep R at Errislannan and Boat Harbour beaches, returning by N shores of Mannin Bay to Derrygimlagh. See Lough Fadda, wild bird haunt. Alcock and Brown memorial nearby.

High Island, *NW of Omey Island, 2 m (3 km) W of Aughrus Point:* site of ruins of monastery of St Feichin, fine views of Connemara coast. No harbour; landing difficult even in fine weather.

Inishbofin Island, *12 m (19 km) NW of Clifden. Mailboat sailings, Cleggan to Inishbofin: Mar–Oct, Mon, Wed, Sat, at 1 p.m. Nov–Feb, Mon, Wed, Fri, at 1 p.m. Details: P. C. O'Halloran, St Joseph's, Inishbofin, tel: Inishbofin 106. Bookings essential. Easter–Sept, further sailings from Cleggan. Details: Pier Bar, tel: Cleggan 26 or Ulick Joyce's Bar, tel: Cleggan 12.* Not a lot to do, but many tremendous seascapes and safe beaches. Two hotels, no shortage of creature comforts. Unspoilt Bofin Harbour is especially attractive. Bicycles, Days Hotel, *tel: Inishbofin 103.*

Kilkieran, *on L102:* St Kieran's Well in cemetery. Pilgrimage, *Sept 9.* Currach racing during summer.

Killary Harbour, *15 m (24 km) NE of Clifden:* Youth Hostel.

Kylemore Lough, *242 bus from Cleggan:* mountains rise almost vertically from its shores. Magnificent 19th c castle on lower slopes now Benedictine convent; in great hall, flag captured by Irish Brigade after battle of Fontenoy. Gothic chapel in grounds. Pottery, *daily, 1 April–30 October 10 a.m.–6 p.m.* Tearoom, craft shop. *Details: Kylemore 2.*

Leenane, *242 bus from Clifden, Galway:* Leenane Hotel, century old coaching inn, renowned flower garden, *tel: Leenane 4/8.*

Letterfrack, *8 m (13 km) NE of Clifden on N59, 242 bus from Clifden, Galway.* Founded by 19th c Quakers as mission settlement. Impressive craft centre, *daily during season.* Excellent bathing strands at nearby Barnaderg Bay.

Maamturk Mountains: *take L100 from Leenane SE to Maam.* Maam Valley Pottery, *Maam: all year, Mon–Sat 10 a.m.–6 p.m.* Adjoining shop. *Tel: (091) 71109.*

Mac Dara's Island, *8 m (13 km) SW of Kilkieran:* ruins of church, grave of St Mac Dara.

Moyard, *5 m (8 km) NW of Clifden on N59:* J. D. McMurray makes handtufted and handknotted carpets, rugs and wallhangings. *Mon–Sat, 10 a.m.–5 p.m., no demonstrations. Tel: Moyard 31.*

Mweenish Island, *near Kilkieran:* sandy beaches. Holy well on S tip. Connected to mainland by bridge.

Omey Island, *6 m (9 km) SW of Cleggan:* can be reached on foot at low tide. Fine strands, pony races in Aug. In sandhills on N side of island, ruins

of Temple Feheen, small 7th c church and college.

Recess, *10 m (16 km) E of Clifden:* Ben Lettery Youth Hostel, *tel: Ballinafad 18.* Connemara Green Marble Shop: large general store with extensive craft shop and very good range of Irish books as well as café, pub and petrol station.

Lough Inagh, *6 m (9 km) N of Recess on minor road to Kylemore:* forest walk, car park, picnic area. Boats: Mrs McAuley, *Inagh Valley Inn, Recess.*

Renvyle Peninsula, *NW of Letterfrack:* Renvyle House Hotel. Run for many years by Oliver St John Gogarty, writer and contemporary of James Joyce. Sports facilities open to visitors: sailing, water skiing, riding, pony trekking, *tel: Renvyle 3.* Ruins of 14th c O'Flaherty castle *1 m (2 km) W of hotel.* Excellent nearby beaches. Renvyle Hill: fine views. **Little Killary Adventure Centre,** *Salruck.* Outdoor sports, *tel: Lettergesh 2.* Bicycles: P. Coyne, *Tullycross, tel: Renvyle 4.*

Roundstone

Roundstone, *14 m (22 km) SE of Clifden on L102, 242 bus from Clifden, Galway.* Quiet village founded in early 19th c by Alexander Nimmo, a Scottish engineer. Almost landlocked harbour. Beach. Riding. Gurteen Beach Trekking Centre, *Errisbeg.* Bicycles: M. J. Ferron, *tel: Roundstone 30.*

St Patrick's Bed and Well, *4 m (6 km) SW of Maam:* take footpath up mountain from Maumeen. Well water believed to have medicinal properties. Pilgrimage last Sun in July.

Salrock, *at head of Little Killary:* tiny, beautiful village, fine view across the Killaries, surrounding mountains magnificent.

Toombeola Bridge, *3 m (5 km) NW of Cashel:* Dominican abbey ruins. Founded 1427 by an O'Flaherty. Riding: The Angler's Return, *tel: Ballinafad 6.*

Dingle

Pop. 1,500, 31 m (50 km) W of Tralee, 42 m (68 km) NW of Killarney, 218 m (350 km) SW of Dublin. EC Thurs. TIO: Dingle 88. July–Aug. Bus enquiries: (066)21211. 186 bus from Tralee.

The main town on the Dingle peninsula, set on an almost landlocked harbour, and a perfect centre for exploring the area's many ancient sites and natural wonders. This fishing town's friendly atmosphere is enhanced by a number of good craft shops, some excellent gourmet restaurants and a plentiful selection of pubs. A very popular resort during the season, especially with Germans. Dingle Regatta: currach races held amid carnival atmosphere, *mid-Aug*. Dingle Races: biggest 'flapper' race for untried horses in Ireland. Complete with fun fair. Great fun, *early Aug*.

Library, *Green Street:* collection of material relating to prominent local patriot Thomas Ashe. *Tues–Sat*. **Dingle Peninsula Heritage Centre,** *John Street*. SO, Daily, 10.30 a.m.–6 p.m.

O'Flaherty's pub, Dingle

O'Flaherty's: very popular old-fashioned pub, stone floor, traditional music during season. Beaches: close to town at Doonsean and Slaidin. Eddie "Hutch" Hutchinson builds currachs at Feothanach near Dingle. *By app*. Bicycles: J. Moriarty, *Main Street, tel: Dingle 66;* Rent-a-Bike, *The Quay, tel: Dingle 46*. Riding: Michael O'Sullivan, *The Quay, tel: Dingle 46*.

AROUND DINGLE

Anascaul, *10 m (16 km) E of Dingle on T68, 186 bus from Dingle*. South Pole Inn, so called because Thomas Crean, who lived here, was the man who found Captain Scott and his companions dead in their tent. Pottery: *Mon–Sat, 9 a.m.–6 p.m. Sun, 2 p.m.–6 p.m. By app*. Walk: N past Anascaul Lake, over slopes of Beenoskee Mountain to Stradbally and Castlegregory.

Ballinskelligs, *Youth Hostel, tel: Ballinskelligs 9*.

Ballydavid, *NE corner of Smerwick Harbour:* see traditional currachs (canvas-covered boats) being built.

Ballyferriter, Teach Siamsa rural theatre workshop: meeting place, the people of West Kerry have an outstanding musical tradition. *June–Sept*. Details: Dingle TIO. Potadoireacht na Caológe pottery, *Clogher: May–Sept, Mon–Sun, 9.30 a.m.–7 p.m. by app*. Shop *same hours, tel: Ballyferriter 44*.

Ballywiheen, *townland 3 m (5 km) NE of Ballyferriter:* Ogham stone and remains of early 12th c church.

Blasket Islands, *W of Slea Head:* only one of the seven islands, the Great Blasket, was ever continuously inhabited and it was abandoned in 1953 after a turn of bad fishing seasons. One of smaller islands, Inishvickillane, is summer home of Irish politician Charles Haughey. During fine weather, the other islands can be visited from Dunquin. *Details: Dingle TIO*.

Brandon Head: good coastal walk to Brandon Point.

Brandon Mountain, *W from Ballybrack following rough track called Saint's Road:* 3,000 ft (900 metres), well worth climbing, St Brendan's Oratory is near top.

Caherconree, *185, 186 bus from Dingle to Camp, 3 m (5 km) climb from Camp. up mountain road to*
Beheenagh, climb W spur. On triangular plateau, explore the old fort, seat of Curaoi Mac Daire, a king of ancient Ireland. Extensive views.

Castlegregory: Cathair na Máirtíneach and Cathair Murphy, two ancient circular stone forts, good beach. Pony trekking: O'Flahertys, *the village*.

Cloghane, *SW corner of Brandon Bay:* fine beach.

Connor Pass, *runs NE from Dingle for some 6 m (10 km):* rises to a height of 1,500 ft (450 metres). Road very narrow and in places only a small stone wall protects you from vast drop to valley below. In fine weather, view over surrounding mountains and rock-strewn valley is incredible. When clouds block the view, it's like being airborne.

Dingle–Dunquin road, spectacular sea views. The road skirts Ventry Harbour; there, you have a choice of routes, the minor road S of Mount Eagle, skirting Slea Head, is the more spectacular. Archaeological remains in this area include over 400 clocáns or beehive huts.

Dun an Oir, *S of Smerwick village on W shore of harbour:* ruins of fort built in 1580. Nearby memorial commemorates massacre of Geraldine and Spanish troops in fort not long after.

Dunbeg Fort, *2 m (3 km) E of Slea Head:* ancient headland fort, rather too spectacularly situated, the outer edges have fallen into the sea. Signposted across fields from coast road.

Dunquin, *187 bus from Dingle (infrequent service)* Entrepreneur, raconteur and traveller, Kruger Kavanagh was a character to end all characters. At his bar, in Dunquin, perched above the sea at the W end of Europe, he was host to personalities from all over the world. Great atmosphere, adjoining guest house. Cottage birthplace of storyteller and folklorist Peig Sayers.

Ferriter's Castle, *2 m (3 km) NW of Ballyferriter:* birthplace of Pierce Ferriter, one of the last Irish chiefs to hold out against Cromwell.

Gallarus Oratory, *2 m (3 km) NE of Ballyferriter:* best preserved early Christian church in Ireland,

Gallarus Oratory

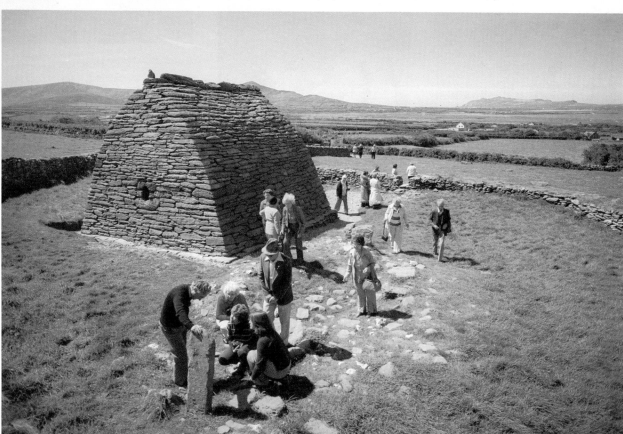

believed to date from 8th c. Built in shape of up-turned boat and still in almost perfect condition.

Gates of Glory, *1 m (1.5 km) W of Dingle Town on way to Slea Head:* two standing stones, nearby milestone a giant standing stone.

Inch, *S Dingle peninsula, 186 bus from Dingle.* Magnificent 4 m (6 km) golden strand at entrance to Castlemaine Bay, one of best bathing beaches in the region.

Minard Castle, *3 m (5 km) SW of Anascaul:* dangerous ruins perched above a cove, but from immediate vicinity, fantastic views.

St Brendan's Oratory, *just S of Ballyferriter:* also ruined Chancellor's House, holy well.

Seven Hogs, or Magharee Islands: ask a boatman at Fahamore to take you across.

Smerwick Harbour, *NW Dingle Peninsula:* good walks along both sides of harbour. To E, land rises up to Ballydavid Head.

Tralee Bay, *N of Camp village:* great sandy beach.

Ventry, *near Dingle:* Bradán Feasa Pottery, *Mon–Fri, 10 a.m.–4 p.m.* Adjoining craft shop and café, *May–Oct, Mon–Sun, 8.30 a.m.–8.30 p.m.* Sandy beach. Bicycles: the Boat Slip.

Ennis

Pop. 7,000, 16 m (26 km) NW of Shannon airport, 42 m (68 km) S of Galway, 145 m (233 km) SW of Dublin. EC Thurs. TIO: (065)281366. All year. Bus enquiries: (065)21038. 111, 120, 122, 124, 219, 226, 227, 228, 229, 231 bus from Galway, Limerick, Shannon.

An interesting town set on the banks of the River Fergus, with narrow, winding streets and a rich historical atmosphere. In addition to having been the unlikely birthplace of the wife of Hector Berlioz, Ennis has been the scene of some notable political 'firsts', such as the election of Daniel O'Connell in 1828 and that of de Valera in 1917. Good centre for touring the Co. Clare coast, including the famous Cliffs of Moher, and the remarkable Burren country for the N. Fleadh Nua: great festival of traditional Irish music, *late May. Details: TIO.* County Clare Show: varied programme, including horse cattle competitions. *Mid-Aug. Details TIO.*

Clare Abbey, *2 m (3 km) SE of Ennis, just off N18:* ruins, including tower of Augustinian abbey founded in 1195.

Killone Abbey, *3 m (5 km) S of Ennis on W shores of Killone Lough:* founded in 12th c by Dónal O'Brien, last king of Munster. St John's Holy Well is near the Abbey; track from abbey still called the 'Pilgrim's Road' after bygone pilgrimages.

Franciscan friary, *off Francis Street:* finished in 1241, completely renovated some 30 years ago. Notable sculptures. Key: nearby Franciscan church.◻ *It is possible that regular opening hours will be introduced in 1984*

De Valera Museum, *Harmony Row:* library and many objects of interest associated with prominent people who had Clare links, including de Valera. *Mon, Tues, Wed, Fri, 11 a.m.–9 p.m. Thurs, 11 a.m.–5.30 p.m. Details: (065)21616.*

O'Connell Monument, *town centre:* site of great 1828 meeting at which Daniel O'Connell was nominated to stand for election in Clare. Also see new de Valera statue. **Railway station:** (unused) old steam engine from the famous now unfortunately extinct West Clare Railway, immortalised by Percy French in his song, *Are you right there, Michael, are you right?*

Lenthall's, *Abbey Street:* delightfully old-fashioned inn, with antique bars and nooks. Denis Maurer, *26 O'Connell Street:* makes gold and silver jewellery. *Mon–Sat, 9 a.m.–6 p.m. Tel: (065) 21088/21974.* Attractive riverside stroll along Harvey's Quay to Wood Quay, returning to Parnell Street. Further upstream, you can take Newbridge Road alongside the river. Swimming

pool: indoor, heated, Sandfield Park, *Gort Road, Tues–Sun. July–Aug, daily. Tel: (065)21604.* Bicycles: Tom Mannion Travel, *O'Connell Street, tel: (065)24211.* Also from Co. Clare Rent-a-Cottage at Ballyvaughan, Broadford, Carrigaholt, Corofin, Feakle. Golf Club, Drumbiggle, *18 holes, tel: (065)24074.*

AROUND ENNIS

Ailwee Cave, *2 m (3 km) SE of Ballyvaughan, just off Ennis Road:* formed 2 million years ago. Quite safe for over 1,000 yards, the strange subterranean landscape includes stalagmites and stalactites, all dazzlingly lit. Ailwee Cave Centre, at entrance, is shaped like Stone Age cairn, restaurant, craft shop. *Mar 1–Oct 31. 10 a.m.–7 p.m. Daily. Winter weekends, otherwise. By arr. Tel: Ballyvaughan 36, Kilfenora 26, Lahinch 150. Lisdoonvarna 77.*

Ballyalla Lake, *2 m (3 km) N of Ennis on Ruan road:* riverside park, picnic area, car park.

Ballyvaughan, *10 m (16 km) NE of Lisdoonvarna, 238 bus from Lisdoonvarna.* Pleasant seaside village with pier, facing Galway Bay. Manus Walsh craft workshop, restaurant. *Tues– Sun. Details: Ballyvaughan 29.* Fine drive to Black Head, Lisdoonvarna and Corkscrew Hill back to Ballyvaughan. Good views N over Galway Bay—especially when the sun's going down.

Bishopsquarter beach, *2 m (3 km) SW of Ballyvaughan:* nearby ruins of Drumcreechy church.

Bridges of Ross: *3 m (5 km) NE of Kilbaha Signposted track from Ross– Moneen–Loop Head road:* pair of arches formed by action of sea on N side of Loop Head peninsula.

Burren, *N of Corofin, E of Lisdoonvarna:* impressive area of limestone outcrops that looks like the moon's surface. Remarkable flora and fauna make it well worth exploring in depth. Being turned into National Park.

Burren, Co. Clare

Cappagh Pier: *take Shannonside road E for about 22 m (35 km):* good views of offshore Scattery and Hog Islands and across to N Kerry coast.

Carrigaholt Castle, *set on headland on S side of Loop Head peninsula:* 14th c, overlooks attractive Carrigaholt harbour.

Cliffs of Moher, *6 m (10 km) NW of Lahinch, TIO: Cliffs of Moher, tel: Lahinch 285 May–Sept.* Little introduction needed. Extending for 5 m (8 km), these thoroughly majestic cliffs are among the West's most striking features. Best seen from O'Brien's Tower, now information centre, craft

shop, observation point. *Early March–Oct 29, weekdays, 10 a.m.–6 p.m. Sun, 12 noon–6 p.m.* The drive N to Black Head, then E to Kinvara along L54/N67, is one of finest coastal routes in Ireland.

Coosheen Folk Museum, *2m (3 km) N of Kilkee:* collection of old household implements dating from 18th c. *SO, 11 a.m.–8 p.m. daily. Details: Kilkee 169.*

Corcomroe Abbey, *6 m (10 km) E of Ballyvaughan at foot of Abbey Hill:* founded in 1182 by King Donal O'Brien. Church still in good condition. Yeats set *The Dreaming of the Bones* here.

Corofin, *9 m (15 km) N of Ennis on L53:* Clare Heritage Centre in converted 18th c Protestant church. Displays, manuscripts, portray life in 19th c West of Ireland. *Mar 17–Oct 31, Mon–Sat, 10 a.m.–5 p.m. Sun, 12 noon–5 p.m. Details: (065)27632.* Boat hire: Michael Burke, *Main Street, tel: (065)27677,* P. Neylon, *Main Street, tel: (067)27683.*

Church door, Kilfenora

Diarmuid and Gráinne's Rock, *N side of Loop Head:* separated from mainland by deep canyon. Tradition says that Cuchulainn jumped this chasm to avoid attentions of witch called Mal. She tried to follow but didn't quite make it.

Doolin, *5 m (8 km) SW of Lisdoonvarna:* small fishing village on sandy bay, famous for its folk music. Trips to Aran Islands in fine weather. *Details: Sea Arann, Lakeview, Lickeen, Kilfenora, tel: Lisdoonvarna 103.*

Dromore, *7 m (11 km) NE of Ennis, near Crusheen:* walks along wooded lakeside, car park, picnic area.

Dysert O'Dea, *3 m (5 km) S of Corofin:* 12th c White Cross of Tola (NM), also round tower.

Ennistymon, *just inland from Lahinch, 228, 229 bus from Ennis.* Delightfully set in wooded valley beside River Cullenagh cascade. Good brown trout fishing, boat trips on river. The Falls Hotel generates its own electricity in ingenious fashion. Willie Daly Riding Centre, *Ballinagaddy.*

Fanore, *S of Black Head:* good bathing.

Gleninagh Castle, *off L54 coast road from Black Head to Ballyvaughan:* four storey L-shaped tower dates from 16th c. (NM). Clearly signposted.

Gragan's Wood, *5 m (8 km) NE of Lisdoonvarna on N67:* forest walks.

Kilbaha: from its tiny harbour, road climbs W for 3 m (5 km) to Loop Head lighthouse. Superb views.

Kilfenora, *7 m (11 km) SE of Lisdoonvarna on L53:*

Cliffs of Moher

Burren Display Centre is best possible introduction to the neighbouring Burren. Flora impressively recreated in silk and wax. Models of birds, butterflies, landscapes, moths. Library has good collection of reference material. Staff will suggest scenic routes for cyclists, drivers, walkers. Adjacent craft shop. *Mar 17–Oct 31, 10 a.m.–6 p.m. daily. Closed 1 p.m.–2 p.m. June, July, Aug, 10 a.m.–7 p.m. No lunch. Winter weekends by arr. Details: Kilfenora 30.* **D**

St Fachtnan's Cathedral (CI): nave used as church, remainder roofless. Doorty Cross and High Cross just W of cathedral. **Donkey Farm,** *Bog Hill,* has many sorts of donkeys, for riding if you wish, *Tues, Thurs, Sat, 10.30 a.m.–6 p.m. Sun, 2 p.m.–6 p.m. Details: Lisdoonvarna 149.* Bicycles: Lynch and Howard.

Kilkee, *35 m (65 km) SW of Ennis. EC Wed. TIO: Kilkee 112. June–Aug. 226, 229 bus from Ennis.* Popular seaside resort with exceptionally safe 1 m (1.5 km) long strand, ideal for bathing. Deep sea and shore angling centre. Professional theatre, *July, Aug, details: TIO.* Children's amusement park. *SO.* Boat trips from pier to see caves and cliffs. Kilkee sub-aqua centre: full skin diving facilities. *Tel: Kilkee 211.* Boats: Manuel di Lucia, *tel: Kilkee 125.* Bicycles: P. Keller, *Circular Road.*

Edmund Point: attractive walk SW to Duggerna Rocks, which protect town from Atlantic, going on to the Amphitheatre. With its tiers of rock-like seats, it is often used for outdoor concerts. Excellent views from nearby Lookout Hill. From

this point, you can return to Kilkee by road or continue past Bishop's Island to Castle Point, from where you can see the coast as far as Loop Head. From East End, fine 5 m (8 km) walk by Blackrock, Chimney Bay to Farrihy Bay and Corbally village, returning by road to Kilkee.

Killimer, *6 m (10 km) E of Kilrush:* Ellen Hanly, the 'Colleen Bawn' is buried in the old graveyard. Her tragic death inspired Gerald Griffin's novel, *The Collegians* on which in turn were based Boucicault's drama, *The Colleen Bawn* and Benedict's opera, *The Lily of Killarney.* Regular daily ferry sailings to Tarbert, Co. Kerry. Details listed under Tarbert in 'Tralee' section. *TIO: Knock 23. June–Aug.*

Kilrush, *27 m (43 km) SW of Ennis. EC. Thurs. 223, 226, 229 bus from Ennis.* Stroll along adjacent Cappagh Pier and enjoy fresh Shannon air. Professional theatre. *July, Aug. Details: Kilkee TIO.* Woodland walks: 1 m (1.5 km) SE of village on N67. Car park, picnic area. Bicycles: Michael Gleeson, *Burton Street.* Kilrush Golf and Sports Club, *Ballykett,* 9 holes, *tel: Kilrush 138.*

Knappogue Castle, *Quin, 6 m (10 km) SE of Ennis on L31:* built 1467, seat of MacNamara family until 1815. In recent years, restored to mediaeval splendour, with craft shop and workshops, forge and replanted gardens and orchards. *Apr 1–Oct 31, mediaeval banquets, 5.45 p.m., 8.45 p.m. nightly. Castle Apr 1–Oct 31, daily, 10 a.m.–5 p.m. Details: (061) 71103/71101.*

Lahinch. *EC. Wed. 117 bus from Galway (summer only), 228, 229 bus from Ennis.* Popular resort with 1 m (1.5 km) long sandy beach at NE corner

of Liscannor Bay. Promenade, sea water swimming pool. Cumann Merriman, annual cultural orgy held late Aug in honour of author of the *Midnight Court,* a bawdy 18th c Irish language epic. *Details: TIO.* Resort Theatre, *July, Aug.* Lahinch Art Gallery, *Main Street, daily.* Entertainment centre: café, cinema, dance hall, pool, traditional music, well situated near beach, *all year, daily.* Bicycles: T. O'Sullivan, *Station Road, tel: Lahinch 12.* Golf Club, 18 holes, *tel: Lahinch 3.*

Lemanagh Castle (NM), *4 m (7 km) E of Kilfenora on L53:* amalgam of 1480 residential tower and early 17th c fortified house.

Liscannor, *just along bay from Lahinch:* small fishing village. John P. Holland, inventor of submarine, born here in Castle Street in 1831. **St Macreehy's:** 12th c church 1 m (1.5 km) E of village on Lahinch road. **Joe McHugh's pub:** mecca for greyhound aficionados, with its collection of trophies. **Clahane shore,** *just W of village,* has safe bathing. Legend says that submerged reef at mouth of Liscannor Bay is site of lost city of Kilstephen. Boats: John Lysaght, *tel: Lahinch 176,* Martin McMahon, *tel: Lahinch 51.*

Lisdoonvarna, *23 m (37 km) NW of Ennis on L53. EC Wed. TIO: Lisdoonvarna 62. Sept. 228 bus from Ennis, 238 bus from Galway.* Ireland's leading spa. Spa Wells Health Centre is principal sulphur spring, with pump house and baths, an ideal way of removing late night impurities from the system. *June–Oct. Details: Lisdoonvarna 23.* Lisdoonvarna Fair: inc. the mating game, when Ireland's shy bachelors seek spouses, *Sept.*

Lemanagh Castle

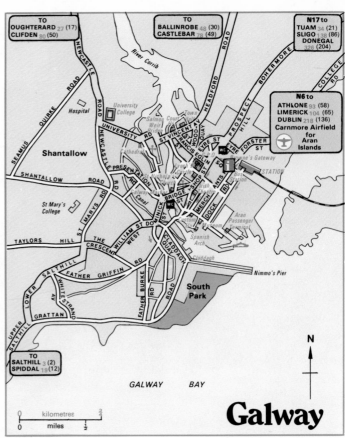

Galway

Three day folk festival, with many top international names, *July, details:* Jim Shannon, Doolin, Co. Clare.

There is an interesting 2 m (3 km) circular walk along the 'Bog' road via the Spectacle Bridge to SW. The bridge, a single span over River Aille, has a round hole in the masonry, same width as the arch. 6 m (10 km) walk NW of town to 15th c ruins of Ballynalacken Castle. The area's cave system is dangerous and should only be explored with help of experienced local guide, *details: TIO.*

Loop Head peninsula, *SW of Kilkee:* good sea views and walks.

Miltown Malbay, *117 (SO), 229 bus from Lahinch.* Scoil Éigse Willie Clancy, in tribute to Clare's greatest piper, *July. Details: Kilkee TIO.* **Silver Strand,** *2 m (3 km) N of Miltown Malbay:* safe bathing. **Slieve Callan,** *6 m (10 km) E of Miltown Malbay:* the highest point in W Clare. It can be climbed from the Miltown Malbay–Inagh L55, *6 m (10 km) E of Miltown Malbay.* Fine views of surrounding countryside. Bicycles: Byrne and Sons, Ennis Road, tel: Miltown Malbay 49.

Moneen Church, *N side of Loop Head peninsula:* contains the 'Little Ark'. In 1850, people of district were refused land for a church and built this box on wheels in which they celebrated Mass on the seashore 'no man's land', between the high and low tide marks.

Mountcashel Castle, *2 m (3 km) N of Sixmilebridge on L11:* built by King of Thomond in late 15th c, recently restored. NM. *Refreshments from 11.30 a.m. daily, dinner and dancing starting 7 p.m. Details: (061)314777.*

Moyasta, *on N67 between Kilrush and Kilkee:* Taylor's pub has changed little this century, with skillets and griddles in old-time kitchen.

Newtown Castle, *2 m (3 km) S of Ballyvaughan:* five storey 16th c tower is round on square base.

Quilty, *4 m (6 km) SW of Miltown Malbay on N67 coast road:* take a currach to Mutton Island, *2 m (3 km) offshore.*

Quin Abbey, *6 m (10 km) E of Ennis:* well-preserved ruins of Franciscan friary founded 1402. Remains of a Norman castle were used to build friary; three of the castle's towers still stand at angles of friary building. You should be able to climb spiral stairs to top of one tower for fine views.

St Brigid's Well, *2 m (3 km) NW of Liscannor:* waters of roadside well said to have curative properties. Pilgrimages *July, Aug.*

Scattery Island, *2 m (3 km) offshore from Cappach Pier, near Kilrush:* 6th c monastic settlement remains include five churches, one round tower. *Guided tours, summer boat service, daily, details: Kilrush 272/275/276.*

Spancilhill, *8 m (13 km) E of Ennis:* Horse Fair, *late June.*

Galway

Pop. 37,000, 135 m (217 km) W of Dublin, 199 m (320 km) SW of Belfast. EC. Thurs. TIO: Áras Fáilte, near railway station. (091)63081. All year. Bus and train enquiries: Ceannt station, (091)62141. 112 bus from Belfast, 117, 120 bus from Cork, 85, 106, 267, 231 from Limerick, 114, 115, 126, 247, from Sligo. Train from Dublin. Coach tours: SO. Details: TIO. Taxis: Eyre Square.

The West's major town, set at the mouth of the River Corrib, on the edge of what is now the western Gaeltacht (Irish-speaking area), Galway was originally a fishing community, which grew prosperous on continental trade. It then supported an affluent merchant class which commissioned many fine buildings, and the visitor with a sense for the past will find much of interest here. The city has long since recovered the vigour it lost during the Famine, and today, it's prosperous but not brash with plenty of pubs and restaurants. Oyster Festival: world oyster opening championships. Much socialising, *Sept, details, TIO.*

Cathedral, *University Road, near salmon weir bridge;* opened 1965, controversial modern design.**D**

Collegiate Church of St Nicholas, *entrance just off*

Shop Street: built by Anglo–Normans in 1320, later enlarged. Tradition has it that Columbus worshipped here before setting out on his voyage of discovery. Excellent restored, many fine carvings and relics from Middle Ages. 'Son et Lumière' performances tell story of Galway and church in enthralling blend of sound and light. *July, Aug only. Tues, Thurs, 9 p.m. Details: TIO.***D**

Reference library, *Hynes Building, St Augustine Street:* much local interest material. *Mon–Sat, tel: (091)62471; 61666.*

Stone Art Gallery, *14 Foster Street:* regular exhibitions—ceramics, graphics, sculptures. *Mon–Sat, 9.30 a.m.–5.30 p.m. Tel: (091)83179.* **University College art gallery:** occasional exhibitions. *Details: (091)7611.* **Kenny Art Gallery,** *Middle Street, tel: (091) 62739.* **Druid Lane Theatre,** *Chapel Lane:* lunch-time, evening performances. Specialises in work by Anglo-Irish writers. *Summer. Details: (091)68617.* **Taibhdhearc na Gaillimhe,** *Middle Street:* regular Irish language productions all year. Fáilte, popular summer presentation of traditional song, music, dance, drama. *Details: (091)62024 after 2 p.m.* **Jesuit Hall,** *Sea Road:* Regular plays and entertainment in English.

Spanish Arch: built 1594 to protect quay where Spanish ships unloaded wares. Spanish Parade continues as Long Walk. Good views of estuary and entrance to docks.**D** **Lynch Memorial,** *Market Street:* Gothic doorway carved with skull and crossbones. According to tradition, the Mayor's son was hanged here for murdering a Spanish visitor in 1493. **Lynch's Castle,** *corner of Shop Street, Abbeygate Street:* incorporated in Allied Irish Bank, late 15th c, one of Ireland's finest surviving town castles. Photographs and texts explain history, *Mon–Fri, 10 a.m.–12.30 p.m.; 1.30 p.m.–3 p.m. Thurs, until 5 p.m.***D**

John F. Kennedy Park, *Eyre Square:* plaque marks where President Kennedy addressed people of Galway in 1963, on receiving freedom of the city. Albert Power's celebrated statue of Pádraig Ó Conaire, pioneer of literary revival earlier this century, also great iron cannon presented to Connaught Rangers at end of Crimean War.**D** **19 Eyre Square,** *(Bank of Ireland):* silver sword and Great Mace. Sword 19th c, 1710 Mace an exceptionally fine piece of Irish silverwork. *Mon–Fri, 10 a.m.–12.30 p.m., 1.30 p.m.–3 p.m. Thurs, until 5 p.m.*

Newtownsmith: pleasant riverside walk to salmon weir bridge. In season, salmon can be seen making their way to Lough Corrib. River Corrib, fine riverside strolls. University Road canal bridge, along tree-lined Upper Canal Road to Lower Canal Road, via Dominick Street to Claddagh Quay. Claddagh was once an individual, Irish-speaking fishing village on W bank of Corrib estuary and home of the Claddagh ring. In the city centre, bounded by Merchant's Road, Shop Street, Cross Street, there are some fine old doorways and windows. In Lydon-House restaurant, 5 Shop Street, interesting carved stones. The city centre lanes, including Buttermilk Lane (off Shop Street), O'Gorman's Lane (behind St Nicholas Collegiate Church) and Kirwan's Lane (off Cross Street) make for interesting rambling.

Royal Tara China, *Tara Hall:* fine bone, china made, decorated, gilded. Visits by app., shop. *All year, Mon–Fri, 9 a.m.–1 p.m.; 2 p.m.–5 p.m. Works closed first two weeks Aug.* Galway Crystal, *Merlin Park: Tours by arr, tel: (091)57311.* Kennys, *High Street, Upper Abbeygate Street:* antiquarian books. *Mon–Sat, 9 a.m.–6 p.m. Details: (091)62739/61014.* O'Gorman's *Shop Street:* wide range of books. Nora Barnacle, later to be wife of James Joyce, worked at O'Gorman's printing works 80 years ago. *Mon–Sat, 9 a.m.–5.30 p.m. 6 p.m. closing Fri.*

Greyhound racing, *New Sports Ground: Feb–Dec, Tues, Fri, 8.30 p.m.* During Galway Race Week at end of July, beginning of Aug, *Mon–Fri. Details: (091)62273.* Galway Airport, *4 m (6 km) NE of Galway:* pleasure flights with Galway Flying Club. *Details: (091)84111.* Boat trips: depart for Lough Corrib from Waterside on E banks of River Corrib. *Daily, 3.30 p.m. SO. Details: Frank Dolan, Riverside, Woodquay, tel: (091)65841.*

AROUND GALWAY

Annaghdown, *8 m (13 km) N of Galway on E shores of Lough Corrib:* ruins of castle and ancient church on monastery site where St Brendan the Navigator said to have died. Nave and chancel can still be seen.

An Spidéal, *243, 244 bus from Galway.* Races, town's major attraction, *June. Details: Galway TIO, (091)63081.* **Church** (C): completed in 1904 in Celtic Romanesque style renowned for architectural excellence.**D** Stone Art Gallery, *Cnocanglas:* ceramics, paintings, sculptures, *Mon–Sat. Sheltered beach.*

Ardamullivan Castle (NM), *5 m (8 km) S of Gort:* ruins of 16th c O'Shaughnessy stronghold.

Ardnageeha, *1 m (1.5 km) W of Cong sawmill on L101:* forest walks, car park, picnic area, good views of Lough Corrib.

Athenry, *15 m (24 km) E of Galway on T4, 235, 236, 241 bus from Galway. Also train.* Its Norman walls are best preserved in Ireland. Five out of six original wall towers survive; only imperious North Gate remains of five mediaeval entrances. **Athenry Castle:** 13th c. Adjacent public park, children's playground. Ruins of Dominican Priory of Ss. Peter and Paul, built in 1241, destroyed by Cromwellians in 1652.

Aughanure Castle, *3 m (5 km) E of Oughterard:* built by O'Flahertys in 16th c. Four storey tower stands on island, protected by fast-flowing stream. Expertly restored. *Mid June–Sept 30, daily, 10 a.m.–1 p.m.; 2 p.m.–7 p.m. otherwise by arr. with caretaker.*

Aughrim, *2 m (3 km) SE of Kilconnell, 237 bus from Ballinasloe (Fri only).* Small village takes name from battle fought on nearby ridge in 1691. Protestant Williamite forces defeated mainly Catholic Irish and French forces, determining future course of Irish history. **Aughrim Museum,** *St Catherine's National School:* two hundred exhibits, including many mementoes of the battle, ancient household utensils, stone axes and number of local archaeological finds. *By arr. Martin Joyce, curator, tel: (0905)3717.*

Ballinasloe, *40 m (64 km) E of Galway on T4, 85, 110, 113, 241 bus from Galway. Also train. Bus and train enquiries: (0905)2105.* Best known for its great October Horse Fair, an eight day carnival. **St Michael's Church** (C), *S of town,* 19th c, stained glass by Harry Clarke.**D**

Ballinasloe Castle: ruins of 14th c structure that commanded strategic brige over River Suck. Swimming pool: indoor, heated, *Station Road, Wed–Sat. Tel: (0905)2293.* Millbrook Riding Centre, *tel: (0905)2372.* Bicycles: P. Clarke, *Dunlo Street, tel: (0905)2417.* Ballinasloe Golf Club, *9 holes, tel: (0905)2126.*

Ballinderry Castle, *2 m (3 km) SE of Tuam,* one of last castles built in Ireland. Good state of repair.

Ballybrit Racecourse, *2 m (3 km) E of Galway:* main races held over five giddy days, *end July, beginning Aug.* Galway Race Week a remarkable social event. *Other races, Sept, Oct. Details: (091)62870.*

Ballykeen Castle, *3 m (5 km) NW of Cong:* ruins of 13th c de Burgos fortress by Lough Mask.

Bermingham House, *2 m (3 km) NE of Tuam off road to Levally Lough:* headquarters of Bermingham and North Galway Hunt. Georgian, magnificent plasterwork and furniture, *weekday aft.*

Carraroe, *W of L100:* many fine beaches, including unique Coral Strand.

Claregalway, *6 m (10 km) NE of Galway on N17 to Tuam, 240, 247, 249 bus from Galway.* Ruins of Franciscan friary built in 1252, suppressed by Henry VIII. By bridge over River Clare, large 15th c de Burgo castle in good repair. Rockmount Riding Centre, *tel: (091) 88147.*

Clarenbridge, *8 m (13 km) SE of Galway on N18:* Burke's Oyster Inn renowned for its oysters. Part of Galway Oyster Festival takes place here, *Sept. (091)86107.*

Clonbur: Petersburg House, largely ruins, once home of Lynch family, one of whose members, John, was a signatory of American Declaration of Independence. Forest walks by S shores of Lough Mask. Take L101 through Cornamona to Leenane on Killary Harbour for one of Connemara's most scenic routes. About 25 m (40 km).

Clonfert Cathedral, *15 m (24 km) NE of Portumna:* original monastery founded by St Brendan the Navigator in 563. Destroyed six times before becoming Augustinian priory in 12th c. Late 12th c doorway is finest example in Ireland of Romanesque style.

Cloondooan Castle, *5 m (8 km) SW of Gort on L55:* once one of strongest in Thomond, now ruined, destroyed after 1586 seige. Nearby is Lough Bunny.

Cong, *S Mayo, between Lough Corrib and Lough Mask, 242 bus from Galway.* 12th c abbey. Rory O'Connor, last High King of Ireland, buried here. Cross of Cong in National Museum, Dublin.

Ashford Castle: 18th c, restored by Sir Benjamin Guinness, of a certain brewing family, now a luxury hotel. On payment of small fee, you can wander round beautiful demesne, see castellated towers and attractive bridge. *Details: Cong 3.*

The Crusheens, *just outside village:* small heaps of crosses. Funeral corteges halt here, a prayer is said and more crosses added. **Cong Caves:** over 40 underground caves in and around village, once places of refuge for highwaymen and patriots. Some can be explored. Cong Salmon Hatchery: *by app. tel: Cong 49.* **Cong Wood:** forest walks, viewing tower. Enter from Cong village, through abbey grounds, across the river. Cong Riding Centre, *tel: Cong 29.* Bicycles: O'Connor's Garage, *tel: Cong 8.*

Coole Demesne, *2 m (3 km) N of Gort, due W of N18, 110, 120, 122, (SO), 124, 231 bus from Galway.* Once home of Lady Gregory, now national forest and wildlife park. Sadly, only ruined walls and stables remain of once fine house where she held literary court with such notables as Sean O'Casey, W. B. Yeats, G. B. Shaw, J. M. Synge, Frank O'Connor. Famous tree, where they carved their initials while taking after dinner air, can be

seen. Picnic areas, forest walks, nature trails. Leaflet detailing trails is available, and nearby Coole Lake still has swans. *Daily.*

Correen, *5 m (8 km) SE of Ballinasloe, on L27:* forest walks.

Corrib View, *2 m (3 km) E of Oughterard:* good views over lake. If this leaves you unsatisfied, follow minor road NW along lakeshore. This peters out 8 m (13 km) from Oughterard, all the while giving excellent views of lake.

De Bermingham Castle, *1 m (1.5 km) W of Dunmore:* 13th c, good state of repair. Also, fine doorway and central tower of nearby Augustinian abbey founded by Walter de Bermingham in 1425.

Derryhivenny Castle (NM), *3 m (5 km) NE of Portumna, just E of T31:* this well-preserved castle, erected in 1653, was one of last built in Ireland.

Dooros Peninsula: fine views of N end of Lough Corrib. Minor road runs to end of peninsula.

Doorus House, *3 m (5 km) NW of Kinvara on shores of Kinvara Bay:* mansion where Count de Basterot, traveller and writer, entertained friends, including Yeats and Lady Gregory on the occasion of the founding of Dublin's Abbey Theatre. Now Youth Hostel. *Tel: (091)37173.*

Drumacoo Church, *12 m (20 km) NW of Gort:* parts of this church of St Sorney may date from 8th c, S doorway is early Gothic, built around 1200.

Dry Canal, *near Cong:* built during great famine 130 years ago. Hundreds of labourers toiled for over four years, but as soon as water was let into the canal, it drained off through porous limestone. Only small section near Lough Mask has any water. Best place to see it is on bridge to N of L101 to Clonbur.

Dunmore, *8 m (13 km) NE of Tuam on N83:* numerous archaeological remains, mainly ring forts.

Fiddaun Castle (NM), *5 m (8 km) SW of Gort:* well preserved O'Shaughnessy fortress.

Furbo, *2 m (3 km) E of An Spidéal:* fine, sandy beach.

Glann, *6 m (10 km) NW of Oughterard on shore of Lough Corrib:* forest walks, car park, picnic area.

Neale, *just NE of Neale House, on L98:* 'Gods of Neale' elaborately carved and inscribed stone, 19th c archaeological hoax.

Gorumna Island, *S of bridge joining Lettermullan Island to S Connemara:* ruin of 16th c castle. Lettermullan stages currach races during summer.

Headford, *18 m (29 km) N of Galway on T40, 120, 124, 242, 249, 259 bus from Galway.* Popular angling centre adjacent to Lough Corrib. Boats can be hired at Greenfield, 4 m (6 km) W of Headford on E shore of lough.

Inchagoill Island, *N reaches of Lough Corrib, 5 m (8 km) SW of Cong.* Boats from Cong, Oughterard. Beautifully wooded island, largest in lake, site of 5th c Teampall Pharaic church, the 9th/10th c Teampall na Naomh (Church of the Saints), and the Stone of Lugna, said to be oldest Christian inscription in Europe, with exception of Rome's catacombs.

Inverin, *18 m (29 km) W of Galway on L100, 243, 244 bus from Galway.* Ruined castle by shore, many sandy beaches nearby. Youth Hostel.

Keelhilla, *8 m (13 km) SW of Kinvara, in N Co. Clare:* was ancient hermitage of St Colman and scene of miracle wherein the feast laid for King Guaire and his nobles flew through the air for the hungry saint.

Kelly's Cave Wood, *1 m (1.5 km) E of Cong on L101:* forest walks, try exploring Kelly's Cave and Captain Webb's Hole.

Kilcolgan, *2 m (3 km) S of Clarenbridge:* Morans Oyster Cottage, old pub famous for its seafood. *Tel: (091)86113.*

Kilconnell, *8 m (13 km) W of Ballinasloe on T4 to Athenry:* Franciscan Friary, founded in 1353, gothic style nave, choir, side aisles, S transept, cloisters, domestic apartments. Instructions for borrowing key on entrance gate. At W end of village 1682 Donnellan memorial cross. (NM).

Kilcornan, *1 m (1.5 km) S of Clarenbridge on N18:* forest walks.

Kilbennan, *3 m (5 km) NW of Tuam, beside L4 to Ballinrobe:* next to ruined 16th c Gothic church of St Benin is an 11th c round tower.

Kilcreevanty, *1 m (1.5 km) E of Kilbennan:* remains of Benedictine nuns' settlement founded about 1200.

Killeeneen, *3 m (5 km) W of N6 at Craughwell:* church is burial place of Raftery, blind Mayo-born poet, who spent much of his life travelling Co. Galway.

Kilmacduagh, *3 m (5 km) SW of Gort:* the monastery founded here in 600 has an impressive array of churches. The nearly round tower, restored a century ago, leans about 2 ft (0.6 metre), Galway's answer to Pisa.

Kiltartan, *1 m (1.5 km) N of Gort:* church of great antiquity. Interesting 15th c altar-tomb.

Kiltiernan, *9 m (15 km) N of Gort, just off N18 to Galway:* ruins of 8th c church inside a large stone enclosure. (NM).

Kinvara

Kinvara, *117, 238 bus from Galway:* charming fishing village in SE corner of Galway Bay. Ideal base for exploring Gort area antiquities and Burren. Traught Strand, 4 m (7 km) sandy beach.

Dunguaire Castle, 16th c, restored, strikingly set on rock at edge of Galway Bay. *Apr 1–Sept 30, daily, 10 a.m.–5 p.m.* mediaeval banquets nightly, *May 15–Sept 30, 5.45 p.m. 9 p.m.* Entertainment includes Irish music, dancing, scenes from plays by writers with local connections, like Lady Gregory. W. B. Yeats, and readings from Raftery the poet. *Details: (091)37108, TIO, Galway, tel: (091)63081, Castle Tours, Shannon Airport, tel: (061)61788.*

Knockaunnageeragh Mountain, *7 m (11 km) NW of Oughterard:* fine views over Lough Corrib.

Knockmaa Hill (Cnoc Má), *6 m (10 km) E of Headford, just S of L98 to Tuam:* traditional home of King Finbarra and Connacht fairies. One legend says it is burial place of Maeve, mythological Queen of Connacht. Excellent views from top.

Knockmoy Abbey, *7 m (11 km) SE of Tuam:* founded in 1189 by Cathal O'Connor, King of Connacht, whose tomb is preserved within the ruins. Traces of ancient murals decorate N wall of chancel. Attractively set by small lake.

Kylebrack, *5 m (8 km) SE of Loughrea on L99:* forest walks.

Labane Church (C), *5 m (8 km) N of Gort on N18 to Galway:* early examples of Dublin School of Stained Glass. The nearby private residence of Tullira Castle was the home of Edward Martyn, the school's founder.

Lake Boliska, *3 m (5 km) N of An Spidéal:* excellent walk here from coast.

Lambert Mansion, *3 m (5 km) NW of Athenry:* ruins of birthplace of Isabelle Lambert, mother of Sir Edward Carson, who led Unionist opposition to Irish Home Rule at beginning of century.

Leaba Phadraig (Patrick's Bed), *between Tuam and Tulynadaly Hill:* altar set in pile of stones. The two indentations have always been bare of grass: they mark where the saint's knees rested while he prayed.

Lisacormack Fort, *1 m (1.5 km) E of Tuam:* largest of the area's many forts.

Loughpark Crannóg, *2 m (3 km) E of Tuam on Rye-hill road:* prehistoric lake dwelling.

Loughrea, *20 m (32 km) E of Galway on N6, 85, 110, 112, 113, 118, 241 bus from Galway.* Delightfully set on N shore of Lough Rea. **St Brendan's Cathedral** (C): this somewhat dull-looking cathedral has fine stained glass windows by Sarah Purser, Evie Hone and embroideries designed by Jack Yeats. Magnificent repository of modern Irish ecclesiastical art. **D Carmelite monastery,** founded by Richard de Burgo, 1300, in excellent repair. Adjacent modern abbey.

GAA Museum, *Dunkellin Street:* many fascinating items illustrate history of GAA in Co. Galway. *By arr., J. P. Cusack, (091)65181 (office); (091)41155 (home).* Author Seamus O'Kelly was born in Loughrea in 1880. This fine but somewhat neglected writer of poetry and drama died in Dublin aged 38. All his books, including *The Weaver's Grave* are currently out of print. House marked with plaque, grave nearby. Boats: Paddy Fitzgerald, Loughrea Sailing Club, *tel: (091)41269;* Denis McCarthy, *Lake Road, tel: (091)41011.* Aille Cross Equitation Centre, *tel: (091)41216.*

Menlough Castle, *2 m (3 km) N of Galway on E bank of River Corrib:* attractive ivy-covered ruin. From Menlough, follow progress of canal to Lough Corrib.

Milltown, *8 m (13 km) NW of Tuam on N17:* admirable walks in pleasant wooded country. Brown trout fishing in River Clare.

Monivea, *6 m (10 km) NE of Galway on L54:* noted for great lawns, once linen bleaching greens. Large estate grounds once belonged to Ffrench family. Key to Ffrench mausoleum from gate lodge. Nearby forest walk.

Mountbellew Demesne, *10 m (16 km) NE of Monivea:* forest walks, car park, picnic area. Mountbellew Golf Club, *9 holes.*

Mount Gable, *near Clonbur:* climb for superb lake views.

Moycullen, *7 m (11 km) NW of Galway on N59. 116(SO), 242 bus from Galway.* Connemara Celtic Crystal. *Mon–Fri, 9.30 a.m.–6 p.m. by app.* Shop, *June–Sept, plus Sat, Sun. Tel: (091)85172.* Connemara Marble Industries, marble jewellery, cutting, adjoining tearoom, shop. *Mon–Sat, 9 a.m.–6 p.m. Tel: (091)85102.*

Moyode Castle, *2 m (3 km) SE of Athenry:* ruined mansion with ancient castle in grounds. Persse family who lived here, together with Persses of Roxboro founded famous Galway Blazers, noted in hunting circles. Liam Mellowes and Galway followers occupied house for several days in 1916 Rising.

Nostaig Fort, *3 m (5 km) NE of Gort:* to W are Caher-glassane Lake and Castle and ancient church of Killomoran.

Oranmore, *5 m (8 km) SE of Galway:* Galway Bay Sailing Centre, sailing, canoeing, wind surfing. *Details: (091)64585.*

Oughterard, *17 m (27 km) NW of Galway, on W side*

of Lough Corrib, *116 bus (SO) from Galway, 242 from Clifden.* Noted angling resort, often called 'Gateway to Connemara'. V'Soske-Joyce, exquisite hand-made carpets, rugs, wall-hangings. *By arr. Tel: (091)82113/82140.* Sections of the old Galway—Clifden railway are suitable for walks. Pony trekking: Canrower Stud, *tel: (091)82120.* Bicycles: T. Tuck, *tel: (091) 82335.* Golf Club, Gurthreeva, *9 holes, tel: (091)82131.* The 10 m (16 km) drive along the N59 to Maam Cross has amazing variety of bog, lake, moorland, mountain scenery. Continue W from Maam Cross along shores of Loughs Shindilla and Ooriid, with Maamturk peaks to N and Twelve Bens to W.

Pallas Castle (NM), *6 m (10 km) W of Portumna, N of T41/L55:* 16th–18th c ruins.

Pigeon Hole, *1 m (1.5 km) N of Cong sawmill on L101 to Clonbur:* steps lead down to atmospheric cave, chasm, underground river. Forest walks in adjoining Pigeon Hole Wood. Car park, picnic area.

Portumna, *40 m (65 km) SE of Galway, 118 bus from Galway (SO), 241 from Galway.* Noted fishing centre for Shannon and Lough Derg. **Portumna Castle** (NM), built in 1609, accidentally destroyed by fire, 1826. N entrance gate designed by Adams, now being restored. Set in Portumna demesne. **Priory:** present remains, largely 15th c, are those which survived Cromwell in 1641.

Portumna Forest Park: this 1,000 acre wildlife sanctuary shelters many species of animal and bird life, including red and fallow deer. Well laid-out nature trail, viewing stands, lakeside observation tower, car park picnic area, information centre. **D** Cruisers: Emerald Star Line, *tel: Portumna 120.*

The Punchbowl, *1 m (1.5 km) SW of Gort, just off N18:* almost perfect crater 100 ft (30 metres) in diameter and almost 150 ft (45 metres) deep. Beagh River flows from nearby Lough Cultra along floor of crater before disappearing. Many other nearby streams come to a similar end.

Rosmuck, *20 m (32 km) SE of Clifden, just off L102, 243, 244 bus from Galway.* Cottage where Patrick Pearse, leader of 1916 Easter Rising, stayed to improve his Irish, he also wrote most of his work here. Signposted. *Daily during summer, otherwise key from house on main road, 100 yards (90 metres) W of turn to cottage.*

Ross Abbey, *2 m (3 km) NW of Headford:* Franciscan friary founded 1357, destroyed by Cromwellians in 1656. Remains of kitchen fish tank, mill, bakery.

Rosturra, *6 m (10 km) SW of Portumna off T41:* forest walks.

Salthill, *W suburb of Galway. TIO, Salthill. (091)63081, May–Sept. Bus from Galway.* One of Ireland's leading seaside resorts, good walks along promenade. Kenny Fine Bindings, *178 Upper Salthill: (091)22752.* **Leisureland,** wide range of indoor sports facilities. Main complex, *June–Sept, daily.* Also special events. Pool, *aft, eve, all year, except Mon, Tues. Details: (091)21455.* Bicycles: Salthill Rentals, *tel: (091)61821, (091)62341– night.* Galway Golf Club, *18 holes, tel: (091)21827.*

Shrule Castle, *on T40 between Headford and Ballinrobe, 120, 259 bus from Ballinasloe, Galway.* Museum, library: items related to local folklife, history and geology. Visitors welcome at any reasonable time.*Tel: (093)21277.*

Thoor Ballylee, *near Gort:* 16th c castle once summer home of W. B. Yeats. *10 a.m.–6 p.m. 1 May–30 Sept, Details: Peterswell 8 or Galway TIO.*

Tirneevin Church, *just N of Kilmacduagh:* exceptionally fine stained glass window by George Campbell, denoting Christ the Sower.

Toberroe, *3 m (5 km) W of Athenry on T4 to Galway:* forest walks.

Toorleitra, *3 m (5 km) W of Woodford:* forest walks.

Tuam, *15 m (24 km) NW of Galway. EC. Thurs. TIO*

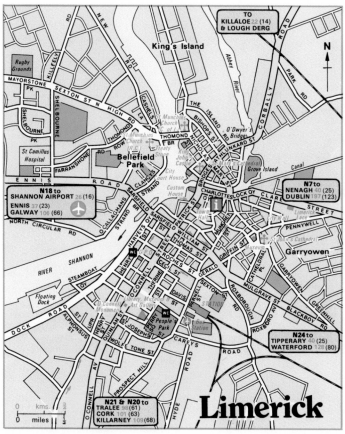

Limerick

tel: (093)24463 July–Aug. Bus enquiries: CIE, Galway. (091)62142. 112, 114, 115, 120, 122, 235, 247, 267 *bus from Galway.* Small market town, formerly major ecclesiastical centre. **Cathedral of the Assumption** (C), built in 1830s. Many fine carvings on windows and tower. In grounds, statue of illustrious 19th c cleric, John McHale, Archbishop of Tuam.**D St Mary's Cathedral** (CI), built in 1860s, incorporates windows and arch of late 12th chancel, 14th c Chapter House at E end.**D** 12th c Cross in Town square.

Mill Museum, *Shop Street:* this, the first industrial museum in West of Ireland, is built round fully operational cornmill and adjacent miller's house. Its kitchen and bedroom are just as they were when miller Mike Farrell and his wife lived here in first decade of century. Small exhibition hall, collection of folk items. *Daily, June–Sept, 10.30 a.m.–12.30 p.m.; 3 p.m.–5 p.m. Otherwise, Dr John A. Claffey, 5 Vicar Street; Jarlath Canney, Canney Bros, The Square, tel: (093)24141.*

Tuam Arts Centre, *Town Hall, The Square:* regular functions, including theatre. Details in local paper. Corrib Craft, *The Mall:* handcrafts traditional Irish furniture. *App. preferred. Details: (093)24113.* Swimming pool: indoor, heated, *Mon–Sun, tel: (093)24554.*D Bicycles: Murphy's Cycle Stores, *tel: (093)24292.* Golf Club, Barnacurragh, *9 holes, tel: (093)24354.*

Tully, *S Connemara:* new church of St Colmcile.

Turoe Stone (NM), *3 m (5 km) N of Loughrea, E of L11 to Bullaun:* 1 st c pillar stone, decorated with Celtic scrollwork.

Limerick

Pop. 65,000, 15 m (24 km) E of Shannon, 123 m (198 km) SW of Dublin. EC Thurs. TIO: Granary Centre, tel: (061)317522. All year. Bus and train enquiries: Colbert Station. (061)42433. 120, 153 *bus from Cork,* 86 *bus from Dublin,* 106, 111, 120, 231 *bus from Galway,* 106, 195 *bus from Killarney,*

106, 111, 220, 227, 231 *bus from Shannon airport. Train from Cork, Dublin, Killarney. Taxis: railway station.*

The fourth largest city in Ireland, and an important market and manufacturing centre, Limerick gives a misleading initial impression of griminess. The city's culture and history will repay careful exploration, especially now that its wide range of monuments and art galleries have been enhanced by an impressive new city museum and the recently established Belltable Arts Centre, arguably the liveliest cultural forum in Ireland outside Dublin.

St John's Cathedral (C), *near St John's Square:* 19th c Gothic building has the tallest spire in Ireland. Ask at Presbytery to see exquisite 15th c mitre and cross.**D St Mary's Cathedral** (CI), *junction of Nicholas Street and Bridge Street:* built 1172 by Donal O'Brien, last King of Munster. Many interesting monuments, 15th c choir stalls. Son et Lumière performances, *early June–mid Sept, Mon, Wed, Fri, Sun, 9.30 p.m.*D **Dominican Church** (C), *Baker Place, Pery Street:* early 19th c, has impressive 17th c statue. Our Lady of Limerick. Note modern fresco over chancel.**D Church of the Holy Rosary,** *Ennis Road, 1 m (1.5 km) from city centre:* its stations of the cross were worked by the craftsmen of Oberammergau in Bavaria. Figure of Blessed Virgin on campanile carved by Oisín Kelly.**D**

Limerick Museum, *1 St John's Square:* paintings and photographs of local scenes, personalities, archaeological finds, coins, many examples from the city's trade history, relics of 1919 Limerick Soviet. Fascinating collection, strongly recommended. *Tues–Sat, 10 a.m.–1 p.m.; 2.15 p.m.–5 p.m. Details: (061)47826.* **Institute for Higher Education,** *Plassy, 3 m (5 km) E of Limerick on N24:* Hunt Collection has about 1,000 items of Irish antiquities and mediaeval art, including Bronze Age implements and an interesting selection of early Christian brooches. *Apr–Sept, Mon–Fri, 9.30 a.m.–5.30 p.m. Otherwise by app., (061)43644.*

Belltable Arts Centre, *69 O'Connell Street:* art exhibitions, theatre, other cultural events. Gallery, *daily except Sun, 9 a.m.–10 p.m.,* Coffee shops *daily, except Sun, 10 a.m.–5.30 p.m.*

Theatre *usually starts at 8 p.m. Details: (061)49866.* **Library and Art Gallery,** *Pery Square, People's Park:* paintings by Keating, Jellett, Walter Osborne, Camille Souter, Percy French, Charles Lamb, etc. Special exhibitions. *Mon–Fri, 10 a.m.–1 p.m.; 2.30 p.m.–8 p.m. Sat, 10 a.m.–1 p.m. Tel: (061)44668.* **Goodwin Galleries,** *74 O'Connell Street:* regular exhibitions. *Mon–Fri, 10.30 a.m.–5 p.m. Closed lunch. Tel: (061)47635.* **Fitz Gallery,** *Upper Cecil Street: Mon–Sat, 10 a.m.–5 p.m. Closed Thurs.* **The Gallery,** *Elsinore, 4 Castletroy:* paintings, wall hangings, sculptures by Anne Fitzgerald. By app., (061)49995.

Walls of Limerick: only portions remain. Best place to see them is at rear of Lelia Street. The two massive gateways at entrance to grounds of St John's hospital are town gate and outer gate of citadel. **Treaty Stone,** *W end of Thomond Bridge:* Treaty of Limerick said to have been signed here in 1691. **St John's Square:** built over 200 years ago, it fell into disrepair. Recently, many of the houses have been restored. **Boru House,** *Mulgrave Street,* childhood home of magnificent and rather neglected writer Kate O'Brien.

Town Hall, *Rutland Street:* portraits of such notables as Daniel O'Connell, Gerald Griffin. *Mon–Fri, office hours.* **The Granary,** *Michael Street:* 230 year old five storey building housing Irish Costume Museum, craft workshops, restaurant, pub. *Details: TIO.* **King John's Castle,** *Thomond Bridge:* traditional Irish entertainment—Seisiún—during summer. Poetry readings. Military museum planned. Snacks during Seisiún performances. *Daily, 10 a.m.–6.30 p.m. Details: (061)49195.* **Limerick Market,** *foot of High Street:* all kinds of bargains, best on *Sat.* **Good Shepherd Convent,** *Clare Street, on Dublin Road:* 150 year old tradition of lace-making, *viewing, Mon–Fri, 9.30 a.m.–1 p.m.; 1 p.m.–5.30 p.m. Details: (061)45178.* Enjoyable walks along both banks of the Shannon and in Mary Street area. Guided walking tours: 1.5 hour duration, taking in most city sights, depart daily from Treaty Stone. SO. *Details: TIO.*

South's, *Quinlan Street:* unchanged over many years, with remarkable antique mirror on wall behind bar. **Punch's,** *Punch's Cross, Dooradoyle:* popular haunt for racing fraternity, nightly sing-

songs at the piano. **Hogan's Thomond House,** *O'Connell Place:* 200 years old, with tiny snug, two mahogany bars.

Limerick Racecourse, *Greenpark:* flat racing and steeplechases all year. *Details: (061)29377/ 27961/29416/ 28972.* Greyhound racing: *Markets Field, Mulgrave Street: Mon, Fri, Sat eve. Details: (061)45170.* Swimming pools: indoor heated, Roxboro Road, *tel: (061)43303;* St Enda's Sports Complex, *Kilmallock Road, daily, closed Fri,* Outdoor: Ennis Road, *opp. Limerick Ryan Hotel and Corbally on River Shannon.* Bicycles: Cresent Cycle Shop, *Dooradoyle, tel: (061)40901;* Limerick Sports Store, *10 William Street, tel: (061)45647/44245;* Noel McMahon and Son, *24 Roches Street, tel: (061)46718;* Nestor Bros, *28 O'Connell Street, tel: (061)44096.* Castletroy Golf Club, *18 holes, tel: (061)45261.* Ballyclough, *18 holes, tel: (061)44083.* Youth Hostel, *1 Pery Square, tel: (061)44672.*

AROUND LIMERICK

Adare, *10 m (16 km) SW of Limerick on N21. TIO: (062)94255 June–Aug. 107 (SO), 195, 208 bus from Limerick.* Claimed to be the prettiest village in Ireland, set in wooded surroundings on W bank of River Maigue. Broad Main Street, thatched cottages, lichen-covered churches. The 15th c Franciscan friary, on slope overlooking river, is Adare's finest monastic ruin. To S is fine old Kilmallock Gate. Golf Club, *18 holes.*

Adare Manor: splendid 19th c house with many fine paintings and pleasure grounds. Closed at time of going to press. *Check with Adair TIO.* George Stacpoole Gallery, *daily.*

Desmond Castle: 13th c ruins overlooking river. Nearby are 11th c ruins of St Nicholas' church and 14th c Desmond Chapel. Adare Iron Works, *Station Road:* see wrought ironwork being made. *All year, Mon–Thurs, 8.30 a.m.–5.15 p.m. Fri, 8.30 a.m.–4 p.m. Tel: (061)94156.* Adare Manor Golf Club, *9 holes, tel: (061)94204.*

Ardagh, *3 m (5 km) N of Newcastle West:* ancient Reerassta ring fort (NM), 8th c Ardagh Chalice found here in 1868, now in National Museum, Dublin.

Ardnacrusha, *5 m (8 km) S of Lough Derg, 203 bus from Limerick.* ESB hydro-electric generating station. *Tours Mon–Thurs all year, except Bank Holidays, 10 a.m.–12 noon; 2 p.m.–4 p.m.Details: (061)45588.*

Ardpatrick, *3 m (5 km) S of Kilfinane:* on summit of hill overlooking tiny village, remains of church, said to have been founded by St Patrick, and round tower.

Askeaton, *16 m (26 km) W of Limerick on N69, 200 bus from Limerick.* Ruins of 15th c Desmond Castle on rocky islet in River Deel, well preserved tower and hall. *Key: Mr Casey, house beside gate.* Also fragments of 13th c St Mary's parish church next to Protestant church. Adjoining ruin is grave of poet Aubrey de Vere. Extensive remains of 15th c Franciscan friary on banks of River Deel. Swimming pool: open air. *June 1–Sept 15, daily.*

Ballinagrane, *2 m (3 km) S of Rathkeale:* Embury–Heck Memorial Church, named in honour of Philip Embury and Barbara Heck, who sailed with a group of Methodists from Limerick in 1760 and founded the Methodist church in America.

Ballinruane/Corronaher, *12 m (20 km) E of Newcastle West:* forest walks.

Ballylanders, *7 m (11 km) E of Kilfinane:* large roofless church, started in late 17th c, with tower forming part of castle.

Barnagh Gap, *4 m (6 km) SW of Newcastle West on N21:* magnificent views over four counties—Limerick, Clare, Tipperary and Kerry.

Beagh Castle, *4 m (6 km) NE of Askeaton:* ruin on shores of Shannon, fine views to airport.

Birdhill, *3 m (5 km) S of Killaloe:* Matt the Thresher's pub full of antiquity.

Broadford, *E Clare, 10 m (16 km) N of Limerick:* good coarse fishing in Doon Lake.

Bruree, *4 m (6 km) W of Kilmallock on L28, 153 bus from Limerick.* De Valera Museum. Numerous personal items, also items on local folklife, history, literature and archaeology. *Sun, Thurs, church holidays, 2.30 p.m.–5 p.m. Other times by*

arr: *Mrs L. Cregan, caretaker, in nearby house.* **D** Old royal forts, some dating from pre-Christian times. Also three 14th c de Lacy castles. Mill wheel near bridge over River Maigue, largest water wheel in the region, used to power adjoining mill.

Bunratty Castle and Folk Park, *8 m (13 km) W of Limerick, off N18 to Shannon Airport. All Limerick–Shannon buses.* Castle built 1460, now restored with one of best collections of 14th–17th c period furniture and furnishings in these islands. *1 Feb–30 Nov daily, 9.30 a.m.–5.30 p.m. Last admission, 4.45 p.m. June, July, Aug, Castle still closes 5.30 p.m., but Folk Park open until 7 p.m.* Mediaeval banquets *twice nightly, 5.45 p.m. and 8.45 p.m. Details: (061)61511.* Folk park in castle grounds has examples of houses from every part of the region and 19th c Irish village street. Also demonstrations of basket making, farriery, candle and bread making in authentically reconstructed setting. Reconstructed smallholdings, complete with genuine farmyard smells. Bunratty House courtyard, *end of park,* exhibition of agricultural machines. *All year, daily, 9.30 a.m.–5 p.m. June–Aug, until 8 p.m. Details: (061)61511.* **D** Durty Nelly's: nearby; very famous pub, very small, loads of atmosphere. Old ranges, open fires, súgán chairs, pianos, cages of live birds. Also seafood restaurant.

Carrigogunnell, *3 m (5 km) W of Mungret:* ruins of large 14th c fort destroyed during second siege of Limerick, 1691.

Castleconnell, *8 m (13 km) NE of Limerick, near Falls of Doonass. 218 bus from Limerick.* Enjoy walks along both banks of Shannon (nature trail signposted) in this famous salmon fishing village. To see the renowned Castleconnell fishing rods being made, contact John Enright. Water skiing: *O'Brien's Bridge, 3 m (5 km) N of Castleconnell. Details:* Brian McCarthy, Shannon Water-Ski Club, *(061)45540.*

Clare Glens, *just N of Glenstal:* Clare River flows through a gorge, making series of falls. Scenic walks signposted.

Craggaunowen Project

Craggaunowen Project, *Sixmilebridge:* fascinating pre-history, mediaeval antiquities, *Apr, May, Sept, Oct, daily, 10 a.m.-5 p.m., June 1-Aug 31, daily, 10 a.m.-6 p.m,* Tel: (061)72178.

Cratloe/Woodcockhill, *7 m (11 km) W of Limerick on N18:* extensive woodland walks, picnic area, car park.

Croom, *7 m (11 km) SE of Adare,* 153 bus from Limerick. Pleasant town on banks of River Maigue. Remains of Croom Castle, 1190 Fitzgerald stronghold. From Tory Hill, 2 m (3 km) NW of town, good views.

Cullaun, *2 m (3 km) NW of Kilkishen, off the L11, 10 m (16 km) NW of Limerick:* forest walks, lakeside picnic area, ruins of Cullaun House.

Curraghchase, *11 m (18 km) W of Limerick on N69, 200 bus from Limerick.* Estate of 19th c poet and author Aubrey de Vere, now National Park. House, with priceless works of art, destroyed in accidental fire in 1941. Tombstone on site where de Vere buried his pets, also earth mound where he sat to write. Gardens and arboretum. Picnic area, car park, caravan park and nature trail.

Cush, *2 m (3 km) N of Kilfinane:* extensive earthworks and burial mounds.

Daar River Gorge, *2 m (3 km) SW of Ardagh:* fine views from ring fort.

Doon Lake, *just off Tulla road, 3 m (5 km) NW of Broadford:* walks, picnic area, lay-by.

Drimmeen/Violet Hill, *1 m (1.5 km) N of Broadford on road to Mountshannon:* woodland walks.

Dromdeeven, *9 m (14 km) NW of Drumcollogher off L71:* forest walks, picnic area, car park.

Drumcollogher, *25 m (40 km) SW of Limerick:* porcelain products, Dresden figurines, *all year, Mon-Fri, 9 a.m.-1 p.m.; 2 p.m.-5 p.m. Closed first two weeks Aug and bank holidays. Details:* (063)9622.

Flagmount, *on E shores of Lough Graney:* lakeside forest walks, car park.

Foynes: climb hill overlooking village to see huge limestone cross built in 19th c to commemorate one Stephen Rice. Foynes-Tarbert N69: fine coastal views along this 12 m (19 km) stretch. Forest walks near village. Picnic area, lay-by, good Shannon views. Sailing: Sean Flynn, *tel: Foynes 178.*

Gallows Hill, *2 m (3 km) above Cratloe village off N18:* viewing point with fine vistas of Shannon estuary and airport 6 m (10 km) W. Picnic area, car park.

Glenaster waterfall, *4 m (6 km) NW of Newcastle West:* from lower Newcastle West-Glin road, cross fields and follow narrow paths to impressive fall on River Daar.

Glenstal Abbey, *9 m (14 km) W of Limerick, near Murroe village on SW slopes of Slievefelim mountains:* Benedictine college, grounds very beautiful in early summer when rhododendrons flower. Monks work at variety of crafts, including beekeeping, sculpture, stonecutting, silver ware. *By arr.,* (061) 81103.**D**

The Graves of the Leinstermen, *4 m (6 km) NE of Ballina:* on slopes of Touninna, highest peak in Arra mountains: a line of vast prehistoric slate slabs. Good views of Lough Derg.

Kildimo, *near Askeaton:* plenty of ruined castles in area. Also, 2 m (3 km) S of Kildimo see ancient oratory of Killulta, believed to be oldest church in Co. Limerick.

Kilfinane, *6 m (10 km) E of Kilmallock,* 212 bus from Limerick. Attractively set in valley surrounded by forests. Rising in background are Ballyhoura and Galtee mountains. See Kilfinane motte, great flat.topped mound encircled by three earthen ramparts. Best views in district from Slieveragh, 1,531 ft (467 metres), just NE of Kilfinane.

Killaloe, *13 m (21 km) NE of Limerick on L12, 206, 218 bus from Limerick.* St Flannan's Cathedral (CI), built 1182, restored recently. Fine Romanesque doorway, in grounds, St Flannan's oratory.**D** Flannan's Cathedral (C), perched on heights above town, in grounds, St Molua's oratory, moved here in 1929 from Friar's Island in Shannon prior to flooding for hydro-electric scheme.**D** Cross Shannon on 13 arch bridge to historic village of Ballina in Co. Tipperary. Cruisers: Atlantis Line, *tel:* (061)76281; Cormacruisers, *tel:* (061)76251: Derg Line Cruisers, *tel:* (061)76264; Lough Derg Day Cruises: *Details:* Limerick TIO.

Killmallock, *21 m (34 km) S of Limerick on T50A, 212 bus from Limerick.* Distinguished ecclesiastical ruins include remains of 13th c Dominican priory, N of town, on banks of River Lubagh. **John's Castle,** *corner of Sarsfield Street and Shears Street:* Peel tower in excellent repair. *Key:* Patrick O'Brien, *43 Milmount.* 400 yard section of old town walls, from rear of C church to Blossom Gate, only one of four gates to survive.

Knocklong, *S Limerick:* good walks on hill near village. Particularly good views from vicinity of Ryves castle ruins on hill. Riding: Willie Gleeson, Ballylooby House, *tel:* (062)53144; Scarteen House.

Lough Graney, *20 m (30 km) N of Limerick:* pleasant lakeside drive N of Feakle village.

Lough Gur, *10 m (16 km) SE of Limerick:* ringed with a remarkable variety of prehistoric remains: dolmens, stone circles, pillar stones, chamber stones, cairns, stone forts. 0.5 m (0.8 km) N of Holycross Road, largest stone circle in Ireland. Ruins of two mediaeval Desmond castles, one E

of lake, other S. Visitor interpretative centre, picnic areas, lakeside walks. During season, conducted walking tours. Centre, *May 1-Sept 30, Mon-Sat, 10 a.m.-1 p.m., 2 p.m.-6 p.m., Sun 2 p.m.-6 p.m. Details: Limerick TIO:***D**

Maghera Mountains, *SW of Lough Graney:* drives, walks. Minor road leads to Lough Ea, nearly 1,000 ft (300 metres) up, while another minor road leads to TV mast. From vicinity, excellent views of E Clare, S Galway.

Manister, *3 m (5 km) E of Croom:* ruins of Monasteranenagh, 12th c Cistercian abbey. Good carvings in church, remains of chapter house, abbey mill. Nearby, see remains of 14th c Rathmore Castle and ruins of ancient Rathmore ring fort.

Mountshannon, *5 m (8 km) NE of Scariff on T41:* fine harbour and pier on SW shores of Lough Derg. From pier hire boat for holy island of Iniscealtra in Lough Derg, with five churches and other remains of early Christian settlement. Sailing: K. Simmons, Iniscealtra Sailing Club, Shore House, Meelick, Whitegate. Mountshannon Youth Hostel, *tel: Mountshannon 9.*

Mungret, *3 m (5 km) S of Limerick on N69, 200 bus from Limerick.* Once site of outstanding monastery and centre of learning, now site of huge cement factory. All that's left of Mungret's 7th c glory are ruins of three churches, all accessible.

Newcastle West, *106, 107 (SO), 195 bus from Limerick,* Desmond castle, interesting remains of 13th c fortress. Also tower house of Glenquin Castle, built 1462, in excellent state of preservation. *Key:* W. Deeley, *nearby farmhouse.* Pleasant walks in the extensive demesne, with wooded parkland open at all times. Monument near church dedicated to W Limerick men who died in War of Independence. **World of Art,** *22 Beechwood Gardens:* Michael O'Dwyer's collection. Paintings of Irish political figures and landscapes. *Mon-Sun, 10.30 a.m.-10 p.m.* Scanlan's Cycle Store, *Maiden Street. Tel:* (069)62472.

Rathkeale, *18 m (29 km) SW of Limerick on N21, 195, 208 bus from Limerick.* Ruins of 13th c Augustinian priory. **Castle Matrix,** built in 1440 on site of ancient Celtic sanctuary to Matrix, their Mother Goddess. Here Edmund Spenser and Walter Raleigh met for first time. Today, 12,000 volume library has rare first editions of some leading Elizabethan poets, including Spenser. In castle, authentic furnishings, objets d'art, historic documents. From 80 ft (24 metre) tower, good view of surrounding counties. Home of Irish International Arts Centre, which holds seminars in graphic arts, poetry, drama. Mediaeval banquets for groups. *Castle and grounds, May 15-Sept 15, Sat-Tues, 1 p.m.-5 p.m. other times by app. Details:* (069) 64284. Riding: The Stables.

Shanagolden, *near Foynes:* ruins of Old Abbey, Augustinian foundation, with fine Gothic W door, two foot-bridges, fishpond, corbelled pigeon house 2 m (3 km) W of village. 2 m (3 km) S, ruins of Shanid Castle, mediaeval Fitzgerald fortress.

Shannon Airport, no facilities for plane spotting, but bar, restaurant, shop open to public. Occasional exhibitions. Regular summer craft fair planned. *Details: Shannon airport TIO,* (061)61664. *All year.* **Ballycaseymore House:** permanent exhibition of region's small industry, arts, crafts. *All year, Mon-Fri, 9.30 a.m.-5 p.m.* Swimming pool: heated, indoor, town centre, *Mon-Sun, details:* (061)61841. Shannon Golf Club, *Shannon Airport,* 18 holes, *tel:* (061)61020.

Tralee

Pop. 15,000, 20 m (32 km) NE of Killarney, 64 m (102 km) SW of Limerick, 187 m (300 km) SW of Dublin. All day closing: Wed. TIO: (066)21288. *All year. Bus and train enquiries:* (066)21211. 106, 117, 173, 194, 195 bus from Killarney. Trains from Cork, Dublin, Killarney.

A lively and attractively laid-out business centre and resort town; good food, good bookshops, and very handy for the Dingle peninsula.

Rose of Tralee Festival: a week of dancing and carousing, *end Aug–early Sept, details: TIO. Féile Pádraig: St Patrick's Week festivities, mid-Mar.*

St John's, (C) *Castle Street:* built 1870. Stations of the Cross by late Sean Keating, 1959 statue of locally-born St Brendan the Navigator.**D Holy Cross Church,** *Princes Street:* designed by Pugin in 19th c. Fine Michael Healy stained glass, sculptured stones from old Dominican abbey in priory.**D**

Rathass church, *1 m (2 km) E of Tralee:* early Christian ruin. In adjoining cemetery, graves of those who died in War of Independence.,

Siamsa Tíre theatre, *Staughton's Row:* marvellous, stimulating Irish folk pageants. *June, Sept, Mon, Thur, 8.30 p.m. July, Aug, Mon, Tues, Thur, Fri, 8.30 p.m. Details: (066) 23049/23055.* **D Dúchas,** *Edward Street:* traditional entertainment nightly during season, *details: TIO.* **D Ballyseedy Memorial,** *2 m (3 km) E of Tralee:* fine bronze by Breton sculptor Jan Goulet, commemorating incident in Civil War.

Sports Centre, *Oakpark:* wide variety of sports, *all year, daily, 10 a.m.–10 p.m., tel: (066) 22442.***D** Racing: five day meeting at Tralee Racecourse during Rose of Tralee festival. *Other races, Mar, June, Nov, details: TIO.* Greyhound racing, *Oakview: Tues, Wed, Fri, 8.15 p.m., closed winter, details: (066) 21416. Tralee Bay sailing: Len Breewood, St Brendan's School of Sailing, Derrymore, tel: (064)30132.* Riding: William J. Riding Centre, *Ballyard, tel: (066) 21840.* Bicycles: E. Caball, *Ashe Street, tel: (066) 22231;* J. Caball and Co., *Staughton's Row, tel: (064) 21654;* Cnoc na Sí Rent a Bike, *Glaise Bheag, Baile na nGall;* Tralee Gas Supplies, *Strand Street, tel: (066) 22018.* Golf Club, *9 holes, tel: (066) 21150.*

AROUND TRALEE

Abbeyfeale, *10 m (16 km) SW of Listowel:* Pontrinard Castle, 14th c Geraldine stronghold, now ruined. Bicycles: Michael Reidy, *Kerry Road, tel: (068) 31175.*

Ardfert, *6 m (10 km) NW of Tralee on L105, 191 bus from Ballybunion, Tralee.* St Brendan's Cathedral, 13th c ruins include nave and choir. **Ardfert Abbey,** *just E of St Brendan's,* Franciscan friary dating from 1253, now ruins. Teampall na nÓigh church ruins and Teampall Griffin, late Gothic church ruins, ogham stone in adjoining graveyard, *near W end of St Brendan's.*

Ballingarry Castle, *4 m (6 km) N of Ballyheigue:* 17th c ruins.

Ballybunion, *21 m (34 km) N of Tralee. TIO: tel, (068) 27202. July, Aug, 191, 194, 195 bus from Tralee.* One of Ireland's top seaside resorts. Plenty of summer fun, highlight the Bachelor Festival, when eligible men meet eligible ladies, *usually June.* **Church of St Augustine:** built in 1877, transferred to present site from nearby Ballyduff in 1957.**D Ballybunion Castle,** *on promontory:* built 1583, now ruins.

The town has many attractive beaches and the caves in the cliffs to the N can be explored at low tide. Seaweed baths: Collins' and Dalys', *mid-May–end Sept, daily.* Riding: Bennett's, tel: (068) 27516. Bicycles: Danna's, *tel: (068) 27278.* Ballybunion Golf Club, *18 holes, tel: (068) 27146.*

Ballyduff, *5 m (8 km) S of Ballybunion on L104:* site of early 13th c Ratoo church. Intact round tower.

Ballygamboon, *2 m (3 km) N of Castlemaine on N70:* forest walks, lay-by, picnic area.

Ballyheigue Castle, *10 m (16 km) NW of Tralee.* Striking 19th c ruins. The nearby beach stretches S for 8 m (13 km) to Banna Strand, one of the country's finest beaches. There is a good walk 5 m (8 km) NW of Kerry Head.

Ballylongford, *8 m (13 km) N of Listowel, 200 bus from Listowel.* Lislaughtin Abbey, *1 m (2 km) N of village,* roofless Franciscan friary. Bicycles: John McCabe, *Bridge Street, tel: Ballylongford 23.*

Barrow Harbour, *5 m (8 km) NW of Fenit:* early 13th c round castle near harbour entrance, good views of Dingle peninsula and NW Kerry coastline.

Carrigafoyle Castle, *2 m (3 km) N of Ballylongford:* partially destroyed by Cromwellian troops in 1649. Climb the spiral staircase for excellent view of Shannon estuary and surrounding countryside.

Casement's Fort, *1 m (2 km) W of Ardfert:* Sir Roger Casement was arrested by this earthen roadside fort after landing at nearby Banna Strand in 1916 with German arms for the Rising. 1 m (2 km) further on, monument commemorates his execution.

Castleisland, *11 m (18 km) E of Tralee on N21:* slight remains of castle built in 1226.

Fenit, *8 m (13 km) W of Tralee.189 bus from Tralee:* notable L-shaped pier. The huge sandstone boulder by the water's edge is an Ice Age relic. Good sea angling and walks.

Fenit Island, *approach by land from Fenit:* ruins of Fenit Castle, built to guard entrance to Barrow Harbour, which had thriving trade with Low Countries four centuries ago.

Finuge, *3 m (5 km) SW of Listowel:* Teach Siamsa Folk Theatre, traditional style Kerry cottage with thatched roof, gatherings of musicians, singers, dancers and players for traditional-style entertainment. *SO, Sat from 9.30 a.m. Details: Finuge 943.***D**

Glanshearoon Hill, *2 m (3 km) E of Castleisland on Abbeyfeale road:* good views of Tralee Bay.

Glin Castle, *30 m (48 km) NE of Tralee on S shore of Shannon, 200 bus from Listowel, 201 bus from Ballybunion (SO).* Built 1780s, seat of Knight of Glin. Interior has fine neo-classical plasterwork. Drawing room, library and unique double flying staircase all have remarkable Adam-style ceilings. Good collection of mid-18th c furniture. Gate shop sells antiques, crafts and home-made food. *Tours by arr. with Mme Fitzgerald, (068) 34173, shop manageress, (068) 34188.* Hamilton's Tower, 19th c, good views of Shannon.

Gunsborough, *4 m (6 km) NW of Listowel:* birthplace of Earl Kitchener of Khartoum, defender of Empire during late 19th, early 20th c.

Kilfergus, *1 m (2 km) SE of Glin:* tombstone of local farmer Timothy Costelloe, who wrote his own epitaph in verse and carved it on the stone.

Kilmurry Castle, *4 m (6 km) E of Castleisland, near Kilmurry crossroads:* 16th c ruin.

Ballybunion

Knockanore Church, *4 m (6 km) E of Ballybunion:* interestingly modern, built 1963–4, sculptures by Oisin Kelly.

Knockanore Hill, *3 m (5 km) E of Ballybunion:* breathtaking views of Shannon, as far as Limerick city.

Leck Castle, *3 m (5 km) N of Ballybunion:* 16th c Fitzgerald fortress, visited by Tennyson in 1842. Access via cliff path.

Lissodigue limestone cave, *3 m (5 km) NE of Fenit:* extends 700 ft (213 metres).

Listowel, *17 m (27 km) N of Tralee on N69, 106, 117, 194, 195, 200 bus from Tralee.* Amazing plaster shop decorations executed by local man Patrick McAuliffe, who died in 1921. Local decorator Francis Chute and his son carry on tradition. Among most striking works are plaster lady on Central Hotel and lion and harp above P. M. Keane's.

Writer's Week, workshops, plays exhibitions, book fair—a must for anyone with literary inclinations, *end June–early July.* Fleadh Cheoil, feast of traditional music and competitions, *late Aug, details: Tralee TIO.* Listowel Races, Harvest Festival, including All Ireland Wren Boys' Competition, *Sept.*

Castle, *town centre:* ruin once belonged to Lords of Kerry, destroyed in 1600. Lartigue Little Theatre, *the Square: details:* D. Hannon. **John B. Keane's pub,** *William Street:* here you may meet the great playwright and storyteller. Bicycles: J. P. Kennelly, *tel: (068) 21285,* J. McKenna, *tel: (068) 21044.*

Lixnaw, *6 m (10 km) SW of Listowel:* ruined 16th c castle of Earls of Kerry.

Tarbert, *4 m (6 km) E of Ballylongford:* car ferry service to Killimer, *every hour on the half hour, daily, all year except Christmas Day, from 7.30 a.m. Apr–Sept., last sailing 9.30 p.m. Sun, from 10.30 a.m. From Killimer, every hour on the hour, daily except Christmas Day. Apr–Sept. 7.00 a.m. to 9.00 p.m. Sun from 9.30 a.m. Details: tel: Kilrush (Co. Clare) 60.*

Tralee Ship Canal: good 3 m (5 km) walk from just S of Tralee to Tralee Bay, alongside canal. Return by minor road, starting where canal enters bay.

Westport

Pop. 3,000, 52 m (84 km) N of Galway, 162 m (261 km) W of Dublin. EC Wed. TIO: (098) 25711/25908. All year. 125, 255 bus from Achill, 123 from Clifden, 120, 124, 259 from Galway, 125 from Sligo, train from Castlebar, Dublin, enquiries: (098) 25218.

Set at head of Clew Bay, which is said to have an island for every day of the year, Westport is an attractive, hilly place with a very continental air. Designed by Georgian period architect James Wyatt the town is a good base for exploring S Mayo. See memorial in mall to Major John MacBride. Horse Show, *June.* Cailin Deas Festival, *Aug. details: TIO.*

Westport House, *1.5 m (2.5 km) outside town:* stately home in beautiful demesne. Georgian house with fine family portraits, old Irish silver, Waterford glass, old furnishings and decorations. Zoo, shopping arcade, fishing, horse caravan holidays, holiday homes. *May 15–Sep 18. May, daily, 2 p.m.–5 p.m., June, July, Aug, daily, 10.30 a.m.–6 p.m., Sept, daily, 2 p.m.–5 p.m. details: (098)25430.*

The Mall: tree-lined boulevard running each side of Carrowbeg River.

Westport Quay: formerly a thriving port, now home of several nautically inclined pubs and restaurants, most notably perhaps the Asgard, an award-winning pub/restaurant with marine type decor and old boat fittings. Climb Tober Hill Street for an excellent view over town.

Sea Angling: Westport Sea Angling Centre. *Tel: (098)25280.* Horse Riding: Drummindoo Riding Centre. *Tel: (098)25616.*

Cruises: P. C. Marine, *tel: (098)25848.* Bicycles: J. P. Breheny and Son, *tel: (098) 25020* Mrs Hopkins, *tel: (098) 25961.* Golf Club, *Ballyknock, Carrowholly, 18 holes, tel: (098) 25113.*

AROUND WESTPORT

Aasleagh Waterfall, *20 m (32 km) S of Westport:* peat-stained fall on Erriff River flanked by glorious mass of rhododendrons.

Balla, *7 m (11 km) SE of Castlebar on N60, 257 bus from Castlebar (infrequent services).* Mediaeval altar, round tower from 7th c monastery founded by St Cronan, holy well and remains of shelter for blind and lame.

Ballinasmalla Abbey, *2 m (3 km) NE of Claremorris off N17 to Knock:* ruins of 13th c Carmelite friary.

Ballinrobe, *259 from Claremorris, Galway, Westport; 124 from Galway, Westport (SO).* Ruins of Augustinian friary, built about 1313, at N end of town. Explore the old canal wharves that form Bowers Walk, in the 19th c, there were great plans, never completed, to link Ballinrobe with Galway and the sea.

Horse racing: *June, Sept; details, Ballinrobe 52/71.* Burke Boats, trips on Loughs Carra and Mask, *tel: Ballinrobe 100.* Riding facilities: Flannery's pub, *tel: Ballinrobe 55.* Bicycles: E. Finlay, *Glebe Street, tel: Ballinrobe 44.* Ballinrobe Golf Club, *9 holes.*

Ballintubber Abbey, *1 m (1.5 km) E of T40 Castlebar–Ballinrobe road:* only church of kind in Ireland where Mass has been said for past 750 years. Founded, by St Patrick in 5th c, present abbey 13th c. Although Cromwell destroyed much of it in 1653, it survived and was restored between 1840 and 1966. Most impressive, well worth visiting.**D Moore Hall,** *near abbey:* ruins of birthplace of George Moore, late 19th early 20th c writer. Fishing in nearby Lough Carra, forest walks, scenic views, car park, picnic area.

Ballycroy, *2 m (3 km) N of Castlehill:* noted angling centre in desolate, largely uninhabited countryside.

Ballyhaunis Abbey, *114, 115 (SO), 247 from Galway, 259 (infrequent service) from Castlebar.* Set amid E Mayo lakes, abandoned during Dissolution, re-roofed early 19th c. Convent of Mercy (C), five Michael Healy windows.**D** Golf club, *9 holes, tel: Ballyhaunis 14.*

Belcarra Folk Museum, *Community Centre, Belcarra, 5 m (8 km) SE of Castlebar:* items relating to local folklife. Visits by arr. Contact either Mrs Maureen Cunningham, *Belcarra 55;* or Miss Ellie Gavin, *Belcarra 100.*

Brackloon, *5 m (8 km) S of Westport on N59:* forest walks.

Breaffy, *3 m (5 km) SW of Castlebar on N60:* forest walks.

Burrishoole Friary, *2 m (3 km) NW of Newport:* built about 1450, tower remains. Nearby, the ruined Carrigahooly Castle.

Caher Island, *S of Clare Island. Sailings by arr. from Roonagh Quay, details: Bay View Hotel, tel: Clare Island 104 or (098) 25380.* Holy Island.

Carrownisky Strand, *5 m (8 km) SW of Louisburgh:* vast, empty, golden beach.

Castlebar, *11 m (18 km) E of Westport on N60. EC Thurs. TIO: (094) 21207. July-Aug. 120, 122, 259 bus from Ballina, Galway, 257 from Claremorris, train from Dublin and Westport, enquiries: Castlebar station, tel: (094) 21222.* Situated where the Castlebar River flows into Castlebar Lough. Its pleasant tree-lined Mall, which once served as a cricket pitch for Lord Lucan and his family is an oasis of calm in a bustling, somewhat plain town.

TIO, (094) 21207. International Walking Festival: *June.* Castlebar International Song Festival: popular music festival draws people from many countries. Good songs, good crack, *Oct, details: TIO, (094) 21207.*

O'Malley Gallery. *Mall:* when completed, will house vast Ernie O'Malley collection of paintings, ceramics, sculptures, *details: TIO, (094) 21207.*
Education Centre: converted chapel. John Wesley laid foundation stone in 1789. Now art, history exhibitions, craft displays, *all year, Mon-Sat, 10.30 a.m.-5 p.m. details: (094) 21769.*

If you enjoy plaque spotting, the Mall is the birthplace of Margaret Burke-Sheridan, internationally famous prima donna: Main Street birthplace of Louis Brennan, inventor of torpedo and monorail; 'Mountainview', Westport Road, birthplace of politician, Charles Haughey.

Castlebar Airport: pleasure flights, *details: (094)*

Croagh Patrick

22853. Sports complex, industrial estate: with new 25 metre pool, *daily, until 10 p.m. details: (094) 22944.* Bicycles: Bourkes Cycle Centre, *Market Square, tel: (094) 22447.* Golf Club, Hawthorn Lodge, *9 holes, tel: (094) 21649.*

Castlehill, *N of Mulrany, via N59:* fine views of Bellacragher and Blacksod Bays.

Castlemagarrett, *1.5 m (2.5 km) S of Claremorris on N17:* forest walks.

Charlestown, *7 m (11 km) NE of Swinford.* Town built by Lord Dillon in 1847. Western Rose Festival, *end July-early Aug.*

Clare Island, *mouth of Clew Bay.* Mail boat sailings from Roonagh Quay, *4 m (6 km) W of Louisburgh, all year. Mon, Wed, Fri, Sat, June 1–Aug 31,* sailings twice daily. Details, Chris O'Grady, Bay View Hotel, *tel: Clare Island 104 or (098) 25380* Remote spot with 160 residents and one hotel, ideal for relaxing. **Clare Abbey,** 15th c, with frescoes. Doonagappul, promontory fort on S cliffs. **Tonadowhy,** *4.5 m (7 km) W of harbour:* disused lighthouse. **Knockmore,** magnificent views of Clew Bay and mountains of Connemara and Mayo.

Claremorris, *E Mayo. 120, 122 bus from Westport, 122 from Castlebar, Galway (SO), 267, 259 from Castlebar, 265 from Ballina, from Galway, Sligo. Train from Ballina, Castlebar, Westport.* Three Aug events: Connacht Donkey Derby; All Ireland Pony Jumping Championship; Town Festival, including band recitals, agricultural show. *Details: Castlebar TIO.*

Clydagh, *3 m (5 km) NE of Castlebar on L134:* salmon and trout fishing, waterfall, forest walks, car park, picnic area.

Collanmore Island, *Clew Bay:* Glenans Sailing Centre, courses, details: Carrowholly 728.

Corraun Peninsula, *near Mulrany:* very fine coastal views. Claggan Mountain, Cuchcamcarragh, Nephin Beg, each over 1,700 ft (500 metres), all worth climbing.

Creevagh Castle, *2 m (3 km) SE of Ballinrobe, off T40:* 15th c ruins.

Croagh Patrick, *5 m (8 km) W of Westport. 264 bus from Westport to Murrisk.* Ireland's holy mountain, a little over an hour's climb from Murrisk on the Westport-Louisburgh road. To do it the hard way, join the mid-summer pilgrimage, *last Sun July.* Spectacular views on clear days.

Eochy's Cairn, *2 m (3 km) E of Lough Mask, near Ballinrobe:* great prehistoric ruined cairn.

Furnace, *between Furnace and Feeagh Loughs, 3 m (5 km) N of Newport, 255 bus from Westport to Newport.* Salmon Research Trust investigates salmon breeding and restocking, *daily, 9 a.m.–5 p.m. tel: (098) 41272.*

Gulf of Aille, *signposted lane from Westport–Partree road, 5 m (8 km) SE of Westport, just W of Aille, 259 bus from Westport to Aille Post Office.* River Aille goes underground reappearing 2.5 m (4 km) E. Caves in nearby cliffs have been partly explored; farmer's permission.

Clare Island

Inishmaine Island, *Lough Mask:* church ruin from 7th c monastery founded by St Cormac (NM).

Inishturk Island, *S of Clare Island:* grand little harbour and beach at Portadoon. Sailings by arr. from Roonagh Quay. *Details:* Bay View Hotel, *tel:* Clare Island 104 or (098) 25380.

Kilgeever Church, *2 m (3 km) E of Louisburgh:* roofless ruins, holy well. Still used by some Croagh Patrick pilgrims. Magnificent views S of Sheeffry Hills.

Killary Harbour: 10 m (16 km) inlet more like Norwegian fjord. Road skirting S side, through fishing village of Leenane, offers tremendous views.

Killeen, *district 5 m (8 km) S of Louisburgh:* many antiquities, including 37 arch clapper footbridge at Bunlahinch, 1 m (1.5 km) W of Killeen Church.

Knock, *7 m (11 km) NE of Claremorris on N17. TIO: Knock, tel: (094) 88174. June–Sept. 265 bus from Castlebar, Claremorris, 267 from Claremorris, Sligo.* Major pilgrimage centre attracting over 2 million pilgrims yearly. Magnificent new basilica next to original church where famous apparation seen in 1879. Our Lady's Domain, to S, beautifully landscaped parklands with trees, shrubs, roses. *Details: (094) 88100, Belcarra 3, (01)775965.* **D** Folk museum: many items on folk life, history, archaeology, religion, *daily, all year.*

Knockranny, *just outside Westport, off T39:* forest walks.

Lapallagh, *5 m (8 km) W of Castlebar off L138 road:* forest walks, viewing point.

Lecanvey, *2 m (3 km) W of Murrisk:* excellent bathing beaches.

Lisnemonaghy, *1 m (1.5 km) N of Kiltimagh in E Mayo:* Tobar na Cuimhne (Well of Memory), holy well whose waters said to improve memory.

Lough Nadirkmore, *6 m (10 km) SW of Touramakeady on W shore of Lough Mask:* small, dramatically set lake surrounded by towering mountains. Start energetic three hour climb to lake at Cappanacreha, *5m (8 km) SW of Touramakeady.*

Louisburgh, *12 m (19 km) W of Westport. TIO, tel: Louisburgh 50. July–Aug. 264 bus from Westport.* Quaint fishing village with good sandy beaches. Founded 1802, probably named after Louisburgh, Nova Scotia. Horse Fair *June* Bicycles: Harneys Garage, *Tel: Louisburgh 5.*

Moanbane Fort, *3.5 m (6 km) SE of Ballyhaunis:* set

---

on N slope of commanding height, good views.

Mulrany, *18 m (29 km) NW of Westport on N59, 255 from Achill Sound, Westport.* Attractive village on isthmus between Blacksod and Clew Bays. Sheltered from Atlantic winds, mild climate encourages giant fuschias and rare plants, such as mediterranean heather. Good bathing beach, sea fishing, boating. Youth Hostel.

Murrisk Abbey, *5 m (8 km) W of Westport off T39: 15th c ruins.*

Mweelrea Mountains, *N shores of Killary Harbour:* three hour climb to Mweelrea summit, five routes to top, most popular from Delphi, just S of Doo Lough on L100. Most dramatic approach by boat from Leenane across harbour. Superb views in clear weather.

Newport: *8 m (12 km) N of Westport on N59. 255 (SO) from Achill Sound, Westport.* Fronted by Clew Bay and sheltered to N by Nephin Beg mountain range. Water skiing facilities, harbour. Youth Hostel.

Old Head, *2 m (3 km) NE of Louisburgh, off T39:* forest walks, spectacular views, car park, picnic area.

Rockfleet Castle, *4 m (6 km) W of Newport, off N59:* 16th c tower house on shores of Clew Bay. When closed see caretaker.

Sheeffry, *14 m (22 km) SW of Westport, on L100 from Louisburgh to Killary Harbour via Doo Lough:* viewing point, car park, picnic area.
Sheeffry Hills, *8 m (13 km) SE of Louisburgh:* two main peaks worth climbing for views.

Srahmore, *N of Lough Feeagh, 5 m (8 km) N of Newport:* forest walks, viewing points, drive alongside River Srahmore.

Straide, *on N5/N58 8 m (13 km) NE of Castlebar, 255, 259 bus from Ballina, Castlebar, Westport.* Birthplace of Michael Davitt, founder of late 19th c Land League. Replica of house from which he and his parents were evicted. Davitt Museum, *June–Sept, daily.* Ruined 13th c Franciscan friary.

Touramakeady Demesne, *by Touramakeady village on W shore of Lough Mask:* forest walks, 2 m (3 km) nature trail, waterfall, good views of lough, car park, picnic area. Boats: Martin Morrin, *tel: Touramakeady 34.*

Turlough, *4 m (6 km) E of Castlebar on N5:* well-preserved round tower with ruined 17th c church.

The NORTH-WEST

Bundoran

Pop. 1,500, 19 m (30 km) S of Donegal, 157 m (252 km) NW of Dublin. EC Thurs. TIO: (072) 41350, July–Aug. Bus enquiries: CIE, Sligo, tel: (071) 2151. 114 bus from Derry, Galway, 290 from Derry, Sligo.

The premier holiday resort in the North West, with a fine strand backed by a promenade. Salmon and trout fishing good in nearby Bunduff and Bundrowes River, as well as in nearby Lough Melvin. First-class sea angling in Donegal Bay. Lobster Festival: lobster landing at quay is followed by sports competitions and festivities, *end June, details: TIO.*

Headlands, dramatic views from both, in clear

---

weather, of S Donegal, Sligo and Mayo. Cliff walk: W of Bundoran, to small, roofless tower called Cassidy's Folly, standing by the sea's edge. Promenade to Rogey, along cliffs N to Aughrus Head with its fantastic rock formations, as far as magnificent Tullan Strand, backed by the Finner sandhills.
Maritime Gallery: work by local artists, *SO, daily, 11 a.m.–8 p.m.* Beach House: museum, art gallery, craft shop, *June–Sept, 12 noon–8 p.m. daily.* St Patrick's Hall: summer season amateur drama by Bundoran Players. Swimming pool: indoor, heated, *daily.* Three outdoor pools, *SO.* Bicycles: Patrick McGloin, *East End, tel: (072) 41383.* Bundoran Golf Club, *18 holes.*

AROUND BUNDORAN

Ard Fothadh, *2 m (3 km) SW of Ballintra:* ancient fort, believed to be the burial place of Hugh MacAinmire, a 6th c High King of Ireland.

Ballintra, *12 m (19 km) NW of Bundoran on N15, 290 bus from Bundoran.* Attractive village set amid drumlins (small, rounded hills). In Brownhill demesne, beside village, River Blackwater flows through caves known as The Pullans. A few hundred yards E of village, at Aghadullagh Old Mill, the river forms a waterfall before flowing through a remarkable chasm.

Ballyshannon, *5 m (8 km) NE of Bundoran on N15. Bus enquiries: (072) 41235. 91, 114, 281, 284, 289, (SO), 290 bus from Bundoran.* Town of great character built on banks of River Erne. Pleasant walks around older parts of town and by river. Lively Folk Festival, *early Aug, details: Bundoran TIO.*

The Mall: William Allingham's birthplace. The cottage where the noted 19th c poet lived is in a decrepit state. In the Allied Irish Bank, you can see his bust, the tall desk at which he once kept accounts and the words he scratched on the windowpane. He is buried in the graveyard of St Anne's just N of the town. Allingham Weekend: poetry reading, competitions, exhibitions of the poet's memorabilia, *usually end Oct. Details: Bundoran TIO.* **Creevy Pier Art Gallery:** works by local artists. *Daily.*

St Mary's of Assaroe, *1 m (2 km) NW of Ballyshannon:* meagre ruins of Cistercian abbey founded in 1184. Just S, grotto-like Catsby Cave, where Mass was celebrated in penal times. The ESB Station fish-pass allows fish to swim upstream—a fascinating sight. *By arr., tel: (072) 65200.* Bicycles: P. B. Stephens, *4/6 Castle Street, tel: (072) 65178.* Swimming pool: indoor, heated, *daily, except Tues.*

Belleek, *4 m (6 km) E of Ballyshannon on L24.* Pottery, begun in 1857, is characteristically creamy porcelain products are renowned the world over. The work requires immense finesse and is absorbing to watch. *Guided tours all year, Mon–Fri. 10.15 a.m.–12 noon; 2.15 p.m.–4 p.m. Closed first two weeks Aug. 'Phone first: Details: Belleek 501.*

Castle Caldwell

Castle Caldwell, *between Boa Island and Belleek, off B136:* demesne and forest on two long peninsulas. By entrance is the Fiddler's Stone, set up in 1770 to commemorate a local fiddler Dennis McCabe. Marvellous lake views. Wildlife observation hides with identification pictures. Castle and chapel ruins, old quay and boathouse.

Kilbarron Castle, *2 m (3 km) S of Rossnowlagh:* 14th c ruins stand majestically on rock promontory overlooking Donegal Bay. Nearby remains of 14th c Kilbarron church.

Kiltyclogher, *4 m (6 km) SE of Lough Melvin:* Festival, mainly traditional events, *July, Details:* Bundoran TIO. Seán MacDiarmada, one of 1916 Rising leaders, commemorated by memorial in village square. Route to his birthplace at Cormone signposted. Megalithic tomb, known locally as Prince Connell's Grave. Between Lough Melvin and Upper Lough Macnean, a series of prehistoric earthworks once said to have divided Ulster from Connacht. Best place to view is just N of Kiltyclogher, where parts straddle the road.

Kinlough, *2 m (3 km) S of Bundoran on T54:* pretty village. Site of interesting prehistoric remains. Forest walks, picnic area, car park. Attractive drive along S shores of Lough Melvin to Rossinver.

Knader, *2 m (3 km) E of Ballyshannon on back road to Belleek:* forest walks, scenic views, picnic area, car park.

Lurgan Carn, *4 m (6 km) SW of Ballintra:* superb views.

Rossnowlagh, *10 m (16 km) N of Bundoran, off N15, 292 bus from Ballyshannon.* Focal point is the magnificent strand, one of Donegal's finest. Surfing enthusiasts have been known to become addicted to the beach. Francican Friary, strikingly modern, with gardens, shrines. **Co Donegal Historical Society Museum,** wide range of local archaeological and folklore items, *all year, daily, 10 a.m.-8 p.m.* **Coolmore Art Gallery:** works by local artists. *Daily.* Boats, canoes: Sand House Hotel, *tel: (072) 65343.*

Tullaghan, *3 m (5 km) SW of Bundoran on N15, 114, 289, 290, bus from 2 m Bundoran.* Co Leitrim's only seaside village. Secluded sandy beaches nearby. The Gallery has collection of metal etchings and steel engravings. *June-Sept, daily, 10 a.m.-5 p.m. Details: (072) 41347.*

Donegal

Pop. 2,000, 19 m (30 km) NE of Bundoran. EC. Wed. TIO: Donegal 148. June-Sept. Bus enquiries: Donegal 101. 114, 290 bus from Derry, Sligo, 91 from Dublin.

Pleasant, if bracing touring centre at the head of Donegal Bay. Many of the natural and historic attractions of S Donegal are within easy reach.

St Patrick's Church of the Four Masters (C): modern, strikingly built with red granite, completed in 1935.

Donegal Abbey, *just S of town:* slight ruins of Franciscan friary founded in 1474 on banks of River Eske. On the N side of Diamond are the ruins of an O'Donnell stronghold (NM), over 500 years old, *accessible at all times.*

Napoleonic anchor *near TIO, quayside:* 15 ft (4.5 metres) long, weights 1.5 tons. Believed to have been left by the French fleet which brought Wolfe Tone back from France for 1798 Rising. Quayside walk: along E bank of River Eske, in direction of abbey. Drumcliffe walk: about 1 m (1.5 km) along W bank of River Eske. Excellent views of Donegal Bay, abbey ruins across river, surrounding woodlands.

Magee Tweed Factory: century old tradition, visitors welcome, *conducted tours all year, Mon-Fri, 11.30 a.m.; 3.30 p.m. Details: Donegal 5.* Donegal Social Club, *Water Street:* indoor sports, visitors welcome, *daily.* Bicycles: C. J. Doherty, *Main Street, tel: Donegal 119.* Donegal Town Golf Club, *Tullycullion, 18 holes, tel:*

Boats at Killybegs

Donegal 108.

AROUND DONEGAL

Aghla Mountain, *5 m (8 km) NE of Glenties:* worth climbing, superb views.

Ardara, *24 m (39 km) NW of Donegal, EC. Wed. 299 bus from Donegal.* One of most interesting towns in Donegal, with wide Main Street and several fascinating small shops in traditional Donegal style. **Church of the Holy Family,** masterly Evie Hone window in W nave depicting the 'Word of God', well worth seeing.

Caves of Maghera, *short distance W of town:* signposted. The hour stroll from village past Drumbarron gives fine view of Loughros Bay and Ardara. Tweed weaving can be seen all year, *Mon-Fri, 9 a.m.-5 p.m.* at John McGill, *Maghera;* William McNelis, *Main Street, tel: Ardara 5.* Bicycles: Donal Byrne, *West End, tel: Ardara 56.*

Ball Hill, *2 m (3 km) SW of Donegal:* Youth Hostel: *tel: Donegal 174.*

Barnesmore Gap, *7 m (11 km) NE of Donegal on N15:* desolate stretch of about 3 m (5 km). Little imagination needed to relive the days of the highwaymen who once roamed here! and if you find the gap too bracing **Biddy O'Barnes pub** has an excellent atmosphere.

Blue Stack Mountains, *7 m (11 km) N of Donegal:* very fine scenery, particularly in Eglish Glen.

Bruckless, *15 m (24 km) W of Donegal on N56, 299 bus from Donegal, Killybegs.* Linen village just before Killybegs.

Carntullagh Head, *near Killybegs:* can be reached by rowing across Killybegs Harbour. Not advised in winter! For boats, contact C. McBrearty, *Church St.*

Carrick, *3 m (5 km) NW of Kilcar on T72A:* starting place for ascent of Slieve League, 1,972 ft (600 metres). Beyond Teelin village, 2 m (3 km) S of Carrick, mountain track leads over Carrigan Head to Bunglass cliffs, which rise sheer from water to height of just over 1,000 ft (305 metres). View from Amharc Mor (literally 'great view') is among the most glorious in the county. After Croaghaun on Achill, these are the greatest sea cliffs in Ireland. Take care, many of the climbs are best left to experienced climbers. Bracing walk of about 10 m (16 km) W as far as Malin Beg. If you wish, continue to Glencolumbkille and Maghera, about 20 m (32 km) in all. Nearby Malinmore has fine strand. Youth Hostel.

Cloghan Lodge, *10 m (16 km) beyond Fintown on Ballybofey road:* salmon leap on the River Finn.

Clonasillagh: *turn N 6 m (10 km) W of Killybegs on T72A:* Forest walks.

Clooney, *5 m (8 km) W of Glenties on Portnoo Road:* forest, lakeside walks, picnic area, car park.

Crocknacunny, *6 m (10 km) N of Pettigo on L84:* excellent scenic views, riverside walks, access to Lough Derg. Picnic area, lay-by.

Crownarad Mountain, *3 m (5 km) W of Killybegs:* 1,621 ft (500 metres) worth climbing, magnificent views.

Derryloughan, *5 m (8 km) N of Glenties on Doochary road:* forest walks near Gweebarra Bay.

Drumanoo Head, *3 m (5 km) S of Killybegs:* minor road extends almost entire distance.

Dunmore Head, *1 m (1.5 km) W of Portnoo:* good views of coast to SW, inc Dawros Head and Crohy Head to NE.

Fintragh Strand, *2 m (3 km) W of Killybegs:* vast, deserted stretch of sand.

Glencolumbkille, *35 m (56 km) W of Donegal at end of T72A, 296 bus from Killybegs.* Fascinating self-help co-operative community, inspired by Fr James McDyer. As he says: 'If you like wild, rugged scenery, uncluttered beaches, a secluded area where you can unwind from modern city life, then Glencolumbkille is for you.' Fairies said to hold festive gatherings hereabouts. 30 thatched cottages to rent. *Details: Glencolumkille 36.*

Folk Museum: cluster of sparely-furnished period cottages near the beach, recalling terrible poverty of the people who endured the worst ravages of landlordism and famine. Other restored buildings inc 'shebeen' (place where poteen was sold), complete with still and a 19th c schoolhouse. Delicious cottage teas, craft shop. *St. Patrick's Day-Oct, daily.*

Straid Gallery: paintings, drawings of particular Donegal interest. SO daily, 10 a.m.-8 p.m. The area is also rich in archaeological remains inc. 5,000 year old court cairns and line of dolmens situated close by the Glenbay Hotel. Many embossed standing stones, ruins of early Christian monastery, beautiful little church in centre of glen.

Glengesh Pass, *between Ardara and Glencolumbkille:* rises spectacularly to 900 ft (274 metres) before plunging to valley. Forest walk, picnic area, car park. Excellent views.

Glenties, *19 m (30 km) NW of Donegal, 295 bus from Ballybofey, Portnoo.* Striking small town set amid woods where two glens meet. Nearby mountain landscapes offer desolate contrast. **Melly's Art Gallery:** landscape oil paintings. *All year, daily, 10 a.m.-8 p.m. Details: Colm Melly, tel: Glenties 100.* Fish Hatchery, by arr., tel: Glenties 41. Drive: take the Fintown road, skirting Lough Finn and Lough Muck, returning through Stracashel Glen. Most attractive 20 m (32 km) route.

Inver Bay, *8 m (13 km) W of Donegal:* excellent sandy bay near Inver village.

Kilcar, *8 m (13 km) W of Killybegs on T72A:* picturesque weaving centre. Visitors welcome at Gaeltarra Eireann factories, Connemara Fabrics and Gaeltarra Snath. *No demonstrations. All year, Mon-Fri, business hours.*

Killybegs, *17 m (27 km) W of Donegal, just off N56, 299 bus from Donegal.* One of Ireland's most important fishing ports, set on a fine natural harbour. Try and be there when the fishing fleet returns, the quaysides are a buzz of activity and the air is alive with gulls. Killybegs International Sea Angling Festival: *usually Aug, coinciding with annual regatta. Details: Donegal TIO.* Bicycles: Morrows, Fintragh.

Donegal Carpets have been hand-weaving carpets, rugs and wall-hangings since end of 19th c. Its wares are found in many famous buildings, from Aras an Uachtarain and Iveagh House, Dublin to the Bank of England, London and the First National City Bank, New York. Extraordinary sight to see the weaving process. Craft shop. *All year, Mon-Fri, 9 a.m.-5 p.m. Closed first two weeks, Aug. Preferably by arr, tel: Killybegs 21.* Bicycles: Morrows, Fintragh.

Lackrom, *4 m (6 km) N of Donegal:* forest walks, good scenic views, car park.

Lough Derg, *10 m (16 km) E of Donegal, access via L84 from Pettigo, 115, 289 bus from Ballyshannon (SO).* Car park 1 m (1.5 km) from the pier for Station Island, lying just offshore. Picnic area, lakeshore drive, forest walks, viewing points, access to St Brigid's Well. Three day pilgrimage to Lough Derg one of most physcally demanding in world, since only one meal a day of dry bread and black tea is permitted. During pilgrimage season, *June-mid-Aug,* pilgrims only allowed on Station Island. Details: The Prior, Lough Derg, Co. Donegal.

Lough Eske, *5 m (8 km) NE of Donegal, off N15:* 15 m (24 km) drive round lough shores gives splendid views of some of Ireland's most beautiful scenery. Forest walks.

Loughros Point, *6 m (10 km) W of Ardara:* fine

views of bays on each side of peninsula and surrounding mountains.

Mountcharles, *4 m (6 km) W of Donegal on N56, 299 bus from Donegal.* Bleak but interesting one street village with excellent views of Donegal Bay from top of nearby hill. Sandy beach 1 m (1.5 km) from village. Jack Furey's: hand embroidery, other hand crafts, *all year, Mon–Sat, 9.30 a.m.–6 p.m.*

Muckross Head, *2 m (4 km) S of Kilcar:* cliffs and caves can be explored at low tide. Fine sandy beach at Traloar.

Murvagh/Mullinasole Strand, *9 m (14 km) SW of Donegal off N15:* forest walks, beach, views.

Narin and Portnoo, *8 m (13 km) N of Ardara, 295, 299 bus from Ballybofey.* Twin villages on S shore of Gweebarra Bay. Chief attraction is Narin's wonderful 1 m (2.5 km) strand. At low tide, you can walk to offshore island of Iniskeel. Golf Club 18 holes.

Port, *2 m (3 km) N of Glencolumbkille:* very isolated, but charming, seaside hamlet, approached by track from Ardara direction.

Rosbeg, *on shores of Dawros Bay:* fine beach, attractive scenery.

St John's Peninsula, *S of Dunkineely:* extends for about 5 m (8 km) into Donegal Bay; a road covers almost entire distance. Exceptional views. Peninsula also has one of finest beaches in Donegal and that's saying something. On W shores, see remains of MacSwyne castle.

Dungloe

Pop. 900, 35 m (56 km) NW of Donegal. TIO: Dungloe 72. July–Aug. Bus enquiries: Londonderry and Lough Swilly Road Services, Letterkenny: tel: (074) 22863. Lough Swilly bus from Letterkenny.

Small town, virtually one street, set on the edge of the Atlantic, capital of The Rosses, a remarkable tract of more than 60,000 acres of rock-strewn land crossed by innumerable streams and dotted with many lakes. Excellent brown trout, sea trout, salmon fishing. The warmth of the welcome you will receive is in direct contrast to the bleakness of the landscape. Mary of Dungloe Festival, *end July, early Aug. Details: Letterkenny TIO.* Bicycles: Rosses Service Depot, *tel: Dungloe 17.*

AROUND DUNGLOE

Arranmore, *3 m (5 km) offshore from Burtonport. Ferry: all year, 11 a.m. daily, weather permitting. Summer, every 20 mins. Details: tel: Arranmore 5.* Largest island off W Donegal coast, with 800 inhabitants. Magnificent trip in fine weather. Striking little villages, such as Illion, where houses rise up from chapel in strand. Magnificent cliffs and caves. **Leabgarrow:** island 'capital', a tiny village on E of island, with fine terraces, harbour, golden strand. Dermot and Mary Toland's craft shop, Gortar, has many island souvenirs, such as 'máirtíns' a house slipper with knitted sock, ideal for Irish winters. **Lough Shure,** *N island,* is Ireland's only rainbow trout lake. **Aphort** *on S* has island's largest strand. Boats: Bridge House, *tel: Arranmore 32.* Youth Hostel.

Bunbeg: tiny, restful fishing village facing Gweedore Bay and sheltered by cliffs. Extensive sandy Magheraclogher strand. Bunbeg drive: inland from village along L82, through village of Gweedore to Dunlewy. Return via Falcarragh, Bloody Foreland. Some of Donegal's most exciting lake and mountain scenery. About 35 m (56 km).

Burtonport, *5 m (8 km) NW of Dungloe on T72, Lough Swilly bus from Letterkenny.* Fishing village noted for its lobster and salmon. Access to Arranmore and smaller islands such as Rutland, Inishfree, Inishmeal. Ask at harbour about boats.

Crohy Head, *4 m (6 km) SW of Dungloe:* fine cliffs and coves. Martello Tower was built in Napoleonic times. Youth Hostel. Maghery Bay has perfect bathing strand.

Cruit Island, *near Kincasslagh:* popular resting point for visitors to W Donegal. Connected by bridge to mainland. Minor road runs to N tip of island.

Errigal Mountain, *near Dunlewy:* 2,466 ft (751 metres), cone shaped, ascend from near Dunlewy Lake, the climb is not too arduous, even for a novice. Magnificent views of much of N Donegal. Errigal Youth Hostel: *Dunlewy, tel: Bunbeg 291.*

Gweedore–Falcarragh: *NW-portion of Donegal,* a stronghold of the Donegal Gaeltacht, or Irish-speaking area.

Keadue Strand, *3 m (5 km) N of Burtonport:* at low tide, short cut across to Kincasslagh village.

Poisoned Glen: *entrance 2 m (3 km) SE of Dunlewy, near ruins of 19th c church.* Glen runs deep into Derryveagh Mountains; at head of glen, sheer cliffs. Name comes from the poisonous vegetation on the lake bank which makes the water unfit to drink.

Talamh Briste (broken earth): landslip near Crohy Head has left a chasm 400 metres long, but only 3 metres wide.

Enniskillen

Pop, 7,000, 27 m (43 km) S of Omagh, 86 m (138 km) SW of Belfast. EC. Wed. TIO: Townhall Street, tel: Enniskillen 23110, all year. Bus enquiries: bus station, Eden Street, tel: Enniskillen 22633. 94, 261 Ulsterbus from Belfast.

County town of Fermanagh, Ulster's lakeland, Enniskillen is attractively set on an island between two channels of the river connecting Upper and Lower Lough Erne. Nearly everywhere in the town you see water and boats of all sizes may be hired for fishing and cruising.

St MacCartan's Cathedral (CI), *Church Street:* dates from 1842, but includes part of 17th c building. Old colours of Enniskillen regiments laid up here.**D Convent Chapel** (C), *Belmore Street:* in Byzantine style, with remarkable nave windows by Michael Healy, Lady Glenavy, Sarah Purser. **St Michael's** (C), *Church Street:* completed 1875. Unusual sculpture of Resurrection above main door.**D Methodist Church,** *Darling Street:* the bulges in the balcony were designed to accommodate crinolines.

Enniskillen Castle, houses two museums: County Museum, devoted mainly to pre-history, with models and dioramas showing lake dwellings and early life in Fermanagh, occasional exhibitions; *Apr–Oct, Mon–Sat, 10 a.m.-12.30 p.m.; 2 p.m.-5 p.m. Nov–Mar, Mon–Fri, 10 a.m.-12.30 p.m.; 2 p.m.-5 p.m.* Regimental Museum, relics of Royal Inniskilling Fusiliers and Inniskilling Dragoons. *Mon–Fri, 9.30 a.m.-12.30 p.m.; 2 p.m.-4.30 p.m.* **Fort Hill,** *E side of town:* good views and abundant walks. Victorian bandstand is rather delightful. Climb 108 steps to top of Cole monument for excellent panorama of Enniskillen and surrounding lakeland. There are walks along the varied length of Main Street, which has six changes of name between the bridges at each end. To N of Main Street, between Water Street and Market Street, a warren of alleys known as Boston conjures up the flavour of the old town.

Lakeland Forum leisure centre, inc. pool, café: *Broad Meadow, tel: Enniskillen 24121.*D Visitor Centre has details of local, expert cave explorers for those visitors wishing to see Fermanagh caves. *tel: Enniskillen 23110.* Lough Erne cruises: daily summer sailings from Round 'O' pier. Both boats have covered deck, bar, refreshments. MV

Endeavour: *details,* Lough Erne Leisure Boating, *Queen Elizabeth Road, Enniskillen, tel: Irvinestown 733/8118.* M V Kestrel, Erne Tours, *24 Willoughby Place, tel: Enniskillen 22882.* Bicycles: Concorde, *Tempo Road, tel: Enniskillen 4775.* P. McNulty, *24/26 Belmore Street, tel: Enniskillen 22423.* Enniskillen Golf Club, *18 holes, tel: Enniskillen 22900.*

AROUND ENNISKILLEN

Ballyconnell Canal, *SE end of Upper Lough Erne:* designed 100 years ago to link Erne to Shannon. It silted up after eight boats made the journey.

Bellanaleck, *4 m (6 km) S of Enniskillen on A409:* picnic areas by shore of Lough Erne.

Boa Island, *N side of Lower Lough Erne, 194 Ulsterbus from Enniskillen.* Joined to mainland by bridge at each end. Near W side in ancient Caldragh cemetery, see two very strange old stone figues, calld 'Janus' statues because they have face on each side. Near E end of Boa, on the jetty, tel. for a boat to Lusty Beg Island, a noted holiday spot.

Brookeborough: Ashbrooke Equestrian School, *tel: Brookeborough 242.*

Bunlougher Forest, *NW of Lisnaskea:* walk to Lough Napeasta.

Carnmore, *7 m (11 km) SE of Brookeborough:* see 32 lakes on a clear day, nearby picnic site. Just E are Doon, Lisnaskea forests.

Castle Archdale Forest, *just N of Rossigh, off B82, 194 Ulsterbus from Enniskillen.* Enchanting country park including ruins of Castle Archdale. Caravan park, fishing stands, picnic area, wildfowl observation stand. Three offshore islands form nature reserve. *All year, daily.* Youth Hostel.

Knockninny Hill

Castle Coole (NT), *2 m (3 km) SE of Enniskillen on A4, 95 Ulsterbus from Enniskillen.* Great Palladian house started in 1790. No expense was spared interior fittings and furniture, the house is considered Ireland's finest classical mansion. Parkland runs down to shores of Lough Coole; the park lake still has a flock of graylag geese established here 300 years ago. House closed until further notice because of renovations. Park open *Apr–Sept, 2 p.m.-6 p.m. Daily, except Fri.*

Clonelly Forest, *3 m (5 km) NW of Kesh on A35:* forest walks, caravan site.

Corradillar Peninsula, *4 m (6 km) SW of Enniskillen:* fishing, picnic sites, walks.

Correl Glen, *entrance nearly opp.that to Lough Navar Forest:* path from waterfall near entrance through woodlands to Carrick Lough.

Crevenish Castle, *2 m (3 km) SW of Kesh:* two and a half storeys and square tower still stand. Good lakeside views.

Derrin Lough, *2 m (3 km) NW of Tempo:* pleasant shore walks. Topped Mountain, 3 m (5 km) SW has path to summit with Bronze Age cairn. Nearby picnic area and attractive lake with superb views.

Devenish Island, *3 m (5 km) NW of Enniskillen:* best-known of 97 islands in Lower Lough Erne. Best-preserved round tower in Ireland can be climbed by internal ladders. Ruins of St Molaise's Oratory, Teampall Mór priory, Augustinian abbey of St Mary. Boats leave Round 'O' pier, Enniskillen, *twice daily, Easter–Sept.*

Ely Forest, *off Enniskillen–Belleek A46:* good walks, along S shores of Lower Lough Erne. At N end of forest, Carrickreagh and Blaney Bays are delightfully secluded and ideal for dropping in by cruiser, if this is your style. Nearby Carrickreagh hilltop viewpoint has good vistas of lake and islands.

Florence Court (NT), *8 m (13 km) SW of Enniskillen on A32, 192 Ulsterbus from Enniskillen.* Three storey 18th c mansion of great charm, linked to flanking pavilions by open arched corridors. Fine paintings, plasterwork, furniture. Demesne has many specimen trees, including the 221 years old yew tree said to have been the stock of all Irish yews. Pleasure gardens give landscaped views over adjoining mountains. Adjoins forest park. *Apr–Sept 30, daily, 2 p.m.–6 p.m. Closed Fri. Open Good Fri,' public holidays on a Fri.* Scenic drive over Cuilcagh plateau to Lower Lough Macnean, about 10 m (16 km).

Glenfarne, *15 m (24 km) SW of Enniskillen on A4/T17, 283 CIE bus from Enniskillen, Sligo.* Extensive forest walks, picnic areas, car parks. Excellent views of Upper and Lower Lough Macnean. Old railway station is poignant reminder of long-closed Enniskillen–Sligo railway.

Inishmacsaint, *W shore of Lower Lough Erne:* great sense of isolation. Unusual High Cross, ruins of 6th c monastery and early church, herd of wild goats. Boat hire at Killadeas for journey across.

Inver Lake, *SW of Rosslea:* good shore walks.

Irvinestown, *194, 296 Ulsterbus from Enniskillen.* Mahon's Hotel has interesting collection of local antiques. *Details: Irvinstown 656/657.*

Kesh Forest, *3 m (5 km) N of Kesh:* good views, walks.

Knockmore Cliffs, *3 m (5 km) N of Derrygonnelly on S side of Lower Lough Erne:* superb views from the top (easily reached from Derrygonnelly road).

Knockninny Hill, *3 m (5 km) N of Derrylin, midway between Enniskillen and Belturbet:* rises steep from the shore, tremendous view from cairn on summit.

Lisnaskea, *95 Ulsterbus from Enniskillen. EC, Thurs.* Pat Cassidy's public house and folk museum is crammed with junk, everything from old stoves to stuffed fish, *all year, Mon–Sat, 11.30 a.m.–11.30 p.m.* Castle Balfour, built early 17th c, Scottish features.

Lough Navar Forest Park, *12 m (19 km) NW of Enniskillen on A46:* vast expanse of woodland. Derrygonnelly is start of impressive 7 m (11 km) forest scenic drive, culminating in 900 ft (270 metre) viewpoint, from where you can see most of Lower Lough Erne, S Donegal, N Sligo. Footpaths, self-guiding nature trails. By entrance, two ancient sweat houses.

Lough Navar: Blackslee, Big and Little Dog, Ballintempo, Belmore Forests all have good long distance walks.

Marble Arch Cave, *3 m (5 km) W of Florence Court:* experienced cavers are still finding deep crevices, as well as exploring vast chambers with stalactites and stalagmites. See natural limestone Marble Arch, Marble Arch Glen.

Monea Castle, *4 m (7 km) inland from Ely Forest:* well-preserved 17th c Plantation fortress. Abandoned in 1750 after a fire.

Pollahuna Cave, *Blacklion, near Belcoo:* recently discovered cave on Cavan–Fermanagh border, can be explored by experienced potholers.

Rossigh, *between Castle Archdale and Killadeas:*

scenic footpath, fishing, car park, on the shores of Lower Lough Erne.

Tempo, *on Enniskillen–Fintona B80:* Pubble Shrub botanical garden. *By arr., Dept of Agriculture, Dundonald House, Belfast BT4 3SB. Tel: Belfast 650111.*

Upper Lough Erne: 57 islands, between Enniskillen and Galloon Bridge, worth exploring if you have a cruiser on the lake. Several interesting days can be spent island pottering.

Upper Lough Macnean, *64 Ulsterbus from Enniskillen to Garrison,* B52 lakeside drive along N shores gives fine views across to Co. Leitrim mountains. Roads continues to tiny hamlet of Garrison.

White Island, *Castle Archdale Bay, 10 m (16 km) NW of Enniskillen. Boat trips from Round 'O' pier, Enniskillen, Easter–Sept, daily.* Eight ancient, famous and inscrutable statues. The question of

Dunfanaghy Beach

their origins continues to cause controversy.

Falcarragh

Pop. 500, 12 m (19 km) NE of Bunbeg, 22 m (35 km) NW of Letterkenny. TIO: Letterkenny, tel: (074) 21160, all year. Bus enquiries: (074) 22863. Lough Swilly bus from Letterkenny.

The bilingual village near the E end of the NW Donegal Gaeltacht is an ideal centre for touring the area's rugged cliffs and mountains. Good trout and salmon fishing in the many streams and lakes; excellent sea fishing.

McKinley's Stone, *1 m (1.5 km) from village:* tradition says that when a local chieftain called McKinley was killed here by Balor of the Mighty Blows from Tory Island, his crystallised blood formed a red vein in the stone. Bicycles: Vincent Carton, Michael Sweeney.

AROUND FALCARRAGH

Ards Forest Park, *2 m (3 km) N of Creeslough on T72:* forest walks, scenic views, swimming, picnic area, car park. **D Ards House,** *4 m (6 km) NE of Creeslough:* now Capuchin Franciscan friary of Ard Mhuire. *By arr., tel: Creeslough 5.*

Ballyness pier, *1 m (1.5 km) N of Falcarragh:* excellent beach in vicinity.

Bloody Foreland: takes its name from the warm reddish colour of the rocks in the setting sun. Fine views of Atlantic and offshore islands. If you have time on your hands, pop into Barnie Melmore's pub, snug against the winds outside.

Carrigart, *at foot of Rosguill Peninsula on T72, Lough Swilly bus from Letterkenny.* Quiet holiday resort with good fishing, excellent beach. Riding: Carrigart Hotel, *tel: (074)53281.*

Creeslough, *6 m (10 km) S of Dunfanaghy, Lough* Swilly bus from Letterkenny. Interesting small village stands on high ground overlooking an inlet from Sheephaven Bay. Duntally Bridge and waterfall, just outside Creeslough, are most attractive. The path of the old Errigal Railway, 28 m (45 km) across NW Donegal to Burtonport, makes a good walkway. Adventure Centre: wide range of outdoor sports, *all year, details: Creeslough 43.*

Doe Castle, *2 m (3 km) NE of Creeslough:* built early 16th c, deserted 1843. Now a fascinating ruin, beautifully set on strip of land running into sea. Access by bridge across moat.

Downings, *3 m (5 km) NW of Carrigart, Lough Swilly bus from Letterkenny.* Well-known sea angling centre. Superb views of Ards Peninsula. Excellent beach. McNutts' tweed factory, *by arr., tel: Downings 15. Closed last week July, first two weeks Aug. Shop all year.* Tra na Rossan Youth Hostel, *tel: Downings 42.*

Dunfanaghy, *Lough Swilly bus from Letterkenny:* popular resort in inlet of Sheephaven Bay, near Horn Head. Strand is 3 m (5 km) long. Nearby Port na Blagh and Marble Hill also have magnificent strands. **The Gallery** is well-known antiques and

Glenveagh Valley

curio shop, *all year, Mon–Sat, 10 a.m.–8 p.m. Sun by arr., tel: (074) 36224.*   Riding: Arnold's Hotel. (074)36208.

Eas Fhionain, *4 m (6 km) E of Falcarragh:* waterfall issuing from rocks oh coast. Associated with St Fionan, the waters are said to have medicinal properties.

Glenveagh Castle and National Park, *11 m (18 km) SE of Falcarragh:* 25,000 acre estate open at all times, splendid Scottish-style mansion, with Victorian furnishings and fine collection of paintings. Outdoor Pursuits Centre: residential accommodation, wide range of outdoor sports, *check with Letterkenny TIO.*

Gortnahork, *2 m (3 km) SW of Falcarragh:* Art and Crafts Centre, *old technical school. July, Aug, daily.* Sub-aqua: McFadden's Hotel, *tel: (074)35101.*

Horn Head, *10 m (16 km) NE of Falcarragh:* cliffs rise out of the sea to height of over 600 ft (180 metres). Splendid views of Atlantic and peaks of Errigal and Muckish. In clear weather, you can

see the Paps of Jura in the Inner Hebrides, 100 m (160 km) NE.

Inishbofin, *3 m (5 km) offshore:* inhabited by about 150 people, a stronghold of Irish language, customs and traditions. Ask at Falcarragh about boats.

Muckish Mountain, *5 m (8 km) SE: 2,197 ft (670 metres),* attracts many climbing enthusiasts.

Lough Glen, *4 m (6 km) E of Creeslough:* delightful lake with fine mountain backdrop.

Rosguill Peninsula, *between Sheephaven and Mulroy Bays:* part of Donegal Gaeltacht. Atlantic Drive round peninsula has some of the finest scenic views in Donegal.

Silver Strand, *Drumnatinney, 3 m (5 km) NE of Falcarragh:* good beach.

Ray Old Church, *2 m (3 km) E of Falcarragh on N56:* site of ancient celtic cross of St Columbkille. Tradition says that the saint hewed the cross from the top of Muckish Mountain and that bad weather stopped him taking it to Tory Island.

Rosapenna, *1 m (1.5 km) from Downings:* fine strand. Golf Club, *18 holes.*

St Columb's, *near Glenveagh:* artist Derek Hill has given the house, overlooking Lough Garton, as a gift to the State. Splendid collection of paintings, china, glass, bric-a-brac, original William Morris wallpaper and a Kokoschka painting. *Details: Letterkenny TIO.*

Tory Island, *9 m (15 km) off coast. Helicopter service:* Irish Helicopters, *Westpoint Hangar, Dublin Airport. Tel: (01) 376473.* Mailboat service: *all year, from Magheroarty Pier, near Gortnahork. Mon, Wed, Fri, 10.30 a.m., returning 9 a.m. following day. Summer boat services are more frequent. Details:* James Ferry, *tel: Falcarragh 37;* Carlton Buchanan, *tel: Downings 48.* Largest of four islands off this part of Donegal 3 m (5 km) long and 1 m (1.5 km) at its greatest breadth, it is largely barren, but its almost sheer cliffs are a fine sight. The population of 200 is often isolated for weeks on end during winter. A trip to the island is an adventure; landing is not easy when the sea is rough and there is no guarantee you will be able to return the same day. Interesting remains: two churches, part of a round tower, 7 ft (2 metre) high Tau Cross. Look out for the work of the island's untrained artists, considered

Gothic style with richly decorated ceilings and impressive windows. 212 ft (65 metres) spire landmark for miles around. The CI Parish Church, *opp. St Eunan's* is 300 years old. Churchyard obelisk in memory of Dr John Kinnean, local Presbyterian minister and 19th c champion of tenants' rights. Swimming pool: indoor, heated, *daily, except Tue.* Bicycles: The Stationery Centre, *Port Road*, tel: (074) 21927. Golf Club, Barnhill, *18 holes*, tel: (074) 21150.

AROUND LETTERKENNY

Ballybofey/Stranorlar, *12 m (19 km) S of Letterkenny on N56. Lough Swilly bus from Letterkenny.* 'Twin' towns connected by bridge over River Finn. Isaac Butt, founder of Home Rule Association, is buried in Stranorlar churchyard. Ballybofey drive: take L75 W, with a choice of routes, either taking the detour near Garranbane Hill, back to Altnapaste or continuing through to Fintown. Following the River Finn the road is quite dramatic and the countryside becomes very wild. From time to time, you may be able to see the old track bed of the late lamented County Donegal railway. Ballybofey and Stranorlar Golf Club, *18 holes, tel: Ballybofey 93.*

Beltany Stone Circle, *2 m (3 km) S of Raphoe:* 64 standing stones, in place since the Bronze Age. Some claim it is older than Stonehenge.

Bunlin Glen, *near Milford:* Bunlin River forms a pretty cascade called the Golan Loop. Near Bunlin Bridge, a second waterfall known as the 'Grey Mare's Tail'.

Carn Hill, *4 m (6 km) S of Ramelton:* excellent viewpoint.

Churchill, *10 m (16 km) W of Letterkenny:* angling centre near beautiful shores of Gartan Lough. Flagstone on hillside W of lake said to mark birthplace of St Colmcille. Forest walks, car park, picnic area. **Glebe Gallery:** *Apr-June, Tues-Sat, 10a.m.-5p.m.; Sun, 1p.m.-5p.m. Jul-Sept, Mon-Sat, 10a.m.-6p.m., Sun, 12p.m.-6p.m.*

Carraig a' Duin (Rock of Doon), *2 m (3 km) W of Kilmacrenan:* flat-topped rock around which clansmen of old gathered when an O'Donnel was to be chosen as chief. Doon Well, at foot, is place of pilgrimage.

Conwal, *2 m (3 km) W of town:* site of ancient monastery. Conwal parish church is very old, several notables lie in its graveyard, inc. Redmond O'Hanlon, the famous 'Rapparee', and his seven sons.

Derryveagh, *3 m (5 km) N of Churchill off L82:* forest walk, good views of Claggan Lough, picnic area, car park.

Drumboe, *200 yds (180 metres) from Stranorlar on T18:* riverside walk, picnic area, car park.

Killydonnell Abbey, *4 m (6 km) SE of Ramelton:* 16th c Franciscan foundation by shores of Lough Swilly, still in reasonable repair.

Kilmacrenan, *7 m (11 km) N of Letterkenny:* ruins of 15th c Franciscan friary. Lough Salt, near village, in very scenic area.

Knockalla Ridge, *between Rathmullan and Portsalon:* good walking territory. Knockalla Coast Road Drive, round Fanad Peninsula, is one of the most spectacular drives in all Donegal. Completed in 1967, the road runs for 8 m (13 km) to Portsalon, giving breathtaking views of Ballymastocker Bay, with its golden beaches. Road goes past Knockalla Fort, which together with Leenan Fort on opp. side of Lough Swilly, was occupied by British garrisons until 1938.

Meenglass, *turn off T18 2 m (3 km) S of Ballybofey:* forest walks.

Meenirroy, *12 m (19 km) W of Letterkenny on L74:* forest walks.

Milford, *10 m (16 km) N of Letterkenny, Lough Swilly bus from Letterkenny.* Tourist and angling centre attractively set at head of Mulroy Bay. Sometimes, small coasters can be seen navigating difficult waters of Mulroy Bay, bound for Milford flour mill.

Monellan, *4 m (6 km) E of Ballybofey:* forest walks

near Crossroads village.

Mongorry, *first R turn NW of Raphoe on Letterkenny Road:* forest walks, good scenic views.

Mullaghagarry, *2 m (3 km) NE of Stranorlar/Ballybofey,* turn L off T18, or R off L80: forest walks, good views over 'twin' towns, picnic areas, car park.

Murren Hill, Dargan Hill, *N Fanad Peninsula:* both worth climbing for excellent views across Mulroy Bay to W and Lough Swilly to E.

Portsalon, *25 m (40 km) N of Letterkenny, Lough Swilly bus from Letterkenny.* Charming, small seaside resort on E side of Fanad Peninsula, set on shores of Ballymastocker Bay. Rita's Bar, by the beach, is famous for its well-preserved traditional interior. Buy a length of tweed with your pint, if you wish. Portsalon Golf Course, *18 holes.* Bunnaton Youth Hostel.

Ramelton, *8 m (13 km) N of Letterkenny on T72, Lough Swilly bus from Letterkenny.* Noted angling centre. The Pool, near the town, is famous for its salmon. Forest walks.

Raphoe, *8 m (13 km) SE of Letterkenny:* busy farming town with square called the Diamond, the pattern of many N towns in Ireland. Cathedral (CI) dates from 1702; alongside are ruins of former bishops' palace. Raphoe Horse Show: *first Mon, Aug.*

Rathmullan, *15 m (24 km) NE of Letterkenny, Lough Swilly bus from Letterkenny.* Historical town that was a main anchorage of the British Fleet during World War I. Town's villas are solid reminders of those far-off navy days. Pier, ruins of 15th c Carmelite friary on outskirts. Rathmullan Sea Angling Festival: *usually June.* Rathmullan Regatta: *early Aug.* Rathmullan Mountains: Croaghan and Crockanaffrin, both just over 1,000 ft (300 metres) high and ideal for climbing.

Rathmullan Wood, *1 m (1.5 km) SW of Rathmullan on L77:* forest walks, fine views over Lough Swilly, picnic areas, car park. Golf Club. Otway, *9 holes.*

Seven Arches, *2 m (3 km) N of Portsalon:* tunnels in the rock that are a striking sight. Further N at Doaghbeg cliffs rise to a great height, with natural Arch of Doaghbeg, big enough to take a boat.

Woodquarter, *2 m (3 km) NW of Milford on T72:* forest walks, excellent views over Mulroy Bay, picnic area, car park.

Folk Festival

seriously by critics of 'primitive' paintings. See West Town, with one shop, and walk along pier, as well as even smaller East Town. Youth Hostel.

Tranarossan, *NE side of Rosguill Peninsula:* one of most picturesquely situated beaches in Co Donegal.

Letterkenny

Pop. 5,000, 21 m (34 km) W of Derry, 32 m (51 km) E of Dungloe. EC. Wed. TIO: (074) 21160, all year. Bus enquiries: Londonderry and Lough Swilly Road Services, tel: (074) 22863. Lough Swilly bus from Derry. 96 from Dublin.

Situated on a hillside overlooking the River Swilly, it has one of the longest Main Streets in Ireland. Good touring centre for N Donegal. International Folk Festival, star-studded week long event, *Aug. Details, TIO.* Donegal International Motor Rally, *June. Details, TIO.*

St Eunan's Cathedral (C): modern building in

Londonderry

Pop. 52,000, 73 m (117 km) W of Belfast, 152 m (245 km) NW of Dublin. EC. Thurs. TIO: Foyle Street, tel: 269501. All year. Bus enquiries: Ulsterbus, Foyle Street bus station, tel: Derry 262261. Also: Londonderry and Lough Swilly Bus Co (for Co. Donegal), Great James Street, tel: Derry 262017. Train enquiries: Waterside station, tel: Derry 242228. Frequent bus services to Belfast, Coleraine, Co. Donegal, Sligo. Also train to Belfast, Coleraine. Taxis: Waterside railway station.

Perhaps more popularly known as Derry (the city's rightful title is a matter of political debate). Settlement began in the 6th c, and certain historical events, such as the lifting of the siege

Londonderry and River Foyle

in 1689, are still recalled with passion. More recently, it has been wracked by some of the most serious disturbances in the present Troubles. A walk from Guildhall Square, through the William Street area as far as Free Derry Corner, with its internationally-known legend, "You are now entering Free Derry," will give a vivid illustration of this intensely Irish city's turmoil. With the old W part of the city rising dour and cramped from the edge of the River Foyle, Derry may appear at first sight to be unwelcoming; closer acquaintance will reveal the very opposite.

Guildhall, *Shipquay Place:* built 1912, fine stained glass windows. Corporation treasures include magnificent collection of Irish plate. *Business hours, Mon–Fri. Also occ. events, such as theatre.*

St Columb's Cathedral (CI), *Bishop Street, City bus A, G.* Memorial window depicts lifting of famous siege. Another window honours noted hymn writer Mrs Frances Alexander. Chapter House has historical objects, inc. padlocks and keys of gates closed by the apprentice boys in 1688. *Daily, 9 a.m.–12.30 p.m.; 2 p.m.– 5 p.m.***D** Nearby Fountain Street has well-preserved wall murals of King William. **St Eugene's Cathedral** (C), *Infirmary Road:* Gothic style, late 19th c. Fine stained glass. Flamboyant, atmospheric building. *Daily.***D Long Tower Church** (C): built in 1784 just outside SW of city walls. Lavishly decorated interior.

Gordon Gallery, *36 Ferrquay Street. Works by prominent local artists. Daily, 11 a.m.–5.30 p.m.* **Orchard Gallery,** *Orchard Street:* regular exhibitions by local artists, also occ. Arts Council exhibitions. Also workshops, meetings, concerts. *Tues–Sat, 11 a.m.–6 p.m. Occ. eve. Details: Derry 269675.* **Magee College,** *Northland Road, City bus B, F.* Occ. theatre, films, other events. *Details: Derry 265621.*

Walls of Derry: only unbroken fortifications in either Ireland or Britain. Walk round open S sections for fine views of city. Also see various cannons facing Guildhall. Below W section lie the Bogside and Creggan estates, internationally renowned during the present Troubles. *Shipquay Street:* walk up one of steepest main streets in world to Diamond with its impressive war memorial. **Craigavon Bridge:** invigorating walk from old city to E side, known as the Waterside, largely residential, good exercise climbing the steep streets. **St Columb's Park,** *Waterside, City bus G.* Fine views of Inishowen Peninsula on Co. Donegal site of Lough Foyle. There are also walks along the quays, through the Georgian-style Clarendon Street area, in Brooke Park and along Northland Road towards the city boundary.

Templemore Sports Complex, *Buncrana Road, City Bus K.* Wide range of indoor and outdoor

sports, inc. pool, conference, function rooms, sauna, bar, restaurant. *Mon–Sun. Details: Derry 265521.* St Columb's Park Activity Centre, *Limavady road: Daily. Details, Derry 243941.* Brooke Park Leisure Centre: *daily, details: Derry 262637.* Lisnagelvin Leisure Centre, inc. pool: *Richhill Park, daily, details: Derry 244442.* Swimming pool: indoor, heated, *William Street, daily, tel: Derry 264459.* City of Derry Golf Club, *18 holes, tel: Derry 242610.*

AROUND DERRY

Ballyarnet, *3 m (5 km) N of Derry, off Buncrana Road:* See site of Amelia Earhart's famous landing after 1932 solo transatlantic flight.

Guildhall windows, Derry

Ballyliffen, *N Inishowen peninsula:* delightful small resort. Nearby, vast sandy stretches of Pollan Strand. Ballyliffen Golf Club, *18 holes, tel: Clonmany 19.*

Banagher Church, *2 m (3 km) SW of Dungiven:* impressive ruin; nave dates from about 1100.

Banagher Forest, *off Draperstown– Feeny B40:* largest in Co Derry, with large artificial Banagher Glen lake, nature reserve.

Buncrana, *W Inishowen, bus enquiries: (077)61340. Lough Swilly bus from Derry.* Seaside resort, fine beach, popular with folk from Derry 13 m (21 km) down the road. The crack's good, especially in summer. **Slieve Snaght Mountain,** *just NE of the town,* worth climbing if you're energetic—it's just over 2,000 ft (600 metres) high. Rewarding views from summit. Walk: via Castle Bridge (O'Doherty's Castle) past Porthaw Bay to Friar Hegarty's Rock, where a local clergyman was executed in 1632. Riding: Bill Doherty, *Main Street.* Bicycles: Hegarty's, *Upper Main Street.* North West Golf Club, *18 holes, Fahan, tel: (077)61027.*

Burt Church, *5 m (8 km) W of the city:* striking circular church designed by Derry architect Liam McCormick, who drew his inspiration from the nearby Grianan of Aileach.

Carndonagh, *N Inishowen. Lough Swilly bus from Derry.* Donagh or St Patrick's Cross stands over 11 ft (3 metres) high and is reputed to be the oldest of its kind in Ireland.

Carrick Rocks, *3 m (5 km) S of Limavady:* charming gorge on River Roe, spanned by foot bridge.

Clonmany, *12 m (19 km) NE of Buncrana on T73:* restful village close to sea. Fine waterfall nearby at Glenevin.

Corby Lynn, *1 m (1.5 km) downstream from Donemana:* attractive walk by waterfall near Tullyard Bridge.

Corick Glen, *3 m (5 km) downstream of Plumbridge:* picturesque meeting point of Glenelly and Owenkillew Rivers.

Culdaff, *on Malin–Moville T73:* Bocan church has 11" (280 mm) high bronze bell dating from 9th or 10th c.

Culmore Point, *3 m (5 km) NE of Derry on A2, Lough Swilly bus from Derry to Moville stops here.* Reconstructed Plantation fort next to lighthouse. Also ruins of old church used by Jacobite army in 1688–89.

Cumber House Riverside Park, *just outside Claudy, 8 m (13 km) SE of Derry, 147, 148 Ulsterbus from Derry.* Nature reserve, picnic area on banks of River Faughan.

Dergalt, *3 m (5 km) from Strabane on Plumbridge road:* birthplace of James Wilson, grandfather of U.S. president Woodrow Wilson. (NT) Original furnishings give good ideal of late 18th c living conditions. *all year, call at farm for admittance.*

Donemana, *7 m (11 km) NE of Strabane on B49, D2 Ulsterbus from Derry. EC, Wed.* Steep-streeted village on banks of Burndennet River. Just S of village is impressively modern St Patrick's church (C), with unusual fibreglass statue of the saint.

Dunaff Head, *4 m (6 km) W of Clonmany:* spectacular sea views.

Dungiven, *20 m (32 km) E of city, 148 Ulsterbus from Derry.* Steeped in history, with several interesting ruins in vicinity. Good game fishing centre.

Dungiven Bawn: remains of early 17th c fortified mansion. Castle has gone, but the surrounding bawn can still be seen. **The Priory,** *just S of town:* founded in 1100 by the O'Cahans, now ruins attractively sited on rock overlooking River Roe.

Eglington, *5 m (8 km) NE of Derry, 143, 152 Ulsterbus from Derry.* Tree-lined village with very English air. Just S is Muff Glen, with woodland walks.

Fahan, *4 m (6 km) S of Buncrana on T73, Lough Swilly bus from Derry to Buncrana stops here.* Attractive little village by shores of Lough Swilly. St Mura's Cross in abbey graveyard. Nearby Inch island connected to mainland by bridge.

Gap of Mamore, *5 m (8 km) NE of Buncrana:* striking views over large part of Inishowen peninsula.

Goles Forest, *near Mount Hamilton, just off B47:* road runs to highest point in forest. Walks, picnic area.

Greencastle, *3 m (5 km) N of Moville, Lough Swilly bus from Derry.* Martello Tower ramparts give fine views over Lough Foyle. Bathing at nearby Shrove Strand.

Grianan of Aileach, *5 m (8 km) W of Derry:* remarkable stone fort built about 1700 BC, yet virtually intact. Excellent views from top of the wall. Turn off main Derry–Buncrana road at Bridgend onto N13 towards Letterkenny. Track from this road runs right to fort.

Learmount Forest, *4 m (7 km) SE of Claudy:* one of NI's most beautiful country parks. Caravanning facilities, Youth Hostel.

Lecamey, *4 m (7 km) NW of Moville:* Sweat House, where in the bad old days, sick people sat amid turf fires and literally sweated it out. Have a look at any time.

Ligfordrum Forest, *4 m (6 km) SE of Strabane on Plumbridge road:* attractive picnic area in disused quarry.

Limavady, *17 m (27 km) E of Derry on A2. EC. Thurs. Bus enquiries: Ulsterbus, Limavady. Tel: Limavady 2101. Train enquiries: Derry 242228. 143 Ulsterbus from Derry. Also train.* Market town with lots of Georgian style. Six-arched Roe Bridge dates back to 1700. Monday market in Main Street good for bargains and banter. **Bellarena Fisheries:** see salmon and trout being smoked, *by arr, Mon–Fri, 10 a.m.–4 p.m., tel: Limavady 481.* Swimming pool: indoor, heated, *Greystone Road, daily, tel: Limavady 4009.* Riding: Mrs R. Smyth, *25 Dowland Road, tel: Limavady 2127.* Limavady Recreation Hall: *9 Greystone Road, daily, tel: Limavady 6279.* Stradreagh Youth Hostel: *4 m (6 km) NE of Limavady.*

Loughermore Forest, *5 m (8 km) NE of Claudy off B69:* splendid walks through wild mountain scenery. At Ballyholly Hill, three stone circles that may have been used as a calendar in 2000 BC.

Magheramore Hill, *2 m (3 km) E of Clonmany:* Bronze Age dolmen with massive capstone.

Malin, *N Inishowen, Lough Swilly bus from Derry.* Sited on Trawbreaga Bay with sandy beach and some of Europe's highest sand dunes, wins Tidy Towns contests with seemingly effortless ease.

Malin Head, Co. Donegal

Malin Head, *8 m (13 km) N of Malin:* most N point in Ireland, with views and winds to match. The 5 m (8 km) long Atlantic Circle drive gives the best views.

Moor Lough, *5 m (8 km) E of Strabane:* attractive walks along sand and gravel shore.

Mount Hamilton, *or Sperrins, 9 m (15 m) E of Plumbridge:* best starting-point for exploring lonely and rugged Sperrin Mountains, including Sawel Mountain 2,240 ft (680 metres). From the hamlet, minor roads run N and S across the mountains.

Moville, *Lough Swilly bus from Derry:* pleasant little seaside town on E shores of Inishowen peninsula. Moville Green is famous for its velvet-like turf; sandy beaches. Moville Regatta: feast of sporting events. *Usually first Mon Aug.* Riding: Redcastle House, *tel: Moville 73.*

Ness Country Park, *near Brackfield on A6:* Burntollet River forms highest waterfall in N. Ireland (about 39 ft, 12 metres). Narrow gorge above the fall is called Shane's Leap, after an 18th c highwayman who escaped from soldiers there. Nature trail, picnic area.

Old Prehen House, *3 m (5 km) S of Derry, near*

Prehen Golf Course, 98, 102 Ulsterbus from Derry. Various works of art, including portrait of James II, who smiles or frowns according to the light. *By prior arr, with Knox family.*

Park village: roads run S into Sperrin Mountains, giving wide choice of scenic routes through some of Ulster's wildest scenery.

Plumbridge, *10 m (16 km) SE of Strabane:* attractively set mountain village, famed for trout fishing in Glenelly River.

River Foyle, *S of Derry:* some 4 m (7 km) of former railway track between bank of river and Letterkenny road has been turned into a pleasant riverside path. The city, on the hills, is very striking seen from the river.

Roe Valley Country Park, *just S of Limavady:* old water mills from great days of linen trade. Riverside, woodland walks. Caravan, picnic sites. Visitors centre with exhibition facilities, restaurant. *Easter–Sept, 10 a.m.–6 p.m. daily.* **D**

Sion Mills, *3 m (5 km) S of Strabane on A5, 97 Ulsterbus from Strabane. EC, Sat.* Originally a model linen village with an exceptionally broad Main Street, it still has great charm. **St Teresa's church** (C), designed in striking style by same architect (Patrick Haughey) as Catholic church in Donemana; there are pleasant walks to village of Carrigullin Lower across Bearney suspension footbridge over River Mourne.

Slievekirk Mountains, *3 m (5 km) NE of Donemana:* old turf track runs up mountain from the Old Glen, Castlewarren, good views of Sperrin Mountains.

Strabane, *14 m (23 km) S of Derry on A5. EC. Thurs. TIO: Lifford Road, tel: Strabane 823333, end May–mid Sept. Bus enquiries: Strabane 2393. 98, 102 Ulsterbus from Derry.* Market town on the banks of the River Mourne. **Gray's Printing Press** (NT), *Main Street:* John Dunlop, who printed the first copies of the American Declaration of Independence in 1776, began his apprenticeship here 20 years earlier at the age of ten. Fine examples of old printing presses and type, including early 19th c Columbian press, topped by a golden eagle. *Daily, except Thu, Sun, public holidays, 2 p.m.–6 p.m.*

Knockavoe Hill, *overlooking the town,* is easy to climb and gives good views as far as Errigal and Muckish Mountains in Co. Donegal. **Strabane Glen:** *1 m (1.5 km) NE of the town,* has good River Foyle views and there are pleasant walks along the Water Mall and banks of River Mourne, also to Lifford, administrative capital of Donegal, literally on the other side of River Finn, Leisure centres: Melvin Hall, *tel: Strabane 882660;* Riverdale centre, inc. pool, *tel: Strabane 886372.* Strabane Golf Club, *18 holes, tel: Strabane 882271.*

Tullagh Bay, *2 m (3 km) NW of Clonmany, N Inishowen:* good beach.

Omagh

Pop. 12,000, 34 m (55 km) S of Derry, 73 m (117 km) W of Belfast, 118 m (190 km) NW of Dublin. EC Wed. Bus enquiries: bus station, Mountjoy Road, tel: Omagh 2711. 79, 98, 273 Ulsterbus from Derry, 273 from Belfast.

The county town of Co. Tyrone, Omagh is set where the Rivers Camowen and Drumragh meet to form the Strule. Its best view is perhaps along the steep and wide High Street, crowned by the choicely-sited, classical style courthouse, behind which stands the modern (C) church, with Gothic style spires. Good salmon, trout, roach fishing in area. Agricultural Show: *first week July.*

Riverside walk: along the banks of the Camowen, past the 'lovers' retreat'. Nearby, see salmon leap 'stairs' in river. Scenic drive to Cookstown over Black Bog, about 27 m (43 km). Turf souvenirs: Owencraft, *Woodside Avenue, by app., tel: Omagh 3097.* Recreation and youth centre: *Old Mountfield Road, daily.* Dergmoney

Riding School, *tel: Omagh 2336;* Mullaghmore Riding School. Omagh Golf Club, *18 holes, tel: Omagh 3160.*

AROUND OMAGH

Ballygawley, *15 m (24 km) SE of Omagh.* **Ulysses S. Grant** (18th President of USA) homestead at Dergenagh due to open shortly. *Details: Dungannon District Council, tel: Dungannon 25311.*

Baronscourt Forest, *3 m (5 km) SW of Newtownstewart on B84:* set on slopes of Bessy Bell Mountain. Japanese sika deer. Nature trail adjacent to Hunting Lodge Hotel. *All year daily during daylight hours.*

Baronscount Estate: home of Duke and Duchess of Abercorn. Gardens and grounds open to organised parties by arr. Attractive deer park dating from 1770's - Japanese Sika deer. Self-catering chalets available all year. Good quality pike fishing. Garden centre open *Mon-Sat, 10a.m.-4.30p.m., Sun 2p.m.-4.30p.m. Details: Baronscourt Estate Office, tel: Newtownstewart 61683.*

Castlederg, *96, 100 Ulsterbus from Omagh:* ruins of Castlesessagh bawn (known locally as Derg Castle), built around 1610, on N bank of River Derg.

Clogher, *15 m (24 km) SE of Omagh on B83. EC, Thurs.* St MacCartan's Cathedral (CI), remodelled 1818. Porch has Clogh-oir, a pagan idol, as well as collection of portraits of former bishops. Good view of Clogher valley from top of tower. *By arr the dean.*

Favour Royal Forest, *3 m (5 km) SE of Augher:* herds of fallow deer, at S end, walk to St Patrick's wishing well and chair.

Fintona, *8 m (13 km) S of Omagh on B122. 87 Ulsterbus from Omagh.* Pleasant walks in wooded park. Golf course next to Ecclesville Park has stone Cow Bridge over Quiggery Water River, all that remains of old coach road.

Gollagh Woods, *on A28 2 m (4 km) E of Augher:* secluded beauty spot on banks of River Blackwater.

Gortin Glen Forest Park, *5 m (8 km) NW of Omagh on B48:* wildfowl enclosure and reserve with Sika deer, nature trails, natural history museum, café, children's play area. On E side of park, extensive views from Mullaghcarn Mountain. Near entrance on B48, the 'magnetic mile' effect will make , our car appear to move uphill—leave the brake off, the road is quite flat! *All year, daily, 10 a.m.–sunset, details: Gortin 217.* Visit nearby Boorin Wood and Gortin Lakes. Youth Hostel in Gortin Village.

Killeter, *5 m (8 km) SW of Castlederg:* isolated but excellent hill, riverside walks. **Killeter Forest,** *just W of Castlederg:* vast upland area is one of the newest and least known forests in NI. You may see red deer. Riverside nature trail, camping site.

Knock-na-Moe Castle Hotel, *Cookstown Road, near Omagh:* Eisenhower and Montgomery Rooms are reminders of secret military planning meetings here involving the two leaders during World War II. *Details: Omagh 3131.*

Knockmany Forest, *12 m (20 km) SE of Omagh on B83:* spread along slopes of Sperrins with good walks, waterfall, splendid viewpoints. On summit of 656 ft (200 metre) hill, see Knockmany chambered cairn, with extraordinary surface designs, believed to date back five or six thousand years.

Leap Bridge, *3 m (5 km) SE of Omagh on B158:* salmon leap on Camowen River and old water mill.

Lough Bradan Forest, *12 m (19 km) W of Omagh, just W of Drumquin on B50:* 5,700 acres of forest. Picnic sites, walks, trout lake. Lough Bradan bog is nature reserve.

Newtownstewart, *9 m (15 km) NW of Omagh on A5. 98 Ulsterbus from Omagh.* Small town attractively set on River Strule. Ruin of Harry Avery's mediaeval castle is 0.4 m (0.8 km) SW of village. The O'Neill chieftain who built the castle wasn't a nice man to know—he is said to have hung 19 men who refused to marry his ugly sister. Ruins of castle, burned in 1689, behind shop at N end of Main Street. The Northern Bank has bloodstained counter, where Thomas Montgomery, a local policeman, murdered William Glass, a bank cashier, in 1871. *Mon–Fri, 10 a.m.–12.30 p.m.; 1.30 p.m.–3.30 p.m.* Newtownstewart Golf Club, *18 holes, tel: Newtownstewart 466.*

Seskinore Forest, *6 m (10 km) S of Omagh on B83:* camping, picnic sites, forest walks. Dept of Agriculture rears pheasants on game farm; see collection of ornamental birds.

Springtown, *2 m (3 km) E of Augher. 85 Ulsterbus from Omagh to Augher.* William Carleton's cottage, where the famous 19th c Irish novelist, spent his youth, is marked by a plaque.

Ulster–American Folk Park, *Camphill, 4 m (6 km) N of Omagh on A5. 98 Ulsterbus from Omagh.* Endowed by Mellons, an American banking family. The cottage from which Thomas Mellon emigrated to America in 1818 is but one of many attractions on this site. Other reconstructed cottages, museum, audio-visual theatre, exhibition galleries detail Irish emigration to the U.S. Farm museum, Old World and New World sections. Former includes meeting house, schoolhouse, forge, country shop. Latter includes log stockade, early Mellon log house at Turtle Creek, Pennsylvania. A full day out. Café, gifts and craft shop, picnic areas. *May–Aug, Mon–Sat, 11 a.m.–6.30 p.m. Sun, 11.30 a.m.–7 p.m. Rest of year, daily, 10.30 a.m.–4.30 p.m. Last admission 1 hr before closing. Closed Sat, Sun, Public Holidays, mid-Oct–mid-March.* **D** *Details: Omagh 3292/3293.*

Sligo

Pop. 15,000, 37 m (59 km) NE of Ballina, 135 m (217 km) NW of Dublin. EC Wed. TIO: Temple Street, tel: (071) 61201, all year. Sligo airport: Strandhill, tel: (071) 7280. Bus, train enquiries: CIE, Mac-Dairmada station, tel: (071) 2152. 125, 268 bus from Ballina, 125 from Belfast, 114, 290 from Derry, 125, 283 from Enniskillen, 114, 115, (SO) 126, 247, 267 from Galway. Train from Carrick-on-Shannon, Longford, Dublin. Coach tours: SO, details, TIO.

The old and flourishing town of Sligo is one of the most attractively set in Ireland, with majestic mountains to the N and the vast, cone-shaped Knocknarea to the S. The town itself is an enticing mixture of modern commerce (complete with good bookshops), ancient history and relatively modern literature: a principal attraction is its connection with W. B. Yeats. Co. Sligo Agricultural Show: *Aug.*

Cathedral of the Immaculate Conception (C), *John Street:* built in Norman style, 1870. **Calry Church,** (CI), *top of Mall:* Gothic style, attractively set above River Garavogue.
Sligo Abbey, *Abbey Street:* founded in 1252 for Dominican Order. Finally destroyed in town's 1641 sacking. After restoration the cloisters are now almost perfect on three sides. Each has 18 beautifully worked arches and elaborately coupled pillars. Key from T. McLoughlin, *6 Abbey Street.*
County Library, *Stephen Street:* includes museum and gallery, with marvellous collection of 20th c Irish art, inc. drawings, by Jack Yeats, J. B. Yeats the elder, George Russell (AE). The museum's Yeats section has a complete collection of his poetical writings, 1889–1936, broadsheets, first editions, paintings, photographs. Centrepiece, his 1923 Nobel Prize for Literature medal. *Daily, 10.30 a.m.–12.30 p.m.; 2.30 p.m.–4.30 p.m. Closed Mondays.*
My Lady's Art Gallery, *Castle Street. Daily, 10.30 a.m.–6 p.m.* **D** **Sligo Art Gallery,** *Yeats Memorial Building, Douglas Hyde Bridge:* frequent visual arts exhibitions, *details: (071) 2693* **Landscape**

Gallery, *Harmony Hill:* key from Mrs R. Cullen, opp. *details (071)3410.* **Hawk's Well Theatre,** *Temple Street:* varied programme in impressive building which combines TIO, *details: (071) 61518–61526.*
Yeats Watch Tower, *corner Adelaide Street, Wine Street:* tops an impressive stone building, once occupied by Pollexfen family, 19th c ship owners. William Pollexfen watched his ships from it and his grandson, W. B. Yeats, spent many happy hours in this eyrie. *Mon–Fri, 9 a.m.–6 p.m.* Yeats International Summer School: full programme of events in and around Sligo. Lectures, seminars on many aspects of the poet's life and work, *Aug. details; Mrs Kathleen Moran, Yeats Society, Yeats Memorial Building, Douglas Hyde Bridge, tel: (071) 2693.*
Hargadon's bar, *O'Connell Street:* unchanged for a century, with glass mirrors, mahogany counters, drawers, and atmosphere all of its own. Sligo Craft Pottery, *Market Yard:* original hand-made pottery. *Daily 10 a.m.–6 p.m.*
Doorly Park: *upstream from town:* good walks and splendid views of Lough Gill and surrounding mountains. College Road: best views in Sligo of Ben Bulben and Knocknarea. Riverside walk: start just by Douglas Hyde bridge, go up pleasant Rockwood Parade alongside the river, continue across Thomas Street into Kennedy Parade, then back past Dominican Abbey. Guided tours leave tourist office, Temple Street, taking in Sligo Abbey, Yeats Museum, Art Gallery, St John's Cathedral, Sligo Cathedral. *July, Aug, Mon–Sat, 11 a.m. Aft, eve by arr.*
Sligo racecourse, *Cleveragh:* one of most beautifully set in Ireland, occ. races, *details: TIO.* Swimming pool: outdoor, Markievicz Road, *daily, tel: (071) 3003.* Woods Cycle Co., *7 Castle Street, tel: (071) 2021,* Conway Bros, *Wine Street. Tel: (071)61240.*

AROUND SLIGO

Abbey Court, *2 m (3 km) NW of Achonry off N17:* ruins of Franciscan friary just outside Lavagh village. A wall vault has burst asunder and a nailed coffin protrudes. Don't come after dark.
Aughris Head, *15 m (24 km) W of Sligo, off N59:* fine views of coast. Aughris is good surfing venue. Nearby Dunmoran Strand a vast, deserted beach.
Ballintogher, *7 m (11 km) SE of Sligo:* Lurgan Stables, *tel: (071) 71327/74150.*
Ballisodare: The Thatch is an old-style Irish pub, with thatched roof, regular Irish nights.
Ballymote, *15 m (24 km) S of Sligo:* Ballymote Castle, by Richard de Burgh, Red Earl of Ulster, extensive ruins flanked by six towers. Remains of Franciscan friary. Remains of 14th c Knights of St John house on shores of Templehouse Lough, 2 m (3 km) SW of village.
Banada Augustinian Abbey, *4 m (6 km) SW of Tubbercurry on Aclare road:* 15th c ruins beautifully sited by River Moy.
Bricklieve Mountains, *6 m (10 km) SE of Ballymote, signposted road leaves LII at Traveller's Rest:* five ridges have prehistoric cairns dating from 2000 BC, known as the Carrowkeel Passage Grave. Whole day can be spent exploring the ridges and cairns. Tremendous sunset views.
Cairns Hill, *2 m (3 km) SE of Sligo:* unusual views of Sligo from summit, with its grass-grown ring fort. Nearby forest walks, picnic area.
Carrowmore Megaliths, *2 m (3 km) SW of Sligo, at foot of Knocknarea:* Bronze Age tombs stretch over 2 m (3 km) of striking countryside, one of the largest such concentrations in Europe. Sligo Riding Centre, *3 m (5 km) SW of Sligo: tel: (071) 2758.*
Cartron, *off Sligo–Dromahaire L16:* forest walks, picnic area, car park.
Castledargan, *5 m (8 km) S of Sligo at Ballygawley:* forest walks.
Collooney, *7 m (11 km) S of Sligo on N4, 247, 267, 275, 288 bus from Sligo.* Innisfree Crystal, see craftsmen hand-cutting glass. *All year, Mon–Fri, 9 a.m.–5.30 p.m. Sat, 10 a.m.–1.30 p.m., details:*

(071) 71340.

Coney Island, *near Rosses Point:* when tide is out, you can walk or drive to island from Strandhill side. Row of pillars marks route. Coney Island, New York, is believed to have been named after it.
Correagh, *5 m (8 km) S of Sligo, off L117:* forest walks.
Creevykeel Court Cairn, *near Cliffony, 15 m (24 km) N of Sligo on N15, 114, 290, bus from Sligo stops nearby.* Best megalithic remains in Ireland. Cairn enclosed by courtyard impressively sited with mountains to S and E.
Deerpark, *4 m (6 km) E of Sligo on Colcagh road:* prehistoric cairn (NM) has galleries opening off each end of an oval court. Excellent views of Lough Gill, forest walks, picnic areas.
Dooney Rock, *4 m (6 km) E of Sligo on L117:* nature trail through woodlands, past shores of Lough Gill to top of rock. On site leaflets detail forest walks, viewing points. Nearby holy well, shrine.
Dromahaire, *10 m (16 km) SE of Sligo:* ruins of Creevelea Franciscan abbey, built 1508. The 17th c Park's Castle is off the L16 just N of village, key at nearby farm. Riding: Lough Gill Caravans, *Drumlease, Glebe House, tel: (071) 74141.*
Drumcliffe, *4 m (6 km) N of Sligo on N15, 290, 291 bus from Sligo.* Churchyard (C) has impressive 11th c cross. On W side of main road, stump of 6th c round tower. W. B. Yeats is buried in churchyard of plain, square towered C of I. Behind the churchyard are the steep cliffs of King's Mountain and the legendary Ben Bulben. Yeats died at Roquebrune in S France in 1939, and his remains were brought home in 1948. On his headstone are carved the immortal words:

> Cast a cold Eye
> On Life, on Death,
> Horseman, pass by!

Old Rectory Gallery, work by local artists, *SO, daily.* Riding: Old Rectory.
Glen of Knocknarea, *0.75 m (1 m) W of Grange House:* chasm in limestone nearly 1 m (2 km) long. Although filled with vegetation, footpath runs through it.
Glencar Lake, *7 m (11 km) NE of Sligo on N16, 125, 283 bus from Sligo.* One waterfall has an impressive unbroken fall of 50 ft (15 metres). Minor road along N shore has best views of upper waterfall.
Gleniff Horseshoe, *near Cliffony:* one of the most spectacular tours in the NW. Road runs round the glen, past Truskmore with its TV mast, giving fine views of towering limestone cliffs. Gleniff on the Horseshoe route has forest walks, picnic area. Turn off at Cliffony, midway between Sligo and Bundoran on N15 in direction of Ballintrillick.
Grange, *10 m (16 km) N of Sligo on N15. 290, 291 bus from Bundoran, Sligo.* Sligo Crystal factory, *all year, Mon–Fri, 8.30 a.m.–5.30 p.m. July, Aug, Sept, also Sun, 2 p.m.–6 p.m. Details: (071) 73251.*
Hazelwood, *3 m (5 km) E of Sligo, 0.5 m (0.8 km) off L116:* scenic views, although views from N shores of Lough Gill not as good as those on the S. Forest walks, picnic area.
Heapstown Cairn, *N end of Lough Arrow, 15 m (24 km) SE of Sligo off N4:* over 200 ft (61 metres) in diameter, said to have been built in one night. Labby Rock, an enormous dolmen, is 2 m (3 km) E of cairn. Nearby Lough Nasool is said to drain dry every 100 years, the last time in 1933.
Innisfree Island: to find the place immortalised by W. B. Yeats, take L117 from Sligo towards Dromahaire, until the signpost for the island, 3 m (5 km) from this point.
Inishmurray Island, *4 m (6 km) off Streedagh Point:* 1 m (2 km) long island, low-lying and bleak. Landing at pier on E side. Substantial ruins of St Molaise's monastery, plundered by Vikings in 807, 11 stations, wells, memorials dotted round island, which was abandoned in Oct, 1947 when the 50 inhabitants moved to the mainland. Boats: Christy Herrity, *Carns:* Joe McGowan; Mullagh-

more, W. A. Mulligan, *tel: (071) 76126.*

Keshcorran Hill, *4 m (6 km) SE of Ballymote, off L11:* caves of Kesh, in hillside, as well as summit, with breathtaking views, are reached by steep path from farmhouse on minor road to Kesh where it runs parallel to main L11.

Knocknarea, *4 m (6 km) SW of Sligo:* huge limestone cone dominates whole area. Queen Maeve, whose likeness adorns Irish £1 note, reputed to be buried in great summit cairn, from where you can enjoy stupendous views. Easy climb on SE side, near Grange House.

Lady's Brae road, *15 m (24 km) SW of Sligo:* spectacular views of Donegal, Mayo Mountains, as well as Ben Bulben, Knocknarea. At Skreen on N59, turn onto minor road up into Ox Mountains, signposted for Lady's Brae.

Lisnalurg, *2 m (3 km) N of Sligo on N15:* one of largest earthwork enclosures in Ireland, covering about 2 acres.

Ben Bulben

Lissadell House, *4 m (6 km) NW of Drumcliffe, 290, 291 bus from Bundoran, Sligo.* 19th c Georgian house, childhood home of Countess Markievicz, a leader in the 1916 Rising, and her sister Eva Gore-Booth. W. B Yeats, regularly slept in bedroom above porch. Dining, music rooms particularly striking. Gardens with masses of daffodils in spring, nearby pine forests, picnic area, access to Drumcliffe Bay. *May 1–Sept 30. Mon–Sat, 2 p.m.–5.15 p.m. Last tour, 4.30 p.m. Details: (071) 73150.* **Ellen's Pub,** Maugherow, full of atmosphere, very popular with Continental visitors.

Lough Gill, *2 m (3 km) E of Sligo:* lake to rival Killarney, 22 islands. Silver bell from Sligo's ruined Dominican Abbey said to lie at bottom of lake. When it peals, only the perfect can hear. Lough Gill cruises depart from Riverside landing stage, near Blue Lagoon lounge, at Doorly Park entrance. *Apr–Dec. Daily departures, June, July, Aug. Details: (071) 2540/2537.* Boat Hire: Frank Armstrong, *14 Riverside, Sligo;* Peter Henry, *tel: (071) 2530.*

Manorhamilton, *15 m (24 km) E of Sligo on N16. 125, 283 bus from Sligo.* Attractive Co Leitrim town with less than 1,000 inhabitants, nestling at the junction of four mountain valleys. Main object of interest is ruined mansion built by Sir Frederick Hamilton in 1638, just N. Wild Rose Festival: Wild Rose Colleen is chosen, various fringe events during week-long festivities, *Aug.*

Mass Hill, *4 m (6 km) W of Tubbercurry:* charming spot in Ox Mountains. Forest walk, scenic drive.

Milltown, *1 m (2 km) W of Manorhamilton:* forest walks.

Mullaghmore, just off N15 between Sligo and

Bundoran: good, sheltered bathing in shadow of Classiebawn Castle. **Annie's bar** is over 200 years old, many fascinating mementoes (including photographs) left behind by visitors. No music, the pint is drawn slowly.

O'Rourke's Table, *3 m (5 km) N of Dromahaire on Manorhamilton road:* prominent rock plateau gives magnificent view of Lough Gill and Yeats Country:

Raghly, *on peninsula at entrance to Drumcliffe Bay:* quiet fishing village, nearby remains of 16th c Dunfore and Ardtermon castles. Just N of village, Tráigh Bhuí, or Yellow Strand, appropriately sandy. Raghly Promontory, excellent views of mountains encircling Sligo Bay.

Rathcarrick/Knocknarea, *2 m (3 km) S of Sligo–Strandhill L132:* scenic views over Sligo Bay, forest walks, picnic area, car park.

Rosses Point, *5 m (8 km) NW of Sligo on L16, 286 bus from Sligo.* Cosy seaside resort with two

Lissadell House

splendid beaches good for swimming. Good views across Drumcliffe Bay. Rosses Point Golf Club, *18 holes, tel: (071) 77171.*

Sessue Gilroy, *20 m (32 km) W of Sligo, turn S towards Lough Easkey at Dromore West: on N59:* fine forest walks and views.

Slish Wood, *S side of Lough Gill, just off L117:*

forest, lakeside walks, paddling pool, picnic area. Sometimes, fallow deer can be seen.

Strandhill, *4 m (6 km) W of Sligo on L132, 285 bus from Sligo.* Coastal resort with two good sandy beaches.

Dolly's Cottage, *285 bus from Sligo:* early 19th c rural house renovated by Strandhill Guild of Irish Countrywomen's Association. *July, Aug, daily, 3 p.m.–5 p.m. July, Aug. Wed aft. country markets. Wed eve, traditional entertainment. Details: (071) 78264.* Strandhill Golf Club, *18 holes, tel: (071) 78188.*

Streedagh, *2 m (3 km) W of Grange:* during spring tide low water, when wind is blowing strongly from S, you may see wreckage of three Spanish Armada galleons, wrecked in 1588 with only one survivor. Nearby ruins of 7th c Staid Abbey, Aghaharrow.

Union Wood, *5 m (8 km) S of Sligo on L3:* forest walks, picnic area overlooking Ballygawley Lough.

The NORTH

Antrim

Pop. 8,000, 17 m (27 km) NE of Belfast, 112 m (180 km) N of Dublin, via Lurgan. EC Wed. Bus enquiries: Ulsterbus depot, Railway Street, tel: Antrim 62729/ 65048. Train enquiries: Antrim 63185. 120 Ulsterbus from Belfast, also train.
A pleasant if unremarkable town at the NE corner of Lough Neagh, founded on the site of an ancient monastery. Although Antrim is largely residential, it has points of interest and excellent sporting facilities. **Round Tower.** About 1,000 years old, remarkably well preserved

Antrim Castle Demesne, fine gardens W of town along Lough Neagh shore, laid out in late 17th c in similar style to Versailles, complete with ornamental waters. Only a tower remains of original castle, burned in 1922, during previous Troubles. Beside it, the Norman motte makes a fine viewpoint. Co. Antrim agricultural show held here in July. *Daily.* **Clotworthy House,** *castle grounds:* theatre, exhibitions, *details Belfast TIO.*
Alexander Irvine's cottage, *Pogue's Entry, off Church Street:* 18th c cottage, childhood home of the author of the 19th c classic, *My Lady of the Chimney Corner.* Interior little changed, key from adjoining shop.

Antrim Forum, *Lough Road:* impressive modern sports centre with extensive facilities, inc. pool, *daily, tel: Antrim 64131.* Avoniel Leisure Centre, *inc. pool: details: Antrim 51565.* Lough Neagh cruises, *Antrim Marina, Sixmilewater, May–Sept, daily, details: Antrim 64131.* Massereene Golf Club, *18 holes, tel: Antrim 62096.*

AROUND ANTRIM

Ballymena, *11 m (18 km) NW of Antrim. EC Wed. (all day). Bus enquiries: bus station, Galgorm Road, tel: Ballymena 2214. Railway enquiries: station, tel: Ballymena 2277. 120 Ulsterbus from Antrim, Belfast, also train.* Prosperous town with a strong Scottish influence, which may account for it having been described, not entirely fairly, as the meanest town in Ireland. Excellent game fishing. **St Patrick's,** *(CI), Castle Street,* is noted for its rich interior and 19th c Art Nouveau windows.**D** From Ballymena roads run through the Braid and Clogh valleys to Antrim moorlands. The coastal routes to Cushendun and Cushendall are very attractive.

Sentry Hill Sports Hall, *Old Ballymoney Road, tel: Ballymena 6101.* Swimming pool: indoor, heated. *Trostan Avenue, Mon–Sat, tel: Ballymena 41427.* Ballymena Golf Club, *18 holes, tel: Broughshane 861487.*

Broughshane, *3 m (5 km) NE of Ballymena on A42, 128 Ulsterbus from Ballymena.* Memorial in Rathcavan churchyard to the locally-born ancestors of General Sam Houston, who brought Texas into the United States. There is a pleasant walk near the village, across the Buttermilk Footbridge by River Braid.

Carnanee, *3 m (5 km) E of Templepatrick, end of lane just N of main Belfast road:* Patterson's water-powered spade mill has been producing spades and shovels for over 200 years. *Business hours, details: Templepatrick 32227.*

Cullybackey, *3 m (5 km) NW of Ballymena on B96, 115 Ulsterbus from Ballymena, also train.* Arthur Cottage, Dreen, home of the parents of Chester Alan Arthur, 21st President of the United States in early 1880s. Fully restored with typical 19th c furnishings, picture gallery, good view of the River Main. *Apr–Sept 30, daily, 2 p.m.–6 p.m. Closed Fri.* 1 m (2 km) N of village on B93 to Glarryford, there is a curious beehive-shaped thatched cottage.

Dunadry Inn, *3 m (5 km) SE of Antrim, 120 Ulsterbus from Antrim.* Created from an 18th c linen mill and its cottages. Axles from the mill's beetling machinery were used to form the gallery's pillars.

Glarryford, *7 m (11 km) of Ballymena on B62/B93:* small village on banks of the River Main. Attractive countryside deserving of wider recognition.

Gracehill, *2 m (3 km) W of Ballymena on A42:* founded by Moravians in 18th c. German Christmas customs still observed in the village church. Ask rector to see Moravian church records.

Kells, *midway between Antrim and Ballymena, 149 Ulsterbus from Ballymena.* Pleasant walk round Diamond and across the old bridge with views over the weir on the Kells Water River. Remains of ancient Augustinian abbey.

Kilgad Lake Fishery, well-stocked with rainbow trout. *Mar–Sept for season subscribers. Details: Kells 891570.*

Newferry, *4 m (6 km) S of Portglenone:* Crosskeys Inn was a favourite watering hole in mail coach days, well over a century ago. Written on the walls, sample fares.

Portglenone, *215 Ulsterbus from Ballymena.* The Cistercian Monastery has its own printing press. *Male visitors only. Details: Portglenone 821211.*

Portglenone Forest, *8 m (13 km) W of Ballymena:* Bannside oak woods, with Augustine Henry trail, in honour of the forestry pioneer born nearby in 1857, and a memorial grove with some of the thousands of trees and shrubs he discovered. Two holy wells. Picnic sites, nature trails. Dunaird Riding School, *Broughshane, tel: Portglenone 821369.*

Slemish Mountain

Randalstown Forest: deer, squirrels and water birds to be seen from hides. *Visiting permits from The Forestry Division, Dundonald House, Belfast BT4 3SB or forester at Tardree.*

Shane's Castle Demesne, *2 m (3 km) W of Antrim on A6T:* steam railway and nature reserve. Locos haul passenger trains on 2 m (3 km) ride round demesne. Two hides by shore of Lough Neagh enable you to see many varieties of water birds. Café, picnic sites. Excellent facilities for a full day out with the children. *Apr–June, Sun, BH. July–Aug, Wed, Sat, Sun, BH. 1 p.m.–6 p.m.* Steam Traction Rally, *July.* Vintage and classic car rally, *end Aug. Details: Antrim 63380.*

Slemish Mountain, *8 m (13 km) E of Ballymena:* volcanic cone which dominates the whole area. Legend says that St Patrick, as a boy slave, herded swine here for his owner, Miluic. Road runs to near top of mountain.

Tardree Forest, *6 m (9 km) of Antrim:* forest walks give good views over Lough Neagh and Slemish. Nature trail. 2 m (3 km) E of forest, Browndod Hill has a Neolithic cairn on summit.

Templepatrick. Templetown Mausoleum built in 1783 by Robert Adams. *Grounds open at all times.* Hartfield Equestrian Centre, *Ballyhartfield Road, Templepatrick. Tel: Ballyclare 41350.*

Toomebridge, *10 m (16 km) W of Antrim on A6T, 210, 211 Ulsterbus from Antrim.* Eel fishery, run as a co-op. Spring is best time to visit, when about 20 million elvers, or baby eels, swim across Atlantic and up the River Bann.

Armagh

Pop. 13,000, 37 m (59 km) SW of Belfast, 85 m (137 m) NW of Dublin. All day closing: Wed. Bus enquiries: Ulsterbus depot, Mall West, tel: Armagh 522266. 51, 61, 251 Ulsterbus from Belfast.

Dominated by its two cathedrals, one Catholic, the other Protestant, for 1500 years Armagh has been the ecclesiastical capital of Ireland. Founded in the 5th c, when St Patrick established his Primatial See here, the city became an internationally renowned centre of learning during the middle ages. Today it retains much of its historic atmosphere and walks round the main sights are very rewarding.

St Patrick's Cathedral (C), set on a hilltop and reached by a fine flight of steps. 19th c Byzantine style, with lavish interior decoration. Red hats of four cardinals hang from Lady Chapel ceiling. **St Patrick's Cathedral** (CI), largely an early 19th c restoration on a 13th c building. Tablet outside N transept marks reputed grave of Brian Boru. **Old Archbishop's Palace** (CI), now district council offices. Fine collection of paintings, classical-style private chapel. *Mon–Fri, 9 a.m.–5 p.m.* **Public Library**, *near CI cathedral:* remarkable institution, founded 1771, with interesting collection, inc. old manuscripts. *Mon–Sat.* **Armagh Friary**, Franciscan, founded 1263–4, longest friary church in Ireland, now ruins. SE edge of city.

Planetarium, *College Hill:* Ireland's only astronomical observatory; public telescope, space equipment (inc. satellite), lectures, films, exhibitions. *Exhibition area, daily, 2 p.m. onwards. July, Aug, imaginative daily shows at 3 p.m., except July 12. Sun, details: Armagh 523689.* **D**

Royal Irish Fusiliers' Regimental Museum, *Sovereign's House, the Mall:* thousands of items detailing the regiment's history. *Mon–Fri, 10 a.m.–12.30 p.m.; 2 p.m.–4.30 p.m. Closed public holidays. Weekends, by arr., tel: Armagh 522911.* **County Museum**, *the Mall:* over 10,000 items, inc. prehistoric implements, local relics. Library, art gallery. Paintings by AE (writer and artist, George Russell, a Lurgan man). Occ. special exhibitions. *Mon–Sat, 10 a.m.–1 p.m.; 2 p.m.–5 p.m. Closed Sun, certain public holidays.* **Cloud Cuckoo Gallery**, *41 Ogle Street, daily.*

The Mall: attractive tree-lined green in the middle of Armagh, constructed on the old racecourse, a peaceful oasis. Jenny's Row, the Seven Houses, Market Square, Scotch Street, Dobbin Street or Castle Street. Folly Glen: pleasant stream-side walk on S side of Armagh. **The Shambles:** pick up a bargain at the various antique shops. Swimming Pool: indoor, heated, *Folly Lane, off Newry Road, Mon–Sat, details: Armagh 522892.* **D** Armagh County Golf Club, *18 holes, tel: Armagh 522501.*

AROUND ARMAGH

Ardress House (NT), *5 m (8 km) E of Moy on B28:* magnificent 17th c farmhouse with fine plasterwork and splendid collection of paintings. Small agricultural museum in farmyard. Garden, picnic area, adventure playground in woods. *Apr–Sept 30, daily, 2 p.m.–6 p.m. Closed Fri. Open Good Fri.*

The Argory, (NT), *4 m (6 km) NE of Moy on Derrycaw road:* fine early 19th c house set in over 300 acres of wooded countryside, overlooking River Blackwater. Rare herd of red Irish cattle, known as moile being preserved here. Lit by an acetylene gas plant in stable yard, house little changed since turn of century. Contents include 1824 organ. *Apr–Sept 30, daily, 2 p.m.–6 p.m. Closed Fri.*

Banbridge, *10 m (16 km) SE of Portadown. EC Thurs. TIO: Information Portakabin, Newry Road, tel: Banbridge 22143. July, Aug. Bus enquiries: 50 Newry Street. Tel: Banbridge 23633. 38, 238 Ulsterbus from Belfast.* Unassuming market town, bisected by underpass in Main Street. Birthplace of Helen Waddell, the noted early 20th c writer.

Downshire Leisure Centre, *daily, tel: Banbridge 23233.*

Benburb, *7 m (11 km) NW of Armagh, 72 Ulsterbus from Armagh.* Servite Priory. Visitors are welcomed to the cheerful cloisters, setting for inter denominational meetings of all kinds. Art gallery, library. Ruins of castle in grounds, poised above River Blackwater. *Details: Benburb 241.*

Blackwater Forest Park, *on opp. bank of River Blackwater to Benburb:* extends for 3 m (5 km), canoeing over weirs, deep pool for sub-aqua

training, fossil hunting area, riverside walks.

Blackwatertown, *5 m (8 km) NW of Armagh on A29/B128, 72 Ulsterbus from Armagh.* Good place to see road bowls, nicknamed 'bullets', being played. Rather like French *boules*, bowls are hurled along the road. Game is confined to counties Armagh and Cork. All-Ireland finals take place here in Aug.

Brantry Forest, *5 m (8 km) W of Benburb, just off B128:* attractive lake, picnic area.

Carnagh Forest, *just S of Keady, on Castleblayney road:* delightful fishing inn overlooks the lake. See woods by jaunting car or pony. Caravan site.

Charlemont Fort, *opp. Moy on the River Blackwater, enter via S side of bridge:* the ruins of earthworks started in 1602 can be followed for most of their length.

Clare Glen, *runs SW from Tandragee for 3 m (5 km), 63 Ulsterbus from Portadown.* Pleasant walks by River Cusher.

Craigavon, new town named after NI's first Prime Minister, set in wooded countryside S of Lough Neagh. Brownlow Recreation Centre, inc. pool, *tel: Craigavon 41333.* Craigavon Golf and Ski Centre, *Turmoyra, S of Oxford Island:* artificial ski slopes, golf putting. Refreshments. *Mon–Sat, tel: Lurgan 41950.* Craigavon Lakes: rowing, sailing, canoeing, regular water sports events. Craigavon Golf Course, *9 holes, tel: Lurgan 3988.* Peacock Gallery, Pinebank House Arts Centre, *Tullygally Road, Craigavon BT65 5BY. Daily. Details: (0762) 41082/41033.*

Fews Forest, *9 m (15 km) S of Armagh on B31:* great walking country where you can stride for miles through forests and along moorland tracks. Fine views over countries Armagh and Down from picnic sites at Carrigatuke and Dead Man's Hill.

Gilford, *5 m (8 km) NE of Tandragee:* marvellous shell garden, *7 Stramore Road. June–Sept, daily except Sat, 1 p.m.–dusk*

Gosford Forest Park, *near Markethill, 40 Ulsterbus from Armagh,* Gosfort Castle closed, but see nearby round tower built by German prisoners-of-war held there during World War II.

Apple-picking in Co. Armagh

Greeve Lough Forest, *4 m (6 km) N of Caledon:* coarse fishing, walks.

Keady, *8 m (13 km) S of Armagh on A29, 69, 278 Ulsterbus from Armagh.* Pleasantly wooded Keady Glen with attractive waterfall.

Loughgall, *5 m (8 km) NW of Armagh on B77:* the apple growing centre of Ireland, rich with orchards. In May, follow signposted tour during apple blossom time. **Orange Order Museum**, *Main Street:* recalls founding of movement here in 1795. *By arr. with caretaker who lives next door.*

Mon–Sat, am & pm. **Loughgall Presbyterian Church**, Ulster poet W. R. Rodgers, was minister here before he devoted himself wholly to writing.

Lurgan, *21 m (34 km) SE of Belfast on M1. All day closing, Wed. Bus enquiries: Ulsterbus, tel: Craigavon 42511. Sureline coaches, tel: Lurgan 22724. Train enquiries: Lurgan 22052. 51, 61, 251 Ulsterbus from Armagh, train from Belfast.* Market town. Small lanes off main streets are remnants of 18th c linen weaving shops. In front of Brownlow House, see monument to Master McGrath, champion racing greyhound. Brownlow Park, boating, fishing. Swimming Pool: indoor, heated, *Robert Street, Mon–Sat, tel: Lurgan 22906.* Lurgan Golf Club, *18 holes, tel: Lurgan 22087.*

Marlcoo Lake, *4 m (6 km) E of Armagh on A51:* crannog or artificial islet, to which Hugh O'Neill, Earl of Tyrone, sent his family for safety at start of his 1595 rebellion. Attractive picnic area.

Middletown, *10 m (16 km) SE of Armagh on A3, 70 Ulsterbus from Armagh.* Enjoyable walk along rather overgrown towpath of long-derelict Ulster Canal.

Moy, *7 m (11 km) N of Armagh on A29, 72, 278 Ulster from Armagh.* Fine tree-lined square. Moy Riding School, *21 Killyman Street, tel: Moy 309.*

Oxford Island, *SE corner of Lough Neagh, 3 m (6 km) from Lurgan:* peninsula and series of bays housing yachting and swimming lido. **Lough Neagh Country Park:** information centre, nature trails. *Mon–Sat.*

Navan Fort, *2 m (3 km) W of Armach on A28:* remains of Eamhain Macha, said to have been built about 300 BC and to have been the most important place in Ireland. No trace of buildings on site. The country's oldest legends, including the Ulster Cycle with its hero Cuchullain, are centred on this area. *Apr 1–Sept 30, Tues–Sat, 10 a.m.–7 p.m. Closed at 1 p.m. for ½ hr lunch Sun, 2 p.m.—7 a.m.*

Portadown, *27 m (43 km) SW of Belfast. All day closing, Thurs. Bus enquiries: tel: Portadown 32323. Train enquiries: Portadown station, tel: Portadown 33051. 61, 65, 251 Ulsterbus from* Armagh, train from Belfast. Market town on the River Bann, and a major coarse fishing centre. Swimming Pool: indoor, heated. Learner and competitive pools, *Thomas Street, Mon–Sat, tel: Portadown 33050.* Portadown Golf Club, *18 holes, tel: Portadown 35356.*

Scarva Demesne, *near Banbridge:* Scarva Sham Fight (a traditional Orange v Green pageant) *July 13.* The Railway Preservation Society of Ireland is reopening a section of the old GNR railway from Scarva for steam train trips, *details: Whitehead 8567.*

Seagahan Dam, *5 m (8 km) W of Markethill:* the edge of Fews Forest, encircled by scenic road with picnic sites. Pleasant, little-known spot.

Tandragee, Golf Club, *18 holes, tel: Tandragee 840727.*

Tannaghmore Garden, *N Craigavon:* Victorian garden, pleasures include an aviary and a children's farm with pony rides.

Tassagh, *2 m (3 km) NW of Keady:* vast disused watermill on Callan River and 11 arches of disused railway viaduct.

Tullygiven Lough, *3 m (4 km) W of Benburb:* popular for picnics and birdwatching.

Tullylish Pottery, *1 m (2 km) E of Gilford off A50:* hand-thrown pottery and other craft lines. *All year. Mon–Sat, 9.30 a.m.–5.30 p.m.* Pot Belly restaurant, *Tues–Sat. Details: Gilford 831404.*

White Hill, *just N of Newtownhamilton, lane from B31:* reputed to have been site of palace of King Lir, whose children were turned into swans by a witch.

Ballycastle

Pop. 3,000, 19 m (30 km) E of Coleraine, 67 m (108 km) NE of Belfast via Antrim Road. EC Wed. TIO: Ballycastle 62024/ 62225, Easter and June–Sept. Bus enquiries: Coleraine bus station, tel: Coleraine 3334. 252 Ulsterbus from Belfast (SO). Also train from Belfast to Ballymoney, then 137, 171 Ulsterbus.

An enormously attractive town on the N Antrim coast, completely unspoiled. Ballycastle proper is 2 m (3 km) inland and connected to the smaller seaside part by a broad, tree-lined avenue. An ideal base for exploring the area's many natural attractions, and host to the lively, two day Ould Lammas Fair, *end of Aug:* many bargains, splendid banter.

White Park Bay

occasional remnants may be seen . Cliffs stretch for 3 m (5 km) W of Ballycastle to Kinbane Head, path for most of way. Loughareema Riding Centre, *tel: Ballycastle 62576.* Golf Club, *18 holes, tel: Ballycastle 62536.* Youth Hostel: *34 North*

The Ould Lammas Fair

Museum, *59 Castle Street:* local glassware, historic domestic utensils, Rathlin Island birds, interesting items from the Spanish Armada galleon, the Girona, wrecked off the N Antrim coast. *SO, details, TIO, June–Sept, tel: Ballycastle 62024/62225.* **Bonamargy Friary,** *(1 km) E of Ballycastle:* attractive ruins on banks of River Margy. Founded about 1500, burned by MacDonnells and Scots in 1584. Restored, but later fell into ruin.

Marconi Memorial, *seafront:* marks the spot where the inventor of wireless telegraphy made his first successful transmission, between Ballycastle and Rathlin Island, in 1898. **Pans Rock,** *E end of Ballycastle beach:* old salt drying pan, reached by footbridge. Walks: around harbour area (boats leave from the pier from Rathlin) and in direction of Fair Head, E of beach. In the 18th c, there was extensive coal-mining in this area;

Street, tel: Ballycastle 62337.

AROUND BALLYCASTLE

Armoy, *6 m (10 km) SW of Ballycastle on A44/B15, 131, 137 Ulsterbus from Ballycastle.* Cairn of Peace marks 1959 world ploughing championships held here. Presbyterian church has spire

Entrance hall, Mount Stewart

like miniature Eiffel tower.

Ballintoy, *5 m (8 km) NE of Ballycastle on B15, 175, 252 (SO) Ulsterbus from Ballycastle.* North Antrim cliff path runs for 11 m (18 km) from here to Runkerry, taking in Giant's Causeway, Dunseverick Castle, White Park Bay. The village has a most attractive harbour: white piers and white beach make fine contrast with black cliffs. Parish church with beautiful Resurrection window. Youth Hostel: *157 Whitepark Road, tel: Bushmills 31745.*

Ballycastle Forest Park, *on slopes of Knocklayd Mountain 3 m (8 km) S of Ballycastle:* scenic drive with splendid views, nature trail.

Ballypatrick Forest, *due S of Murlough Bay, near A2:* walks by Corratavy River, scenic drives, nature trails, picnic area. Ponies for hire at farm by entrance.

Ballyvoy, *2 m (3 km) E of Ballycastle on A2:* small road leads from village to hill, planned walks across summit.

Carrick-a-Rede Rope Bridge, *5 m (8 km) W of Ballycastle, near B15 coast road, 172, 252 (SO) Ulsterbus from Ballycastle.* Crossing the swaying bridge, made of planks and wires, from mainland to small offshore island, is an exhilarating experience. Magnificent coastal views if you dare look-up. *Bridge erected early May, taken down mid-Sept.*

Fair Head, *4 m (6 km) NE of Ballycastle:* one of most rugged spots on N coast with wonderful! views of Rathlin Island and SW Scotland.

Glenshesk, *E of Knocklayd Mountain:* well-wooded lanes, ideal for rambles. Attractive riverside walk by waterfall called John Henry's Steps. Breen Wood Nature Reserve has old oak trees. No yellow ribbons!

Kilbane Castle, *4 m (6 km) NW of Ballycastle off B15:* from ruins on long narrow promontory, excellent sea and cliff views. Picnic area.

Loughareema, *vanishing lake on A2 from Ballycastle to Cushendun:* the lake can suddenly dry, as quickly as if someone pulled the plug.

Murlough Bay, *just E of Fair Head:* unspoilt bay in National Trust care. Small ,winding road runs down from Ballylucan, on main road; on way to shore, see monument to Sir Roger Casement.

Port Bradden, *W end of White Park Bay, 172, 252 (SO) Ulsterbus from Ballycastle to Ballintoy.* Tiny hamlet with smallest church in Ireland, 11 ft × 6 ft (3 × 2 metres).

Rathlin Island, *8 m (13 km) N of Ballycastle: between NI and Scotland's Mull of Kintyre:* visited by prehistoric man, and latterly by Robert the Bruce, who, while hiding in a cave here was inspired by a spider's persistence to recover the Scottish throne. Nearly all the coastline is formed by cliffs, but the island itself is almost flat, so walking is no hardship. Pop. about 100. Guesthouse. Crossings: *ask at pier or TIO, 61 Castle Street, Ballycastle, tel: Ballycastle 62024/62225.*

Brockley, remains of stone-age settlement and the prehistoric mound fort of Doonmore. **Knockans,** *between Brockley and the harbour:* traces of an early Christian monastic settlement. The West Lighthouse is best place to see island's enormous bird population, and near the East Lighthouse, cement blocks with title 'Lloyds' mark the base of the wireless mast set up for Marconi in 1898.

Grace Staples' Cave, *below Kinbane Castle:* cuts through the entire cliff. Boat only, ask at Ballycastle Pier or Ballintoy Harbour.

Torr Head, *E end of Murlough Bay:* desolate spot with excellent views of North Channel. Scotland is only 12 m (19 km) away. Narrow coastal road runs N from Cushendun or road from Murlough Bay.

White Park Bay, *2 m (3 km) W of Ballintoy on B146. 172, 252 (SO) Ulsterbus from Ballycastle to Ballintoy.* The bay's half-moon beach is one of finest in the north. Youth Hostel. Also has bicyles for hire.

Bangor

Pop. 40,000, 13 m (21 km) NE of Belfast, 118 m (190 km) N of Dublin, via Belfast. EC Thur. TIO: The Esplanade, tel: Bangor 472092, June–Aug 31. Bus enquiries: Abbey Street bus station, tel: Bangor 474143. Train enquiries: railway station, tel: Bangor 474143. 1 Ulsterbus from Belfast, also train. Coach tours: SO, details TIO.

Originally the site of a rich and influential monastery founded in 559 by St Comgall and devastated, three centuries later, by the Danes, Bangor today is a popular, pleasant and prosperous seaside town extending along the sandy bays of Bangor and Ballyholme. Plenty of indoor entertainments, with a number of nightspots, and excellent shopping.

Bangor Abbey, *at entrance to town, just off main Belfast road:* there are traces of the original monastery but most of its stone was used in the building of the present church, in 1617. **Town Hall,** *Castle Park:* ancient bell of Bangor Abbey and facsimile of Bangor Antiphonary, oldest datable document written in Irish 1,300 years ago, by arr., recreation officer. The town has a fine aboretum.**D Ward Park,** *on Donaghadee side of Bangor:* attractions include nature trail, children's zoo, bowls, putting, *all year, daily.* **Promenade,** complete with traditional seaside amusements, sunken Gardens at E end, Marine Gardens at W.

Summer theatre, *Central Avenue:* full range of entertainments, *tel: Bangor 475729.* Sea Cruises, daily during summer at 10.30 a.m., 2.30 p.m., 7.30 p.m. from harbour, weather permitting. Swimming pool: heated, indoor, *Castle Park Avenue, tel: Bangor 462271;* outdoor, Pickie Pool, on front.**D** Bicycles: G. P. Marshall & Son, *Abbey Street, tel: Bangor 460467.* Ballymacormick Riding School, *Ballycormick Road, tel: Bangor 458020.* Golf Clubs: Carnalea, *18 holes, tel: Bangor 461368;* Clandeboye, *36 holes, tel: Bangor 465767.*

AROUND BANGOR

Ballycopeland Windmill, *1 m (2 km) W of Millisle, 7 Ulsterbus from Belfast to Millisle.* 18th c hilltop cornmill in perfect working order. *Apr–Oct, Tues–Sat, 10 a.m.–6 p.m. Closed lunch. Sun. 2 p.m.–6 p.m. Nov–Mar, Sat, 10 a.m.–4 p.m. Closed lunch. Sun, 2 p.m.–4 p.m.*

Ballyhalbert: *10 m (16 km) S of Donaghadee, 9, 10 Ulsterbus from Belfast.* Small fishing village on E coast of Ards peninsula: a string of cottages beside a beach, with small, attractive harbour and a shore walk 1 m (2 km) SE to Burr Point, most E point in Ireland. Pass Celtic standing stone, ruins of old church.

Ballyholme beach: *1 m (2 km) stretch on E side of Bangor,* with a promenade made for strolling.

Ballycormick Point, pleasant shoreline walks at the entrance to Belfast Lough. Enter from the Ballyholme end of Bangor promenade or from the Watch House, Groomsport Harbour.

Ballywalter. *5 m (8 km) S of Millisle, 7, 9, 10 Ulsterbus from Belfast.* Small seaside village with good beaches and harbour. The A2 coastal route offers excellent views and there is an attractive inland walk 1 m (2 km) NW, as far as the 'White Church'.

Comber, *4 m (6 km) SW of Newtownards on A21, 11 Ulsterbus from Belfast. EC, Wed.* Fine central square and village green. Its renowned whiskey distillery closed down after the war, but some of the local pubs still have a few precious bottles. Millbridge Riding School, *Ballystockart, tel: Comber 872508.* Lewis Lowry, *129 Glen Road, Comber 872508.* Breezemount Riding School, *Green Road, Conlig, tel: Bangor 463784.*

Copeland Islands, *N of Donaghadee:* now deserted. Lighthouse Island (NT) is a bird sanctuary, boats from Donaghadee. *By arr., NT, tel: Saintfield 510721.*

Crawfordsburn Country Park: beach, camp site, café, car park. Its shore path forms part of the 'Ulster Way' walk.**D** The Crawfordsburn Inn, *1, 2 Ulsterbus from Bangor:* dates from 1614 and retains much of its old-world atmosphere. Clandeboye, Game and Country Fair, *June–July.*

Donaghadee, *6 m (10 km) SE of Bangor on A2/B21, 7 Ulsterbus from Belfast. EC, Thurs.* A most attractive and relaxing seaside town, full of character and characters, built around an imposing harbour. Good sea fishing. **Grace Neill's bar,** facing harbour, was built in 1611 and happily retains its historic atmoshere. Peter the Great of Russia was entertained here in 1697 during his Grand Tour of western Europe. It also sheltered Keats. The laneways in the town centre still have a little of the old French-style atmosphere and there are good views of the town and harbour from the castle-like moat, used for storing explosives during the harbour's construction. Short sea cruises: *10.30 a.m., 2.30 p.m., 7.30 p.m. daily, SO.* Donaghadee Golf Club, *18 holes, tel: Donaghadee 883624.*

Glastry Clay Ponds, *near Ballyhalbert:* educational nature reserve with work tables and informative displays. Ideal for children of all ages. *All year, details: A. Irvine, Benito, Castle Ward, Strangford. Tel: Strangford 253.***D**

Greyabbey, *7 m (11 km) S of Newtownards on A20. 9, 10 Ulsterbus from Newtownards. EC, Thurs* Well-preserved ruins of Cistercian abbey founded in 1193. The grounds, filled with masses of trees and flowers are an equally striking sight. *Apr–Sept, Tues–Sat, 10 a.m.–7 p.m.; Closed at 1 p.m. for ½ hr lunch. Sun, 2 p.m.-7 p.m. Oct.-Mar, Sat, 10 a.m.-1 p.m.; 1.30 p.m.-4 p.m. Sun, 2 p.m.-4 p.m.* Greyabbey Riding Centre, *30 Carrowdore Road, tel: Greyabbey 274.*

Groomsport, *3 m (5 km) E of Bangor, 3 Ulsterbus from Bangor. EC Thurs* Old-world village with beach and promenade. Cockle Row has a summer exhibition of works by local artists.

Helen's Bay, *3 m (5 km) W of Bangor, 1, 2 Ulsterbus from Bangor, also train. EC, Thurs.* Small resort on S shore of Belfast Lough. Pleasant walk from the baronial-style railway station to the beach.

Mahee Island, *N end of Strangford Lough:* ruins of 1570 castle. Nendrum monastic site has impressive early Christian ruins and the elevated location gives fine views over the lough. Connected to Reagh Island (with bird observation hides) and mainland near Killinchy by a causeway.

Millisle, *2 m (3 km) S of Donaghadee, 7 Ulsterbus from Belfast EC Thurs.* Long, sandy beach.

Mount Stewart, and the **Temple of the Winds,** *5 m (8 km) SE of Newtownards on A20, 9, 9A, 10 Ulsterbus from Newtownards.* Great 18th c house, Irish seat of the Londonderry family. House interiors most imposing, as are the formal and informal gardens, with lakes, woodlands, terraces. Temple built on lines of the temple of same name in Athens. House, with its stately interior plasterwork, is often described as the gem of Ulster architecture. *House and Temple, Apr–Sept 30, daily. Also Good Fri. Gardens, Apr–Oct 31, 12 noon-6 p.m. daily, details: Greyabbey 387.*

Newtownards, *6 m (10 km) S of Bangor on A21. EC Thur. Bus enquiries: Regent Street bus station, tel: Newtownards 812391. 5, 7 Ulsterbus from Belfast.* Thriving manufacturing and market town, founded in the 17th c.

Movilla Abbey, *1 m (2 km) E of town on B172,* nothing remains of the original 6th c monastery, present ruins are of a 15th c church; Dominican friary ruins, near the old market cross, E end of High Street. Handsome 18th c Town Hall.
The **Ulster Flying Club,** airfield just A off A21, pleasure flights, *details Newtownards 813327.* The Ards Shopping Centre is the largest in Ireland. Swimming pool: indoor, heated, *daily Newtownards 812837.*

Orlock Head, *2 m (3 km) E of Groomsport:* marks entrance to Belfast Lough.

Ringhaddy, *just SW of Killinchy:* jetty, set in

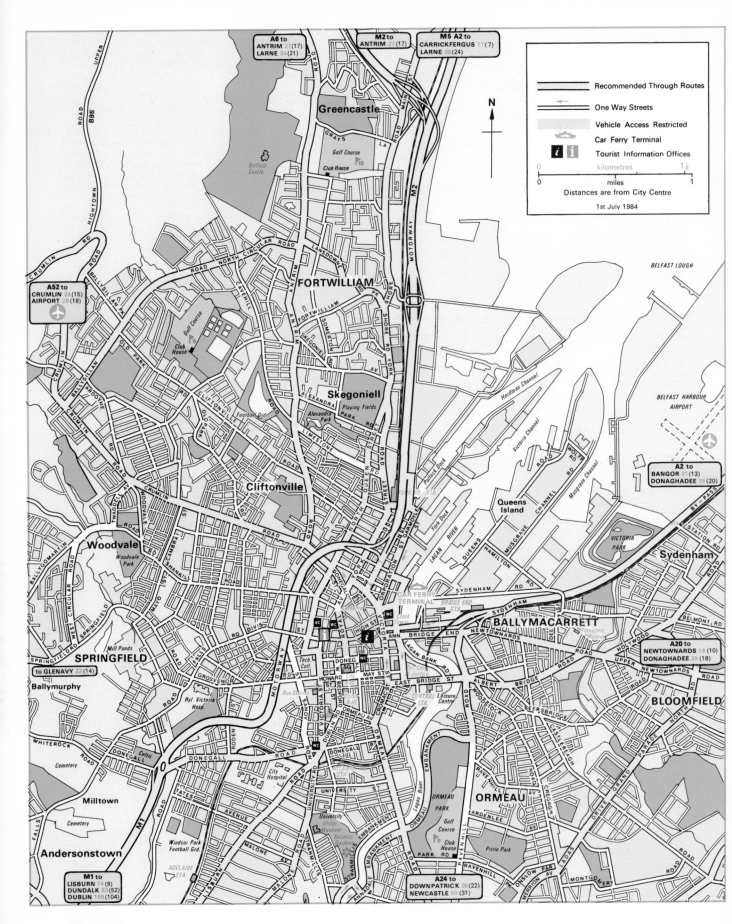

Belfast

superb countryside, approached by a tiny, winding road.

Scrabo Tower, *set on a hilltop 2 m (3 km) SW of Newtownards W of A21.* Built in 1857 as memorial to the third Marquis of Londonderry. Superb view point at top of tower; display tells story of Scrabo Hill and surrounding countryside. *Details, tel: Belfast 768716.* Surrounding area a country park. Excellent views over the Ards peninsula and Strangford Lough. *Details: Newtownards 811491. Scrabo Golf Club, 18 holes, tel: Newtownards 812355.*

Belfast

Pop. 360,000, 104 m (167 km) N of Dublin. Six day shopping. TIO: Northern Ireland Tourist Board, High Street, tel: 231221, all year, Belfast Airport, tel: Crumlin 52103, all year. Irish Tourist Board: 53 Castle Street, Belfast, tel: 227888. If travelling within the city boundary always use Citybus (red). Ulsterbus (blue), runs no internal city service. Good Ulsterbus services to all parts of N. Ireland. Bus enquiries: Great Victoria Street bus station, tel: 220011. Train from Dublin. Also trains to Bangor, Larne, Derry. Train enquiries: Central Station, tel: 235282. Taxis: Donegall Square East, Central Station, York Road Station. Coach tours: SO Details: TIO/Ulsterbus, tel: 220011. Youth Hostel: 11 Saintfield Road, tel: 647865.

Capital of Northern Ireland, attractively situated on the Lagan estuary at the foot of the Antrim plateau. Despite its relative decline as an industrial force, and more particularly the toll taken by The Troubles, Belfast is a vigorous city, much of which is extremely pleasing to the eye. It also has a fine cultural tradition which is not always recognised, and its museums and art galleries repay close inspection.

Major Festivals: Belfast Arts Festival: three week culture feast, with something for everyone. Local and international artists, enormous variety of music, theatre, film, *Nov, details: Belfast 665577 or Belfast TIO.* Circuit of Ireland international car rally: start and finish, *Apr.* Royal Ulster Agricultural Society, Kings Hall, Balmoral: annual agricultural show, *May.* July 12 Parades: marking the anniversary of the Battle of the Boyne in 1690. Ancient Order of Hibernians' parades, *Aug 15.*

City Hall

celing. **Unitarian church,** *Rosemary Street:* fine plasterwork, woodwork.

The city has many other fine religious buildings, mostly from the second half of the 19th c, when some seventy new churches were established. Perhaps the most notable are Fitzroy Presbyterian (1872), *University Street;* St Mary's (1869), *Crumlin Road;* St Thomas's (1870), *Lisburn Road;* Elmwood Hall, deconsecrated church, *by Botanic Gardens;* the small, delightful St Matthew's, *Woodvale Road,* which includes an imitation round tower; St Mark's *Dundela,*

Queen's University

CATHEDRALS & CHURCHES

St Anne's Cathedral (CI), *Donegall Street:* plain but impressive modern building. **St Malachy's Church** (C), *Alfred Street:* excellent fan-vaulted

completed in 1878 to design by William Butterfield.

NOTABLE BUILDINGS

City Hall, *Donegall Square:* handsome structure with a fine marble interior, wall murals, excellent

city views from dome. *Guided tours, Fri, 10.30 a.m. Details: 220202.***D Stormont,** *E Belfast, 22, 23 Citybus to Massey Avenue, 16, 17, 20 to main entrance.* Commanding building in 300 acres of gardens, seat of the NI parliament from 1921–72. Superb views from terrace, good walks. Stormont Castle, recently the NI Prime Minister's official residence, is nearby. **Belfast Castle,** *N*

Victorian Palm House, Botanic Gardens

Belfast, 2, 3, 4, 5, 6, 45 Citybus. Attractive walks in extensive grounds; if you feel nimble, a shepherd's path winds up Cave Hill to McArt's Fort on the summit.

Custom House, *High Street:* majestically proportioned building set where the culverted Farset joins the Lagan. Anthony Trollope worked here as a surveyor's clerk in 1841. **Royal Courts of Justice,** *Chichester Street:* a substantial structure, in Portland Stone, opened in 1933 as a gift from Westminster.

Linen Hall Library, *Donegall Square North:* late 18th c, now fully refurbished very strong on Irish interest material, occasional exhibitions. *Tues-Fri, Sat a.m. Details: 224579.* **Queen's University,** *University Road:* founded 1849, attractive main building; library with over 750,000 books, various collections, including Hamilton Harty music. By arr., librarian.**D**

MUSEUMS

Ulster Museum and Art Gallery, *Stranmillis Road, 65, 69, 71 Citybus.* Distinguished collection of art and antiquities, including treasure from the *Girona,* a Spanish Armada galleon wrecked off N Antrim coast. Coelacanth, rare preserved specimen of "living fossil" fish. Permanent art collection featuring many fine modern works and such Irish artists as William Conor, Jack B Yeats, Colin Middleton, George Campbell. Sculpture by Henry Moore, Barbara Hepworth, F. E. McWilliam. Visiting exhibitions. Engineering hall has working examples of old machinery. Monthly poster lists all museum activities. *Café. Mon–Fri, 10 a.m.–5 p.m. Sat, 1 p.m.–5 p.m. Sun, 2 p.m.–5 p.m. Details 668251.* **D Transport Museum,** *Witham Street, off Newtownards Road, 16, 20, 21, 22, 24, 26 Citybus.* Marvellous collection of railway rolling stock, cars, motor bicycles, trams, horse-drawn vehicles. Highlight is the 'Maeve' steam engine built for former Great Southern Railways. *Mon–Sat, 10 a.m.–5 p.m. Bank holidays. Details: 51519.*

GALLERIES

Caldwell Gallery, *Bradbury Place. 41, 52, 59, 65, 69, 71, 83, 85, 89 Citybus.* Large, attractive basement gallery with regular exhibitions by Irish and British artists, *Mon–Fri, 10 a.m.–5 p.m. Tel: 223226.* **D Arts Council Gallery,** *Bedford House, Bedford Street:* frequent exhibitions by local and international artists, *Mon–Sat, 10 a.m.–5 p.m. Details: 663591.* **Octagon Gallery,** *Lower Crescent. 83, 85 Citybus.* Regular exhibitions of paintings, sculpture, craft work from local sources. *Tues–Sat, 11 a.m.–5 p.m. Tel: 246259.* **Malone Gallery,** *32 Malone Road, 71 Citybus.* Regular exhibitions with special emphasis on young, local artists, *Mon–Fri, 10 a.m.–5 p.m. Tel: 662169.* **Bell Gallery,** *13 Adelaide Park. 71 Citybus.* Irish artists' work, rare editions of Irish books, crafts, antique furniture, *Mon–Fri, 10 a.m.–5 p.m. Sat, 10 a.m.–1 p.m. Tel: 662998.* **Gallery 667,** *667 Lisburn Road:* occasional exhibitions.

THEATRES

Grand Opera House, *Gt Victoria Street:* designed by 19th c theatre architect Frank Matcham, reopened in 1980 after a thorough refurbishing. Gloriously rococo interior complete with old-style stage safety curtain. Drama, opera, ballet, pantomime. *Details: 241919.* **Lyric Players' Theatre,** *Ridgeway Street, Stranmillis, 69 Citybus.* Fine, modern theatre offers modern and classical drama, with a generally Irish emphasis. Food bar, occasional lectures, recitals. *Details: 60081.* **Arts Theatre,** *Botanic Avenue. 83, 85 Citybus.* Wide range of drama, seasonal childrens' shows, rock musicals, emphasis on entertainment. *Details: 224936.* **Group Theatre,** *Bedford Street:* amateur drama. *Details: 229685.*

ROUND & ABOUT

Belfast Zoo, *Antrim Road:* superb collection of animals and birds, a magnet for children. Guided tours, film shows, lectures. *Mar–Oct, 10 a.m.–6 p.m. daily. Nov–Feb, 10 a.m.–4 p.m. daily. Last admission 1 hr before closing. Café. Details: 776277.***D**
Falls Road/Shankill Road, *Belfast, 13, 14, 15, 39, 55, 63 Citybus.* World famous, not to say notorious, the militantly Unionist Shankill, and Nationalist Falls are areas of considerable personality, and not without appeal. In the City centre the narrow passageways between Ann Street and High Street still have a little of their original 18th c atmosphere and at **Harland and Wolff** *(16, 20, 21, 22, 24, 26 Citybus),* where the 'Titanic' was built, you will find 'Goliath' and 'Samson' the world's 2nd and 3rd biggest cranes. *By arr. PR Dept.* University area: pleasant walks, including University Square, Upper and Lower Crescent. *Gilnahirk Road, E Belfast, 76, 77 Citybus to Gilnahirk Road:* good 20 minute climb up into Castlereagh Hills, with superb views over N Co. Down, as far as Isle of Man in clear weather. *Belmont Road, E Belfast, 22, 23 Citybus to Belmont Road:* invigorating walks into Holywood

Hills. **Albert Clock:** *High Street.* built 1851.
Variety Market, *next to Law Courts, Chichester Street.* All kinds of everything. *Every Fri.***D** **Smithfield Market,** *behind Royal Avenue:* the present prefabricated shops lack the character of the old market, burned down some years ago, but the bargains are as good.
The Crown Liquor Saloon (NT), *Great Victoria Street:* high Victorian style pub, snugs, gloriously over-the-top glass and tilework and a thoroughly distinctive atmosphere. **Robinsons,** *next door:* snugs, tile work, good Guinness and interesting old prints. **Kelly's Cellars,** *Bank Place, off Royal Avenue:* one of Belfast's oldest pubs, dating back some 200 years, with character to match.
Kings Hall, *Balmoral, 59 Citybus or Train.* Exhibition centre, *details TIO.* **Ulster Hall,** *Bedford Street:* regular Ulster Orchestra, rock and pop concerts. *Orchestral bookings: Arts Council Gallery, Bedford Street, tel: 663591.*

PARKS

Botanic Gardens, *near Ulster Museum, 69, 71, 83, 85 Citybus.* Acres of pleasant space, highlight is the Victorian Palm House, an elegant structure in curved glass. *Daily from 7.30 a.m. to lighting-up time.***D** Dixon Park, *Upper Malone, S Belfast, 71 Citybus.* Setting for internationally renowned rose trials every summer. **Ormeau Park,** *78, 82, 83, 85 Citybus.* Fine expanse between Ormeau and Ravenhill Roads. **Old Waterworks,** *Antrim Road, 2, 3, 4, 5, 6, 45 Citybus.* Now an attractive park with waterfalls and bridges. **Minnowburn Beeches,** *on S fringe of Belfast, in Lagan valley:* good walks in fields, woodland, open spaces, best approached on B205 to Shaw's Bridge. **Lagan Regional Park,** starts at Molly Ward locks on Stranmillis embankment, near Botanic gardens, and continues for 8 m (13 km) to Lisburn; including Barnett's demesne, *71 Citybus:* delightfully wooded park overlooking river Lagan. **Hazelwood park,** *next to zoo:* delightful setting with lake. Summer entertainment.

SPORT

Ravenhill Road, city's major rugby venue. **Windsor Park,** NI's main football stadium, *tel: 223703.* Greyhound racing: **Dunmore Park,** *Antrim Road. Tues, Thurs, Sat, 8 p.m. Details: 776232.*
Leisure Centres: Andersonstown Road, *tel: 625211 (inc. pool);* Avoniel Road, *tel: 51565;* Ballysillan Road, *tel: 721040 (inc. pool);* Beechmount, *Falls Road, tel: 228631;* Divis Community Centre, *Ardmullan Place;* Grosvenor Centre, *Grosvenor Road, tel: 240050;* Loughside Centre, *Shore Road, tel: 781524/5;* Maysfield, *East Bridge Street, tel: 241633 (inc. pool);* Olympia Centre, *Boucher Road, tel: 233369;* Ormeau Park Centre, *tel: 58024;* Queen's University Physical Education Centre, *Botanic Park, tel: 661111, extn. 4317;* Shankill Road, *tel: 241434 (inc. pool);* Stadium Recreation Centre, *Shankill Road, tel: 222439. All daily.* Swimming pools: Falls Baths, *tel: 224906;* Grove Baths, *tel: 748599;* Montgomery Road Baths, *tel: 50777.* Ormeau Avenue Baths, *tel: 221904;* Templemore Avenue Baths, *tel: 57540. All daily.* Castlereagh Equestrian Centre, *Rocky Road, Cregagh, tel: 793005.* Laurel Hill Riding Centre, *Gilnahirk, tel: 792469/Castlereagh 556.* Longhurst Stables, *172 Upper Malone Road, tel: 614265.*
Golf Clubs: Balmoral, *18 holes, tel: 668514.* Belvoir Park, *18 holes, tel: 643693.* Dunmurry, *18 holes, tel: 610834.* Fortwilliam, *18 holes, tel: 770980.* Knock, *18 holes, tel: Dundonald 3251.* Knockbracken, *18 holes, tel: 643554.* Malone, *18 and 9 holes, tel: 612758.* Shandon Park, *18 holes, tel: 793730.*

AROUND BELFAST

Aghagallon, *near SE corner of Lough Neagh,* turn off M1 motorway near Lurgan, B12 N of Aghagallon: gardener's folly over 100 years old. Don't get lost in the maze! Nearby water-driven mill still in perfect working order. **Aghalee,** *1 m (1.5 km) NW of Aghagallon,* Sureline Coaches 6A from

Lurgan. Neat little village with award-winning looks. **Bartin's Bay,** *just W of Aghalee:* see baskets being made from willows grown around nearby Lough Beg. *Details: Thomas Mulholland, tel: Aghalee 217.*

Ballynahinch, *15 m (24 km) SE of Belfast on A24T, 18, 20 Ulsterbus from Belfast. EC, Mon or Fri.* Harris's old water-driven corn mill by Ballynahinch River. *Viewing, by arr: Ballynahinch 2479.*

Belvoir Park, *Newtownbreda, 13 Ulsterbus from Belfast.* Norman motte, remains of 14th c Breda Old Church, golf course, forest caravan site.

Cairn Wood, *5 m (8 km) E of Belfast just off B170:* forest high in Craigantlet Hills, nature trail, picnic area.

Collin Glen, *W of Belfast, at top of Glen Road:* 50 acres of wild woodland, with streams that run down from Black Mountain and Colin Mountain. Paradise of trees and wild flowers.

Crumlin, *10 m (16 km) W of Belfast on A52, 23, 103, 106, 107, 109 Ulsterbus from Belfast. Train from Belfast. EC, Tues or Sat.* Quiet, pleasant village at head of wooded Crumlin Glen. Good walks alongside tiny Crumlin River which forms cascades after the weir. The Glen has a 'Cockle House', a 19th c folly built partly as a house, partly as a cave. Largest opening faces Mecca! 13th c church ruins, by Pound bridge over river. **Quail and Ornamental Pheasant Garden,** *2 Crumlin Road. All year, daily, 2 p.m.–6 p.m. Closed Thurs. Sun by arr. Tel: Crumlin 52900.* **Nutts Corner** motor cycle races. *Details: Belfast T10.*

Cultra, *1 Ulsterbus from Belfast.* Ulster Folk and Transport Museum, will provide a very full day out in search of Ulster's social and economic history. Cultra Manor has displays of domestic objects, furniture and crafts, with 19th c photographs and William Conor paintings. Reference library. In surrounding park, reconstructed rural buildings, city streets, spade mill, linen scutch mill, blacksmith's forge, weaver's house. Transport section documents over 200 years of Irish transport, including the 1893 Carrickfergus-built 'Result' schooner, old aircraft, donkey creels and pony traps. *May–Sept. Mon–Sat, 11 a.m.–6 p.m. Sun, 2 p.m.–6 p.m. Oct–Apr, Mon–Sat, 11 a.m.–5 p.m., Sun, 2 p.m.–5 p.m. Details: Holywood 5411.***D**

Down Royal Racecourse, *the Maze, near Lisburn:* regular races including the Ulster Harp Derby, *July 13. Details: Maze 621256.***D**

Dromore, *17 m (27 km) SW of Belfast on A1T, 38, 238 Ulsterbus from Belfast. All day closing, Thurs.* Interesting market town, with ancient stocks in square; Cl cathedral with 1613 Bible; Dromore Mound, a great Norman earthwork.

Dundonald, *just E of Belfast on A20, 5, 7, 8, 9, 10 Ulsterbus from Belfast. Also 16, 17, 20 Citybus. EC, Thurs* Striking Norman motte, old village, surrounded by parkland. Birr House Riding Centre, *Whinney Hill, tel: Holywood 5858.*

Edenderry, *just S of Belfast:* 19th c mill village.

Gawley's Gate, *near SE corner of Lough Neagh:* Sail Inn, a thatched post office and pub. Canal runs from yard to nearby lough.

Giant's Ring, *Ballylesson, S of Edenderry:* neolithic earthwork, over 600 ft (200 metres) in diameter. Most impressive, as is another ancient earthwork nearby, Fort Hill. From Farrell's Fort on hilltop, fine views of Belfast.

Glenavy, *2 m (3 km) S of Crumlin on A26, train from Belfast.* Pretty, one-street village sloping down to Glenavy River.

Hillsborough, *3 m (5 km) S of Lisburn on A1T, 38, 238 Ulsterbus from Belfast. EC, Sat.* Charming village, steep main street, Northern Ireland's antiques and crafts centre. **Fort,** massive structure, 17th c. *Apr 1–Sept 30, Mon–Sat, 10 a.m.–6 p.m. Sun, 2 p.m.–6 p.m. Closed, Tues, Oct–Mar, 10 a.m.–4 p.m. Sun, 2 p.m.–5 p.m. Closed, Tues.* Custodian of fort will show visitors round pretty 1760 **Market House.** *Details, tel: Hillsborough 683285.* **Hillsborough parish church**

(CI), *Belfast road:* imposing 1773 building. Sir Hamilton Harty buried in churchyard. **Fairfort House.** *Ballynahinch Street:* plaque marks Harty's childhood. home.

Shambles Art Centre: summer exhibitions. Hillsborough park: ideal for walking. Ballyknock Riding School, *38 Ballyknock Road, tel: Dromore 692144.*

Holywood, *6 m (9 km) NE of Belfast, 1 Ulsterbus from Belfast, also train. EC. Wed.* Pleasant seaside town on S shores of Belfast Lough. **Old Priory Church,** *High Street:* roofless ruins, partly dating from 13th c. Variety of good walks: around back of town, up into Holywood hills; along the esplanade, start of a 5.5 m (9 km) coastal path to Bangor; from Redburn House, wooded walks, good views of Belfast hills.
Grendor Gallery, *116 High Street:* regular exhibitions by local artists. *Mon–Fri, 10.30 a.m.–12.30 p.m.; 2 p.m.–5 p.m. Sat, 10.30 a.m.–12.30 p.m., tel: Holywood 4670.* Seapark, by sea-shore, tennis courts and other sports facilities. Holywood Golf Club, *18 holes, tel: Holywood 2138.*

Jordanstown, *163, 166 Ulsterbus from Belfast.* Northern Ireland Polytechnic. Occasional public arts performances.**D** Swimming pool: indoor, heated. *Tel: Whiteabbey 65131.*

Knockbreda, *just S of Belfast:* 18th c, parish church (CI), Georgian, in delightfully sylvan surroundings.

Lisburn, *8 m (13 km) SW of Belfast. All day closing: Wed. Bus enquiries: Smithfield Square, tel: Lisburn 2091/2092. Train enquiries: Lisburn 2294. 23 Ulsterbus from Belfast, also train.* Busy market town. **Christ Church Cathedral,** *Market Square:* early 18th c, a most interesting building.
Lisburn Museum, *The Assembly Rooms, Market Square:* impressive new museum with material reflecting local archaeology and history. Art gallery, exhibitions, *Tues–Fri, 10 a.m.–4.45 p.m. Details: Lisburn 72624.* Castle Gardens, between cathedral and River Lagan. Pleasant walks in delightful surroundings. Wallace Park, wooded area to N of town, ideal for walks and picnics.

Grove Leisure Centre, *15 Ballinderry Park, daily, tel: Lisburn 71131.* Glenmore Activity Centre, *43 Glenmore Park, Hilden, daily, tel: Lisburn 2830.* Bicycles: Lisburn Cycle Shop, *Railway Street, tel: Lisburn 2066.* Swimming pool: indoor, heated, *Market Place, Mon–Sun, details: Lisburn 2306.***D** Lisburn Golf Club, *18 holes, tel: Lisburn 77216.***D**

Magheraknock Fort, *3 m (5 km) NW of Ballynahinch:* United Irishmen made their last stand here, late 18th c. Good views over N Down.
Magheralin, *1 m (1.5 km) SW of Moira, 51, 61, 251 Ulsterbus from Belfast.* Holy Trinity parish church (CI), excellent stained glass windows.
Moira, *7m (11 km) SW of Lisburn, 51, 61, 251 Ulsterbus from Belfast.* St John's parish church (CI) at head of imposing avenue from wooded park, which has foundations of castle of former Earls of Moira.

Newtownabbey: Valley Leisure Centre, inc. pool, *40 Church Road, tel: Whiteabbey 61211.***D**

Ram's Island, *off Sandy Bay, W of B12 near Glenavy. Train from Belfast to Glenavy.* Interesting Lough Neagh island, complete with stump of round tower. Wooded bird sanctuary. Ideal for a peaceful picnic. Boat hire: Tunny Cut, between Glenavy and Aghalee.

Rowallane, (NT), *11 m (18 km) SE of Belfast on A7, 15 Ulsterbus from Belfast.* Famous garden developed from wasteland over the past 100 years; 50 acres of gardens, shrubs and plants. Best date spring and autumn, although early summer most colourful. *Apr. Mon–Fri, 9 a.m.–6 p.m. Sat, Sun, 2 p.m.–6 p.m. May, June, Mon–Fri, 9 a.m.–9 p.m. Sat, Sun, 2 p.m.–6 p.m. July–Oct, Mon–Fri, 9 a.m.–6 p.m. Sat, Sun, 2 p.m.–6 p.m. Details: Saintfield 510721.***D**

Spa, *3 m (5 km) S of Ballynahinch on Castlewellan road, 18, 20 Ulsterbus from Belfast.* Regency spa

house, old pump house now looked after by Masonic Order. By arr. Recreation Dept., Down District Council, *tel: Downpatrick 4331.*

Carrickfergus

Pop. 19,000, 11 m (18 km) NE of Belfast, 14 m (22 km) S of Larne. EC Wed. TIO: Castle Green, tel: Carrickfergus 63604, end June-Aug. Bus enquiries: Circular Road bus station, Larne, tel: Larne 2345. Train enquiries: Carrickfergus station, tel: Carrickfergus 63286. 183 Ulsterbus from Belfast, also train.
Carrickfergus Castle: built 1180 in military occupation until 1928. Best preserved Norman castle in Ireland. Now magnificently set museum. Interesting relics of three local regiments and illustrations of numerous episodes in Irish history. Splendid Great Hall, chilling dungeons, fine views from battlements. *Apr–Sept, Mon–Sat, 10 a.m.–6 p.m. Sun, 2 p.m.–6 p.m. Last admission 3.30 p.m. Oct–Mar, Mon–Sat, 10 a.m.–4 p.m. Sun, 2 p.m.–4 p.m. Last admission 3.30 p.m. Otherwise by arr. with caretaker.*
St. Nicholas' (CI), *off Market Place:* Founded in 12th century, four interesting stained glass windows, by Lady Glenavy, Catherine O'Brien, Ethel Rhind. Near church, small section of old town wall. **Andrew Jackson Centre,** American Trail *E outskirts of town:* early 18th c Irish cottage. Adjacent to the site of the ancestral home of Andrew Jackson, 7th President of the US of A 1829-37. Homestead and display gallery depicting the lifetyle of the area. *Oct–Mar, daily 10 a.m.-1 p.m., 2 p.m.–5 p.m., Apr–Sept, same times plus 6 p.m.-8 p.m.* **Dobbin's Inn,** *High Street:* 17th c pub has interesting relics of old town, inc. huge fireplace. Ask to see secret passage that runs to castle. **Louis MacNeice Plaque.** *North Road:* the distinguished poet lived in the town from two years of age until he went to Cambridge University. His father was rector of St Nicholas' church, commemorative plaque on rectory gate. Guided Walkabout Tours of town. *All year, by arr. Borough Council, tel: Carrickfergus 63604.* Carrickfergus Festival *end July/early Aug.*
Harbour, *just W of castle;* plenty of seaborne activity. Rowing boats may be hired. Walks along the wide promenade and in Marine Gardens. Shaftesbury Park, walks, putting etc. **Carrickfergus Marina:** largest in Ireland, capacity 300 berths, completely serviced by water, electricity and optional telephone; 130 berths available from 1 April 1985. Other amenities and services include boat sales and repairs, chandlery supplies, fuel berth, hoist, restaurant and tourist caravan park. *Tel: Carrickfergus 66666.* Leisure Centre offers a comprehensive range of indoor activities for all ages. Includes two swimming pools, squash courts and outdoor tennis courts. *Kennedy Drive, daily, tel: Carrickfergus 65711.* Golf Club, *18 holes, tel: Carrickfergus 63713.*

AROUND CARRICKFERGUS

Ballyboley Forest, *4 m (6 km) N of Ballyclare off A36:* Dept of Agriculture caravan site, lake, viewpoint.

Ballycarry, *2 m (3 km) N of Whitehead, just W of A2, 168 Ulsterbus from Whitehead. EC, Sat.* Quiet hilltop village. Ruins of Ireland's first Presbyterian church, built 1613; grave of James Orr (1770-1816), poet and United Irishman.
Ballyclare, *10 m (16 km) SW of Larne. EC, Thurs.* Annual fair, *end May.* Extensive pre-Christian settlements. Whitepark Equestrian Centre, *Ballycorr Road, tel: Ballyclare 23088.* Beeches, *171 Ballycorr Road, tel: Ballyclare 22441.* Ballyclare Golf Club, *9 holes, tel: Ballyclare 22696.*

Ballyeaston, *1 m (2 km) N of Ballyclare, 153, 156 Ulsterbus from Belfast to Ballyclare.* Attractive village on steep hill.

Bellahill, *2 m (3 km) W of Whitehead:* see exterior of Dalways' built around 1609 and N. Ireland's best preserved plantation house.

Glenoe, *on Ballycarry-Larne B149:* most attractive NT beauty spot, with woods, whitewashed houses and Glenoe Glen with four waterfalls.

Glynn, *foot of Glenoe Glen:* picturesque village with old corn mill and dam. From old church, footbridge spans River Glynn.

'Holestone', *2 m (3 km) NW of Ballyclare:* Bronze Age megalith perched on a hill top. It has a small hole, through which a woman's hand may pass, but not a man's. In the past, couples plighted their troth by clasping hands through the hole.

Islandmagee: *peninsula 7 m long, 2 m wide (11 × 3 km),* 169 Ulsterbus from Whitehead. Fine cliffs on the E side, with the Gobbins (about 200 ft–60 metres) swarming with seabirds. Brown's Bay, Ferris Bay are popular bathing, picnic spots. **Portmuck,** *N tip of peninsula:* sandy cove and harbour reached by corkscrew road. Ruins of ancient castle, said to have been home of a Magee chief, on headland to E. Try your luck with a delicately poised **Rocking Stone,** a glacial boulder on the rocky shore E of Brown's Bay. Nearby Druid's Chair dolmen. Ashfield Riding Centre, *tel: Whitehead 73413.* Island Golf Club, *9 holes, tel: Islandmagee 228.*

Kilroot, *4 m (6 km) NE of Carrickfergus, 163 Ulsterbus from Carrickfergus.* Ruins of church where youthful Jonathan Swift was 18th c incumbent.

Kilwaughter, *3 m (5 km) SW of Larne:* roads to N and W of village give good views of scenic uplands.

Knockagh Monument, *2 m (3 km) SW of Carrickfergus:* one of the best vantage points in area. Approach by path through golf course or by road on N side, which runs almost to the top of the cliffs.

Larne, *21 m (34 km) NE of Belfast. EC, Tues. TIO: Victoria Road, tel: Larne 2313, all year. Larne Harbour, tel: Larne 2270, Easter–Sept 30. Bus enquiries: tel: Larne 2345. Train enquiries: tel: Larne 2347. 156 Ulsterbus from Belfast, also train.* Ferry service to Islandmagee, daily, first sailing 7 a.m., last 9 p.m. Apr–Sept. Ferry services to Cairnryan and Stranraer in Scotland. The gateway to the Glens of Antrim, with three interesting old churches: St Cedma's *Inver* (16th c). First Presbyterian Church, *Bridge Street* (17th c). Unitarian Church, *Ballymena Road* (17th c.).
District Historical Centre, *Cross Street,* exhibits include 1900 country kitchen, with open peat hearth, dresser, grandfather clock; old smithy, with anvil, hand bellows, tools; photographs. *All year, Tues–Sat, 2 p.m.–6 p.m.* Walks: Chaine Memorial Park, seashore promontory, sickle-shaped Curran promontory S of harbour. Swimming pool: heated, indoor, *Tower Road, daily, tel: Larne 3478.***D** Golf Club, *18 holes, tel: Ballygally 324.*

Whitehead, *5 m (8 km) NE of Carrickfergus on A2. EC, Thurs, Bus enquiries: tel: Larne 2345. Train enquiries: tel: Whitehead 72377. 163, 168 Ulsterbus from Belfast, also train.* Attractive seaside town, with good walks along promenade E towards Black Head, from where you can enjoy fine views over Belfast Lough. The Irish Railway Preservation Society has preserved several old steam locos and carriages. Summer trips, and excursions to various parts of Ireland. *Details: Whitehead 78567.***D** Whitehead Golf Club, *18 holes, tel: Whitehead 72792.*

Coleraine

Pop. 15,000, 31 m (50 km) NE of Derry, 54 m (87 km) NW of Belfast. All day closing, Thurs. Bus enquiries: bus station, tel: Coleraine 3334. Train enquiries: tel: Coleraine 2263. 221 Ulsterbus from Belfast, Derry, also train.

Dunluce Castle

Carrickfergus Castle

Said to have been given its name by St Patrick in the 5th c, Coleraine became a small city during the Middle Ages, and though there are few remains from this period, there are a number from its second incarnation, as a plantation town, including remnants of the 1641 seige, also fine Georgian houses and streets. Recently it became a university town, with the controversial siting here of the University of Ulster.

St Patrick's Church, (CI), *town centre:* see mark on N wall where cannon ball hit building during 1641.**D Town Hall:** relics include sword presented by Irish Society in 1616. *Mon–Fri, by arr.* **Tropical Bird Garden,** *Ballymoney Road: daily.* Walks: good along both banks of River Bann. Anderson Park, *by river,* a quiet if windy oasis by the main shopping area. Ballysally, *on N side of University:* marina, caravan camp, café. Swimming pool: indoor heated, *Railway Road, daily, tel: Coleraine 3439.* Bicycles: Coleraine Motorcycles and Cycle Centre, *8 Newmarket Street, tel: Coleraine 52655*

Wars I and II. *Term time, Mon–Fri, 9 a.m.–10 p.m. Sat, 9 a.m.–1 p.m. Vacations, Mon–Fri, 9 a.m.–5 p.m.* **Riverside Theatre,** amateur and professional productions, touring art exhibitions in foyer. *Details and bookings, tel: Coleraine 51388.* Guy Wilson Daffodil Garden, with almost 1,500 varieties of daffodil, the world's most comprehensive collection.

AROUND COLERAINE

Ballymoney, *8 m (12 km) SE of Coleraine. All day closing, Mon. TIO: Lower Main Street tel: Bushmills 31343, June–Sept. Bus and train enquiries: Ballymoney Railway Station, tel: 63241.* 119, 171, 173, 218 Ulsterbus from Coleraine, also train. Two interesting churches: Our Lady and St Patrick, (C), built of local basalt, fine stained glass windows. Trinity Presbyterian Church, built 1884 by Home Rule advocate Rev. J. B. Armour. Riada Leisure Centre, inc. pool, *Carryduff Road, daily, tel: Ballymoney 65792.* Roe Valley Recreation Centre, inc. pool, *Greystone Road, daily, tel: 6279/4009.*

Ulsterbus from Coleraine. EC. Thurs Old Bushmills Whiskey Distillery has world's oldest distillery licence dating from 1609. Attractively set by St Columb's Rill. *Mon, Wed, Thur, tours at 10.30 a.m., 2.30 p.m. Tel first, Bushmills 31521.* Open-topped Bushmills bus runs from Coleraine to Giant's Causeway, *June–August, daily. Bushfoot Golf Club, 9 holes, tel: Bushmills 31317.*

Camus High Cross, *4 m (6 km) S of Coleraine on A54:* weather-worn cross in Camus old graveyard on W bank of River Bann, site of former monastery. Camus Woods, by riverside, good picnic spot.

Castlerock, *8 m (13 km) NW of Coleraine, TIO: Main Street, tel: Castlerock 258, July, Aug.* 134 Ulsterbus from Coleraine, also train. *EC, Wed or Sat.* Bracing seaside village just W of Bann estuary. Good beach. Open air swimming pool. Castlerock Golf Club, *18 holes, tel: Castlerock 314.*

Causeway Safari Pleasure Park, *4 m (6 km) N of Ballymoney, 132 Ulsterbus from Portrush, 137 from Ballycastle, 171 from Coleraine.* Lions and other exotic wildlife roaming extensive parkland. Keep the car windows closed while you're driving round, in case they feel like a snack! Curio shop, picnic area, restaurant, *Apr–May, weekends only June–Aug, daily, 11 a.m.–6.30 p.m. details, tel: Dervock 41474.*

The Cutts, *2 m (3 km) S of Coleraine:* salmon leap. Nearby, Somerset forest recreation area. Also huge Mountsandel mound on E bank of Bann, site of a 1st c royal palace.

Dervock, *5 m (7 km) NE of Ballymoney, 171 Ulsterbus from Coleraine, EC, Sat.* Farm outhouse at Conagher was home of great-great-grandfather of US president William McKinley, assassinated in 1901. **Downhill Castle,** *near Mussenden Temple:* built about 1780 and once the setting of magnificent social gatherings and a great art collection. Impressive even in its dilapidation. **Downhill Forest,** *W of Downhill Demesne:* good walks in Dept of Agriculture property. Nearby Portadvantage Cove is haven of peace.

Dundarave, *just N of Bushmills:* splendid Georgian house with sumptuous interior. By arr. only. *Details: Recreation Officer, tel: Ballycastle 62225/22565.*

Dunluce Castle, *midway between Giant's Causeway and Portrush, 132, 138, 172, 252 Ulsterbus from Bushmills, Portrush.* Magnificent ruins on crag above sea, dating from about 1300. Part of the castle fell into the sea in 1639, taking with it several unfortunate servants who happened to be in the kitchen at the time. Two years later it was abandoned.

Today is it one of the most massive and romantic ruins in Ireland, with spectacular views. Ruins of old church just S. *Apr–Sept, Tues–Sat, 10 a.m.–1 p.m.; 2 p.m.–6 p.m. Sun, 2 p.m.–6 p.m. Oct–Mar, Tues–Sat, 10 a.m.–1 p.m.; 2 p.m.–5 p.m. Sun, 2 p.m.–5 p.m.*

Giant's Causeway

University of Ulster: many arts events throughout the year. Concerts in Diamond Hall, smaller recitals and visual arts exhibitions in the Octogon. *Guided tours mid July–mid Aug, Wed, 11 a.m. Details and bookings, Cashier's Office, tel: Coleraine 4141 extn 278.* Library of some 200,000 volumes inc. Denis Johnston manuscripts, much material relating to World

Bellarena, *5 m (8 km) N of Limavady:* 'Miners' Marks', two small towers mark where first Ordnance Survey of Ireland and Britain was begun in 1834.

Bishop's Road: starts in Downhill village and climbs to Eagle Hill and Binevenagh. Excellent views of Donegail and Scottish coast from Gortmore picnic area.

Bushmills, *3 m (5 km) S of Giant's Causeway, 138*

Glenelly Valley

Dunseverick Castle, *E end of Giant's Causeway:* slight ruins of one of Ireland's earliest castles dating from about 500, perched on a high crag.

Garvagh, *11 m (16 km) S of Coleraine on A29, 116 Ulsterbus from Coleraine.* Attractive village on Agivey River. Garvagh Forest has wooded recreation area, caravan site.

Giant's Causeway, *9 m (12 km) E of Portrush on B146, 172 Ulsterbus from Portrush.* Ireland's best-known tourist attraction. A fascinating, often spectacular landscape of six-sided basalt columns. The tallest, in the Giant's Organ, are about 36 ft (12 metres) high. Information Centre, shop. Also picture boards telling the 'Girona' (Spanish Armada galleon) story. Café. Bus from car park to Windy Gap. *Geological Walk: 3 m (5 km),* signposted, illustrated information panels, an excellent way of seeing area's geology.

Kilrea, *6 m (9 km) SE of Garvagh:* Movanagher Fish Farm. *By arr, tel: Kilrea 40533.*

Liffock, *just outside Castlerock, 134 Ulsterbus from Coleraine.* 17th c Hezlett House built without foundations on flat rock. Unusual roof. *Apr–Sept 30, daily, 2 p.m.–6 p.m. except Fri. Open Good Fri, all public holidays.*

Magilligan Strand, *134 Ulsterbus from Coleraine to Castlerock, also train.* Ireland's longest strand runs from 6 m (10 km), starting just W of Castlerock; also Martello Tower, built during Napoleonic Wars.

Mussenden Temple, *entrance by Bishop's Gate, 5 m (8 km) W of Coleraine on A2, 136 Ulsterbus from Coleraine.* Built 1783, spectacularly sited above Magilligan Strand. Excellent walks in nearby glen, particularly in early summer when the daffodils and rhododendrons are in full bloom. *Apr–Sept 30, daily, except Fri.*

Pleaskin Head, *to E of Giant's Causeway:* magnificent panorama of whole N Antrim coast and parts of SW Scottish coast in clear weather.

Portballintrae, *2 m (3 km) SW of Giant's Causeway, loop road from A2. TIO: Tel: Bushmills 31672, July, Aug. 138 Ulsterbus from Coleraine, Portrush.* Pleasant, secluded seaside village with harbour and beach. Boat excursions from harbour, *SO.*

Portcoon Cave, *W end of Giant's Causeway cliffs:* beautiful internal colouring, enter from landward side.

Portnabo slipway, *near Giant's Causeway entrance:* boats to view Causeway coast caves from sea. *SO.*

Portrush, *6 m (19 km) N of Coleraine on A29. EC, Wed. TIO: Town Hall, tel: Portrush 823333, Easter–Sept, 30 Bus enquiries; Coleraine bus station, tel: Portrush 8223/5. 140 Ulsterbus from Coleraine, also train. 'Portrush Flyer, July, Aug.* Resort town set on a peninsula jutting into the ocean, with attractive terraces and a bustling, seaside atmosphere. Railway station of architectural interest. Many summer entertainments, including Town Hall theatre, fishing, bowling, swimming. Good beaches at east and west strand.

Portandoo Countryside Centre, *Bath Road:* Interpretative, information centre, *Tel: Portrush 823600.***D**

Cliff walks W towards Portstewart. E to Dunluce. At E end of chalk White Rocks, car park, picnic area with fine coastal views. Walk to top of Ramore Head for invigorating views. Daily summer boat trips leaving from harbour, round offshore Skerry Islands. **Barry's,** seafront: *huge amusement arcade, details: Portrush 822340.* **Royal Portrush Golf Club:** Dunluce course, *18 holes:* Valley course, *18 holes, tel: Portrush 822311.* Rathmore Golf Club, *18 holes, tel: Portrush 822990.*

Portstewart, *4 m (6 km) SW of Portrush. EC, Thurs, except summer. TIO: Town Hall, tel: Portstewart 2286, July, Aug. Bus enquiries: Coleraine bus station, tel: Coleraine 3334. Train enquiries: Portrush Railway Station, tel: Portrush 8223/5. 140 Ulsterbus from Coleraine, also train.* The main streets of this attractive Victorian-style town form an Atlantic promenade, winding round

rocky bays, with shore paths at each end. Magnificent 2 m (3 km) long strand between town and River Bann.

Flowerfield Arts Centre, regular exhibitions of local art and craft, *daily, details: TIO.* Boat excursions from harbour, *SO.* Two 18 holes golf courses, *details: Portstewart 2015.*

Bann Estuary Wildlife Sanctuary, *3 m (5 km) E of Castlerock:* observation hide with illustrative panels. The River Bann is navigable by boats with draughts of up to 3 ft (1 metre) all the way from sea to Portadown, crossing Lough Neagh. Unusual, little-used way of seeing a cross-section of Ulster life.

Slaghtaverty Dolmen, *on hill slope 3 m (5 km) S of Garvagh:* legend has it that this is last resting place of Abhartach, a dwarf with magical powers who was killed by a neighbouring chieftain and buried upside down to silence his ghost.

Cookstown

Pop. 7,000, 46 m (74 km) W of Belfast, 53 m (85 km) SE of Derry. All day closing, Wed. Bus enquiries: Dungannon bus office, tel: Dungannon 22251. 80, 110, 120, 210, 273 Ulsterbus from Belfast, 80, 82 from Dungannon.

Renowned for its main street (two miles long and fifty metres wide) and its interesting old-fashioned pubs, which are particularly lively on market days; the River Ballinderry, just S of town, is one of best trout rivers in NI.

Killymoon Castle: *at golf club, SE of town:* fine exterior, built in 1803 to design of John Nash, architect of the extravagant Brighton Pavilion in S England. *Derryloran Parish Church (CI), S of end of Main Street:* also designed Nash. Catholic church, *town centre:* spire of Gothic-style building is landmark for miles around. Adjoining convent chapel contains interesting modern church art. Swimming pool: heated, indoor, *Fountain Road, daily, tel: Cookstown 63853.***D** Killymoon Golf Club, *18 holes, tel: Cookstown 62254.*

AROUND COOKSTOWN

Arboe Cross, *W shores of Lough Neagh, take B73 E from Cookstown for 10 m (16 km) to lake shore, then turn R down minor road for 1 m (2 km):* best preserved 10th c High Cross in NI; nearby, ruins of old churches, 6th c abbey.

Ballyronan, *4 m (6 km) SE of Magherafelt:* popular sailing spot. Lough Neagh pleasure steamers call here. Walks along lake shore, bathing and picnic areas.

Beaghmore Stone Circles, *4 m (6 km) NW of Drum Manor, approach by small road running N from Dunnamore hamlet:* six stone circles, also cairns, dating back 4,000 years. Their original purpose is obscure.

Cady, *3 m (5 km) S of Cookstown:* Andrew Warnock's bagpipe-making workshop. *By arr. Tel: Cookstown 63615.***D**

Carndaisy Wood and Glen, *3 m (5 km) NW of Moneymore:* many good picnic spots, to N road corkscrews almost to summit to Slieve Gallion. This is one of the most spectacular and least-known drives in the entire North.

Castledawson, *3 m (5 km) SE of village, at mouth of Moyola River. All day closing, Mon.* Lough Neagh's best sandy beach. Due to commercial sand extraction, not suitable for swimming. Between Castledawson and river mouth, picturesque bridge. Nearby picnic area. Fishing, Moyola Park Golf Club, *18 holes, tel: Castledawson 468.*

Church Island, *Lough Beg, 2 m (3 km) NE of Castledawson:* tower with spire built by 18th c bishop, ruins of earlier church. Island approached on foot over watery meadows.

Coagh, *5 m (8 km) E of Cookstown on B73:*

delightful crossroads village. From main Hanover Square, cross over bridge to enormous Clochtogle dolmen.

Coney Island, *SW corner of Lough Neagh:* wooded islet with ruined keep at mouth of Blackwater River. Nearby Brackagh Bog fenlands of interest to naturalists.

Davagh Forest, *8 m (13 km) NW of Cookstown:* vaguely Wild Westish with gravelly bed of Broughderg River. From Beleevnamore Mountain, you can see most parts of NI on a clear day. Many nature trails, picnic areas.

Drum Manor Forest Park, *4 m (6 km) W of Cookstown on A505:* butterfly gardens, delightful spot enclosed by old walls where rare species can be seen in summer. Demonstration shrub garden for blind, wildfowl ponds. Nature trail, picnic area, camping, caravan sites, information centre, café.**D**

Dungannon, *11 m (18 km) S of Cookstown. EC, Wed. Bus enquiries: Bus Office, Market Square, Dungannon. Tel: Dungannon 22251. 261 Ulsterbus from Belfast, Enniskillen.* Walk up steep streets to Castle Hill, from where there are excellent views of the countryside between Lough Neagh and Sperrins. Tyrone Crystal makes a fine range of glassware. *Factory tours, Easter onwards. Mon–Fri. By app. only. Groups preferred. Details: Dungannon 25335.* Greyhound racing: Oak Park. *Regular weekly meetings. Details: Dungannon 20223.* Swimming pool: indoor, heated, *Circular Road, daily, tel: Dungannon 3490/2331.* Dungannon Golf Club, *18 holes, tel: Dungannon 22098.*

Glenshane Pass, *NW of Maghera on A6:* spectacular drive. Usually first road in Ireland to be snowed under in bad winter weather. Forest at top of pass for those interested in camping, orienteering.

Iniscarn Forest, *NE face of Slieve Gallion, 2 m (3 km) from Desertmartin:* from car park, footpath follows winding stream to near mountain top.

Lough Fea, *5 m (8 km) N of Cookstown on B162:* set high in the hills, its shores are ideal for picnics.

Loughry Agricultural College, *3 m (5 km) S of Cookstown:* plantation mansion much visited by Swift. He is said to have written part of *Gulliver's Travels* in the summerhouse. House has portraits of Stella, Vanessa. *By app. the principal, tel: Cookstown 62491.*

Magherafelt, *N of Cookstown on A29 then A54. All day closing, Tues.* Swimming pool: indoor, heated, *Greenvale, daily, tel: Magherafelt 2796.* Drumbally Riding Centre, *Desertmartin. Tel: Magherafelt 32003.*

Moneymore, *4 m (6 km) NW of Cookstown on A29, 110, 120 Ulsterbus from Cookstown.* Pleasant Georgian-style village reconstructed in early 19th c. Go through archway in centre of village in broad market yard, surrounded by old corn stores with balconies.

Parkanaur Forest Park, *3 m (5 km) W of Dungannon.* Woodland trails, deer park, camp and caravan sites, picnic places, car park. Farm buildings of original estate restored to initial character. *Details: tel: Belfast 650111, extn 456.*

Peatlands Park, *The Birches, N of M1 Loughall exit:* Peat faces, rhododendrons, small lake.

Pomeroy, *7 m (11 km) SW of Cookstown, 86 Ulsterbus from Dungannon.* Tyrone's highest village, surrounded by fine moorland and mountain scenery. Market, *in Square, every second Tues.*

Reuben's Glen, *2 m (3 km) S of Desertmartin, just off A29:* roadside beauty spot with woodland stream.

Saltersstown, *2 m (3 km) S of Ballyronan:* three centuries ago, the Salters' Company planned to build a town here on the NW shores of Lough Neagh. It stayed a plan and all you can see today are a bawn wall with towers and the gables of a small castle.

Springhill House, *(NT) 1 m (2 km) outside*

Moneymore on Coagh road, 110, 120 Ulsterbus from Cookstown. Excellent example of settler's manor house, complete with furniture and one of Ulster's most regularly authenticated ghosts. Cottar's kitchen with bygone utensils. Costume museum. Gardens, woodland walks. Apr–Sept 30, daily, 2 p.m.–6 p.m. Closed Fri. Open Good Fri, public holidays on a Fri. Nearby Manor House Hotel, Moneymore, has special menu for Springhill visitors.**D**

Stewartstown, 5 m (8 km) SE of Cookstown on B520, 80 Ulsterbus from Cookstown. EC. Thurs. Fine cobbled square with little shops and houses. Drumcairne Forest, 2 m (3 km) E has Italian terrace, picnic sites. Old warehouses surround derelict canal basin. Other reminders of once prosperous Tyrone mining industry include coal workings to the S of the village. About 2 m (3 km) NW, in Newmills direction, see ruined arches, remains of 'dry wherries', where the old canal barges had to be hauled over dry land.

Tobermore, 3 m (5 km) SW of Maghera: small village with delightfully 'unplanned' narrow streets, has won many best-kept village prizes. Several picnic areas.

Traad Point, just N of Ballyronan: good sandy beach on shores of Lough Neagh.

Tullahogue Hill, 3 m (5 km) S of Cookstown, just off B520: from summit, fine view over much of Tyrone. Fine hilltop enclosure, the crowning place of the O'Neills, Ulster chiefs for five centuries until 17th c.

Washing Bay, due E of Coalisland: popular with birdwatchers and swimmers.

Wellbrook Beetling Mill (NT), near Drum Manor Forest Park: 18th c mill, with great wheel and sluices, on Ballinderry River, restored to full working order. Most impressive, if noisy, process. Nearby walks along river banks and mill race. Apr–Sept 30, daily, 2 p.m.–6 p.m. Closed Fri.

Cushendall

Pop. 700, 4 m (6 km) S of Cushendun. EC. Tues. TIO: Mill Street, tel: Cushendall 415, June–Sept. Bus enquiries: Larne bus station, tel: Larne 2345. 162 Ulsterbus from Larne, 252 from Ballycastle, Larne (SO).

Capital of the Glens of Antrim, and one of the most distinctively Irish parts of NI. The village, largely created by a wealthy 19th c landowner Francis Turnly, is a charming little place, the ideal introduction to the scenic delights of the Glens. Game fishing.

Parish church (C), riverbank: built 1832, Michael Healy stained glass window. Mill Street: old corn mill, formerly powered by River Dall. Small, sandy beach. Youth Hostel: Layde Road, tel: Cushendall 344.

AROUND CUSHENDALL

Antrim Coast Road (A2): from Larne to Cushendun, with some of the most impressive coastal scenery in Ireland. The mountain roads leading off the Cushendall—Cushendun A2 offer good views.

Ballygally, 5 m (8 km) N of Larne, 162 Ulsterbus from Larne. Beach well-preserved mill on inland side of village. Youth Hostel.

Carnlough, 3 m (5 km) NW of Glenarm. EC. Thurs, except July, Aug. TIO: Post Office, Harbour Road, tel: Carnlough 328, all year. 162 Ulsterbus from Larne. Pretty little Glens village with fine beach and harbour. Walk: up Waterfall Road to see old limekiln building with tall white chimneys, relic of a bygone era. Also see Cranny Falls. A track leads out onto the great expanse of Garron Moorland.

Cushendun, 5 m (8 km) N of Cushendall on A2, 162 Ulsterbus from Cushendall. EC. Tues. Most N

Glens village, and one of the most attractive, with cottages built in Cornish style to design of Clough Williams Ellis, who also designed the nearby 'Glenmona', home of Lord Cushendun.

Cave House, just S of village: can only be approached by road through natural cave. Now a holiday retreat, but worth going to see, unusual entrance. 1 m (1.5 km) N of Castle Carra ruins, on Torr Head road, see modern cross on a cairn, commemorating a bloody 16th c clan feud. Next to it is a large monument to Sir Roger Casement. Sandstone cliffs to S of village have many caves. Boat from Cushendun Harbour. Just outside Cushendun, a path leads from Milltown houses alongside Brabla Burn to moors. Delightful walk, but it you want even more silence, head for Tornamoney Burn, 2 m (3.5 km) N of Brabla.

Garron Point, midway between Cushendall and Carnlough, 162 Ulsterbus from Cushendall, Carnlough. At its summit, an old earth fort, at foot of cliffs, a tiny harbour. Just N, White Lady, a chalk carving by the coastal road, from here, take lane to tiny hamlet of Galboly, set in Swiss-like scenery. Old quay, used for shipping limestone, is 0.5 m (0.8 km) W of White Lady.

Glenaan, 3 m (5 km) W of Cushendall: where the road up the glen joins the road to Glendun, past Beagh's Forest. Splendidly desolate, open, wild countryside.

Glenariff Glen: stretches inland for some 5 m (8 km) from Waterfoot, 162 Ulsterbus from Cushendall to Waterfoot. Known as the 'Queen of the Nine Glens', Glenariff was described by Thackeray as 'Switzerland in miniature'. Steep mountains rise on both sides of glen, which narrows to a deep, wooded gorge. Path winds along the glen, crossing the river by means of rustic footbridges, enabling you to see the waterfalls. Also viewing places, but be careful in wet weather, when paths are very slippery. Glenariff Forest Park: charming walks at head of Glenariff, Café, visitor centre. A 26 m (42 km) path, part of Ulster Way, runs from head of glen to Ballycastle. A good walk! Glenariff: Feis na nGleann, Community Carnival Week, July.

Glenariff Forest Park, near head of Glenariff Glen, on N side: look out for disused station, relic of the narrow gauge railway that once ran to Ballymena, and the flat slabs that once formed the ancient Black Causeway from the Bann Valley to the Antrim coast.

Glenarm, 162, 252 Ulsterbus from Larne, 252 from Ballycastle. EC. Wed. Most S village in Glens of Antrim has pleasing aspect, but suffers under the full force of an Ulster Sunday. The public park runs for some 4 m (7 km) beside Glenarm River, up the glen, complete with waterfalls. Good salmon and trout river. The back roads W of the village make for interesting sorties into the mountains.

Glendun (C), 1 m (1.5 km) beyond Knocknagarry Bridge: St. Patrick's Church, with Sweethearts' Stone. John McAlaster, who died in 1803 at the age of 18 after falling from a ship's rigging weeks before he was to marry, is buried here. His broken-hearted sweetheart was said to have cut the inscriptions on the grave's flat headstone.

Glendun Viaduct, 3 m (5 km) E of Cushendun on A2: most impressive structure on whole Antrim coast road. From the viaduct, good views down the glen. Fuchsia adds to the vista. Vicinity has good salmon and trout fishing.

Layde, 1 m (1.5 km) N of Cushendall: Layde Old Church ruins in a little valley overlooking the sea. Road to churchyard passes ornamental well that once provided the village's water supply. Walk: along cliff path down to beach.

Sallagh Braes, 3 m (5 km) SW of Ballygally: fine ampitheatre of crags, from which there are fine views as far as Ailsa Craig, the vast cone-shaped rock off the Ayrshire coast.

Tiveragh Hill, 1 m (1.5 km) NW of Cushendall: known locally as the 'fairy hill'. Good climbing.

Waterfoot, 1 m (1.5 km) S of Cushendall, 162 Ulsterbus from Cushendall. Set at mouth of Glenariff River on Red Bay, so called because of

the red sandstone washed down in nearby streams. 16th c ruins of Red Bay Castle are poised on cliffs above bay. Glens of Antrim Feis, July. Walks: starting at the White Arch, follow the course of the old railway track, once used for shipping iron ore to Cumberland and Scotland. Today, it's a pleasant walk along SE side of the glen.

White Bay, 2 m (3 km) SE of Glenarm on A2: see tiny fossilied marine creatures, as well as flints, in the rock. Car park, picnic area.

Monaghan

Pop. 5,500, 17 m (27 km) SW of Armagh, 54 m (87 km) SW of Belfast, 75 m (120 km) NW of Dublin. EC Thurs. TIO: (047) 81122, June–Sept. Bus enquiries: (047) 82377. 89 bus from Derry, 89, 90, 93, 94 from Dublin.

The county town of Monaghan has a distinctly Northern air, hardly surprising since it is in the historic province of Ulster. Surrounding area dotted with lakes, ideal coarse fishing country.

St Macartan's Cathedral, (C) S of town centre: imposing 19th c structure in Gothic Revival style.**D County Museum**, The Courthouse: many fascinating exhibits including prehistoric stone and metal weapons, pottery and ornaments, 18th c military material, Carrickmacross and Clones lace, police equipment, butter churns, baking irons, coins, maps, photographs. Canal, railway relics. Highlight is 14th c Cross of Clogher. Short-term art, history exhibitions. All year, Tues–Sat, 10 a.m.–1 p.m.: 2 p.m.–5 p.m. Closed Mon, public holidays. June, July, Aug, Sun, 2 p.m.–6 p.m. Details: (047) 82211.**D**

Ulster Canal: good walks along disused banks. **Rossmore Forest Park**, 1 m (2 km) S of town, off L44: car park, picnic site, lakeside and forest walks, fishing, nature trails. From Rossmore Castle site, panoramic views.**D** Canoeing, hill walking, rock climbing: Anne and Brendan Lillit, tel: (047) 81721. Swimming pool: indoor heated, Clones Road, daily, Bicycles: E. Clerkin, Main Street, tel: (047) 81434; Patrick McCoy, Dublin Street, tel: (047) 81283. Rossmore Golf Club, 9 holes, tel: (047) 81316.

AROUND MONAGHAN

Annaghmakerrig, off L40, 5 m (8 km) NW of Cootehill: car park, picnic area, forest walks.

Ballybay, 9 m (14 km) SE of Monaghan: Billy Fox Memorial Park, picnic area, forest walks.

Bellamont Dartry, 1 m (2 km) N of Cootehill, off L48: car park, picnic area, forest walks.

Black Island, E outskirts of Castleblayney, 14 m (22 km) SW of Monaghan on N2: pleasant lakeside walks here and along shores of Lough Muckno.

Carrickmacross, 28 m (45 km) SE of Monaghan on N2: lacemaking displays at St Louis convent, daily. Carrickmacross Golf Club, Nuremore, 9 holes.

Castleblayney, Hope Castle and grounds, Lough Muckno, being taken into public ownership.

Castleshane, 5 m (8 km) E of Monaghan on N2: forest walks, attractive Castleshane Waterfall.

Clones, 12 m (19 km) SW of Monaghan on N54, 27, 85 bus from Cavan, 93 from Dublin, 112 from Armagh, 128 from Enniskillen. Ancient Celtic cross in Diamond. 75 ft (22 metre) high round tower in graveyard near Cavan road and Early Bronze Age court cairn. Sarcophagus dates back to early Christian times. Exact origins unknown but worth a close look. Key from nearby Patton's pub. Derelict Ulster Canal skirts town. Bicycles: J. Reilly, the Diamond. Clones Golf Club, Hilton Park, 9 holes, tel: Scotshouse 17.

Concra, 2 m (3 km) SE of Castleblayney on T22: forest walks, fishing.

Dún a' Ri Forest Park, 6 m (10 km) SW of Carrickma-cross, 1 m (2 km) N of Kingscourt on L35: 560 acres, and numerous amenities: picnic site,

View from Lurigethan, Antrim Coast

monastery founded by St Deogh. Stump of round tower, 42 ft (13 metres) high. **Inniskeen Museum** includes Patrick Kavanagh section. The great poet and novelist was born in village and is buried in nearby cemetery. Museum also features relics of old Great Northern Railway, which ran through village. *May–Sept, Sun, 3 p.m.–6 p.m.* McNello's pub includes photos of poet, chair he regularly sat on.

Kingscourt: St Mary's (C) has fine Evie Hone windows. The Ascension was one of her favourite works.**D**

Mannan Castle, *4 m (6 km) N of Carrickmacross:* 12th c hilltop motte and bailey.

Tirgarvan, *2 m (3 km) W of Carrickmacross:* interesting limestone caves.

planned walks, nature trails. 'Romantic Glen' of Cabra River runs full length of park, other features include ruins of military barracks, waterfall. Wishing Well.**D**

Glaslough. *6 m (10 km) NE of Monaghan on L5:* Castle Leslie Residential Equestrian Centre, horse riders have the run of entire 1,000 acre estate. Interesting Italian gardens. *Details: (047) 81700.*

Inniskeen, *midway between Carrickmacross and Dundalk, just N of T24, 2 bus from Carrickmacross, 3 bus from Dundalk.* Ruins of 6th c

Newcastle

Pop. 5,000, 13 m (21 km) SE of Downpatrick, 31 m (50 km) SE of Belfast. EC Thurs. TIO: 61 Central Promenade, tel: Newcastle 22222, July, Aug. Bus enquiries: bus station, tel: Newcastle 22296. 18, 20 Ulsterbus from Belfast. Coach tours: SO, details TIO.

One of Northern Ireland's top seaside resorts, beautifully situated, with the great sandy beaches of Dundrum Bay backed by the towering Slieve Donard Mountain. Plenty of sport, including fishing, golf, pony trekking.

Our Lady of the Assumption Church (C), *near N end of Downs Park:* circular, with striking interior design.**D Grant Gallery:** Irish and international paintings, sculpture, *daily, details: Newcastle 22349.* Newcastle Centre: impressive range of indoor entertainments, sport, café, lounge. Ideal for when it rains, especially with children, *daily, details: Newcastle 22222.***D** Promenade Gardens: see fountain commemorating Percy French, who wrote the song *The Mountains of Mourne.* Castle

Newcastle

Park: wide range of sporting activities. Summer concerts, open air entertainment.

Donard Park: rises up the slopes of Slieve Donard and Shanlieve. For an interesting walk, follow the Glen River from the town centre car park through Donard Park and forest up the path to the Saddle, a col between Slieve Donard and Slieve Commedagh. Above the second bridge is an old stone-built ice house. Bicycles: W. McClure, *17 Dundrum Road, tel: Newcastle 23262.* Newcastle Riding Centre, *35 Carnacavill Road, tel: Newcastle 22694.* Royal County Down Golf Club, *18 holes, tel: Newcastle 23314.* Youth Hostel: *134 Downs Road, tel: Newcastle 22133.*

AROUND NEWCASTLE

Annalong, *8 m (13 km) S of Newcastle on A2, 37 Ulsterbus from Newcastle. EC, Thurs.* Charming fishing village. Walk round harbour, often filled with fishing boats, before relaxing in a quayside pub. Early 19 th c **Cornmill** being reconstructed. Due to open early summer, 1984. Will be first water-driven cornmill in N. Ireland open to public. *Details: Newry and Mourne District Council, tel: Newry 5411.*

Bloody Bridge, *2 m (4 km) S of Newcastle, just W of A2, 37 Ulsterbus from Newcastle.* Scene of 1641 massacre of Protestants. NT has provided car park, coastal walk. Nearby is Maggie's Leap, a narrow chasm so-called because a young lady of that name jumped across while carrying a basket of eggs to avoid a persistent suitor. Donard Cove is only accessible by boat from Newcastle.

Brontë Country, *between Rathfriland and Banbridge:* rolling hills and bushy dells, homeland of father and many uncles and aunts of the three novelist sisters. Brontë trails is signposted. Emdale, 3 m (5 km) SE of Loughbrickland; ruin of cottage where Brontë's father, Patrick, was born is marked by plaque. Drumballyroney is 3 m (5 km) NE of Rathfriland. On the hilltop can be seen church where Rev. Thomas Tighe coached Patrick for Cambridge and also school where he taught. In churchyard, graves of some six of his brothers and sisters. Magherally, 3 m (5 km) NE of Banbridge: ruined

Murlough Sand Dunes, near Dundrum

Annalong Harbour

church where grandparents of Brontë sisters were married. Also grave of novelist Helen Waddell, who wrote *Peter Abélard,* the touching story of Abelard and Heloise.

Bryansford, *2 m (3 km) NE of Newcastle, 34 Ulsterbus from Newcastle.* Row of fine stone cottages. Modern nature study centre. On B180 just outside village. Lord Limerick's Follies, two peculiar towers, topped with glacier-shaped granite stones. *1 m (1.5 km) NE, on B180,* ruins of St Donard's old church inside rath. Also stump of round tower.**D**

Castlewellan, *5 m (8 km) NW of Newcastle on A50, 17, 18 Ulsterbus from Newcastle. All day closing, Thurs.* Pleasant-looking market town. Mon is market day; every second Mon, the town's fair takes place. Walk the length of the broad Main Street, taking in both Upper and Lower Squares.

Castlewellan Forest Park, *just N of Castlewellan:* over 1,000 acres with outstanding wildlife. Signposted walks. Camping, caravan sites. Slievenaslat is a slight mountain that can be scaled on foot or horseback. Arboretum has may trees and plants from all over the world and is considered one of the finest in the world. 18th c farmstead, with courtyards, barns, belfries. Café.**D**

Castlewellan Lakes: *five within 5 m (8 km) radius of town:* all good for fishing and lakeside walks; Castlewellan, Ballylough, Ballyward, Ballymagreehan, Lough Island Reavy. Last-named has easiest acces; S end is alongside A25, about 4 m (6 km) SW of Castlewellan. Near E end of this lake, Drumena Cashel is one of best-preserved ringforts (early defended homesteads) in N. Ireland. Mount Pleasant Riding Centre, *Upper Clarkhill, tel: Castlewellan 651;* Newcastle Riding Centre, *35 Carnaville Road, tel: Newcastle 22694.*

Clough, *just S of Seaford, 18, 20 Ulsterbus from*

Castle Ward

Newcastle. Crossroads village with well-preserved Norman motte and bailey, ruin of small castle.

Dromara, *5 m (8 km) SW of Ballynahinch, 27 Uisterbus from Ballynahinch EC, Sat.* Lovely and secluded, with attractive old bridges over infant River Lagan. Good walks. Mossvale Riding Centre, *18 Church Road, tel: Dromara 279.*

Drumkeeragh Forest, *10 m (16 km) N of Newcastle, W of B175:* comparatively new, with outstanding views of Slieve Croob Mountain to S. Caravan site.

Dundrum, *3 m (5 km) N of Newcastle, 18, 20 Ulsterbus from Newcastle. EC, Thurs.* Attractive seaside village. Dundrum Castle: built by Normans, late 12th c, now substantial ruins. *Apr 1–Sept 30, Tues-Sat, 10 a.m.–6 p.m. Closed lunch.*

Sun, 1.50 p.m.–6 p.m. Oct 1–Mar 31, hours as above, but closes 4 p.m.

Katesbridge, between Castlewellan and Banbridge on A50: delightful little village o banks of Upper Bann River. Norman motte by river, also picnic area. Blacksmith's forge, by old bridge, has been run by Morgan fimily for five generations, see horseshoes being shaped on the anvil, amid clatter of sparks.

Legananny Dolmen, 4 m (7 km) S of Dromara on slopes of Cratlieve Mountain: considered the most graceful Stone Age monument in Northern Ireland.

Loughinisland, 7 m (11 km) SE of Ballynahinch on A24T, 18, 20 Ulsterbus from Newcastle. Ruins of three ancient churches on lake islet connected to mainland by causeway. Oldest church probably pre-dates 11th c.

Minerstown Beach, E shores of Dundrum Bay: splendidly situated. Tyrella Strand is W continuation of this beach, magnificent 4 m (6 km) stretch, firm enough for driving.

Mountains of Mourne: rise up in spectacular fashion behind Annalong. Minor roads lead from village, but since no roads cross the centre of the range, you must walk to see main peaks at close quarters. **Slieve Donard,** 2,796 ft (850 metre), the highest mountain, is worth climbing, especially on clear day, when there are views to Donegal and Wicklow in Ireland, Isle of Man, NW England, N Wales mountains. Takes about 2 hours from Newcastle, following route of old tramway from near harbour. At summit, slight remains of 5th c oratory built by St Domhanghort, who gave the mountain its name. Mourne Coastal Path: runs S for 4 m (6 km) along seashore from Bloody Bridge, at the foot of Slieve Donard. Most exhilarating: another path follows course of Bloody River into the mountains.

Murlough National Nature Reserve, 1 m (1.5 km) S of Dundrum, 18, 20 Ulsterbus from Newcastle. Impressive place where you may see badgers or find a Stone Age arrowhead. Illustrations of birds and flowers to guide walkers, special guided tours. For permits for restricted areas, contact the warden, tel: Dundrum 311/467. Information centre has changing displays about the area. Always open.**D**

Rathfriland, 4 m (6 km) S of Katesbridge, 36 Ulsterbus from Newcastle. EC, Thurs. Small plantation town set on a hill, steep streets rising to square. Old buildings include Quaker meeting house. Kinnahalla Youth Hostel: Hilltown, tel: Rathfriland 289.

Rourke's Park, 2 m (3 km) N of Annalong, 37 Ulsterbus from Newcastle to Annalong. Forest recreation area in valley of Annalong River. Excellent starting point for mountain walks, taking in Slieve Binian, Blue Lough, great cave of Cove mountain, Brandy Pad. Car park.

Seaforde, on Newcastle–Ballynahinch A24T, 18, 20 Ulsterbus from Newcastle. Seaforde House demesne may be visited by prior arr.

Slievenaman, 4 m (6 km) W of Newcastle: Youth Hostel.

Slievenamoney Hill, 5 m (8 km) N of Castlewellan: granite cross on summit marks the fact that Franciscan friars found refuge nearby during 17th and 18th c Penal times.

Tollymore Forest Park, near Bryansford: impressive and enjoyable, 1,200 acres, with Gothic follies, arboretum, caravan, camping site, café, exhibition hall. Hermitage is random collection of stones forming cave-like room on banks of River Shimna. Many planned walks, varying in length from 1 to 8 m (1.5–13 km).**D**

Portaferry

Pop. 1,600, 25 m (40 km) S of Belfast EC, Thurs. Bus enquiries: Downpatrick bus station, tel:

Downpatrick 2384. Ferry enquiries: Strangford 637. 9, 9A, 10 Ulsterbus from Belfast. Ferry from Strangford.

A most attractive seaside village near the S end of the Ards Peninsula, facing Strangford across the narrow waters at Strangford Lough entrance. The long waterfront has a mixture of Scots-style cottages and some Georgian houses, a most pleasing prospect enhanced by the charming old-world inns. Good sea angling centre, especially for giant skate.

Templecranny Old Church, off Church Street: belfry and one gable left. **Portaferry House:** ruins of 16th c castle in grounds. Queen's University marine biology station and aquarium, Strand Street: by arr., tel: Portaferry 230. Car ferry to Strangford: daily at half hour intervals between about 7.30 a.m. and 10.30 p.m. 10 minute trip, details: Strangford 637. Boats: at quayside for trips round Strangford Lough and its innu merable islands.

AROUND PORTAFERRY

Ardglass, 7 m (11 km) SE of Downpatrick. 16 Ulsterbus from Downpatrick EC, Thurs. Main fishing port of this part of Co. Down. Walks around inner and outer harbour. **Ardtole Church,** 0.5 m (0.8 km) N of town: 15th c ruin on height overlooking sea.

Jordan's Castle, 15th c structure by harbour. July 1–Aug 31, Tues–Sat, 10 a.m.–7 p.m. Closed 1 p.m. ½ hr. lunch. Sun, 2 p.m.–7 p.m. Apr, May, June, Sept, 10 a.m.–7 p.m., Sun, 2 p.m.–7 p.m. Rest of year by arr. Isabella's Tower, just N of town: 19th c folly on a hilltop. Ardglass Golf Club, 18 holes, tel: Ardglass 841219.

Ardkeen Promontory, E shore of Strangford Lough, 4 m (7 km) N of Portaferry. 9, 9A, 10 Ulsterbus from Portaferry. Foundations of 12th c Ardkeen Castle. 200 years ago the stones were used to build a nearby mansion, of which one large wall still stands.

Ballyhornan, 5 m (8 km) S of Strangford on A2. 16 Ulsterbus from Downpatrick. Growing coastal hamlet with two fine beaches in vicinity. Just S, you can walk over to Gun's Island. You may see seals on the coast here.

Ballynoe Stone Circle, 3 m (5 km) S of Downpatrick: large standing stones enclose a Neolithic burial mound, most impressive.

Ballyquintin Point, S point of Ards Peninsula: on E side, Temple Cowey has foundations of very early church and three tiny springs still visited by pilgrims, who leave votive offerings. Off the Point, don't be surprised to see seals basking on rocks at Bar Hall Bay.

Ballywhite Hill, 2 m (4 km) N of Portaferry: highest point of Ards Peninsula, fine views.

Bankmore Hill, 1.5 m (2 km) S of Portaferry: overlooks the narrows at entrance to Strangford Lough, with its permanent whirlpool.

Castle Ward (NT), near Strangford: most unusual house, part classical, part Strawberry Hill 'Gothic', apparently because Lord and Lady Bangor could not agree on the design of their new house. Lady Bangor's gothick boudoir is most eccentric and well worth seeing. Victorian laundry offers fascinating glimpse of great-grandma's wash day. Landscaped grounds include old Castle Ward, 15th c tower house, formal garden, Temple Water with Greek temple folly, nature trails, tearooms caravan park, wildfowl collection. Castleward theatre, regular perfomances. House, Apr–Sept 30. daily, 2 p.m.–6 p.m. Closed Fri. Open Good Fri, public holidays on a Fri. Grounds and wildfowl collection, all year, daily, 9 a.m.–sunset. Details: Strangford 204.**D**

Cloughey, 2 m (3 km) SW of Portavogie. 9, 9A, 10 Ulsterbus from Portaferry. EC, Thurs. Village set on shores of beautiful sandfringed bay. Just behind village is ruin of Kirkistown Castle, built 1622.

Downpatrick, 9 m (14 km) W of Strangford All day closing, Wed. Bus enquiries: bus station, tel: Downpatrick 2384. 15 Ulsterbus from Belfast. County town of Down. St Patrick said to be buried

in churchyard of Down Cathedral at top of English Street. Fine walk along Georgian Mall beside cathedral.

Downpatrick Museum: general and local items, check with: Downpatrick 5218. Quoile Pondage is pleasant 3 m (5 km) stretch of river turned into lake by barrage. Starting from the old stone bridge in the town, the winding lakeside path gives pleasant views of Quoile Castle ruins and old quays. NT nature reserve. Fishing stands, picnic areas.**D** Downpatrick Racecourse: about six meetings a year, details: Carryduff 812663. Leisure Centre, inc. pool: Market Street, tel: Downpatrick 3426.**D** Downpatrick Golf Club, 9 holes, tel: Downpatrick 2152.

Inch Abbey, 2 m (3 km) NW of Downpatrick: founded by Cistercians about 1180, now impressive ruin. Apr 1–Sept 30, Tues–Sat, 10 a.m.–7 p.m. Closed at 1 p.m. for ½ hr. lunch. Sun, 2 p.m.–4 p.m.

Inishargy, 1.5 m (2 km) NE of Kircubbin: Haws Brae Lane is an old road running S and sufficiently high to give good views of Strangford Lough and sea, 3 m (5 km) to E.

Kearney, near S tip of Ards Peninsula: delightful 19th c fishing village, restored by NT. Pleasant walks along rocky shore.

Kilclief Castle: on Strangford side of Lough entrance: 15th c castle. June–Sept, Tues–Sat, 10 a.m.–7 p.m. Closed at 1 p.m. for ½ hr. lunch. Sun, 2 p.m.–7 p.m. Rest of year by arr.

Killough, 2 m (4 km) SW of Ardglass. 16 Ulsterbus from Downpatrick. One long street lined with sycamore trees, has quite a continental air. Pleasant walk round harbour area, taking in partly 18th c parish church, old warehouses. On hilltop to S of village, tower of former windmill.

Killyleagh, 14 Ulsterbus from Downpatrick. All day closing, Thurs. Delightful village on W shore of Strangford Lough, 4 m (6 km) from Strangford as the crow flies, but 15 m (24 km) by road via Downpatrick because of River Quoile estuary flowing into the lough. Pleasant walks around Killyleagh's broad streets and up to gates of the castle. Interesting harbour area.

Kircubbin, 7 m (11 km) N of Portaferry on A20. 9, 9A Ulsterbus from Portaferry. EC. Thurs. Attractive lough-side village and sailing centre.

Kirkistown, just inland from Portavogie: motor and motorcycle racing circuit, details: Portavogie 325.**D**

Millin Bay, just S of Kearney: Tara Fort on hilltop overlooking bay is impressive Celtic defensive farmstead.

Mound of Downpatrick, just NW of town: hillock raised in 12th c for castle construction. Ideal for a light climb.

Portavogie, 7 m (11 km) NE of Portaferry. 9 10 Ulsterbus from Portaferry. EC, Thurs. Main fishing village of Ards Peninsula. Harbour often filled with fishing boats. Occasional evening quayside fish auctions, two beaches.

St John's Point, just S of Killough: rugged coastal walk, stretches for some 2 m (4 km). See ruins of 10th c church.

Saul, 2 m (3 km) NE of Downpatrick: St Patrick landed here.in 432 to begin his Irish mission and said to have died here in 493. Modern memorial church of St Patrick (CI) on height above village. 1 m (1.5 km) W is Sliabh Padraig hill, topped by a huge granite figure of the Saint.

Strangford, ferry enquiries: Strangford 637. 16 Ulsterbus from Downpatrick. Ferry from Portaferry. EC Wed. Attractive little harbour area facing Portaferry across the mouth of Strangford Lough. Strangford Castle: imposing 16th c edifice. Open by arr with caretaker. Strangford Lough Wildlife Scheme: seven refuge areas around lough shores, also hides, for watching many varieties of water birds. Permits: A. Irvine, warden, Castle Ward, Strangford, tel: Strangford 253. Strangford Riding School, Castleward Road, tel: Strangford 329.

Struel Wells, 1.5 m (2.5 km) S of Saul, near Downpatrick: once a popular place of pilgrimage. St

Patrick said to have blessed the wells. Site includes ruined church, drinking well, eye well, ruins of bathouses for men and women (no mixed bathing!). *Open all year.*

Rostrevor

Pop. 2,100, 1 m (1.5 km) by ferry from Omeath, 9 m (14 km) SE of Newry. EC Wed. Bus enquiries: Edward Street bus depot, Newry, tel: Newry 3531. 39 Ulsterbus from Newry. EC Wed.

A small, delightfully nostalgic seaside town with a clear Victorian influence. An excellent centre for exploring Carlingford Lough and the Mountains of Mourne, just N behind the town.

Rostrevor Forest, *behind the town:* from car park, 0.5 m (0.8 km) walk to viewpoint with panorama of lough. More strenuously, there is a walk to Cloghmore (Big Stone), perched at 900 ft (820 metres), on a spur of Slievemartin. Another path to Cloghmore goes from shore level across the Oakwood and Fidders' Green. For a more leisurely stroll try the square, with its ancient trees and the area along the front.

AROUND ROSTREVOR

Ballykeel, *just N of Mullaghbawn:* fine Stone Age dolmen.

Bessbrook, *3 m (5 km) NW of Newry. 41 Ulsterbus from Newry.* Good walks round main College and Charlemont squares. Also see huge old mill, with dam, sluices, weirs. As the town was founded just over 100 years ago by a Quaker linen manufacturer, there isn't a pub in sight. However, if you visit the nearby hamlet of Camlough, it has six to compensate. Walk: from old tramway depot, follow route of long closed track through woodlands and past several old mills into Newry.

'Bush Town', *3 m (5 km) E of Hilltown on B27:* fairy thorn tree is largest in north of Ireland, in triangle is formed by junction of Bryansford and Kilkeel roads.

Cairnhill House, *1 m (1.5 km) NE of Newry on the B8/A25:* weeping wych elm tree in garden has greatest spread of foliage in Ireland, 232 ft (71 metres).

Camlough Lake, *2 m (3 km) SW of Bessbrook, off B30:* paths by NE shore, excellent climb to top of nearby Camlough Mountain, 1,389 ft (420 metres).

Cassy Water Valley, *5 m (8 km) E of Rostrevor:* one of the best walks in the Mournes. Kilfeaghan dolmen is W of lane leading up the valley.

Cloghoge, *3 m (5 km) S of Newry:* start of fine walk to top of Flagstaff Hill, excellent views. Return through Newry Forest to canal side.

Cranfield Point, *4 m (6 km) SW of Kilkeel:* fine beach and dunes popular with campers and caravanners.

Derrymore House, *1 m (1.5 km) S of Bessbrook on A25:* late 18th c thatched manor house with interesting furnishing. 1800 Act of Union between Ireland and Britain said to have been drafted here. 48 acre park open daily. *House by arr., National Trust, Rowallane, Saintfield, Ballynahinch, Co. Down BT24 7LM. Tel: Saintfield 510721.*

Dunnaval Beach, *2 m (3 km) S of Kilkeel:* very secluded.

Fairy Glen, *2 m (3 km) N of Rostrevor:* delightfully scenic, with small waterfalls on Kilbroney River and rustic paths, ideal for a quiet stroll.

Greencastle, *just NE of Cranfield Point:* well-preserved ruin of 13th c Norman castle, built at same time as Carlingford Castle, across the lough. *Apr 1–Sept 30, Tues–Sat, 10 a.m.–7 p.m. Closed 1 p.m. for ½ hr. lunch Sun, 2 p.m.–7 p.m. Closed rest of year.*

Hilltown, *8 m (13 km) N of Rostrevor on B25. 33 Ulsterbus from Newry.* Its numerous pubs are reminder of the village's brandy-smuggling past.

Attractive tree-lined square.

Kilkeel, *10 m (16 km) E of Rostrevor on A2. EC, Thurs. Sept.–May, all day. TIO: Town Hall, tel: Kilkeel 63092, July, Aug. 39 Ulsterbus from Newry.* Main fishing port of S Down. Winding streets, stepped footpaths, many old houses ot great character, and an interesting harbour area. Water in granite trough at 14th c church ruins at town centre said to cure warts. Kilkeel Golf Club, *9 holes, tel: Kilkeel 62296/62293.*

Killevy, *3 m (5 km) S of Camlough:* site of one of Ireland's most important early nunneries, founded late 5th c.

Killowen, *2 m (3 km) E of Rostrevor:* good bathing beach.

Mount Norris, *on Bessbrook–Markethill B133:* attractive little village with good walks 2 m (3 km) W of Shaw's Lake. NT wooded glen with trout stream and waterfall is 3 m (5 km) SW. Just S of glen, in old burial ground of Ballymoyer, is the grave of Florence MacMoyer an informer who brought about the execution of St Oliver Plunkett and was so detested that her grave was heaped with stones. Sometimes a stone or two is still added.

Mullaghbawn, *W side of Slieve Gullion:* small museum, furnished in traditional S Armagh farmhouse style, displays of old instruments and pictures. *Summer weekends or by arr., caretaker lives nearby.*

Narrow Water Castle, *2 m (3 km) on Newry side of Warrenpoint:* 16th c ruins on rock connected with shore by causeway. *Apr–Sept 30, Tues–Sat, 10 a.m.–7 p.m. Closed 1 p.m. for ½ hr lunch. Sun, 2 p.m.–7 p.m. Oct 1–Mar 31, Sat, 10 a.m.–4 p.m. Closed 1 p.m. for ½ hr. lunch. Sun, 2 p.m.–4 p.m.*

Newry, *10 m (16 km) NW of Rostrevor EC. Wed. TIO: Bridge Street, tel: Newry 61748, July, Aug. Bus enquiries: Edward Street bus depot, tel: Newry 3531. 39 Ulsterbus from Rostrevor, 38, 45, 238 from Belfast.* Though much scarred by the Troubles, the town has many interesting features and is a good shopping centre. The Clanrye River and canal cross the town, and the canal quaysides have interesting 18th c warehouses. **Cathedral of Ss. Patrick and Colman** (C), *Hill Street:* dates from 1825 with interesting mosaics and stained glass. **St Patrick's Church** (CI), *Church Street:* incorporates part of 16th c tower. **Newry Arts Centre Museum,** *Bank Parade:* range of artistic activities, also museum, with interesting local exhibits. *Mon–Sat, 9 a.m.–4.30 p.m., details: Newry 61244.*

Newry Canal: being reopened for boating, good coarse angling. Kilmorey Park, *between Stream Street and Cowan Street:* attractively wooded. Swimming pool: heated, indoor, *Clanrye Avenue, daily, tel: Newry 3481.* Newry Golf Club, *18 holes, tel: Newry 3871.*

Poyntzpass: follow banks of canal 4 m (6 km) S of Jerrettspass, passing hump-backed bridges and locks.

Silent Valley, *5 m (8 km) N of Kilkeel, off B27:* two huge reservoirs for supplying water to Belfast. Approach by 3 m (5 km) long lakeside road to dam. Good park between entrance gates and Silent Valley dam. From Ben Crom dam, walk up to fine viewpoints above the lakes. *Reservoir permit: Dept. of Environment, tel: Belfast 768716.*

Slieve Gullion, *5 m (8 km) SW of Newry:* massive 'whale-backed' mountain. Fine scenic drive. From summit, with its ancient passage grave and wild goats, you can see smoke of both Dublin and Belfast on a really clear day. Adjoining forest has caravan site, picnic areas, walks to viewpoints. SE side of mountain, Hawthorn Hill, has nature and crafts exhibition centre, *all year, daily, 10 a.m.–sunset.*

Spelga Dam, *4 m (6 km) SW of Hilltown:* try the 'magnetic mile' effect similar to that at Gortin Forest Park in Tyrone. Your car will appear to go uphill when facing downhill and vice versa; breathtaking views. The road also runs N past Fofanny Reservoir, from where a loop road goes E across Trassey River, the start of the popular walk up the wide river valley to Hare's Gap. Youth

Hostel at Kinnahalla, Near Spelga Reservoir.

Warrenpoint, *3 m (5 km) W of Rostrevor. EC. Wed. winter only. TIO: Information Office, Boating Pool, tel: Warrenpoint 2256, July, Aug. 39 Ulsterbus from Newry.* Spacious resort with fine square and tree-lined promenade, two piers ideal for fishing, walking. Summer events include open air art exhibition. Market in square, *Sun.* Summer boat excursions to Omeath.

Town Hall Museum has interesting collection of Victoriana, including old postcards of area, old prints, glass negatives, silver, mementoes of old Warrenpoint railway. Domestic and farm hardware. *All year, Mon–Fri, 9 a.m.–5 p.m. July, Aug, Sat, Sun, 2.30 p.m.–4.30 p.m. Details: Warrenpoint 2256.* Warrenpoint Golf Club, *18 holes, tel: Warrenpoint 2219.*

The MID-LANDS

Carlow

Pop. 10,000, 52 m (84 km) SW of Dublin, 25 km (40 km) SE of Portlaoise, 24 m (38 km) NE of Kilkenny. EC Thurs. TIO: (0503) 31554, July, Aug. Bus and train enquiries: (0503) 31633. 53 bus from Dublin, 56 from Dublin and Kilkenny. Train from Dublin and Kilkenny.

A pleasant, modest town, a former Anglo-Norman stronghold, and 'capital' of the second smallest county in Ireland. Though recently industrialised, it retains a quiet air, and there are interesting walks to be had around older streets and along the River Barrow, where it is joined by the Burrin tributary, forming a four angled lake.

Cathedral of the assumption, (C), *off Tullow Street:* consecrated in 1833, this Gothic-style edifice has Hogan marble monument to Bishop Doyle, a 19th c writer on politics and current affairs under the pen-name 'JKL', James of Kildare and Leighlin'. Stained glass windows by Harry Clarke. **D Carlow Castle,** *near Barrow bridge:* ruins of Norman castle, W wall and two flanking towers. Captured by Cromwell in 1650 and later returned to Earl of Thomond. In 1814, Dr Middleton, a local physician, tried to convert it to a lunatic asylum and put explosives in walls to reduce their thickness. In the event, most of the castle had to be demolished for safety reasons. Access with permission, through adjacent Corcoran's Mineral Water factory. *Mon–Fri.* **Courthouse,** *junction of Dublin Street and Dublin Road:* design of this 19th c building lifted from the Parthenon.

Museum, *Haymarket:* old theatre full of fascinating local curios. Reconstructed forge and kitchen. Military and religious items, also relics of carpenter's and cooper's trades. Enter through yard at side of Town Hall, *daily, inc Sat, Sun; SO. Otherwise, Sun aft, details: (0503)31532 or Alec Burns, College Street.* **Library,** *Dublin Street:* very interesting collection of local antiquarian books. *Mon–Fri, details: (0503)31126.* Technical College Library, Kilkenny Road: see equipment used by John Tyndall, 19th c founder of science of thermodynamics, *term time, Mon–Fri, 9 a.m.–5 p.m. Check with librarian first, tel: (0503) 31324.* See Ballinabranna.

Oak Park, *2 m (3 km) N of Carlow:* Agricultural Research Institute run by An Foras Taluntais. 300 acres of woodland lakes, wildfowl sanctuary, visitors welcome. *Mon–Fri, 9 a.m.–5 p.m. Details:*

(0503)21222. Walks in vicinity of Haymarket, also S along Barrow towpath to Clogrennan or N along E bank of river. Swimming pool: outdoor, heated, *Athy Road Park, daily, June, July, Aug.* Bicycles: A. E. Coleman, *Dublin Street, tel: (0503) 41273.* Golf Club, *18 holes, tel: (0503) 31695.*

AROUND CARLOW

Ballinabranna, *near Carlow:* plaque on Old School to famous 19th c physicist, John Tyndall, who had primary education here.

Ballymoon Castle, *2 m (3 km) E of Muine Bheag:* probably built between 1290 and 1310. According to local tradition, never finished. Although in ruins, doorways and fireplace of great hall in excellent condition.

Browne's Hill Demesne, *2 m (3 km) E of Carlow on L7:* magnificent dolmen, the 100 ton capstone is largest in Ireland.

Duckett's Grove Castle, *between Tullow and Castledermot on L31A:* built in 1830, burned down in 1933. Majestic ruins. Owner, Miss Frances Brady, runs nearby riding school.

Killeshin, *3 m (5 km) W of Carlow on L31:* magnificent Romanesque doorway, all that remains of 6th c monastery founded by St Diarmuid. Nearby is old rath called Castlequarter, with striking view of Barrow Valley. In clear weather, you will see nine counties.

Leighlinbridge, *7 m (11 km) S of Carlow on N9:* W half of 16th c tower, access via nearby house. See Great Mound with circular moat, off *Kilkenny Road:* site of ancient palace of Kings of Leinster. Village marks edge of ancient 'pale'.

Muine Bheag, (Bagenalstown), *11 m (18 km) S of Carlow, 53, 56 bus from Carlow, also train.* The anglicised name comes from Walter bagenal of Dunleckney, who tried to build a town of great architectural splendour, called Bersaille. Task never completed. Carrigbeg Riding Establishment, *tel: (053)21157.*

St Mullins, *9 m (15 km) S of Borris:* beautifully situated village on E bank of River Barrow. Monastic remains include St Mullins' Abbey and 7th c ruins of St Moling's monastery. Pleasant walks in village and nearby woodlands. Good coarse fishing.

Tullow, *7 m (12 km) SE of Carlow:* annual show, *Aug 15,* horse and cattle competitions, goats' and pets' contests, trade displays, usually including a Bible society stand. Costumed riders take part in horse and trap competitions. All good, clean fun.

Windy Gap, *on N80 between Carlow and Stradbally:* striking views.

Carrick-on-Shannon

Pop. 2,000, 30 m (48 km) SE of Sligo, 101 m (162 km) NW of Dublin. EC Wed. TIO: (078)20170, May–Sep. Bus and train enquiries: (078)20036. 126, 275 bus from Athlone, Sligo, 277 from Drumshanbo. Train from Dublin, Sligo.

Leitrim has the smallest population of any county in Ireland and Carrick-on-Shannon is the smallest county town. A noted angling centre, and the mecca of Shannon cruising. Attractive walk from river banks to town centre. Shannon Boat Rally: *late July, details: TIO.*

Costelloe Chapel: reputed to be the second smallest in the world. No interior fittings, apart from altar and stained glass window. Canoes: Kennedys, Jamestown Bridge. Cruisers: Athlone Cruisers; Carrick Craft, *The Marina, tel: (078)20236:* Emerald Star Line, *tel: (078)20234:* Flagline (1972), *The Marina, tel: (078)20172:* Weaver Boats, *St Patrick's Park, tel: (078)20204.* Swimming pool: outdoor, heated, *summer, daily.* Bicycles: Patrick Geraghty, *Main Street;* Mrs. F. Holt, *Bridge Street.*

AROUND CARRICK-ON-SHANNON

Aghrane, *10 m (16 km) SW of Roscommon, near Ballygar on N63:* forest walks, picnic area, lay-by parking.

Arigna Mountains, *W of Lough Allen:* one of Ireland's few coal mining areas. Route round mountains clearly signposted, superb views of Leitrim countryside.

Ballinamore, *15 m (24 km) NE of Carrick, 85 bus from Enniskillen, Longford, 282 from Drumshanbo, Longford.* Pleasantly set amid hills and near Garadice Lake, ideal centre for angling, golfing, horse riding. Boats: *details, TIO, Ballinamore, tel: 91. June–Sept.* Tully Farm Riding Centre, *tel: Ballinamore 177.* Rent-a-Bike, *High Street, tel: Ballinamore 91.*

Ballintober Castle, *8 m (13 km) NW of Roscommon on N60:* chief seat of the O'Conors, now an impressive ruin.

Boyle, *9 m (14 km) W of Carrick on N4. EC Wed, July, Aug, rest of year, all day. TIO: tel: Boyle 145, June–Sept. Bus, train enquiries: Boyle 27. 126, 275 bus from Carrick. Train from Carrick.* Cistercian Abbey, founded 1161, ruins near river on N side of town. Nave, choir, transepts still in good repair. Among domestic buildings, kitchen and hospitium are best preserved. *Mid-June–mid-Sept, daily, 10 a.m.–6 p.m. Rest of year key with caretaker.* Boats: Peter Blishen, Lakeshore Restaurant, *tel: Boyle 214;* M. Burke, Knockvicar, *tel: Cootehall 12;* Mrs A. Harrington, Glencarne House, *Ardcarne, tel: Cootehall 13;* Mrs K. Mattimoe, *Lakeview, Shannon Cruisers, tel: Cootehall 7;* Bicycles: M. E. Sheerin, *Main Street, tel: Boyle 10.*

St Canice's Cathedral

Castlerea, *19 m (30 km) NW of Roscommon on N60. Train enquiries: Castlerea 31. 247 bus from Galway. Train from Athlone, Castlebar.* Attractive town on wooded reach of River Suck. People's Park has sports facilities, inc. swimming pool. **Clonalis,** *just W of town:* great 19th c manor, unique great houses of Ireland in being owned by a Gaelic family. Drawing room is comfortably Victorian, library has 19th c portraits and many fine books. Private chapel. Museum, inc. Carolan's harp and portrait, Gaelic manuscripts, glass porcelain, Victorian costumes, Sheraton furniture. *May, June, Sat, Sun, 2 p.m.–5.30 p.m. daily except Mon 1 July–9 Sept, 11 a.m.–1 p.m., 2 p.m.–5.30 p.m. Other times by arr. Castlerea 118.* Bicycles: T. Bruen, *Main Street, tel: Castlerea 73.*

Clooneyquin, *3 m (5 km) SW of Elphin on N61:* birthplace of Percy French, noted song writer and entertainer.

Derrycarne, *just N of N4 at Dromod:* attractive picnic area with access to Shannon.

Dromod, *10 m (16 km) SE of Carrick:* Breffni Inn: friendly, family-run pub, described as Ireland's cleanest.

Dromonona, *2 m (4 km) W of Boyle on L133:* site of one of largest dolmens in Ireland, measuring 14 × 11 ft (4.5 × 3.3 metres).

Drumshanbo, *8 m (13 km) N of Carrick on T54, 277 bus from Carrick, 282 from Dromod Railway Station.* Angling centre near S end of Lough Allen, reputed to have best pike in N Europe. An Tostal Festival: everything Irish, dancing, music, singing, *June, details: Carrick TIO.* J. M. Mooney, *Carrick Road, tel: Drumshanbo 13,* has interesting documents relating to area and runs information service for visitors. Swimming pool: outdoor, heated. *All year, daily.*

Drumsna, *5 m (8 km) SE of Carrick.* Woodcarving Centre, *Main Street, daily, 10 a.m.–6 p.m. Tel: Drumsna 25, in advance.* Huge ancient earthworks of Doon just S of village.

Doughill/Slieve Bán, *5 m (8 km) S of Strokestown:* forest walks, viewing points.

Dunamon Castle, *4 m (6 km) S of Oran on Roscommon–Ballymoe N60:* very similar style to Bunratty, occupied by Divine Word Missionaries. *By arr, tel: (093)7222.*

Elphin, *8 m (13 km) SW of Carrick-on-Shannon:* cathedral town. Smith Hill, *1 m (1.5 km) NW,* held to be birthplace of Oliver Goldsmith.

Fenagh abbey, *3 m (5 km) S of Ballinamore:* ruins of Gothic church, only remains of monastery founded by St Columba.

Frenchpark, *8 m (13 km) SW of Boyle on L11:* Douglas Hyde, founder of the Gaelic League and first president of Ireland was born at Ratra House 3 m (5 km) to W, now a shell in the middle of a field. His grave is in the old Protestant churchyard about 1 m (1.5 km) W, on S side of N5. Remains of 13th c Dominican Cloonshanville Abbey.

Hill of Rathcroghan, *6 m (10 km) SE of Frenchpark:* ancient palace of kings of Connacht once stood here. 0.5 m (0.8 km) SW is cave of Owneygrat, The Cave of the Cats, in ancient times considered to be the entrance to the Other World.

Keadue, *4 m (6 km) NE of Lough Key 277 bus from Carrick:* Turlough O'Carolan, last of the Irish bards, is buried in Kilronan Abbey cemetery, near N shore of Lough Meelagh, just W of village. O'Carolan Festival, ten days of events, musical and sporting, *early Aug. Details: Boyle TIO.*

Kilronan Forest, *turn L 1 m (1.5 km) NW of Keadue:* attractive walks midway between Lough Allen and Lough Key.

Knockateen, *1 m (2.5 km) W of Tarmon Church on W side of Lough Allen:* scenic views, forest walk, picnic area, car park.

Lanesborough, *boats:* Mr. Watts, *tel: (043)21202,* Mr. Ryan, *Cois Abhann, tel: (043) 21111.* Thornfield Riding School, *Rathcline, tel: (0902) 21265.*

Lavagh, *near Drumkeeran:* forest walks, picnic area, car park.

Lough Allen, the 30 m (48 km) lakeside road gives fine if sometimes bleak views of lake.

Lough Gara, *8 m (13 km) of Ballymote off L133:* on W side of lake are the well-preserved ruins of Moygara Castle.

Lough Key Forest Park, *2 m (3 km) E of Boyle on N4:* one of Ireland's most beautiful. Walks through extensive forest area, with detailed and most interesting nature trail. Bog Gardens, a moss of rhododendrons and azaleas in early summer, feature many peat-loving plants and shrubs. Deer enclosure. Attractive gazebo gives excellent views of lake and islands. Fine views from Moylurg Tower, on hill where mansion once stood—destroyed by accidental fire in 1957. One of house's subterranean passageways has been restored and lit. Restaurant and shop open during summer. Picnic area, caravan park, camping site, fishing, swimming, water sports. Boats from the shop, *tel: Boyle 214.* Lake cruises, *tel: Cootehall 7.***D**

Mote Park, *(Big Wood), 3 m (5 km) SE of Roscommon on N61:* forest walks.

Oran, *9 m (14 km) NW of Roscommon on N60, 248 bus from Roscommon.* Stump of round tower, meagre remains of pre-Romanesque church, all that is left of early monastery.

Roscommon, *27 m (43 km) S of Carrick. EC Thurs. TIO: (0903) 6356, June–Sept. Bus, train enquiries: (0903)6201. 240 bus from Longford, 248 from Athlone, 275 from Boyle. Train from Athlone.* County town of Co Roscommon, several interesting ruins. Indoor heated swimming pool. Horseracing. **Roscommon Castle,** *13th c,* attractively set on hillside. Dominican Friary, founded 1253, main ruins, church with N transept. The old jail, town square, once had a female hangman (hangperson?). Now houses more peaceable TIO.

Derrydonnel, forest walks *1 m (2.5 km) S.* Racing: *details: (0903) 6231.* Swimming pool: indoor, heated, *Abbey Street, daily. Tel: (0903) 6306.*

Slieve Bawn Hills, *E of Strokestown:* worth climbing for views over plains of Roscommon and River Shannon.

Source of the Shannon: *from Dowra, at N end of Lough Allen, take L43 N for about 4 m (6 km), turn R for about 2 m (3 km).* Source is signposted; ½ m (0.8 km) climb.

Strokestown, *12 m (19 km) S of Carrick, 126, 275 bus from Roscommon.* Slieve Bawn co-op handcrafts market, wide range of craft produce, silverware, rush and basket making. *All year, Mon–Fri, 9.30 a.m.–6 p.m. Details: Strokestown 58.* IDA Craft Centre Workshops. *Mon–Fri, 9.30 a.m.–6 p.m. Details tel: Strokestown 197.* Riding: Mrs H. Cox, Churchview House, *tel: Strokestown 47.*

Cavan

Pop. 3,500, 71 m (114 km) NW of Dublin, 19 m (30 km) SW of Clones. All day closing: Mon. TIO: (049) 31942, June–Sept. Bus enquiries: CIE, Cavan, tel: (049) 31353. 91 and 95 bus from Dublin, 24 and 91 from Enniskillen, 112 from Belfast and Galway, 85 and 112 from Lurgan and Portadown.

A delightful small town, attractively set among low hills. Its many nearby lakes offer excellent coarse fishing.

St Mary's Franciscan Abbey, *Abbey street (rear of Post Office):* founded by Giolla Iosa O'Reilly in

1300, only belfry tower remains. Adjacent park. Cavan Crystal, *Dublin Road:* see fascinating spectacle of blowing and handcutting glass, *closed first two weeks Aug. details: (049) 31800.* Sports Centre: special events, *details, TIO.* Bicycles: Wheels, *Farnham Street, tel: (049) 31831.* Golf Club, *18 holes, tel: (049) 31283.* Cavan Equestrian Centre, *tel: (049) 32017.*

AROUND CAVAN

Baileborough, *18 m (30 km) SW of Cavan on L24, 3 bus from Cavan.* Excellent coarse fishing in five neighbouring lakes. **Castle Lake,** car park, picnic place, forest walks.

Belturbet, *8 m (12 km) N of Cavan:* Show: showjumping, agricultural events, *mid-Aug.* Book-A-Boat, *tel: Belturbet 2147.* Belturbet Golf Club, *9 holes, tel: (0492) 2287.*

Butlersbridge, *4 m (6 km) N of Cavan on N3.* Derragarra Inn Folk Museum: items include a curious Victorian vacuum cleaner and an 1820 horse drawn hearse. Adjacent thatched cottage is exact reproduction of old style Irish homestead, complete with open turf fire, settle bed and dancing stone. Nearby is award-winning Derragarra Inn. *Mon–Fri, 10 a.m.–7 p.m.; Sun, 3 p.m.–6 p.m. All year. Details: (049) 31003.*

Castlehamilton, *1 km N of Killeshandra on T52:* forest walks.

Castlesaunderson, *8 m (13 km) N of Cavan off T52 near junction with TIO:* car park, picnic area, forest walks.

Cohaw, *3 m (5 km) SE of Cootehill on L46 to Shercock:* good example of prehistoric double court cairn, which looks as if two single cairns were placed back to back.

Corronagh, *on S shore of Lough Ramor:* car park, picnic area walks with good lake views.

Cuilcagh House, *3 m (5 km) NE of Virginia, beside Cuileagh Lough:* site of house and mound called Stella's Bower, where Jonathan Swift has inspiration for *Gulliver's Travels.*

Headford/Deerpark, *1 m (2 km) W of Virginia off L49:* pleasant walks through broadleaf and conifer woodland.

attractively set by shores of River Erne and Lough Oughter. Excellent course fishing area. Car park, picnic area, boating, swimming, forest walks, nature trails, shop, restaurant, marina.

Mulrick, *2 m (3 km) SW of Gowna village in S Cavan:* forest walks with fine views of Lough Gowna.

Murmod Hill, *2 m (3 km) N of Virginia:* fine vantage point Lough Ramor.

Oldcastle: local parish church with relic of St Oliver Plunkett.**D**

Cornafean, *8 m (13 km) SW of Cavan and 2 m (3 km) off L15 Cavan–Killeshandra road:* Corr House, the Pighouse Collection, housed in a converted pighouse, a fascinating collection of local curios including three legged pots, wooden porringers and cow bells. *All year. by arr.,* Mrs Phyllis Faris, *tel: (049) 37248.*

Rann Ford, *4 m (6 km) W of Cavan on River Erne system:* Cloughhoughter Castle, well preserved 13th/14th c circular tower castle, attractive picnic site.

St Colmcille's Abbey, *5 m (8 km) SW of Belturbet, T52 Milltown, minor road to N shore of Derrybrick Lake:* although founded in 6th c, present ruins are 14th c, also round tower, in exceptionally beautiful setting.

Shantemon Hill, *4 m (6 km) NE of Cavan:* row of pillars on N slope of hill marks inauguration place of O'Reillys, ancient Lords of east Breifne.

Slieve Rushen Mountain, *2 m (3 km) NW of Ballyconnell:* from summit excellent views of much of Erne system.

Virginia, *19 m (31 km) SW of Cavan, 24 bus from Cavan.* Excellent coarse fishing in adjacent Lough Ramor and neighbouring lakes and rivers. Bicycles: S. Kellett.

Kilkenny

Kilkenny Castle

Kilmore, *3 m (5 km) W of Cavan on old Killeshandra Road:* 12th c Romanesque door built into cathedral, (NM).

Loughcrew Hills, *8 m (13 km) S of Virginia:* about 30 prehistoric passages graves. Excellent views across central plain to western mountains.

Killinkere, *5 m (8 km) W of Virginia:* birthplace of General Sheridan, American civil war hero.

Killykeen Forest Park, *2 m (3 km) E of Killeshandra and 8 m (13 km) W of Cavan turn NW off L15:*

km) NW of Rosslare, 120 m (193 km) NE of Killarney. EC. Thurs. TIO: The Parade, opp Castle, (056) 21755, all year. Bus and train enquiries, (056) 22024. 56, 99, 102 bus from Dublin, 56 bus from Waterford. Train from Dublin, Waterford.

This ancient city, set attractively on the banks of the river Nore, has a distinguished and colourful past. The Confederate Irish Parliament regularly sat here, the Lord Lieutenant had a residence in the town and during the 17th c it came close to upstaging Dublin as an administrative centre. It wears its history well however, the atmosphere is relaxed and peaceful, and though the town really ought to be lingered over, it can be explored in a day. Arts Week: multi-media arts event, including music in St Canice's Cathedral, exhibitions in Kilkenny Castle Modern Art Gallery, readings, theatre, fringe performances. *End Aug, early Sept. Details: (056) 22118.*

St Canice's Cathedral (CI): 13th c, one of most beautiful in Ireland. From tower, magnificent views of city and much of county. *All year, daily, 9 a.m.-6 p.m. Closed 1 p.m.-2 p.m.* **Black Abbey,** *Abbey Street:* built 1225, nave and transept restored as Dominican church.**D** Museum: *next door to abbey, in presbytery.* Probably smallest museum in Ireland, with many religious items, such as a liturgical directory printed in Paris in 1475 and one of oldest books in existence. Ring Presbytery doorbell.

Kilkenny Castle: built in early 13th c, rebuilt many times since. Guided tours. Formal gardens, parklands, children's playground, modern Art Gallery with regular exhibitions, *Mid-June-Sept 30, daily, 10 a.m.-7 p.m. Rest of year, Tues-Sat, 10 a.m.-1 p.m.; 2 p.m.-5 p.m. Sun, 2 p.m.-5 p.m. Park daily from 10 a.m. Details: (056)21450.***D**

Black Freren Gate, *near Black Abbey:* only remaining medieval gate. **St Canice's Library,** *just N of Cathedral:* some 3,000 books, many 16th and 17th c, *by arr. with librarian.* **Tholsel,** *High Street:* Corporation regalia, including 1609 Mayor's sword and 1677 Mace, old records and charters. *By arr. with Town Clerk.*

Kilkenny Design Workshops, *opp. Castle:* permanent display of glassware, jewellery, woven goods. Workshops not open. *Mon-Sat, 9 a.m.-1 p.m.; 2 p.m.-6 p.m. Tel: (056)22118.* **Roberts' Bookshop,** *Kieran St:* Good on local history books. Rudolf Heltzel, *The Parade:* makes gold, silver jewellery. *Mon-Fri, 9 a.m.-5.30 p.m. Tel: (056)21497.* Smithwick's Brewery: *guided tours, May 1-Sept 30, Mon-Fri, 3 p.m. Details (056)21014.*

Rothe House, *Parliament Street:* 1594 Tudor merchant's house, meticulously restored. Museum, with many items of local historical and cultural interest, such as old pikes, old picture postcards and 1850 Kilkenny-made double bass. On top floor, see amazingly restored ceiling, held together by dowels. Not a single nail was used. *Apr 1-Oct 31, Mon-Sat, 10.30 a.m.-12.30 p.m.; 3 p.m.-5 p.m. Sun, 3 p.m.-5 p.m. Other times on request. Details: (056) 22893.*

Kyteler's Inn, *St Kieran's Street:* Dame Alice Kyteler, a noted witch, said to have been born here 1280. Building has been an inn since 1324. Restored, with restaurant and bar, so you can contemplate the magical happenings of old in modern comfort, *tel: (056) 21064/21888.* **Tynan's Bridge House Bar,** *near Castle:* authentic Edwardian interior, with marble counter, gaslights. Outstanding traditional front looks onto river.

High Street, the slips (alleys) and lanes between here and St Kieran's Street are worth exploring, as are lanes off far side of Parliament Street and High Street. Interesting walks from John's Bridge, below castle walls, along riverside path into open country. In opp. direction, along John's Quay towards St Canice's.

Greyhound racing: *St James's Park,* regular meetings, *details: (056) 21214.* Swimming pool: indoor, heated. *Michael Street, daily, except Mon, Fri, details: (056) 21380.* Kilkenny Equestrian Centre, *Castleinch,* Bicycles: John Wall, *88 Maudlin Street, tel: (056) 21236.* Golf Club, Glendine, *18 holes, tel: (056) 22125.*

AROUND KILKENNY

Ballylarkin Castle, *2 m (3 km) SW of Freshford:* slight remains. Nearby Bishops' Tree, where according to local history, seven bishops were murdered.

Ballyragget, *7 m (11 km) W of Castlecomer on L110:* attractively set on upper reaches of River Nore. Remains of large 15th c Ormonde castle.

Bishopswood, *2 m (3 km) SW of Durrow on N8:* forest walks, picnic area, car park.

Brandon Hill, *near Graiguenamanagh:* well worth climbing for the patchwork views of Barrow

valley, also forest walks.

Baunriach Summit, *8 m (13 km) SE of Castlecomer:* dizzy views of Barrow valley from Carlow to New Ross.

Callan, *10 m (16 km) SW of Kilkenny. 59, 99, 102 bus from Kilkenny.* Birthplace of Edmund Ignatius Rice, founder of Irish Christian Brothers. The preserved farmhouse at Westcourt, where he was born in 1847, and adjacent monastery and chapel, are open to visitors. *Daily, 9.30 a.m.-6 p.m. Details: Br Nixon, CBS, Callan, tel: (056) 25141.***D** Kilkenny Crystal Company: glass cutting. *All year, Mon-Fri, 8.30 a.m.-5.30 p.m. Weekends by arr. Details: (056) 25132.* Callan Golf Club, *9 holes, tel: (056) 25136.*

Castlecomer, *12 m (20 km) N of Kilkenny on N78, 56, 102 bus from Kilkenny.* Attractive town, despite nearby coalmining. Planned and built to classical design about 1636,It retains its good looks and handsome boulevard of lime trees. Pleasant walks in vicinity. **Reddy's pub:** coalminers' museum, with helmets, tools, photographs.

Castlemorris, *3 m (5 km) W of Knocktopher on L32:* forest walk, lay-by, picnic area.

Clara Castle, *6 m (10 km) NE of Kilkenny, turn off N10 before Coolgrange:* 15th c fortified residence impresively set below mountains. Huge six storey tower, secret chambers and a 'murder hole'. *Key from cottage opp.*

Clashganny, *3 m (5 km) S of Borris on L184:* walks by River Barrow and canal, car park, picnic area.

Drummin, *2 m (3 km) S of St Mullins:* forest walks, views of nearby River Barrow.

Bennettsbridge, *5 m (8 km) SE of Kilkenny on T20, 56, 75 bus from Kilkenny.* Attractively set on banks of River Nore. Fine stone bridge across river.

Dunmore Cave, *7 m (11 km) N of Kilkenny on N78, 56, 102 bus from Kilkenny.* One of finest limestone caves in Ireland, with a number of large chambers and magnificent dripstone formations. Most striking is 'Market Cross' stalagmite, over 20 ft (6 metres) high. Equipped with lighting and viewing galleries, full guide service. *Mid-June-mid-Sept. Daily, 11 a.m.-12.45 p.m.; 2 p.m.-7.15 p.m. Otherwise, 11 a.m.-12.45 p.m.; 2 p.m.-4.45 p.m. Oct-mid-Feb, closes 4 p.m., details: (056) 27726.*

Fertagh, *4 m (6 km) N of Urlingford:* 100 ft (30 metre) round tower, intact but for part of roof.

Flagmount, *8 m (13 km) E of Kilkenny, just N of N10.* O'Neill's stone-built pub has delightful shopfront, leaded glass windows and antique mahogany bar.

Foulksrath Castle, *8 m (13 km) NW of Kilkenny on N77:* an Anglo-Norman foundation, now an extravagant Youth Hostel. *Tel: (056) 27674.*

Freshford, *8 m (13 km) NW of Kilkenny on T19, 215 bus from Kilkenny.* Delightful village with tree-lined square, built in gap in Slieveardagh Hills.

Gowran, *8 m (13 km) E of Kilkenny, on N10, 56 bus from Kilkenny.* Parish church built about 1225. Many interesting monuments. Gowran marble workshops: Jim Harding, *tel: (056) 26177;* Kilkenny Stone and Marble, *tel: (056) 26233.* Gowran racecourse: *details: (056) 26126.*

Graiguenamanagh, *20 m (32 km) SE of Kilkenny, 53 bus from Carlow.* Attractive village set on banks of River Barrow by Brandon Hill, amid beautiful woodlands. **Duiske Abbey:** the largest Cistercian foundation in Ireland, built between 1207 and 1240. Restored to its original glory and now used as parish church.**D** Ryan's Pub: one of the last of the old-style pub/grocers. Tremendous atmosphere.

Cahill Crafts, *High Street:* spinning wheels, weaving looms, *tel: (0503) 24166.* Cushendale Mills make fine quality woven woollen goods, *Mon-Sat, 9 a.m.-5.30 p.m. Closed first two weeks Aug. Shop all year, details: (0503) 24118.* Duiske Handcut Glass, *High Street, daily, tel: (0503) 24174.* Forest walks by canal bank. Youth Hostel.

Inistioge, *5 m (8 km) SE of Thomastown on T20, 75*

bus from Kilkenny. Thoroughly attractive village set in striking part of Nore valley. Tree-lined square. Excellent walks through surrounding countryside. Norman castle remains on rock above river. **Augustinian priory:** founded 1210, nave, tower, Lady Chapel remain. Island View, just S of village on New Ross road, as attractive as its name implies. Oldcourt Equestrian Centre.

Jenkinstown, *6 m (10 km) N of Kilkenny on N78:* pleasant walk beside Dinin River. Car park, picnic area.

Jerpoint Abbey, *2 m (3 km) SW of Thomastown, on N9:* Cistercian foundation dating from 12th c and one of finest monastic ruins in Ireland. *Mid-June-Sept, 30, daily, 10 a.m.1 p.m.; 2 p.m.-7 p.m., otherwise by arr.* Key from caretaker, Mrs Wallace, *in adjacent house.*

Johnstown, *17 m (27 km) W of Kilkenny:* Osmond Bennett's collection of veteran cars will send enthusiasts into raptures. His pride and joy is a 1901 Di Dion Bouton, reckoned to be the oldest veteran car in Ireland. *By app., Johnstown Garage, tel: (056) 31274.*

Kells Priory, *8 m (13 km) S of Kilkenny on L26:* founded 12th c. Ruins cover 5 acres, running down to King's River. Car park, picnic area.

Kilcooley Abbey, *on NW slopes of Slieveardagh Hills, 4 m (6 km) S of Urlingford:* founded in 1200 as sister abbey of Jerpoint. Remains include church, dovecot.

Killamery, *5 m (8 km) SW of Callan:* outstanding 8th c High Cross. Although much bruised by the weather, carvings can be clearly seen.

Kilree, *2 m (3 km) S of Kells:* ancient round tower, granite Celtic Cross.

River Barrow, *near Graiguenamanagh:* riverside walks, car park, picnic area.

Thomastown, *11 m (18 km) S of Kilkenny, 56, 75, 118 bus from Kilkenny, also train.* Busy market town on banks of River Nore. Ballylynch and Mountjuliet demesne, ideal for walks. Take a stroll down river bank to 13th c Grennan Castle. Captured by Cromwell and now an imposing ruin. Double daffodils grow on lawn between castle and river. **Ryan's Garage:** many interesting old enamel signs. Vocational School Equitation Centre, *tel: (056) 24112.* **The Water Garden:** small but utterly peaceful garden, with trees, shrubs, aquatic plants. Café. *May 1-Sept 30, daily, 10 a.m.-6 p.m. Details: (056) 24478.*

Tincashel crossroads, *2 m (3 km) SE of Urlingford:* see a grand total of 12 castles from here.

Trenchmore, *2 m (3 km) S of Callan on N78:* forest walks, lay-by, picnic area.

Ullard, *3 m (5 km) N of Graiguenamanagh:* attractive site near River Barrow with ancient church ruins, tall, sculptured cross.

Urlingford, *16 m (25 km) W of Kilkenny on T19, 102, 118 (SO), 215 bus from Kilkenny.* Many monuments. District flat and boggy, but surprisingly extensive views even from low hills.

Woodlands, *3 m (5 km) S of Kilkenny on N78, turn R at Tennypark:* forest walk, lay-by, picnic area.

Woodstock Park, *1 m (1.5 km) S of Inistioge, turn R off T20:* forest walks, arboretum, car park, picnic area.

Mullingar

Pop. 7,000, 50 m (80 km) NW of Dublin, 32 m (51 km) SE of Longford. EC Wed. TIO: (044)48650, all year. Bus and train enquiries: CIE, (044)48274. Buses from Dublin, also train.

The county town of Westmeath and centre of Ireland's top cattle raising area, so the steaks are normally good! Too often, visitors rush through the Midlands, convinced there are no sights on offer, however the quiet, unpretentious countryside around Mullingar deserves closer study.

Cathedral of Christ the King: striking structure built in 1936. See Mosaics of Ss. Patrick and Anne by Russian artist Boris Anrep, near high altar. Ecclesiastical museum above sacristy normally closed: sacristan for permission.**D**

Military and Historical Museum, *Columb Barracks:* many items relating to the Army in Mullingar, as well as UN service in Congo, Cyprus, Lebanon. *Mon–Fri, 9 a.m.–4.30 p.m. by arr. Officer in charge, tel: (044) 8391.* **Library** *Dublin Road:* world's largest collection of Goldsmith first editions. *Mon–Fri, 9.30 a.m.–5.30 p.m. Closed 1 p.m.–2 p.m.*

Market House, *Market Square:* plans to turn summer folk museum into permanent collection. *Details: TIO, (044) 48761.* **Canton Casey's:** claimed to be the oldest pub in Midlands, dating back 200 years. Little changed interior, with old order books and ancient mirrors. **Greville Arms Hotel:** see realistic likeness of James Joyce, who had Mullingar connections, in the hotel reception area. Royal Canal: good walks along towpath. Town park: enjoyable walks just off town centre. Greyhound track, *Kilbeggan Road: Tues, Sat, 8.30 p.m. Details: (044) 48348.* Swimming pool: indoor, heated, Annebrook, *off Austin Friar Street, daily, tel: (044) 80262.* Bicycles: Kenny Bicycle Shop. *Springfield Terrace, tel: (044) 41671.* Golf Club, Belvedere, *18 holes, tel: (044) 48629.*

AROUND MULLINGAR

Abbeyshrule Airfield, *15 m (24 km) W of Mullingar on L18:* pleasure flights. Annual air show, early Aug. Details: (044) 5424/5459. **Abbeyshrule Cistercian Abbey,** *4 m (6 km) NE of Ballymahon, Co. Longford:* founded about 1200. Remains include choir and part of church nave.

Athlone: *EC Thur. TIO: (0902) 2866, all year.* Bus and train enquiries: (0902) 2651. 47 and 110 bus from Dublin, 46, 85, 110, 112 and 113 from Galway, 85 from Mullingar. Train from Dublin, Galway.

Historic town on Shannon banks, at the boundary between provinces of Leinster and Connacht. Good fishing and cruising centre. **Church of Ss. Peter and Paul:** (C) renaissance twin spires and dome, on W bank of river.**D** Ruins of 13th c Franciscan abbey. *Abbey Road.*

Athlone Castle:(NM) *W bank of Shannon:* 13th c, from loopholes in curtain wall, good town views. Museum has many interesting items relating to town and district, *June–Aug, Mon–Sat, 11 a.m.–1 p.m.; 3 p.m.–6 p.m.* **Library,** *by bridge over Shannon:* many fine volumes of local interest, including books on McCormack and Goldsmith. Occasional exhibitions, art shows, *details: (0902) 2166.*

Des Earl's, *O'Connell Street:* pub with small kitchen and dairy decked out in the old style, complete with traditional values like spinning wheel, oil lamps and fire fan. Good riverside walks, clearly signposted. See also parts of old town walls at Railway View on E side of river.

Swimming pool: indoor, heated, *Retreat Heights, daily.* Outdoor swimming in Lough Ree. Athlone Cruisers, Shancurragh, *tel: (0902) 35163.* Smaller boats widely available. Bicycles: Hardimans, *48 Connaught Street.* Michael Hardimans, *Irishtown, tel: (0902) 2951.* Athlone Golf Club, *Hodson's Bay, 18 holes, tel: (0902) 20731.*

Auburn, *8 m (13 km) NW of Athlone on N55:* ruins of Oliver Goldsmith's boyhood residence.

Barley Harbour, *near Newtowncashel, on E shore of Lough Ree:* home of Michael Casey, artist in bog oak. It takes several years from when he fishes pieces of oak from bog until they dry and are suitable for working. Worth a call. *Mon–Sat, 9 a.m.–5 p.m., all year.*

Belvedere, *2 m (3 km) S of Lynn, on NE shore of Lough Ennell:* great Gothic 'jealous wall' built by former Lord Belvedere to prevent his wife seeing her brother-in-law's mansion nearby. He believed his wife was having an affair with his brother. Gardens occasionally open to public.

Carrick Wood, *the shore of Lough Ennell, 6 m (10*

km) SE of Mullingar, take T9 Kilbeggan road: forest walks by the shores of Lough Ennell.

Castlepollard, *13 m (21 km) N of Mullingar on TIO.* Tullynally Castle: seat of Pakenhams, Earls of Longford, for over 300 years. 30 acres of lawns, woods and walled garden set above Lough Derravaragh. In castle courtyard, Victorian kitchens and laundries now 'life below stairs' museum. *Gardens, June 1–Sept 30, daily except Sat, 2.30 p.m.–5 p.m. Castle tours, groups only, by app. Details: (044) 61159.*

Centre of Ireland: at least two claimants! One spot is round tower-like structure on hill, *2 m (3 km) NE of Glasson,* the other a pillar stone on island off W shore of Lough Ree, *4 m (6 km) NE of Athlone and directly opposite Hodson Bay Hotel.*

Clonfin, *4 m (6 km) W of Granard on T15:* Memorial to 1921 ambush carried out by North Longford Flying Column, led by General Sean MacEoin, 'Blacksmith of Ballinalee'.

Clonmellon, *19 m (31 km) NE of Mullingar:* ruins of 18th c castle, home of Sir Benjamin Chapman who designed the village. Obelisk next to castle commemorates a relative, Sir Walter Raleigh, who introduced the potato to Ireland.

Cloondara, *4 m (6 km) W of Longford on N5 to Strokestown:* site of forgotten Richmond Harbour, where Royal Canal joins Camlin River and thence the Shannon. Tall warehouses and derelict locks create atmospheric setting. In Cloondara, delightful village of many bridges, Teach Cheoil (Irish music house) stages performances of Irish music during summer. Visitors cordially welcomed. *Details: Longford, TIO, tel: (043) 46566.***D**

Delvin, *13 m (21 km) NE of Mullingar:* ruins of 12th c Delvin Castle (NM), built by Hugh de Lacy, Lord of Meath.

Derrycassan: *4 m (6 km) N of Granard:* turn W of Gowna road: forest walks.

Edgeworthstown, (Mostrim), *8 m (13 km) E of Longford on N4, 47 and 87 bus from Longford or Mullingar.* Long association with Edgeworth family, whose best-known member was novelist Maria.

Fore: *3 m (5 km) E of Castlepollard:* Seven Wonders of Fore. Monastery in a bog: 13th c Benedictine Abbey of Ss. Feichin and Taurin, more like a castle: now in ruins, it had miraculous underground water supply, so no need for millrace (counts as two miracles). Tree with three branches: said never to have had more than three branches, in honour of Holy Trinity. Water that never boils: from spring by three branch tree. Never boils, ill luck said to overtake anyone who tries. Stone raised by St Feichin's prayer: huge lintel stone on low W door of St Feichin's church said to have been raised by

him. Anchorite in stone: just outside village, on Castlepollard road, anchorite's cell by partly restored 6th c St Feichin's church. Also large motte, to E of village, on lower slopes of Ben of Fore. **Abbey pub,** paintings of seven wonders of Fore. Owners Michael and Beatrice Coffey mines of information.

Granard, *16 m (26 km) NE of Longford, 44 bus from Dublin:* prominent motte on SW side of town topped by statue of St Patrick. Riding facilities, Glendara, *tel: Granard 6599.*

Hill of Ardagh, *4 m (6 km) SW of Edgeworthstown:* good views across Lough Ree.

Levingston: *2 m (3 km) N of Mullingar:* St Bridget's Well, stations and small oratory, signposted; fish farm at same location. *tel: (044) 48115.*

Lilliput House, *SW shores of Lough Ennell:* ruins of house once visited by Jonathan Swift; said to have helped inspire *Gulliver's Travels.*

Longford, *27 m (43 km) NW of Mullingar.* All day closing Thur. TIO: (043) 46566. June–Sept. Bus and train enquiries: (043) 45208. 85, 113 bus from Athlone, 47, 87 from Mullingar. Train from Dublin, Mullingar, Sligo.

County and market town on S bank of Camlin River. Lough Forbes, good for perch and pike, and the River Shannon, are within reach. See ruined *Harbour Row* home and printing works of **Vincent Gill,** great eccentric who ran *Longford News* newspaper from start in 1936 until not long before his death in 1976.

St Mel's Cathedral (C), a striking 19th c renaissance building, with ecclesiastical museum, inc. vestments and objects dating to before penal days, *all year, Mon, 11 a.m.–1 p.m.; Wed, 11 a.m.–1 p.m.; Sat, 1 p.m.–3 p.m.; Sun, 4 p.m.–6 p.m.* **Dann's** fascinating and antique poster printing works, *Market Square. By app.* Greyhound racing: Longford Park, details: (043) 6441. Swimming pool: indoor, heated, *Market Square, daily all year, tel: (043) 6536.* Bicycles: E. Denniston, Central Cycle Stores, *Sallymount Street. Tel: (043) 46345.* Longford Golf Club, *18 holes, Glack, tel: (43) 6310.*

Multyfarnham Abbey: (C) *7 m (11 km) N of Mullingar, 47 bus:* Franciscan, largely 15th c., restored in recent years. In grounds of adjoining college, elaborate life-size stations of the cross.

Newcastle Demesne: *1 m (2 km) E of Ballymahon.* Forest walks.

Rahan, *3 m (5 km) S of Kinnegad, on River Boyne:* forest walks, picnic place, lay-by.

Rathconnell Hill, *2 m (3 km) NE of Mullingar off N52 to Delvin:* fine views. Nearby ruins of Rathconnell Court. Four small, attractive lakes to W and NW.

Rinndown Peninsula, *8 m (13 km) N of Athlone on W*

Japanese Gardens

shore of Lough Ree, just E of Lecarrow: minor road from Lecarrow continues as track to lakeside where ruins of castle, church and other 13th c buildings combine to make one of the most eerie places in Ireland. Don't go at nightfall.

Ross: turn left 5 m (7 km) E of Finea on Mountnugent road: forest walks along the S shore of Lough Sheelin.

Lough Ree: day cruises during summer months. Aloha Cruisers, 5 Retreat Heights, Athlone. Tel: (0902) 2849.

Lynn/Kilpatrick: off T9, 1 m (2 km) S of Mullingar: walks, forest walks, around Butler's Bridge, across Lacy's Canal, and further W.

Moatfarrell: 2 m (3 km) NW of Edgeworthstown: remains of motte and bailey.

Mullaghmeen: 5 m (8 km) E of Finea on Oldcastle road: forest walks.

St Munna's Church (NM), 6 m (9 km) NE of Mullingar: 15th c structure with four storey, castle-like tower and battlements. Caretaker in house opp. graveyard.

Slanemore Hill, 4 m (6 km) NW of Mullingar: 499 ft (152 metres), three tumuli on summit, fine views of locality, including nearby Lough Owel.

Tang, on N55 Athlone-Ballymahon road: in heart of Goldsmith country. Flagstone of 'Busy Mill' that once stood nearby, mentioned by Goldsmith, is now doorstep of the Three Jolly Pigeons pub.

Uisneach Hill, (NM) 12 m (20 km) W of Mullingar off L4 to Ballymore: ancient seat of High Kings of Ireland. Burial mounds and fort on hilltop. From here, on clear day, you can see 20 of Ireland's 32 counties. Large limestone boulder to W, the Cat-stone, was common centre of Ireland's five early provinces.

Naas

Pop. 10,000, 21 km (34 km) SW of Dublin on the N7. No EC. TIO: Tel: (045)97636. July–Aug. Bus enquiries: CIE, Dublin. (01) 787777. Frequent buses from Dublin.

In early times, Naas was the seat of the Kings of Leinster, and the North Mote, off Main Street, was the site of the ancient royal palace—indeed St Patrick is said to have camped on the site of the present Church of Ireland. Today Naas, county town of Co Kildare, is peaceful and prosperous.

Corban Art Gallery, St Corban's Lane: regular exhibitions by local artists. Mon-Fri, 11 a.m.-5 p.m. Sat, Sun, 3 p.m.-5 p.m. **D** Kelly Pottery, 36 Woodlands: Mon-Fri, 10 a.m.-1 p.m.; 2 p.m.-5 p.m. Sat, 10 a.m.-1 p.m. Walks: behind courthouse in Main Street and around the canal harbour basin. You can also walk along Grand Canal towpath. Just SE of Naas, see park, with lake, between Blessington and Ballymore Eustace roads.

Mondello Park, 6 m (9 km) NE of Naas: motor racing, details: (045)60151. Naas Racecourse, (045)97391. Swimming pool: indoor, heated. Fair Green. all. year, Tues-Thur, Sat, Sun. Brittas Lodge Riding Stables, tel: (01)582162: Kellett Riding School, tel: (045)97208/9299. Bicycles: John Cahill, Sallins Road, tel: (045)9655. Golf Club, Kerdiffstown, 9 holes, tel: (045) 97509.

AROUND NAAS

Athy: 13 m (13 km) SW of Naas, market town, set on formerly strategic ford. **Dominican church** (C) built near River Barrow in 1963-5. Pentagon shape with striking interior design. Impact heightened by George Campbell's stations of the cross and Bríd Ní Rinn's statues, high altar crucifix.**D** Woodstock Castle, just N of town: 13th c ruins on W bank of River Barrow. Bicycles: Duthie Large Ltd, tel: (0507)21414. Athy Golf Club, 9 holes, tel: (0507)31729.

Ballingee, 1 m (2 km) W of Wicklow Gap on L107: car park, picnic area, forest walk, scenic views from Annalecky Bridge.

Ballitore, 3 m (4 km) N of Moone, off T51: old meeting house of once flourishing Quaker settlement now library and museum with interesting collection of mainly Quaker material. SO, daily, inc Sun aft., details: (01)778088.

Baltinglass, 19 m (30 km) SW of Blessington on T42, 49 bus from Naas. See impressive ruins of 12 c Baltinglass Abbey on banks of River Slaney. Abbey was sister foundation of Mellifont, Co. Louth. **Baltinglass Hill,** 1 m (2 km) E of Baltinglass: Remains of large Bronze Age cairn, good views.

Baltyboys, near Blessington Lakes: Youth Hostel.

Blackwood, 4 m (6 km) N of Athy on the Kildare road: forest walks.

Blessington, 65 bus from Crampton Quay, Dublin: pleasant strolls from this tree-lined village to shores of Poulaphouca Reservoir.

Brittas: Slade Valley Golf Club, 18 holes, tel: (01)582207.

Carbury Hill, 4 m (6 km) E of Edenderry: fine views of Midland plain from where the T41 to Enfield crosses the shoulder of the hill.

Carnalway Church, (C), 2 m (3 km) NE of Kilcullen: 1922 window of St Hubert by Harry Clarke.**D**

Castleruddery Transport Museum, just S of Donard on banks of River Slaney, 65 bus from Dublin. Some 70 old vehicles, including buses, lorries, trams, trolley buses, oldest is 1921 Leyland fire engine. Details: (01)311287/977543.

Celbridge, 67 bus from Aston Quay, Dublin: Celbridge Abbey once home of Esther Van Homrigh, Swift's Vanessa, now residence of Hospitaller Brothers of St John of God, who run it as St Raphael's School for Mentally Handicapped Children. The brothers will be happy to show you over house; also see Vanessa's pleasure grounds along banks of Liffey. Tel: (01) 288161.**D**

Castletown House: 18th c mansion fully restored by Irish Georgian Society. Splendid approach along 800 metre lime tree avenue. In house, see Long Gallery (with Venetian chandeliers), main hall and staircase (with Italian plasterwork), Print Room and Red Drawing Room. Festival of Music in Great Irish Houses held here, June. House, Nov-Mar, Sun, 2 p.m.-5 p.m., Apr-Sept, Wed, Sat, Sun, 2 p.m.-6 p.m. Groups at any time by arr. tel; (01)288252. Donacomper Riding School, tel: (01)288221. **Conolly's Folly,** 2 m (3 km) NW of Castletown House: 140 ft (40 metre) triumphal arch built in 1740 to provide relief work. Temple Mills House: 100 vintage cars and motor cycles from United States, France, Germany and England. By app. only, tel: (01)288297.

Curragh, E of Kildare, 52, 55, 57 bus from Busaras, Dublin. Race trains from Heuston station, Dublin. Curragh Racecourse: several meetings during year. Best-known is Irish Sweeps Derby, June, details: (045)41205. **Curragh Camp:** ask to see marvellous 1920 armoured car, the 'Slievenamon', used by Michael Collins on his way to Beal na mBláth in 1922. Permission: Officer Commanding, (045)41301. Frenchfurze Riding Stables, Maddenstown, tel: (045)41275. Curragh Golf Club, 18 holes, tel: (045)41238.

Donadea Forest Park, 5 m (8 km) SW of Kilcock on L181: car park, picnic place, castle ruins, lake, forest walks. Nature trails inc. for disabled. Information centre, shop. Sat, Sun, 12 p.m.-6 p.m.

Donard, 11 m (16 km) S of Naas: Ballinclea Youth Hostel: tel: (045)53657.**D**

Donnelly's Hollow, 3 m (4 km) NW of Kilcullen, beside L19: here the famous boxer beat English champion George Cooper in December, 1815. Long line of footprints said to have been made by Donnelly.

Dunstown, 4 m (6 km) W of Naas on L25: car park, picnic place, forest walks.

Edenderry, 13 m (20 km) NW of Naas: market town, originally built largely by Marquis of Downshire.

Swimming pool: indoor, heated. St Conleth's Road, Tues-Sun, details: (0405)31294.**D** Bicycles: J. Moran, O'Connell Square. (0405)31583 Edenderry Golf Club, 9 holes, tel: (0405)31072.

Glen Ding, 1 m (2 km) from Blessington on L181 to Naas; picnic place, forest walks.

Glen of Imaal, 6 m (10 km) S of Poulaphouca Lake: walks in four forests, Leitrim, Knickeen, Knockamunnion, Stranahely. Five entrances to these forests on roads from Seskin Bridge and Ballinaclea to Knickeen Ford. Parts of glen used as army firing ranges—watch for the 'Danger' signs.

Hill of Allen, 8 m (13 km) NE of Kildare Town, off L180: famous in Irish legend as the otherworld seat of Fionn MacCumhail. Tower, 676 ft (206 metres) summit, built by Sir George Aylmer in mid-19th c. Path to top of hill, good views.

Hollywood Glen, S of Poulaphouca: 2 m (3 km) of natural delights. Fine views from top of nearby Church Mountain. At far end of glen, at Woodenboley, car park, forest walks, picnic area.

Irish Pewter Mill, Timolin, Moone: restored pewter craft making in Ireland, factory tours, Mon-Fri. Adjoining craft centre, Mon-Fri, 9.30 a.m.-5.30 p.m. Sat, 10.30 a.m.-5 p.m. all year, details: (0507)24164.

Jigginstown House, 1 m (2 km) SW of Naas, by N7 to Kildare: begun in 1632. If it had been finished, this would have been Ireland's largest private residence.

Kilcock, 46, 110 bus from Busaras, Dublin, Kilcock Art Gallery, School Street: work by contemporary Irish artists. All year, Mon-Sat, 10 a.m.-5 p.m. Tel: (01)287619.**D**

Kilcullen, 8 m (13 km) SW of Naas on N9, 53 and 56 bus from Naas. If you're of a mind to, see arm of early 19th c prize fighter, Dan Donnelly, in glass case at Hide-Out bar by crossroads. They serve good lunches, tel: (045)81232. W Attractive walk by Liffeyside, picnic area. Bicycles: T. J. Kelly, Naas Road, tel: (045)81388.

Kildare, 8 m (13 km) SE of Naas, bus from Busaras, Dublin: St Brigid's Cathedral (CI), 19th c restoration of 13th c structure. Opening times posted in window of verger's house, beside churchyard gate. Nearby round tower has staircase to top. By app. Dean Paterson, Dean's House, Curragh Camp, tel: (045)41654. Bicycles: John Kearney, Crosskeys, tel: (045)21457. Cill Dara Golf Club, 9 holes, tel: (045)21433.

Kilkea Castle/Mullaghreelin, 3 m (4 km) N of Castledermot on Castledermot-Athy road: car park, picnic place, ring fort, forest walk to Wishing Well.

Leinster Aqueduct, 3 m (5 km) N of Naas and just W of Sallins: late 18th c engineering feat carries Grand Canal over River Liffey in great style. Long sections of towpath in this area are ideal for walking.

Lugnagroagh, S of bridge at Poulaphouca, Valleymount road: car park, picnic place, forest walk, viewing points.

Lyons Hill, 3 m (4 km) S of Celbridge: one of early seats of kings of Leinster, tremendous views.

Maynooth, 9 m (14 km) N of Naas, 66 bus from Aston Quay, Dublin. **St Patrick's College:** chapel, library, sacristy, museum, with ecclesiastical and scientific sections. 15th c chalices, induction coil, horse shoeing machine and Maynooth battery, invented by Rev. Dr Nicholas Callan, 19th c professor of science here. To see museum, call at gate lodge. College and grounds, mid-June-mid-Sept, details: (01)285222. **Maynooth Castle,** near St Patrick's College gates: see 12th c ruins, including gatehouse, keep, great hall. Key: Castleview House, opp. all reasonable times.

Monasterevin, 6 m (10 km) W of Kildare: walks along Grand Canal towpath.

Moone, 8 m (12 km) E of Athy: high cross with 51 sculptured panels showing biblical scenes, one of most famous in Ireland.

Moore Abbey, *just S of Monasterevin on L18:* car park, forest walks, picnic place. Mansion was once home of famous tenor, Count John McCormack. Now a convent; closed to public.

National Stud, *1 m (2 km) E of Kildare:* ideal for half-day out. National Stud: *Easter Sun–Oct.* **Irish Horse Museum,** *in grounds of National Stud:* traces evolution of horse in Ireland. Highlight is Arkle's skeleton. **Japanese Gardens:** laid out in 1906, they symbolise life of man from cradle to grave. Also plant souvenir shop, selling bonsai trees. Museum and Gardens, *Easter–Oct, Mon–Fri, 10.30 a.m.–12.30 p.m.; 2 p.m.–5 p.m. Sat, 10.30 a.m.–12.15 p.m.; 2 p.m.–5.30 p.m. Sun, 2 p.m.–5.30 p.m., details: (045)21251.* **D**

Michael O'Dwyer's cottage, *SW side of Glen of Imaal at Derrynamuck on Rathdangan road:* furnished just as it was when he escaped from British forces in 1799. Key at entrance on main road.

Oughterard Hill, *6 m (9 km) NE of Naas:* ruins of ancient monastery and stump of round tower. Fine views over Kildare plain.

Poulaphouca, *6 m (10 km) SE of Naas, 65 bus from Bachelor's Walk, Dublin.* Liffey cataracts, not quite Niagara, but some good falls near bridge. Water skiing, Golden Falls Water Ski Club, *tel: (01)806733.*

Punchestown Standing Stone, *3 m (5 km) E of Naas:* one of finest examples in Ireland. Racecourse *(045)97704.*

Reban Cástle, *3 m (5 km) NW of Athy:* ruins of 13th c fortress on a yet more ancient site, marked on Ptolemy's 2nd c map of Ireland.

Russborough, *near Blessington, 65 bus from Crampton Quay, Dublin.* Beit art collection includes works by Goya, Rubens, Velasquez, Vermeer. Guided tours round Palladian house, built 1740–1750 to see Irish silver, magnificent Francini plasterwork. Basement has superb collection of miniature steam locomotives. Woodland gardens open when rhododendrons are in bloom. Craft shop, tea room. Special events, including Festival of Music in great Irish Houses, June. House, *Easter–Oct 31; Sun, Bank Holidays, 2.30 p.m.–5.30 p.m. Also June, July, Aug, Wed, 2.30 p.m.–5.30 p.m. Also July, Aug, Sat, 2.30 p.m.–5.30 p.m.* Groups by arr. Woodland Garden, *late spring, early summer, details (045)65239.*

Stratford-on-Slaney, *4 m (6 km) NE of Baltinglass,* ruins of 18th c weaving village on W side of Little Slaney River.

Valleymount, *5 m (8 km) S of Blessington:* Glenbride Youth Hostel: *tel: (045)67111.*

Vicarstown, *6 m (9 km) S of Monasterevin:* paddle boats for hire on Grand Canal in summer, also canalside amenity area. *Details: (0502)25252.*

Wicklow Gap: follow L107 through magnificent mountain scenery to Laragh, near Glendalough.

Wolfe Tone's grave, *near Clane, 4 m (6 km) N of Naas:* evocative location in beautiful countryside.

Wonderful Barn, *1 m (2 km) SW of Leixlip, 67 bus from Middle Abbey Street, Dublin.* 1743 five storey building built for Lady Conolly of nearby Castletown House, conical in shape, tapering to top, outside staircase.

Navan

Pop. 5,000, 30 m (48 km) NW of Dublin and 17 m (27 km) W of Drogheda. EC Thurs. Bus enquiries: CIE, Drogheda, tel: (041) 38583. 23 bus from Drogheda, 24 bus from Dublin.

This hilly town, set at the confluence of the Boyne and the Blackwater, was once a walled and fortified outpost of the Pale. Today, thanks to mining developments, it enjoys a new prosperity. Good fishing.

Athlumney House, *2 m (3 km) S of Navan, by*

River Boyne: impressive remains of four storey 15th c castle with attached 17th c Tudor house. Tradition has it that the last occupier, Sir Launcelot Dowdall, set it on fire rather than have it shelter William of Orange. *Key from convent opp.* **Dunmoe Castle,** *3 m (5 km) NE of Navan:* 16th c ruin, burned down in 1799. Good views of the Boyne. **Navan motte,** *on W side of town:* excellent vantage point. **Kilcarne Bridge,** *Dublin Road, just outside Navan:* at time of writing this historic structure is threatened with demolition. **Town Hall,** *Watergate Street:* erected circa 1800 and used as police station until 1978. Renovated and re-opened as new Municipal Offices in 1983. **Donaghmore Round Tower,** *2 m (3 km) NE of Navan on Slane road:* on early Christian site, reputedly founded by St Patrick. Nearby remains of 15th c church, Fair Green (C), Blackcastle and St Mary's (CI) are also worth exploring.

Oriel Gallery, *opp. St Mary's:* local drawings and paintings. *Daily, July–Sep. Otherwise by arr. Patrick Reel in adjacent shop.* **D** Navan Trade Centre, *Trim Road:* frequent exhibitions and other events, *details: (046)23377/23388.*

Navan Racecourse, *details: (046)21350.* Greyhound racing: *Trim Road, every Wed, Thur eve.* Swimming pool: indoor, heated, *Commons Road, all year, daily, details: (046)23001.* **D** Royal Tara Golf Club, *18 holes, tel: (046)25244.*

AROUND NAVAN

Athboy, *8 m (13 km) NW of Trim on L3, 113 bus from Navan.* Protestant church has 15th c tomb with effigies of armoured knight and wife.

Beauparc, *4 m (6 km) NE of Navan:* Bridge of Boyne Youth Hostel, *tel: (046)24119.*

Bective Abbey, *5 m (8 km) S of Navan on T26:* founded as a Cistercian house in 12th c. Ruins of original chapter house and church, also remnants of fortified house into which abbey was converted after the Dissolution.

Castlerickard, *8 m (14 km) SW of Trim, just off T26:* see Swift Mausoleum, large, pyramid-shaped structure next to church.

Corronaugh, *turn N off T35 3 m (5 km) S of Virginia or E off L49 3 m (5 km) SW of Virginia:* walks along the S shore of Lough Ramor, car park, picnic area.

Donore Castle, *8 m (13 km) SW of Trim on T26 to Kinnegad:* said to have been built in early 15th c to qualify for £10 grant from Henry VI. Nothing new about housing subsidies! In good condition. *Key from cottage opp.*

Hill of Lloyd, *2 m (3 km) W of Kells along L142 to Crossakeel:* the hill's lighthouse-shaped tower was built in 1791 in memory of Sir Thomas Taylor by the first Earl of Bective, his son. Pleasant walk through fields; views over Co. Meath are excellent.

Hill of Tailte, *near Donaghpatrick village, just off N3 road:* site of one of four ancient palaces built by King Tuathal. Venue of *Aonach Tailteann,* Olympic Games of ancient Ireland which were founded in prehistoric times and lasted until 12th c.

Hill of Tara, *6 m (10 km) S of Navan, 1 m (1.5 km) W of N3 Dublin–Navan road. 20, 40, 43 bus from Dublin, Navan.* One of the most historic places in Ireland, formerly cultural and religious capital. Although only simple earthworks remain, it's worth walking to the top to sense the history and sample the stunning view.

Hill of Ward, *1 m (1.5 km) E of Athboy, just off L14 in Navan direction:* reputed location of Palace of Tlachtga, site of famous ancient festival. In 1168, on occasion of national synod of prelates and kings, 13,000 horsemen said to have thronged nearby roads. Fine views from summit.

Kells (Ceanannus Mór), *10 m (16 km) NW of Navan. EC Wed. 23 bus from Drogheda, 24, 43, 91 from Dublin, Navan.* Ancient town in River Blackwater valley. Originally, the site of an important 6th c monastic settlement founded by St Colmcille. Pleasant and interesting walks up and down hilly central streets.

St Columba's Church, *top of Market Street:* most impressive building in the town, built on site of original settlement. The magnificent Book of Kells was written here and in the church gallery, there are facsimiles of the Book, reproduction pages from the Book of Durrow and large scale photographs of the Columban site. In the grounds, a round tower, self-standing spire and four High Crosses. The town's fifth, Market Cross, is in centre of Kells. St Columcille's House, a high roofed monastic building similar to St Kevin's Church, Glendalough, is just outside the churchyard. *Key from house opp.* Swimming pool: indoor, heated, *Navan Road, daily, tel: (046)40551.*

Laracor, *2 m (3 km) S of Trim on L25:* Jonathan Swift was once rector here. The present C of I is said to occupy the site of Swift's church; the communion silver he used is preserved. Nearby, on Trim road, remains of cottage occupied by Swift's 'Stella' (Esther Johnson).

Lough Bracken, *1 m (1.5 km) SW of Drumconrath in N Meath:* forest walks, fishing, car park, picnic area.

Mount Oriel: *2 m (3 km) NW of Collon on N2 Slane-Ardee road:* worthwhile views from 810 ft. (246 metre) hill.

Moynalty, *4 m (6 km) N of Kells:* Field Day, with steam-driven agricultural machinery, old agricultural implements on show, *mid-Aug.*

Newtown Trim, *1 m (1.5 km) E of Trim on N bank of River Boyne:* vast ruin, once the abbeys of Ss. Peter and Paul. Stand at the gate in the hedge facing the ruin and shout; a flawless echo will return from the ruins.

Skreen Hill, *7 m (11 km) S of Navan, 1 m (1.5 km) E of N3 Dublin–Navan road:* climb to ruined tower on summit for good views.

Slane, *15, 23 bus from Drogheda. 92 93 bus from Dublin:* Janeville, the cottage birthplace of poet Francis Ledwidge killed at Ypres in 1917. Now restored as Ledwidge museum. *Daily..*

Slane Castle: only restaurant and night club open to public, ruins of Gothic church in grounds.

Slane Hill, *1 m (1.5 km) N of Slane:* 500 ft (152 metre) hill where St Patrick lit historic Paschal Fire in 5th c, proclaiming Christianity throughout Ireland. Remains of 16th c church and school on site of an ancient church founded by St Patrick. Excellent views take in whole Boyne valley from Trim to Drogheda.

Summerhill, *6 m (10 km) SE of Trim:* forest walks, car park, picnic area.

Tallon's Mill, *5 m (8 km) NW of Navan on N3 Navan–Kells road:* 18th c mill in perfect working order; special channels have been built to ensure plentiful supply of water.

Trim, *9 m (14 km) SW of Navan on T26. EC Thurs. 44 and 45 bus from Dublin.* Rich in history, contains perhaps more antiquities than any other town in Ireland. **St Patrick's Cathedral** (CI), with fine baptismal font, 11th c tower and mediaeval gravestones.**D**

Yellow Steeple, *opp. Castle:* part of 13th c St Mary's Abbey, destroyed in 1649 to prevent it falling to Cromwell.

Trim Castle: built by Hugh de Lacy in 1172, largest Anglo—Irish fortress in country, well preserved ruins cover large area.

Town Hall, *Castle Street:* ask to see the interesting Corporation records, they date from 1659. *Mon–Fri, business hours, details: (046)31238.*

Education Centre, *Castle Street:* regular exhibitions of historic and local interest material. *All year, Mon–Fri, 10 a.m.–1 p.m.; 2.30 p.m.–5 p.m. Details: (046)31158.* **D** Swimming pool: indoor, heated, *daily, tel: (046)31140.*

Rock of Cashel

Thurles

Pop. 10,000, 13 m (21 km) N of Cashel, 25 m (40 km) NE of Tipperary, 92 m (148 km) SW of Dublin. EC Wed. TIO: Nenagh, (067) 31610, all year. Bus and train enquiries: (0504) 21733. 215 bus from Limerick, train from Cork, Dublin, Limerick.

Market town pleasantly situated on the banks of the River Suir. Once an Anglo-Norman town, you can see the remnants of two castles at the main bridge and near Liberty Square. Interesting shopfronts, including Sweeney, Baker and Grocer, Mitchel Street, good town and riverside walks.

Cathedral (C): interior richly decorated with marble. Its campanile is a landmark for miles around. **D** Interesting modern Church of St Joseph and St Brigid at *Bothar na Naomh, near railway station.* **Hayes Hotel,** *Liberty Square:* historic building where Gaelic Athletic Association was founded in 1884. Library: fine collection of Co Tipperary historical material, *Mon–Sat.*
Racing, *2 m (3 km) NW of Thurles, off T21:* regular meetings, *details: Nenagh TIO:* Greyhound racing, *Thurles track: Tues, Sat, eve, details:* (0504) 21003. Swimming pool: indoor, heated, *Mon–sun, details:* (0504) 22349. Golf Club, 18 holes, tel: (0504) 222426. Shamrock Bus Service, tel: (0504) 21622; coach tours of area.

AROUND THURLES

Athassel Abbey, 2 m (3 km) SE of Thomastown: 12th c Augustinian foundation on W banks of River Suir, ruins consist of church, cloister, monastic buildings.

Ballinacourty, on Tipperary–Lisvernane scenic route, 1 m (2 km) from Christ the King statue: forest walks, viewing points over Glen of Aherlow, car park, picnic area.

Ballinahow Castle, 3 m (5 km) from Thurles on Newport road: 16th c fortress of rare circular design. Signposted access via farmyard.

Ballydavid Wood, 4 m (6 km) SE of Tipperary on N24: forest walks, picnic area, car park. Ballydavid Wood Youth Hostel, tel: (062) 54148.

Barna Castle, 2 m (3 km) SW of Templemore: circular five storey keep, 60 ft (18 metres) high. Spiral staircase to battlements. View from top outstanding.

Bishop's Wood, 1.5 m (2 km) NE of Dundrum on L119: forest walks, lay-by, picnic area, entrance near Bishopswood school.

Brittas Castle, 2 m (3 km) N of Thurles: 19th c structure begun as copy of Warwick Castle. Work stopped after owner killed by lump of falling masonry. A house has since been built within the foundations.

Cahir, S. Tipperary. EC Thur. TIO: Cahir Castle July–Aug, tel: Cahir (052)41453. 85, 86, bus from Roscrea, 101, 146 bus from Clonmel.

Small, quiet town with many outstanding Georgian buildings. Good salmon and trout fishing. Excellent centre for climbing the Galtee Mountains.
Cahir Castle: magnificent structure, built 1142, excellently restored. Massive keep, spacious courtyard and hall, high enclosing walls. Now architectural interpretative centre. *mid-June–30 Sept, 10 a.m.–7 p.m. daily. Otherwise, Tues–Sat, 10 a.m.–5 p.m. Closed 1 p.m.–2 p.m. Sun, 2 p.m.–5 p.m.,* guided tours, *details: TIO.* 13th c abbey ruins in attractive setting beside River Suir. Keating's shop, just opp. Cahir Castle, claims to be last in Ireland using pre-decimal coinage.
Cahir Park, 1.5 m (2 km) S of Cahir on L184: forest and riverside walks by River Suir (very beautiful here and spanned by cast iron bridge), scenic views, car park, picnic area. Ornate Swiss cottage designed by Nash. Cahir Cycle Clinic, Barrack Street, tel: (052) 41592. Cahir Park Golf Club, 9 holes, tel: (052)41474.

Cashel, 13 m (21 km) S of Thurles. TIO: (062) 61333. All year. 86, bus from Thurles. Small but attractive country town with points of interest other than the Rock of Cashel. Also see outstanding traditional shopfronts, inc Meany's pub. Variety of craft workshops. Town Hall has small local museum, *daily, Mon–Fri.* Cashel Folk Village, Chapel Lane, Dominic Street. *Daily.* Good centre for exploring historical riches of Co. Tipperary. Salmon and trout fishing centre.
Hore abbey, just W of Rock of Cashel: Cistercian foundation. Dominican friary ruins, *Chapel Lane, near base of Rock.* Cashel Palace Hotel: formerly palace of Church of Ireland archbishops, built in Queen Anne style in 1730. Splendid interiors, magnificent lounge hall with original panelling and carving, spacious Adam drawing room. Hotel's food and wine match sumptuous interiors.
Diocesan Library, in precincts of CI cathedral: one of the finest collection of 16th and 17th c books in Ireland, as well as ancient maps. By arr.. *Very Rev. David Woodworth, The Deanery, tel:* (062) 61232. CI cathedral is spartan; in contrast, C

church alive with exotic statues. Old leper hospital ruins 1 m (2 km) S of town.
Rock of Cashel: this magnificent rock is one of Ireland's great historic sites. Main features are 12th c round tower, in good condition; Cormac's Chapel, styled as miniature cathedral; St Patrick's Cross; the cathedral of St Patrick and the Hall of Vicars Choral, which you pass through on entering the grounds. It is easy to spend hours scrambling round these fascinating ruins. Full guide service. *Mid-June–Sept 30, daily, 9 a.m.–7 p.m. Rest of year, Tues–Sat, 10 a.m.–1 p.m.; 2 p.m.–5 p.m. Sun, 2 p.m.–5 p.m., details:* (062) 61437.

Cordangan and Bansha West, 1 m (2 km) from Bansha and 5 m (8 km) SE of Tipperary on N24: forest walks, viewing points, picnic area, car park.

Derrynaflan, 2 m (3 km) SE of Horse and Jockey on N8: impressive ruins of 13th c church on grassy mound in middle of peat bog. From near Heathview House, follow track across the bog. Outstanding archaeological treasures unearthed here in 1980.

Devil's Bit Mountain, 4 m (6 km) NW of Templemore: take the road to near summit for splendid views over N Tipperary. Legend says that the nearby gap in range was formed when the Devil spat out the Rock of Cashel, to S.

Dromineer, 6 m (10 km) NW of Nenagh: Lough Derg's finest resort. Sail Inn has great nautical atmosphere. Boats: Mrs J. Roberts, tel: (067) 24114. Teddy Knight's Sailing Centre, tel: (067) 24295. Matt Ryan, Nenagh, tel: (067) 31336.

Dundrum, 8 m (12 km) NE of Tipperary town on L119: forest walks. 1 m (1.5 km) SW of village forest walks, nature trail, game sanctuary at Marl Bog.

Dunmore, 1 m (2 km) NE of Durrow, off N8: forest walks.

Durrow, 20 m (32 km) NE of Thurles: attractive setting on banks of Erkina River. Ruins of village's early monastic foundation are in churchyard.

Fethard, 9 m (14 km) NW of Clonmel: remains of priory on site of Augustinian foundation. Keeps of three castles, including the interesting Fethard Castle, in town centre. Most of town walls and flanking towers survive. **Folk, farm and transport museum,** old railway station, Fethard-Cashel L111: over 1,000 exhibits of farm life and transport. *Summer, daily, 10 a.m.–6 p.m., otherwise Sat, Sun, 1 p.m.–6 p.m. Details (052)31516.*

Galbally, 8 m (12 km) SW of Tipperary town: Hillcrest House Riding Centre, tel: (062)57915.

Garrykennedy, 8 m (13 km) NW of Nenagh: boats for hire on Lough Derg at pier.

Glen of Aherlow, immediately S of Tipperary: noted beauty spot. On N side of glen, minor road runs across wooded slopes of Sliabh na Muc: the views here are tremendous.

Clonmacnoise

Glengarra, *8 m (13 km) SW of Cahir on N8:* forest and riverside walks alongside Burncourt River. Nature trail, note unusual tree and shrub species. Picnic area, car park.

Gortavoher, *4 m (6 km) S of Tipperary, on Tipperary–Lisvernane road:* forest walks, car park. Picnic area offers extensive views over Glen of Aherlow.

Gort-na-Clay Castle, *7 m (11 km) E of Rathdowney:* in 1660, the prison of Thomas, Black Earl of Ormond.

Holy Cross Abbey, *4 m (6 km) S of Thurles on W bank of River Suir.* 215 bus from Thurles. SO. Founded in 1168 by the Benedictines and shortly afterwards transferred to the Cistercians. After standing roofless for generations, it was completely restored (1975) and is now used as a parish church. *Daily, 9.30 a.m.–6 p.m. Details: (0504)43241.*

Horse and Jockey, *8 m (12 km) NE of Cashel on NB:* interesting painting of horse with jockey on gable wall of pub.

Kilbreedy Castle, *5 m (8 km) E of Rathdowney:* also nearby Cullahill Castle and church, built in 15th c. A main Fitzpatrick stronghold.

Kilcash Castle, *follow N76 8 m (12 km) NE of Clonmel, turn L to Ballypatrick, 1m (2 km) N of Ballypatrick crossroads, turn R and continue for about 1 m (2 km):* set on the SE slopes of Slievenamon, striking views from ivy-covered ruins.

Killurney, *beside Kilcash village, off by-road next to Killurney school:* forest walks, viewing points.

Knockelly Castle, *3 m (5 km) NE of Fethard:* magnificent ruins, including a tower and walled bawn, set on a high hill.

Knocknacree, *1.5 m (2 km) NE of Cloughjordan on Shinrone road, 10 m (16 km) NE of Nenagh:* forest walks.

Knockshigowna, *7 m (11 km) SW of Birr:* panoramic views from summit.

Kylecrew Mill, *on Thurles–Bouladuff–Annfield road:* interesting 19th c all-timber, water-powered mill.

Leigh, *6 m (10 km) E of Thurles:* ruins of two churches on site of 6th c Liathmore monastery.

Limerick Junction Racecourse, *108, 213 bus, train from Limerick: regular races, details: (062) 51357.*

Loughmore Castle, *3 m (5 km) S of Templemore:* well-preserved 16th c tower with later additions. Can be seen at all reasonable times.

Mona Incha Abbey, *2 m (3 km) E of Roscrea:* dates 1,300 years, now fashionable as a pilgrimage centre. 12th c church remains, interesting High Cross.

Moor Abbey, *near Galbally village, just off L119 at W of Glen of Aherlow:* ruins of 13th c foundation, only the church survives: in SW angle of nave, stairway leads to upper wall.

Motte of Knockgraffon, *4 m (6 km) N of Cahir:* shaped like pyramid and said to have been crowning place of Kings of Munster before their seat was transferred to Cashel.

Mount St Joseph's: Cistercian monastery, *2 m (3 km) W of Roscrea, just off L34:* daughter house of Mount Melleray, Co. Waterford and charmingly set on banks of Little Brosna River. Ireland's only silk farm. *By arr., (0505) 21711.*

Mountain Lodge, *8 m (13 km) SW of Cahir:* Youth Hostel.

Mullinahone, *10 m (16 km) NE of Fethard:* see house in Fethard Street where 19th c novelist Charles Joseph Kickham lived. Celtic Cross over his grave in local C church.

Nenagh, *24 m (39 km) NE of Thurles. EC Wed. TIO: (067) 31610, all year. 85, 86, 218 bus from Limerick. Train from Limerick. Bus and train enquiries: (067) 31232.* Chief town of N Tipperary and bustling centre of rich agricultural district. **Nenagh District Heritage Centre:** house of governor of old county gaol has been turned into fascinating reconstruction of area's history. Also

temporary exhibitions. *June-Aug, Mon-Sat, 10.30 a.m.-5.30 p.m., Tues, Thurs, 7 p.m.-9 p.m., Sun, 2.30 p.m.-5.30 p.m. Rest of year, daily, 2.30 p.m.-5.30 p.m., Tues, Thurs, 7 p.m.-9 p.m.* 13th c Franciscan friary, ruins, *Abbey Street,* **Nenagh Castle:** impressive circular keep which formed part of larger castle built around 1200. Keep, *all year, key:* caretaker, Ballyartella Woolen Mills. *Mon-Fri, 9.30 a.m.-1 p.m.; 2 p.m.-5.30 p.m. Sat, 9.30 a.m.-12.30 p.m. Details: (067) 31055.* Swimming pool: indoor, heated, *Tues-Sun. Tel: (067) 31788.* C W Bicycles: Central Garage, *Pearse Street, tel: (067) 31293.*

Rockwell College, *4 m (6 km) S of Cashel on N8, near New Inn village:* visitors are welcome in the beautiful grounds and will be shown over the college. *Details: (062) 61444.*

Roscrea, *21 m (34 km) N of Thurles. EC Wed. 85, 86, 218 bus from Limerick. Train from Limerick, Nenagh: enquiries: (0903) 21198.* Pleasant market town with interesting historical ruins, good centre for walking and climbing in Slieve Bloom Mountains.
   Damer House: neglected early 18th c building saved from demolition in 1975 and since completely restored. Richly decorated and carved staircase, much good furniture, fine paintings, relics of life in old Roscrea. Heritage Centre, guided tours, slide shows. *1 Apr-31 Oct, weekdays 10 a.m.-5 p.m., Sat., Sun 2 p.m.-6 p.m. June, July, August, open till 6 p.m. Details: (0505) 21850.*
   Roscrea Castle, *near Damer House:* built 1281, reconstructed 1332. Gate tower, two other towers, parts of walls remain. *Hours as Damer House, otherwise key in adjoining County Council office.* **St Cronan's Monastery**, divided in two by main road. In E portion, a High Cross. In W part, round tower and remains of cathedral church. There are remains of a 15th c *Franciscan friary* partly incorporated into St Cronan's Church. Opp. Glebe View Garage see ruins of primitive Methodists' meeting place. Pleasant walk along the Mall, on opp. site of Moneen river.

Cistercian College, fine museum, items on folklife, archaeology, history, natural history. *Not usually open, but ask the monks, tel: (0505) 21061.* Bicyles: Michael England, *tel: (0505) 21776.* Roscrea Golf Club, *9 holes, tel: (0505) 21130.*

St Patrick's Stone, *Grange, 1 m (2 km) S of Cahir:* roadside boulder with imprint of Saint's knees.

Salesian Convent, *Brosna, 5 m (8 km) NW of Roscrea:* fine terraced gardens with ornamental waters, *by arr., (0505) 47136.*

Scaragh, *2 m (3 km) W of Cahir, off N24:*forest walks, viewing points.

Silvermine Mountains, *S of Nenagh:* many fine climbs. For panoramic views, visit Step viewing point near Silvermines village, car park, picnic area.

Slievenamon Mountain, *6 m (10 km) SE of Fethard:* superb views from summit reward for energetic climb.

Soloheadbeg, *4 m (6 km) N of Tipperary:* first shots in War of Independence fired here, January, 1919. Memorial to event at Solohead Cross.

Templemore Park, *9 m (14 km) N of Thurles on N62. 85, 86 bus from Thurles, train from Dublin, Limerick.* Remains of Templemore Abbey and Black Castle. Swimming pool, nature trail.

Terryglass, *NE shores of Lough Derg:* village of great character, with century-old stone church and 13th c Old Court castle. Picnic area, boating facilities. **Paddy's pub**, very old, with lots of atmosphere, enchanced by mirrors on the wall and stove in middle of lounge. Ideal for relaxing after Lough Derg cruising.

The Thatched Cottage, *2 m (3 km) from Nenagh on Dromineer Road:* 150 year old with thatched roof and traditional Irish hospitality, restaurant, *details: (067) 31155.*

Thomastown Castle, *6 m (10 km) E of Tipperary, on N74:* birthplace of Father Mathew, Capuchin apostle of temperance, now a ruin. His statue is

at adjoining Thomastown crossroads.

Timoney Standing Stones, *4 m (6 km) SE of Roscrea in townlands of Timoney Hills and Cullaun:* nearly 300 scattered over 100 acres.

Tipperary, *25 m (40 km) SW of Thurles. EC Wed. TIO: (062) 51457, July, Aug. Bus and train enquiries: (062) 51206. 107, 213 bus, train from Limerick.* Farming town with interesting historical remains. Fine old shopfronts in Church Street, Main Street, O'Brien Street. Brown trout fishing. Good centre for climbing and hill walking on Slievenamuck and Galtee Mountains.
   St Michael's Church (C). Impressive Gothic style with a number of distinctive architectural features, including W door. Chancel arch of 13th c Augustinian abbey in grounds of Christian Brothers' school. Also ruins of 17th c Abbey Schools. Motte of Norman motte-and-bailey castle on sandhill just N of town. Monument to Charles Kickham, 19th c patriot, poet, novelist. Also Manchester Martyrs' memorial. Sean Treacy Memorial Pool, *Bank Place, daily. Tel: (062) 51806/51817.* Bicycles: J. J. O'Carroll, *10 James's Street, tel: (062) 51229.* Tipperary Golf Club, *9 holes, tel: (062) 51119.*

Toomevara Folk Museum, *10 m (16 km) E of Nenagh on N7. 86, 127, 218 bus from Nenagh.* Many items used in rural Ireland over the centuries. *Daily, at all reasonable times. Key next door.*

Toureen, *4 m (6 km) N of Cahir, off N24:* forest walks.

Tullamore

Pop. 8,500, 25 m (40 km) SE of Athlone, 28 m (45 km) NE of Roscrea, 60 m (96 km) W of Dublin, EC Mon. TIOs: Athlone, (0902) 72866, all year. Birr, tel: Birr 206. Bus and train enquiries: (0506) 21431. 51, 100 bus from Dublin. Also train.

A quiet, modest town whose development owes much to the laying out of the Grand Canal in 1798. Probably the single most exciting event in Tullamore's history occurred in May, 1785, when a hot air balloon caught fire durings its ascent and crashed, setting fire to a third of the town.
   St Catherine's, *Hop Hill, Portarlington Road:* fine 1818 Gothic church on impressive hill site. **Irish Mist Distillery:** the world-famous liqueur is produced here, video presentation and product sampling, *Mon-Fri, 3 p.m.-5.30 p.m., details, (0506) 21399.* W Scally's Drapery Shop, *Columcille Street:* built 1911–14 after a design seen in Brussels.

There is an interesting walk from Chapel Street to Convent Road, on S bank of Grand Canal; Chapel Street has the town's last farmyard. Also Harbour Street, round the old canal harbour and back by canalside Convent Road. S bank of canal continues past Irish Mist factory to Kilbride Street. If you are in the SE outskirts, walk along the Clonminch Road, to see the site of the 1854 railway station, never popular because of its distance from town and only used for ten years.
   Grand Canal, Shannon cruises: Celtic Canal Cruisers Ltd, *24th Lock, tel: (0506) 21861.* Swimming pool, *daily, details: (0506) 21867.* Bicycles: C. McCabe, *Church Street, tel: (0506) 21717.* Golf Club, *18 holes, tel: (0506) 21439.* Buckley's Riding Centre. *tel (0506)53507.*

AROUND TULLAMORE

Abbeyleix, *9 m (14 km) S of Portlaoise on N8 Dublin-Cork road, 52 bus from Portarlington. 73, 102 bus from Kilkenny.* Woodlands, gardens, miles of quiet leafy paths and riverside scenery. 1773 house closed to public, but see formal terrace gardens on W front; Paradise Gardens, almost well 'natural' garden, full of trees, shrubs and in May, June bluebells. Avenue of lime trees and American Garden with magnolias. Tomb of Malachy O'More, last king of Leix, 12th c Monks' Bridge, riverside walks by Nore. Café and craft shop. *Easter–September 30. Daily, 2.30 p.m.–6.30 p.m. Details: (0502) 31227/31162.*

Dunne's Craft Centre, *Cork Road, Abbeyleix. Open daily, tel: (0502)31395.*

Ballycowen Castle, *4 m (6 km) W of Tullamore on N bank of Grand Canal:* originally mediaeval, present ruins largely those of 1626 fortified house. Remains of two 6th c churches (NM) at Rahan.

Banagher, *22 m (25 km) SW of Tullamore, 51 bus from Tullamore, 214 bus from Birr.* Remains of 17th c English-built batteries which commanded crossing of River Shannon. Crannog Pottery; tearooms, craft shop. *May–Sept, Mon–Sat, 9.30 a.m.–8 p.m. Sun, 2.30 p.m.–6.30 p.m Oct–Apr, Mon–Sat, 9.30 a.m.–6 p.m. Details: Banagher 24. W Cruiser hire: Silverline Cruisers, tel: Banagher 112; Carrick Craft, tel: Banagher 187.*

Belmont, *near Clara, Co. Offaly,* riding facilities: Moyston Riding Centre *tel: Belmont 4.*

Birr, *23 m (37 km) SW of Tullamore. All day closing: Thur. TIO: Birr 206. June–Sept. Bus enquiries: Birr 8. 51 bus from Tullamore, 52 from Portlaoise, 100 from Dublin, 214 from Nenagh.* Attractive town full of graceful Georgian architecture. Spend a day exploring town and castle grounds. Birr Vintage Festival: great festivities, *Aug, details: TIO, Birr 206.*

Birr Castle: home of Earl of Countess of Rosse, gardens open to the public. Ornamental lake, arboretum, displays of trees, shrubs, flowers, inc. 200 year old box hedges, claimed to be tallest in world. See walls and tube of great mid-19th c Birr telescope, for 80 years, largest in the world. Museum, section on scientific discoveries of Sir Charles Parsons, *all year, daily, 9 a.m.–1 p.m.; 2 p.m.–6 p.m. or dusk. Details: Birr 56.* D

Crottys' Church, *Castle Street:* relic of early 19th c Catholic schism, when Fr Michael Crotty set up an independent church. **Seffin Stone**, *John's Mall:* believed to be Megalithic; also Crimean Gun, presented to Birr in 1858 for services rendered in Crimean War. Riverside walk along banks of Camcor, also Mill Island mid-river park.

Pleasure flights: Midland Flying Club, Birr Airfield. Swimming pool: indoor, heated, *Wilmer Road, Tues–Sat, all year, details: Birr 343. C W* Bicycles: P. L. Dolan and Sons, *Main Street, tel: Birr 6.* Birr Golf Club, *The Glens, 18 holes, tel: Birr 82.*

Brittas, *1 m (2 km) W of Clonaslee on L116:* car park, picnic area, forest walk.

Bunreagh, *7 m (11 km) NW of Mountrath on Kinnitty road:* car park, picnic place, forest walks, viewing points, scenic route over Slieve Bloom Mountains.

Castle Bernard, *near Kinnitty:* 19th c building owned by Department of Lands. On terrace, carved shaft of high cross, (NM).

Cadamstown, *3 m (5 km) NE of Kinnitty on T9:* Silver River ravines, old mill, bridge of Ardara, ruins of St Luna's Abbey. Just NE of village, megalithic Giant's Grave, by arr. local forestry officials, *tel: Kinnity 5/20.*

Carrick Hill, *just off L108 adjoining Portalington:* car park, picnic place, forest walk.

Clonenagh, *1.5 m (3 km) E of Mountrath on N7 to Portlaoise:* St Fintan's Well, embedded in trunk of large roadside tree, said to have arrived there miraculously.

Clonmacnoise, *4 m (6 km) N of Shannonbridge on Offaly bank of River Shannon:* one of Ireland's great holy places, monastery founded in 548 and for nearly 1,000 years, renowned as centre of piety and learning. Raided many times and finally abandoned in 1552. Cathedral, seven church ruins, two round towers, castle ruins. Ancient Pilgrim's Road, fragments of 11th c causeway to cemetery, still in use. Jetty for cruisers. *mid-June–30 Sept daily 10 a.m.–7 p.m. Otherwise by app. with caretaker. Guided tours. TIO at site entrance SO, tel: (0905) 4134.*

Clononey Castle, *2 m (3 km) NW of Cloghan on L27 to Shannonbridge:* well preserved tower, 17th c bawn.

Coolbanagher Church, *6 m (9 km) NE of Portlaoise,*

near Emo on L26: very striking late 18th c interior by Gandon, who also designed Custom House, Dublin. *By arr.*, Rev. Philip Day, *tel: (0502) 24143.*

Croghan Hill, *10 m (16 km) NE of Tullamore:* good views, nearby village of Tyrellspass won a 1976 European Architectural Heritage Year award.

Durrow Abbey, *4 m (6 km) N of Tullamore on T9 to Kilbeggan:* little remains of St Colmcille's monastery, origin of 7th c Book of Durrow (now in Trinity College), but see holy well and Durrow High Cross, with panels showing Biblical themes.

Dysart Forest Park, *5 m (8 km) E of Portlaoise on T16:* attractive views.

Emo Court Garden, *2 m (3 km) NE of Coolbanagher church:* specimen trees, shrubs, imposing lake. Late 18th c Gandon house only open to special interest groups. *Gardens, Easter–Oct 31, Sat, Sun, BH, 2.30 p.m.–5.30 p.m.* D

Emo Park, *5 m (7 km) S of Portarlington:* forest walks.

Festival Field, *4 m (6 km) SW of Clonaslee off L116 to Mountmellick:* attractive high moorland with picnic area.

Forelacka Glen, *2 m (3 km) SE of Kinnitty:* lively mountain stream.

Garry Castle, *1.5 m (3 km) SE of Banagher:* ruins of former MacCoghlan stronghold.

Garryhinch, *4 m (6 km) W of Portarlington:* forest, riverside walks, car park, picnic area.

Glenbarrow, *12 m (19 km) S of Tullamore:* six waterfalls, riverside walk by exuberant River Barrow. Car park, picnic area. Good climbers can tackle nearby Ridge of Capard, superb views.

Glendine East, *N of Camross village on S side of Slieve Bloom Mountains:* attractive natural site by Killeen River, car park. If you feel energetic, it's an hour's climb to Glendine Gap, 2,000 ft (600 metres). On far side, the open glen of Glendine West.

Glendineoregan, *2 m (3 km) S of Clonaslee:* car park, viewing point, forest walks, scenic route over Slieve Bloom mountains. Just SE, at the Cut and Glen Bordowin (car park and viewing point), impressive mountain pass. Slieve Bloom orienteering maps: Slieve Bloom Association, *tel: Kinnitty 36;* Curragh Orienteers, *7 French Furze, Kildare,* enclose large SAE. Pony trekking: Capard Trekking Centre, *tel: (0502) 28514.*

Glenletter, *5 m (8 km) SE of Kinnitty on Kinnitty–Mountrath road:* car park, picnic area, viewing point, forest walks. Source of Silver River, attractive viewing points along Hogan's Road.

Gloster, *7 m (11 km) SE of Birr off T32:* pleasant lakeside forest walks here and at Goldengrove, 3 m (5 km) further along T32.

Glynsk mountain, *NE of Kinnitty.* Forest walks, viewing points.

Haywood House, 1 m (2 km) NE of Ballinakill, on Abbeyleix– Ballyragget road. Magnificent Italianate gardens designed by Sir Edward Lutyens. Now a Salesian missionary college; grounds *by arr., tel: (0502) 34334.*

Kilbeggan, *7 m (11 km) N of Tullamore, 46 bus from Athlone.* Horse racing. *details: tel: (0506) 32176/32125.*

Kilcormac, *10 m (16 km) NE of Birr:* C church with carved wooden 16th c *Pieta*, buried in bog for 60 years during Penal times, in order to keep it safe. D

Kinnitty, *8 m (13 km) E of Birr on L116, 52 bus from Birr.* Charming village at foot of Slieve Bloom Mountains. As William Bulfin, in the 19th c *Rambles in Erin*, wrote: 'Kinnitty is probably the most beautifully situated village I have ever seen, embowered in woods, a sheltered Eden in the hills.' The L116 over the mountains is a most striking route into Co.Laois.

Lea Castle, *2.5 m (4 km) E of Portarlington, between Grand Canal and River Barrow:* once a stronghold of Fitzgeralds, barons of Offaly,

destroyed in 17th c.

Leap Castle, *6 m (9 km) SE of Birr on T9 Kinnitty–Roscrea road:* remains of 16th c. stronghold of the Ely O'Carrolls—said to be most haunted in Ireland, with 24 ghosts.

Lime Kiln Grove, *E of Kinnitty, turn S off L116, continue for 2.5 m (4 km):* forest walks, picnic area.

Lynally, *4 m (6 km) SW of Tullamore:* 6 th c monastery ruins.

Monicknew, *7 m (11 km) N of Mountrath on Mountrath– Clonaslee road:* forest walks, viewing points, scenic route over Slieve Bloom mountains, 1.25 m (2 km) nature trail taking in Monicknew bridge, built as Roman arch. From car park at the Cut, direct climb to summit of Wolftrap mountain.

Oughaval, *1 m (2 km) SE of Stradbally:* car park, forest walks, picnic area.

Portarlington, *17 m (27 km) SW of Tullamore:* once home of a strong Huguenot community. French Week, *Sept,* celebrates Portarlington's colourful history, events include snail eating. *All day closing Mon.*

'French' Church of Ireland, *just off town square:* interesting graveyard, Huguenot records, French silver. Viewing by arr.: Rev. E. C. J. Woods, *tel: (0502) 23144.* The town's ESB station was the first in Ireland to use turf for electricity generation. *By arr., tel: (0502) 23145.* Swimming pool: indoor, heated, *daily, except Tues, details: (0502) 23149.*

Portlaoise, *17 m (28 km) SE of Tullamore:* Veteran Car Museum, *Ivyleigh:* dozen veteran cars plus other early transport items, visitors welcome, but tel: Mr and Mrs Denis Lucey in advance, *(0502) 21244.* Portlaoise Sports Centre, *daily.* Moneyballytyrell swimming pool, *daily, details: (0502) 21710.* Bicycles: M. Kavanagh, *Railway Street.* Heath Golf Club, *18 holes, tel: (0502) 26533.*

Rahan, *5 m (8 km) W of Tullamore:* remains of 6th c monastery, three ruined churches, roofed church with fine rose window.

Rahugh, *5 m (8 km) NE of Tullamore on Grand Canal banks:* holy well, nearby St Hugh's tombstone is said to be good for headaches.

Rathdaire, *1 m (1.5 km) S of Ballybrittas, near Portarlington:* forest walks.

Rock of Dunamase, *3.5 m (6 km) E of Portlaoise:* ruined fortress perched atop 150 ft (46 metres) rock is magnificent in its desolation. Great views over Midland plain.

Rosenallis, *4 m (6 km) NW of Mountmellick:* oldest Quaker burial ground in Ireland.

Shannon Harbour, *20 m (32 km) W of Tullamore:* a forlorn sight, with deserted quaysides, empty warehouses, façade of once lavish canal hotel: loads of atmosphere. Alternatively, the Grand Canal area is usually thick with craft. **Harbour Bar:** traditional country pub, with grocery provision drawers, 1887 GAA roll of honour and interesting paintings.

Sheffield Forest Park: *3 m (5 km) SE of Portlaoise on L26:* forest walks.

Sragh Castle, *just W of Tullamore on N bank of Grand Canal:* 1588 ruin with dungeons and murder holes.

Stradbally, *6 m (10 km) E of Portlaoise on T16, 56 bus from Carlow or Kilkenny.* Irish Steam Preservation Society Museum, traction engines, rollers, *all year,* with Richard Byrne, who lives nearby. Narrow gauge railway in grounds of Stradbally Hall, *SO,* Steam Rally, *first weekend Aug, details:* Mrs Olive Condell, *tel: (0502) 25136.* D

Tihilly, *1 m (1.5 km) NW of Tullamore:* mediaeval ruins, church and interesting High Cross.

Timahoe Round Tower, *8 m (13 km) SE of Portlaoise:* built in 1100, one of finest in Ireland. Nearby ruins of castle and abbey.

Togher Forest Park: *2 m (3 km) S of Portlaoise on by-road off T14:* forest walks.

Index to Places

103

Dublin

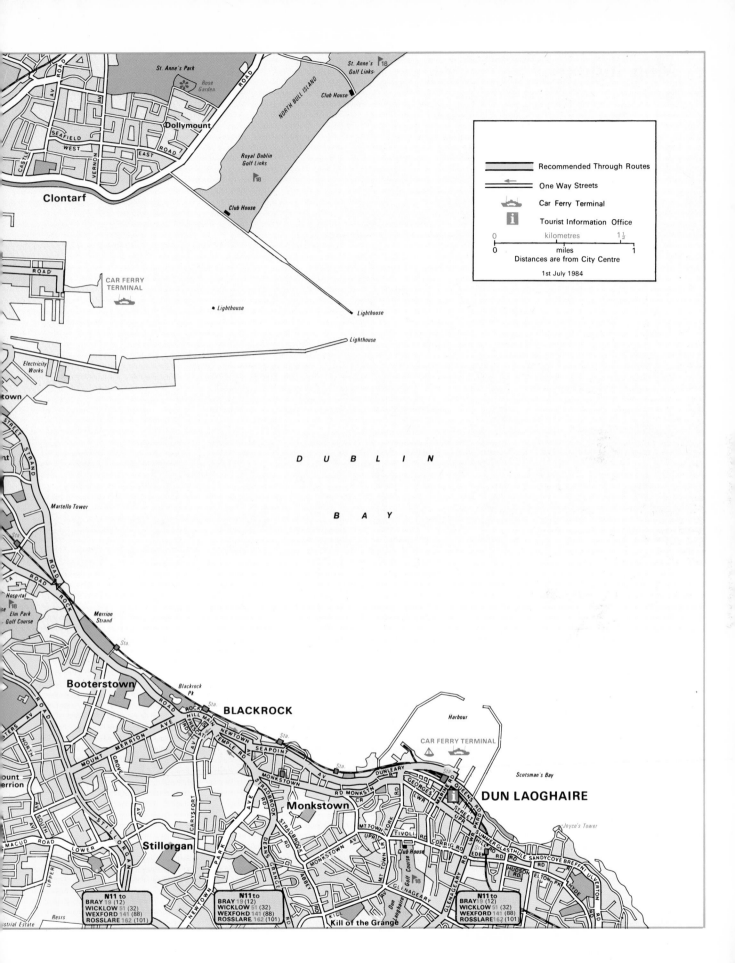

St. Anne's Park

Rose Garden

Dollymount

NORTH BULL ISLAND

St. Anne's Golf Links

Club House

Royal Dublin Golf Links

Club House

SEAFIELD WEST

VERNON

EAST

ROAD

Clontarf

ROAD

CAR FERRY TERMINAL

Electricity Works

Lighthouse

Lighthouse

Lighthouse

D U B L I N

B A Y

Martello Tower

Hospital

Elm Park Golf Course

Merrion Strand

Sta.

Booterstown

Blackrock Pk

Sta.

BLACKROCK

Harbour

CAR FERRY TERMINAL

Scotsman's Bay

Mount Merrion

Mount Merrion

Monkstown

Stillorgan

Club House

DUN LAOGHAIRE

Joyce's Tower

GLASTHULE SANDYCOVE BREFFNI ULVERTON

Kill of the Grange

N11 to
BRAY 19 (12)
WICKLOW 51 (32)
WEXFORD 141 (88)
ROSSLARE 162 (101)

N11 to
BRAY 19 (12)
WICKLOW 51 (32)
WEXFOHD 141 (88)
ROSSLARE 162 (101)

N11 to
BRAY 19 (12)
WICKLOW 51 (32)
WEXFORD 141 (88)
ROSSLARE 162 (101)

Map Index

Banbridge *Down* **7 F 1**
Bandon *Cork* **13 G 5**
Bandon, R *Cork* **13 F 5**
Bangor *Down* **3 G 5**
Bangor Erris *Mayo* **4 C 2**
Bann, R *Armagh/Down* **7 E 1**
Bann, R *Derry/Armagh* **3 E 4**
Bann, R *Wexford* **11 E 5**
Bannow Bay *Wexford* **15 F 3**
Banteer *Cork* **13 G 2**
Bantry *Cork* **13 E 5**
Bantry Bay *Cork* **12 D 5**
Bansha *Tipperary* **9 H 6**
Barefield *Clare* **9 E 4**
Barna *Galway* **8 D 2**
Barnatra *Mayo* **4 B 2**
Barnesmore Gap *Donegal* **1 H 5**
Barraduff *Kerry* **13 E 3**
Barrow, R *Leinster* **15 E 2**
Bartragh I *Mayo* **4 D 2**
Baurtregaum, mt *Kerry* **12 D 2**
Bawnboy *Cavan* **6 A 3**
Beagh, L *Donegal* **1 H 3**
Béal an Atha *see* Ballina
Béal Átha na Sluaighe *see* Ballinasloe
Bealaclugga *Clare* **9 E 2**
Bealalaw Bridge *Kerry* **12 C 3**
Bear I *Cork* **12 C 5**
Beara, pen *Kerry/Cork* **12 D 4**
Beaufort *Kerry* **12 D 3**
Beenmore, mt *Kerry* **12 C 3**
Beennageeha, mt *Kerry* **12 D 1**
Beenoskee, mt *Kerry* **12 C 2**
Beg, L *Derry/Antrim* **3 E 4**
Begooly *Cork* **13 H 5**
Belclare *Galway* **5 E 6**
Belcoo *Fermanagh* **6 B 2**
Belderg *Mayo* **4 C 2**
Belfast *Antrim* **3 F 6**
Belfast, L *Antrim/Down* **3 G 5**
Belhavel, L *Leitrim* **5 G 2**
Bellacorick *Mayo* **4 C 3**
Bellaghy *Derry* **3 E 4**
Bellahy *Sligo* **5 F 3**
Bellanagare *Roscommon* **5 G 4**
Bellanaleck *Fermanagh* **6 A 2**
Bellavally Gap *Cavan* **6 A 2**
Bellavary *Mayo* **4 D 4**
Belleek *Fermanagh* **1 G 6**
Belleeks *Armagh* **7 E 2**
Bellmullet *Mayo* **4 B 2**
Beltra *Mayo* **4 D 4**
Beltra *Sligo* **5 F 2**
Beltra, L *Mayo* **4 D 4**
Belturbet *Cavan* **6 B 3**
Benbane Hd *Antrim* **3 E 2**
Benbaun, mt *Galway* **4 B 6**
Benbrack, mt *Cavan* **6 A 3**
Benbulbin *Sligo* **5 G 1**
Benburb *Tyrone* **6 D 1**
Benbury, mt *Mayo* **4 B 5**
Bencorr, mt *Galway* **4 B 6**
Bencroy, mt *Leitrim* **5 H 3**
Bengorm, mt *Mayo* **4 C 5**
Bennettsbridge *Kilkenny* **10 C 5**
Benwee Hd *Mayo* **16 B 1**
Benwee, mt *Mayo* **4 C 5**
Beragh *Tyrone* **2 C 6**
Bessbrook *Armagh* **7 E 2**
Betraghboy Bay *Galway* **8 B 1**
Binevenagh *Derry* **2 D 3**
Binghamstown *Mayo* **4 B 2**
Birdhill *Tipperary* **9 G 4**
Birr *Offaly* **9 H 3**
Birreencorragh *Mayo* **4 C 3**
Black Hd *Antrim* **3 G 4**
Black Hd *Clare* **8 D 2**
Blacklion *Cavan* **5 H 2**
Blackrock *Louth* **7 E 3**
Blacksod Bay *Mayo* **4 B 3**
Blackstairs Mt
Carlow/Wexford **10 D 6**
Blackstairs Mountains
Carlow/Wexford **10 D 6**
Blackwater *Wexford* **15 H 2**
Blackwater, R *Meath* **6 D 5**
Blackwater, R *Munster* **14 B 3**
Blackwater, R *Tyrone* **6 C 1**
Blanchardstown *Dublin* **11 E 1**
Blarney *Cork* **13 H 3**
Blasket Sound *Kerry* **12 A 3**
Blennerville *Kerry* **12 D 2**
Blessington *Wicklow* **11 E 2**
Bloody Foreland *Donegal* **1 G 2**
Blue Ball *Offaly* **10 A 2**
Blue Stack, mt *Donegal* **1 G 5**
Blue Stack Mts *Donegal* **1 G 5**
Blueford *Cork* **13 F 2**
Boa I *Fermanagh* **1 H 6**
Boderg, L *Roscommon* **5 H 4**
Bodyke *Clare* **9 F 4**
Bofin, L *Galway* **4 C 6**
Bofin, L. *Roscommon* **5 H 4**
Boggeragh Mts *Cork* **13 F 3**
Boherbue *Cork* **13 F 2**
Bohermeen *Meath* **6 C 5**
Bohola *Mayo* **5 E 4**
Bolus Hd *Kerry* **12 B 4**
Booley Hills *Kilkenny* **14 D 1**
Borris *Carlow* **10 D 5**
Borris-in-Ossory *Laois* **10 A 4**
Borrisokane *Tipperary* **9 H 3**
Borrisoleigh *Tipperary* **9 H 5**
Boughil, mt *Kerry* **12 D 3**
Bourn Vincent Park *Kerry* **13 E 3**
Boyle *Roscommon* **5 G 3**
Boyne, R *Meath* **7 E 5**
Brackley, L *Cavan* **6 A 3**
Bracknagh *Offaly* **10 C 2**
Brandon *Kerry* **12 C 1**
Brandon B *Kerry* **12 C 1**
Brandon Hd *Kerry* **12 B 1**
Brandon Hill *Kilkenny* **10 D 6**
Brandon Mt *Kerry* **12 B 2**
Brandon Pk *Kerry* **12 B 2**
Bray *Wicklow* **11 F 2**
Bray Hd *Kerry* **12 B 4**
Bray Hd *Wicklow* **11 F 2**
Bré *see* Bray
Brick, R *Kerry* **12 D 1**
Bride, R *Cork/W'ford* **14 B 4**
Brideswell Roscommon **5 H 6**
Bridgend *Donegal* **2 B 3**
Bridget, L *Clare* **9 F 4**
Bridgetown *Wexford* **15 G 3**
Brittas *Dublin* **11 E 2**
Brittas B *Wicklow* **11 F 4**
Broad Haven, B *Mayo* **4 B 1**
Broadford *Clare* **9 F 4**
Broadford *Limerick* **13 F 1**
Brookeborough *Fermanagh* **6 B 1**
Broomfield *Monaghan* **6 D 3**
Brosna, R *W'meath/Offaly* **10 A 2**
Broughshane *Antrim* **3 F 4**
Bruff *Limerick* **9 F 6**
Bullagon Pt *Louth* **7 F 3**
Bullaun *Galway* **9 F 2**
Bull Pt *Antrim* **3 E 2**
Bunatrahir *Mayo* **4 D 1**
Bunaveela L *Mayo* **4 C 3**
Bunbeg *Donegal* **1 G 3**
Bunclody *Wexford* **11 E 5**
Buncrana *Donegal* **2 B 2**
Bundoran *Donegal* **1 G 6**
Bunmahon *Waterford* **14 D 3**
Bunnahowen *Mayo* **4 B 2**
Bunnanadden *Sligo* **5 F 3**
Bunny, L *Clare* **8 D 3**
Bunnyconnellan *Mayo* **5 E 3**
Burnfoot *Donegal* **2 B 3**
Burren, dist *Clare* **8 D 3**
Burrin *Clare* **9 E 2**
Burtonport *Donegal* **1 F 3**
Bush, R *Antrim* **3 E 3**
Bushmills *Antrim* **3 E 2**
Butler's Bridge *Cavan* **6 B 3**
Butlerstown *Cork* **13 G 5**
Buttevant *Cork* **13 G 2**

Caha, mt *Kerry* **12 D 4**
Caha Mts *Cork/Kerry* **12 D 5**
Caher I *Galway* **4 B 5**
Caherbarnagh, mt *Cork* **13 F 3**
Caherconlish *Limerick* **9 F 5**
Caherconree, mt *Kerry* **12 C 2**
Caherdaniel *Kerry* **12 C 4**
Cahersiveen *Kerry* **12 B 3**
Cahir *Tipperary* **14 B 2**
Cahore Pt *Wexford* **11 F 6**
Caisléan an Bharraigh *see* Castlebar
Caledon *Tyrone* **6 D 1**
Callan *Kilkenny* **10 B 6**
Callan, R *Armagh* **6 D 1**
Caltra *Galway* **5 G 6**
Camaross *Wexford* **15 F 2**
Camlough *Armagh* **7 E 2**
Camolin *Wexford* **11 E 5**
Camowen, R *Tyrone* **2 C 6**
Camp *Kerry* **12 C 2**
Campile *Wexford* **15 F 3**
Cape Clear *Cork* **12 D 6**
Cappamore *Limerick* **9 G 5**
Cappoquin *Waterford* **14 C 3**
Caragh L *Kerry* **12 D 3**
Carbury *Kildare* **10 D 1**
Cark Mt *Donegal* **1 H 4**
Carlanstown *Meath* **6 D 5**
Carlingford *Louth* **7 F 3**
Carlingford L *Down/Louth* **7 F 3**
Carlow *Carlow* **10 D 4**
Carn *Derry* **2 D 4**
Carna *Galway* **8 B 1**
Carnagh *Armagh* **6 D 2**
Carncastle *Antrim* **3 G 4**
Carndonagh *Donegal* **2 B 2**
Carnew *Wicklow* **11 E 5**
Carney *Sligo* **5 F 1**
Carnlough *Antrim* **3 F 3**
Carnlough B *Antrim* **3 F 3**
Carnsore Pt *Wexford* **15 H 3**
Carra, L *Mayo* **4 D 5**
Carragh *Kildare* **10 D 2**
Carraig na Siúire *see* Carrick-on-Suir
Carran, mt *Kerry* **13 E 4**
Carraroe *Galway* **8 C 1**
Carrauntoohil, mt *Kerry* **12 D 3**
Carrick *Donegal* **1 F 5**
Carrick *Wexford* **15 F 3**
Carrick-on-Shannon
Leit/Roscommon **5 H 4**
Carrick-on-Suir *Tipperary* **14 D 2**
Carrickbeg *Waterford* **14 D 2**
Carrickboy *Longford* **6 A 5**
Carrickfergus *Antrim* **3 G 5**
Carrickmacross *Monaghan* **6 D 3**
Carrickmore *Tyrone* **2 C 6**
Carrig *Tipperary* **9 H 3**
Carrig I *Kerry* **8 C 5**
Carrigadrohid Res. *Cork* **13 G 4**
Carrigaholt *Clare* **8 B 5**
Carrigaline *Cork* **14 A 5**
Carrigallen *Leitrim* **6 A 3**
Carriganimmy *Cork* **13 F 3**
Carrigans *Donegal* **2 B 4**
Carrigart *Donegal* **1 H 2**
Carrigatuke, mt *Armagh* **7 E 2**
Carrigfadda, mt *Cork* **13 F 5**
Carrowkeel *Donegal* **2 C 2**
Carrowmore L *Mayo* **4 C 2**
Carryduff *Down* **3 G 6**
Cashel *Tipperary* **10 A 6**
Cashen, R *Kerry* **8 B 6**
Cashlaundrumlahan, mt
Galway **9 F 3**
Castlebar *Mayo* **4 D 4**
Castlebar L *Mayo* **4 D 4**
Castlebellingham *Louth* **7 E 4**
Castleblayney *Monaghan* **6 D 3**
Castlebridge *Wexford* **15 G 2**
Castlecomer *Kilkenny* **10 C 4**
Castlecor *Cork* **13 G 2**
Castlederg *Tyrone* **2 A 5**
Castledermot *Laois* **10 D 4**
Castleellis *Wexford* **11 E 6**
Castlefinn *Donegal* **2 B 4**
Castlegregory *Kerry* **12 C 2**
Castlehill *Mayo* **4 B 3**
Castlecaulfield *Tyrone* **2 D 6**
Castledawson *Derry* **3 E 5**
Castleisland *Kerry* **13 E 2**
Castlemaine *Kerry* **12 D 2**
Castlemaine Harbour *Kerry* **12 D 2**
Castlemartyr *Cork* **14 B 5**
Castleplunket *Roscommon* **5 G 5**
Castlepollard *Westmeath* **6 B 5**
Castlerea *Roscommon* **5 G 5**
Castlerock *Derry* **2 D 2**
Castletown *Laois* **10 B 3**
Castletown *Westmeath* **10 B 1**
Castletown Bere *Cork* **12 C 5**
Castletownroche *Cork* **13 H 2**
Castletownsend *Cork* **13 F 6**
Castlewellan *Down* **7 G 2**
Castlewellan Forest Park
Down **7 F 1**
Catherine, L *Tyrone* **2 B 5**
Causeway *Kerry* **8 B 6**
Cavan *Cavan* **6 B 3**
Cavangarven *Monaghan* **6 C 2**
Cavetown L *Roscommon* **5 G 4**
Ceanannus Mór *Meath* **6 D 5**
Ceatharlach *see* Carlow
Celbridge *Kildare* **11 E 1**
Chapeltown *Down* **7 H 2**
Charlemont *Armagh* **2 D 6**
Charlestown *Mayo* **5 F 3**
Churchtown *Wexford* **15 F 3**
Cill Airne *see* Killarney
Cill Chainnigh *see* Kilkenny
Clady *Tyrone* **2 B 4**
Clanabogan *Tyrone* **2 B 6**
Clane *Kildare* **10 D 1**
Clara *Offaly* **10 A 1**
Clare I *Galway* **4 B 4**
Clare, R *Galway* **5 E 6**
Clarecastle *Clare* **9 E 4**
Clareen *Offaly* **10 A 3**
Claregalway *Galway* **9 E 1**
Claremorris *Mayo* **5 E 5**
Clarinbridge *Galway* **9 E 2**
Clashmore *Waterford* **14 C 4**
Claudy *Derry* **2 C 4**
Clear I *Cork* **13 E 6**
Clew Bay *Mayo* **4 B 4**
Clifden *Galway* **4 B 6**
Cliffoney *Sligo* **1 F 6**
Clogh *Antrim* **3 E 3**
Clogh *Kilkenny* **10 C 4**
Clogh *Wexford* **11 F 5**
Clogh Mills *Antrim* **3 E 3**
Cloghan *Donegal* **1 H 4**
Cloghan *Offaly* **10 A 2**
Cloghan *Westmeath* **6 C 6**
Cloghane *Kerry* **12 B 2**
Cloghaneely, reg *Donegal* **1 G 3**
Clogheen *Waterford* **14 B 3**
Clogher *Tyrone* **6 C 1**
Clogher Hd *Louth* **7 F 4**
Clogher Head *Louth* **7 F 4**
Cloghey *Down* **7 H 1**
Cloghran *Dublin* **7 E 6**
Clohamon *Wexford* **11 E 5**
Clonakilty *Cork* **13 G 5**
Clonakilty B *Cork* **13 G 6**
Clonard *Meath* **6 C 6**
Clonaslee *Laois* **10 B 2**
Clonbern *Galway* **5 F 6**
Clonbullogue *Offaly* **10 C 2**
Clonea *Waterford* **14 D 3**
Clonee *Meath* **11 E 1**
Clonegal *Carlow* **11 E 5**
Clones *Monaghan* **6 C 2**
Clonfert *Galway* **9 H 2**
Clonmany *Donegal* **2 B 2**
Clonmel *Tipp/Waterford* **14 C 2**
Clonmellon *Westmeath* **6 C 5**
Clonmore *Carlow* **11 E 4**
Clonmore *Tipperary* **10 A 4**
Clonoulty *Tipperary* **9 H 5**
Clonroche *Wexford* **10 D 6**
Clontarf *Dublin* **11 F 1**
Clontibret *Monaghan* **6 D 2**
Clonygowan *Offaly* **10 C 2**
Cloonacool *Sligo* **5 F 3**
Cloonagh L *Roscommon* **5 F 4**
Cloonaghlin, L *Kerry* **12 C 4**
Cloonbannin *Cork* **13 F 2**
Cloondara *Longford* **6 A 5**
Cloone *Leitrim* **6 A 4**
Cloonee Loughs *Kerry* **12 D 4**
Cloonfad *Roscommon* **5 F 5**
Cloonkeen *Mayo* **4 D 4**
Cloonlara *Clare* **9 F 5**
Clough *Down* **7 G 2**
Cloughjordan *Tipperary* **9 H 4**
Cloyne *Cork* **14 B 5**
Cluain Meala *see* Clonmel
Coachford *Cork* **13 G 4**
Coagh *Tyrone* **2 D 5**
Coalisland *Tyrone* **2 D 6**
Cóbh *Cork* **14 A 5**
Cod's Hd *Cork* **12 C 5**
Coleraine *Derry* **2 D 3**
Collin Top, mt *Antrim* **3 F 3**
Collon *Louth* **7 E 5**
Collooney *Sligo* **5 G 2**
Collorus *Kerry* **12 C 4**
Colly, mt *Kerry* **12 C 3**
Comber *Down* **3 G 6**
Comeragh Mts *Waterford* **14 C 2**
Cong *Mayo* **4 D 6**
Conlig *Down* **3 G 5**
Conn, L *Mayo* **4 D 3**
Connemara, reg *Galway* **4 B 6**
Connor *Antrim* **3 F 4**
Convoy *Donegal* **2 A 4**
Cookstown *Tyrone* **2 D 5**
Coolaney *Sligo* **5 F 2**
Coolbawn *Tipperary* **9 G 3**
Coole *Westmeath* **6 B 5**
Coolgreany *Wexford* **11 F 4**
Coolmore *Donegal* **1 G 6**
Coomacarrea, mt *Kerry* **12 C 3**
Cooraclare *Clare* **8 C 5**
Cootehill *Cavan* **6 C 3**
Copeland I *Down* **3 H 5**
Coppeen *Cork* **13 F 4**
Coralstown *Westmeath* **6 C 6**
Corcaigh *see* Cork
Cork *Cork* **13 H 4**
Cork Harbour *Cork* **14 A 5**
Cornafulla *Roscommon* **9 H 1**
Cornamona *Galway* **4 C 6**
Corofin *Clare* **9 E 3**
Corraun Peninsula *Mayo* **4 B 4**
Corrib, L *Galway/Mayo* **4 D 6**
Corrig Mt *Dublin* **11 E 2**
Costelloe *Galway* **8 C 1**
Courtmacsherry *Cork* **13 G 5**
Courtmacsherry B *Cork* **13 G 5**
Courtown Harbour *Wexford* **11 F 5**
Craanford *Wexford* **11 E 5**
Craigavon *Armagh* **3 E 6**
Craigue *Laois* **10 D 4**
Crana, R *Donegal* **2 B 2**
Cranfield Pt *Down* **7 F 3**
Craughwell *Galway* **9 F 2**
Crawfordsburn *Down* **3 G 5**
Creegh *Clare* **8 C 5**
Creeslough *Donegal* **1 H 3**
Creggan *Tyrone* **2 C 5**
Cregganbaun *Mayo* **4 B 5**
Creggs *Galway* **5 G 6**
Crinkill *Offaly* **10 A 3**
Croagh Patrick, mt *Mayo* **4 C 5**
Croaghanmoira *Wicklow* **11 E 4**
Croaghann, mt *Mayo* **4 A 3**
Croaghleheen, mt *Donegal* **1 G 4**
Crockets Town *Mayo* **5 E 2**
Crohy Hd *Donegal* **1 F 4**
Cromane *Kerry* **12 C 2**
Crooked Wood *Westmeath* **6 B 6**
Crookhaven *Cork* **12 D 6**
Crookstown *Cork* **13 G 4**
Croom *Limerick* **9 F 6**
Cross *Mayo* **4 D 6**
Crossakiel *Meath* **6 C 5**
Crossbarry *Cork* **13 G 4**
Crossdoney *Cavan* **6 B 4**
Crossgar *Down* **7 G 1**

Crosshaven *Cork* **14 A5**
Crosskeys *Kildare* **10 C3**
Crossmaglen *Armagh* **7 E3**
Crossmolina *Mayo* **4 D3**
Croughaun Hill *Waterford* **14 D3**
Crownarad, mt *Donegal* **1 F5**
Crumlin *Antrim* **3 F5**
Crumlin *Dublin* **11 F1**
Crusheen *Clare* **9 E4**
Cuilcagh, mt *Fermanagh* **6 A2**
Culdaff *Donegal* **2 C2**
Cullahill *Laois* **10 B4**
Cullaunyheeda L *Clare* **9 E4**
Cullaville *Armagh* **6 D3**
Culleens *Sligo* **5 E2**
Cullenagh, R *Clare* **8 D4**
Cullin, L *Mayo* **4 D3**
Cullybackey *Antrim* **3 E4**
Cullyhanna *Armagh* **7 E3**
Culmore *Donegal* **2 B3**
Cummer *Galway* **5 E6**
Curracloe *Wexford* **15 H2**
Curragh *Kildare* **10 D2**
Curragh, The *Kildare* **10 D2**
Curraglass *Cork* **14 B4**
Currane *Kerry* **12 C4**
Curry *Sligo* **5 F3**
Cushcamcarragh, mt *Mayo* **4 C3**
Cushendall *Antrim* **3 F3**
Cushendun *Antrim* **3 F3**
Cusher *Armagh* **7 E1**
Cushina *Offaly* **10 C2**
Cutra, L *Galway* **9 F3**

Dahybann, L *Mayo* **4 C3**
Daingeen *Offaly* **10 B1**
Dalgan, R *Mayo/Roscommon* **5 E5**
Dalkey *Dublin* **11 F2**
Dalua, R *Cork* **13 F2**
Dalystown *Galway* **9 G2**
Darby's Bridge *Kerry* **12 C3**
Darragh *Clare* **9 E4**
Dart, mt *Tyrone* **2 C4**
Dartry Mts *Sligo* **5 G1**
Dawros Hd *Donegal* **1 F4**
Deadmans Hill *Armagh* **7 E2**
Dee, R *Louth* **7 E4**
Deel, R *Limerick* **9 E6**
Deel, R *Mayo* **4 D3**
Deel, R *Meath/W'meath* **6 C6**
Deele, R *Donegal* **2 B4**
Deer I *Clare* **9 E5**
Delgany *Wicklow* **11 F2**
Delvin *Westmeath* **6 C6**
Derg, L *Donegal* **1 H5**
Derg, Lough *Tipperary/Clare/Galway* **9 G4**
Derg, R *Tyrone* **2 B5**
Dernacreeve *Cavan* **6 A2**
Derneen, R *Wicklow/Carlow* **11 E5**
Derravaragh, L *Westmeath* **6 B5**
Derriana, L *Kerry* **12 C4**
Derrybeg *Donegal* **1 G3**
Derrybrian *Galway* **9 F3**
Derrygonnelly *Fermanagh* **6 A1**
Derryhick L *Mayo* **4 D4**
Derrykeighan *Antrim* **3 E2**
Derrylin *Fermanagh* **6 B2**
Derrymore *Kerry* **12 D2**
Derrynane Nat. Hist. Pk *Kerry* **12 B4**
Derrynasaggart Mts *Cork/Kerry* **13 E4**
Derryrush *Galway* **8 C1**
Derryveagh Mts *Donegal* **1 G4**
Dervock *Antrim* **3 E3**
Desertmartin *Derry* **2 D5**
Devil's Bit Mt *Tipperary* **9 H4**
Devil's Mother, mt *Galway* **4 C5**
Dingle *Kerry* **12 B2**
Dingle B *Kerry* **12 B3**
Dingle, pen *Kerry* **12 C2**
Dinin, R *Kilkenny* **10 C5**
Divis, mt *Antrim* **3 F5**
Djouce Mt *Wicklow* **11 F2**
Doagh *Antrim* **3 F5**
Doagh I *Donegal* **2 B2**
Dolla *Tipperary* **9 G4**
Donabate *Dublin* **7 F6**
Donadea *Kildare* **10 D1**
Donaghadee *Down* **3 H5**
Donaghcloney *Down* **7 F1**
Donaghmore *Laois* **10 A4**
Donaghmore *Tyrone* **2 D6**
Donard *Wicklow* **11 E3**
Donegal *Donegal* **1 G5**
Donegal B *Donegal* **1 F6**
Donegal Pt *Clare* **8 C5**
Doneraile *Cork* **13 H2**
Donoughmore *Cork* **13 G3**
Doo L *Clare* **8 D4**
Dooagh *Mayo* **4 A3**
Doocastle *Mayo* **5 F3**
Doochary *Donegal* **1 G4**
Doogort *Mayo* **4 B3**
Doolin Pt *Clare* **8 C3**
Doon *Limerick* **9 G5**
Doon, L *Clare* **9 F4**
Doonbeg *Clare* **8 C5**
Doonbeg B *Clare* **8 C4**
Doonbeg, R *Clare* **8 C5**
Doorin Pt *Donegal* **1 G6**
Doulus Hd *Kerry* **12 B3**
Downhill *Derry* **2 D2**
Downpatrick *Down* **7 G1**
Downpatrick Hd *Mayo* **4 D1**
Dowra *Leitrim* **5 H2**
Drains B *Antrim* **3 G4**
Drangan *Tipperary* **10 B6**
Draperstown *Derry* **2 D4**
Drimoleague *Cork* **13 E5**
Drinagh *Cork* **13 F5**
Dripsey *Cork* **13 G4**
Drogheda *Louth* **7 E5**
Droichead Atha *see* Drogheda
Droichead Nua *Kildare* **10 D2**
Dromahair *Leitrim* **5 G2**
Dromara *Down* **7 F1**
Dromard *Sligo* **5 F2**
Dromin *Louth* **7 E4**
Dromina *Cork* **13 G1**
Drommahane *Cork* **13 G3**
Dromod *Leitrim* **5 H4**
Dromore *Down* **7 F1**
Dromore *Tyrone* **2 B6**
Dromore West *Sligo* **5 E2**
Drum *Monaghan* **6 C3**
Drum Hills *Waterford* **14 C4**
Drumahoe *Derry* **2 B3**
Drumcard *Fermanagh* **6 A2**
Drumcliffe *Sligo* **5 G1**
Drumcollogher *Limerick* **13 G1**
Drumconrath *Meath* **6 D4**
Drumfree *Donegal* **2 B2**
Drumharlow, L *Roscommon* **5 H3**
Drumkeeragh Forest *Down* **7 G1**
Drumkeerin *Leitrim* **5 H2**
Drumlish *Roscommon* **6 A4**
Drumquin *Tyrone* **1 G5**
Drumshanbo *Leitrim* **5 H3**
Drumsna *Leitrim* **5 H3**
Duagh *Kerry* **8 C6**
Dublin *Dublin* **11 F1**
Dublin B *Dublin* **11 F1**
Duleek *Meath* **7 E5**
Dún Dealgan *see* Dundalk
Dún Garbhán *see* Dungarvan
Dunaff Hd *Donegal* **2 B2**
Dunany Pt *Louth* **7 F4**
Dunboyne *Meath* **11 E1**
Duncannon *Wexford* **15 F3**
Duncannon Bridge *Cork* **13 F3**
Duncormick *Wexford* **15 G3**
Dundalk *Louth* **7 E3**
Dundalk B *Louth* **7 E3**
Dundonald *Down* **3 G6**
Dundonnell *Roscommon* **9 G1**
Dundrum *Down* **7 G2**
Dundrum *Tipperary* **9 H6**
Dundrum B *Down* **7 G2**
Dunfanaghy *Donegal* **1 H2**
Dungannon *Tyrone* **2 D6**
Dungarvan *Kilkenny* **10 C6**
Dungarvan *Waterford* **14 C4**
Dungarvan Harbour *Waterford* **14 D4**
Dungiven *Derry* **2 D4**
Dungloe *Donegal* **1 G4**
Dungourney *Cork* **14 B4**
Dunkellin, R *Galway* **9 E2**
Dunkerrin *Offaly* **9 H4**
Dunkineely *Donegal* **1 G5**
Dunkitt *Kilkenny* **15 E2**
Dunlavin *Wicklow* **10 D3**
Dunleer *Louth* **7 E4**
Dunloe, Gap of *Kerry* **12 D3**
Dunmanus Bay *Cork* **12 D6**
Dunmanway *Cork* **13 F5**
Dunmore *Galway* **5 F5**
Dunmore East *Waterford* **15 E3**
Dunmurry *Antrim* **3 F6**
Dunnamanagh *Derry* **2 B4**
Dunohill *Tipperary* **9 H6**
Dunquin *Kerry* **12 B2**
Dunshaughlin *Meath* **7 E6**
Durlas *see* Thurles
Durrow *Laois* **10 B4**
Durrus *Cork* **13 E5**
Dursey Hd *Cork* **12 B5**
Dursey Island *Cork* **12 B5**
Duvillaun More, I *Mayo* **4 A3**
Dyan *Tyrone* **6 D1**
Dysart *Kildare* **10 D1**

Eagle Mt *Down* **7 F2**
Eagle, Mt *Kerry* **12 B2**
Eagle, Mt *Kerry* **13 E2**
Eagles Hill *Kerry* **12 C4**
Easky *Sligo* **5 E2**
Easky, L *Sligo* **5 E2**
Easky, R *Sligo* **5 E2**
Eddy I *Galway* **9 E2**
Eden *Antrim* **3 G5**
Edenderry *Offaly* **10 C1**
Ederny *Fermanagh* **2 A6**
Edgeworthstown *Longford* **6 A5**
Egish, L *Monaghan* **6 D3**
Eglinton *Derry* **2 C3**
Elphin *Roscommon* **5 G4**
Elton *Limerick* **9 G6**
Emly *Tipperary* **9 G6**
Emmoo *Roscommon* **5 H5**
Emyvale *Monaghan* **6 C1**
Enfield *Meath* **10 D1**
Ennell, L *Westmeath* **6 B6**
Ennis *Clare* **9 E4**
Enniscorthy *Wexford* **11 E6**
Enniskean *Cork* **13 F5**
Enniskerry *Wicklow* **11 F2**
Enniskillen *Fermanagh* **6 A1**
Ennistymon *Clare* **8 D3**
Eochaill *see* Youghal
Erne, L., Lower *Fermanagh* **1 H6**
Erne, L. Upper *Fermanagh* **6 B2**
Erne, R *Fermanagh* **1 G6**
Erriff, R *Mayo* **4 C5**
Errigal, mt *Donegal* **1 G3**
Errill *Laois* **10 A4**
Erris Hd *Mayo* **4 B1**
Errit L *Roscommon* **5 F4**
Eske, L *Donegal* **1 G5**
Eyeries *Cork* **12 C5**
Eyrecourt *Galway* **9 H2**

Fahan *Donegal* **2 B3**
Fair Head *Antrim* **3 F2**
Fairy, R *Tyrone* **2 B5**
Falcarragh *Donegal* **1 G2**
Fanad Hd *Donegal* **2 A2**
Fane, R *Louth* **7 E3**
Fardross Forest *Tyrone* **6 B1**
Farranfore *Kerry* **13 E2**
Fathom Wood *Louth* **7 E3**
Faughan, R *Derry* **2 C4**
Feakle *Clare* **9 F4**
Feale, R *Kerry* **8 B6**
Fedamore *Limerick* **9 F6**
Fee, L *Galway* **4 B6**
Feeagh, L *Mayo* **4 C4**
Feenagh *Limerick* **13 G1**
Feeny *Derry* **2 C4**
Fenagh *Carlow* **10 D5**
Fenagh *Leitrim* **6 A3**
Fenit *Kerry* **12 D1**
Ferbane *Offaly* **10 A2**
Fergus, R *Clare* **9 E5**
Fermoy *Cork* **14 A3**
Fern, L *Donegal* **2 A3**
Ferns *Wexford* **11 E5**
Ferrybank *Wicklow* **11 F4**
Fethard *Tipperary* **10 A6**
Fethard *Wexford* **15 F3**
Fiddown *Kilkenny* **14 D2**
Finea *Westmeath* **6 B5**
Finn, L *Donegal* **1 G4**
Finn, R *Donegal* **2 A4**
Fintona *Tyrone* **2 B6**
Fintown *Donegal* **1 G4**
Fintragh B *Donegal* **1 F5**
Finuge *Kerry* **8 C6**
Fivemiletown *Tyrone* **6 B1**
Flagmount *Clare* **9 F3**
Foilclogh, mt *Kerry* **12 B3**
Fontstown *Kildare* **10 D3**
Forbes L *Leit/Long/Roscommon* **5 H5**
Ford *Wexford* **11 B6**
Foxford *Mayo* **5 E3**
Foygh *Longford* **6 A6**
Foyle, L *Donegal/Derry* **2 C3**
Foyle, R *Donegal/Tyrone/Derry* **2 B4**
Foynes *Limerick* **8 D5**
Freemount *Cork* **13 G2**
Frenchpark *Roscommon* **5 G4**
Freshford *Kilkenny* **10 B5**
Funshinagh, L *Roscommon* **5 H6**
Furnace, L *Mayo* **4 C4**
Furraleigh *Waterford* **14 D3**

Gabriel, Mt *Cork* **12 D6**
Gaillimh *see* Galway
Galey, R *Kerry* **8 C6**
Galley Hd *Cork* **13 F6**
Galmoy *Killkenny* **10 B4**
Galros *Offaly* **10 A2**
Galty Mts *Tipp/Lim* **14 A2**
Galway *Galway* **9 E2**
Galway Bay *Galway/Clare* **8 D2**
Gara, L *Sligo/Roscommon* **5 G4**
Garadice L *Leitrim* **6 A3**
Garlowcross *Meath* **7 E5**
Garrison *Fermanagh* **5 H1**
Garristown *Dublin* **7 E6**
Garron Pt *Antrim* **3 F3**
Gartan, L *Donegal* **1 H3**
Garvagh *Derry* **2 D3**
Garvagh *Leitrim* **6 A3**
Gaugin Mt *Donegal* **1 H4**
Gaybrook *Westmeath* **6 B6**
Geashill *Offaly* **10 B2**
George, L *Clare* **9 E3**
Gerahies *Cork* **12 D5**
Giant's Causeway, prom *Antrim* **3 E2**
Gilford *Down* **7 E1**
Gill, L *Sligo* **5 G2**
Glanaruddery Mts *Kerry* **13 E1**
Glandore *Cork* **13 F6**
Glanmire *Cork* **13 H4**
Glanmore, L *Kerry* **12 D5**
Glanworth *Cork* **14 A3**
Glashabeg *Kerry* **12 B2**
Glaslough *Monaghan* **6 D1**
Glassan *Westmeath* **6 A6**
Glassdrummond *Down* **7 G2**
Glen B *Donegal* **1 E5**
Glen L *Donegal* **1 H3**
Glenade L *Leitrim* **5 G1**
Glenamaddy *Galway* **5 F5**
Glenamoy *Mayo* **4 C2**
Glenamoy, R *Mayo* **4 C2**
Glenariff *Antrim* **3 F3**
Glenariff Forest Park *Antrim* **3 F3**
Glenarm *Antrim* **3 F3**
Glenarm, R *Antrim* **3 F4**
Glenavy *Antrim* **3 F6**
Glenbeg L *Cork* **12 C5**
Glenbeigh *Kerry* **12 C3**
Glencar L *Sligo/Leit* **5 G1**
Glencolumbkille *Donegal* **1 E5**
Glencullen *Dublin* **11 F2**
Glendalough, R *Wicklow* **11 E3**
Glendun, R *Antrim* **3 F3**
Glenealy *Wicklow* **11 F3**
Gleneely *Donegal* **2 C2**
Glenfarne *Leitrim* **5 H2**
Glengad Hd *Donegal* **2 C1**
Glengariff *Cork* **12 D4**
Glengavlen *Cavan* **6 A2**
Glengormley *Antrim* **3 F5**
Glenicmurrin L *Galway* **8 C1**
Glenmore *Kilkenny* **15 E2**
Glenoe *Antrim* **3 G4**
Glenshane Pass *Derry* **2 D4**
Glenties *Donegal* **1 G4**
Glenveagh National Park *Donegal* **1 H2**
Glenville *Cork* **13 H3**
Glin *Limerick* **8 D6**
Glinn, L *Roscommon* **5 F4**
Glinsk *Galway* **8 B1**
Glyde, R *Louth* **7 E3**
Glynn *Antrim* **3 G4**
Glynn *Carlow* **10 D6**
Gola I *Donegal* **1 F3**
Golam Hd *Galway* **8 B2**
Golden *Tipperary* **9 H6**
Golden Vale *Tipperary* **9 G5**
Goleen *Cork* **12 D6**
Goresbridge *Kilkenny* **10 C5**
Gorey *Wexford* **11 F5**
Gormanston *Meath* **7 F5**
Gort *Galway* **9 E3**
Gortahork *Donegal* **1 G3**
Gorteen *Galway* **9 F1**
Gorteen *Sligo* **5 F3**
Gorteen *Waterford* **14 C4**
Gorteeny *Galway* **9 G3**
Gortin *Tyrone* **2 C5**
Gortin Glen *Tyrone* **2 C5**
Gortin Glen Forest Park *Tyrone* **2 C5**
Gorumna I *Galway* **8 C2**
Gosford Forest Park *Armagh* **7 E1**
Gougane Barra Forest Park *Cork* **13 E4**
Gowna, Lough *Cavan/Roscommon* **6 A4**
Gowran *Kilkenny* **10 C5**
Graiguenamanagh *Kilkenny* **10 D6**
Granard *Longford* **6 B5**
Grand Canal *Irish Rep.* **11 E2**
Graney, L *Clare* **9 F3**
Grange *Kilkenny* **10 B5**
Grange *Louth* **7 F3**
Grange *Sligo* **5 F1**
Grange *Waterford* **14 C4**
Grangebellow *Louth* **7 E4**
Grangeford *Carlow* **10 D4**
Gt Blasket I *Kerry* **12 A2**
Great I *Cork* **14 A5**
Gt Sugar Loaf, mt *Wicklow* **11 F2**
Greencastle *Donegal* **2 C2**
Greencastle *Down* **7 F3**
Greenore *Louth* **7 F3**
Greenore Pt *Wexford* **15 H3**
Greese, R *Kilddre* **10 D4**
Grey Pt *Down* **3 G5**
Greyabbey *Down* **3 H6**
Greystones *Wicklow* **11 F2**
Groomsport *Down* **3 H5**
Guitane, L *Kerry* **13 E3**
Gullaba Hill *Kerry* **13 E4**
Gur, L *Limerick* **9 F6**
Gweebarra B *Donegal* **1 F4**

Gweedore, reg Donegal 1 G3
Gweedore Donegal 1 G3
Gweesalia Mayo 4 B3

Hacketstown Carlow 11 E 4
Hags Hd Clare 8 C3
Halltown Meath 6 D5
Hamiltonsbawn Armagh 7 E 1
Harrow, The Wexford 11 E 6
Headford Galway 5 E 6
Helvick Hd Waterford 14 D4
Herbertstown Limerick 9 F 6
Hillsborough Down 3 F 6
Hilltown Down 7 F 2
Hollyford Tipperary 9 H5
Hollymount Mayo 5 E 5
Hollywood Wicklow 11 E 3
Holycross Tipperary 10 A5
Holywood Down 3 G5
Hook Hd Wexford 15 F 3
Horn Hd Donegal 1 H2
Horseleap Offaly 10 B 1
Horseleap Cross Roads Galway 5 F 6
Hospital Limerick 9 G6
Howth Dublin 11 F 1
Hungry Hill Cork 12 D5
Hurlers Cross Clare 9 E 5

Iar Connagh, dist Galway 8 C 1
Ilen, R Cork 13 E 5
Inagh Clare 8 D4
Inagh, L Galway 4 C6
Inch Kerry 12 C2
Inch Wexford 11 F 5
Inch I Donegal 2 B3
Inchicronan Clare 9 E 4
Inchigeelagh Cork 13 F 4
Inchquin L Clare 8 D3
Inis *see* Ennis
Inis Córthaidh *see* Enniscorthy
Inishark Galway 4 A5
Inishbofin Galway 4 A5
Inishbofin, I Donegal 1 G2
Inisheer, I Galway 8 C3
Inishkea N, I Mayo 4 A2
Inishkea S, I Mayo 4 A2
Inishmaan, I Galway 8 C3
Inishmore, I Galway 8 C2
Inishmurray Sligo 1 F 6
Inishowen, dist Donegal 2 B2
Inishowen Hd Donegal 2 C2
Inishtooskert, I Kerry 12 A2
Inishturk Galway 4 A5
Inishvickillane, I Kerry 12 A3
Inistioge Kilkenny 10 C6
Inniscarra Res. Cork 13 G4
Inniscrone Sligo 5 E 2
Innishannon Cork 13 G4
Inny, R Kerry 12 C4
Inny, R Long/W'meath 6 B6
Inver Donegal 1 G5
Inverin Galway 8 C2
Ireland's Eye, I Dublin 11 F 1
Iron, L Westmeath 6 B6
Iron Mountains Leit/Cavan 5 H3
Irvinestown Fermanagh 2 A6
Island Magee Antrim 3 G4
Islandeady L. Mayo 4 D4
Iveragh, pen Kerry 12 C3

Jamestown Leitrim 5 H4
John F. Kennedy Memorial Park
Wexford 15 F 2
Johnstown Kildare 10 D1
Johnstown Kilkenny 10 B5
Jonesborough Armagh 7 E 3
Joyces Country, dist Galway 4 C6
Julianstown Meath 7 F 5

Kanturk Cork 13 G2
Katesbridge Down 7 F 1
Keadeen Mt Wicklow 11 E 3
Keadue Roscommon 5 H3
Keady Armagh 6 D2
Kealkill Cork 13 E 4
Keel Mayo 4 B3
Keel L Donegal 1 H3
Keenagh Longford 6 A6
Keeper Hill *see* Slievekimalta
Kells Antrim 3 F 4
Kells *see* Ceanannus Mór
Kells Kilkenny 10 C6
Kells, R Antrim 3 F 4
Kenmare Kerry 12 D4
Kenmare River Kerry/Cork 12 C4
Kerry Hd Kerry 8 B6
Kerrykeel Donegal 2 A2
Kesh Fermanagh 2 A6
Key, L Roscommon 5 G3
Kid, Mt Cork 13 E 5
Kilala Mayo 4 D2
Kilbaha Clare 8 B5
Kilbeggan Westmeath 10 B 1
Kilbehenny Limerick 14 B3
Kilberry Kildare 10 C3
Kilberry Meath 6 D5
Kilbride Meath 7 E 6
Kilbride Wicklow 11 E 2
Kilbride Wicklow 11 F 4
Kilbrittain Cork 13 G5
Kilcar Donegal 1 F 5
Kilchreest Galway 9 F 2
Kilcock Kildare 10 D1
Kilcolgan Galway 9 E 2
Kilconnell Galway 9 G1
Kilconny Cavan 6 B3
Kilcoole Wicklow 11 F 3
Kilcormac Offaly 10 A2
Kilcrohane Cork 12 D5
Kilcrow, R Galway 9 G2
Kilcullen Kildare 10 D2
Kildalkey Meath 6 D6
Kildare Kildare 10 D2
Kildavin Carlow 10 D5
Kildorrery Cork 13 H2
Kilfenora Clare 8 D3
Kilfinane Limerick 13 H1
Kilflynn Kerry 12 D1
Kilgarvan Kerry 12 E 4
Kilglass L Roscommon 5 H4
Kilgowan Kildare 10 D3
Kilkea Kildare 10 D3
Kilkee Clare 8 C5
Kilkeel Down 7 F 3
Kilkelly Mayo 5 E 4
Kilkenny Kilkenny 10 C5
Kilkerrin Galway 5 F 6
Kilkieran Galway 8 C1
Kilkinlea Limerick 13 E 1
Kilkishen Clare 9 F 4
Kill Kildare 11 E 2
Kill Waterford 14 D3
Killadeas Fermanagh 2 A6
Killadoon Galway 4 B5
Killadysert Clare 8 D5
Killala B Mayo/Sligo 4 D2
Killaloe Clare 9 G4
Killanne Wexford 10 D6
Killargue Leitrim 5 G2
Killarney Kerry 13 E 3
Killary Harbour Mayo/Galway 4 B5
Killashandra Cavan 6 B3
Killashee Longford 5 H5
Killateeaun Mayo 4 D5
Killavullen Cork 13 H2
Killeagh Cork 14 B5
Killeigh Offaly 10 B2
Killen Tyrone 2 A5
Killena Wexford 11 F 5
Killenaule Tipperary 10 A6
Killerig Carlow 10 D4
Killeter Tyrone 2 A5
Killimer Clare 8 C5
Killimor Galway 9 G2
Killinaboy Clare 9 E 3
Killinick Wexford 15 G3
Killmalock Limerick 13 H1
Killmessan Meath 6 D6
Killough Down 7 H2
Killucan Westmeath 6 C6
Killurin Wexford 15 G2
Killybegs Donegal 1 F 5
Killygordon Donegal 2 A4
Killykeen Forest Park Cavan 6 B3
Killylea Armagh 6 D1
Killyleagh Down 7 G1
Kilmacanogue Wicklow 11 F 2
Kilmacrennan Donegal 1 H3
Kilmacthomas Waterford 14 D3
Kilmaganny Kilkenny 10 B6
Kilmaine Mayo 4 D6
Kilmaley Clare 8 D4
Kilmanagh Kilkenny 10 B5
Kilmeague Kildare 10 D2
Kilmeedy Limerick 9 E 6
Kilmichael Pt Wexford 11 F 5
Kilmihill Clare 8 D5
Kilmona Cork 13 H3
Kilmore Quay Wexford 15 G3
Kilmurry Clare 9 F 4
Kilmurry McMahon Clare 8 D5
Kilnaleck Cavan 6 B4
Kilrea Derry 3 E 4
Kilorglin Kerry 12 D2
Kilreekill Galway 9 G2
Kilronan Galway 8 C2
Kilross Tipperary 9 G6
Kilrush Clare 8 C5
Kilsaran Louth 7 E 4
Kilsheelan Tipperary 14 D2
Kiltartan Galway 9 E 3
Kiltealy Wexford 10 D6
Kilteel Kildare 11 E 2
Kiltegan Wicklow 11 E 4
Kiltimagh Mayo 5 E 4
Kiltoom Roscommon 5 H6
Kiltormer Galway 9 G2
Kiltulla Galway 9 F 2
Kiltullagh, L Galway 5 F 6
Kiltyclogher Leitrim 5 H1
Kilworth Cork 14 A3
Kilworth Mts Cork 14 A3
Kinale, L Longford 6 B5
Kings R Kilkenny 10 B6
Kingscourt Cavan 6 D4
Kinlough Leitrim 1 G6
Kinnegad Westmeath 6 C6
Kinnitty Offaly 10 A3
Kinsale Cork 13 H5
Kinsale Harbour Cork 13 H5
Kinsale, Old Head of Cork 13 H5
Kinsalebeg Waterford 14 C4
Kinvara Galway 9 E 2
Kippure, mt Wicklow 11 E 2
Kircubbin Down 3 H6
Kitmurvy Galway 8 B2
Knightstown Kerry 12 B3
Knock Clare 8 D5
Knock Mayo 5 E 4
Knockacummer, mt Cork 13 F 2
Knockaderry Limerick 8 E 6
Knockadoon Hd Cork 14 D5
Knockalla Mt Donegal 2 A2
Knockalongy, mt Sligo 5 F 2
Knockanaffrin Waterford 14 D3
Knockananna Wicklow 11 E 4
Knockanarrigan Wicklow 11 E 3
Knockanefeune Kerry 13 E 2
Knockanevin Cork 13 H1
Knockboy, mt Cork/Kerry 13 E 4
Knockbrack, mt Kerry 13 E 3
Knockbrandon Wexford 11 E 5
Knockbrett Tipperary 10 A6
Knockcroghery Roscommon 5 H6
Knockfeha, mt Kerry 13 E 2
Knocklayd, mt Antrim 3 E 2
Knockmealdown Mts
Tipperary/Waterford 14 B3
Knockmore Mayo 4 D3
Knocknaboul Kerry 13 E 2
Knocknadober, mt Kerry 12 B3
Knocknagashel Kerry 13 E 1
Knocknagree Cork 13 F 2
Knocknagullion, mt Kerry 12 D4
Knocknalina Mayo 4 B2
Knocknamaddree, mt Cork 12 D6
Knocknaskagh, mt Cork 13 H3
Knocktopher Kilkenny 10 C6

Labasheeda Clare 8 D5
Lack Fermanagh 2 B6
Lady's Island L Wexford 15 G3
Lagan, R Down/Antrim 3 F 6
Lagan, R Down/Antrim 7 F 1
Laghey Donegal 1 G5
Laghtgeorge Galway 9 E 1
Lahardane Mayo 4 D3
Lahinch Clare 8 D4
Lambay I Dublin 7 G6
Lamb's Hd Kerry 12 B4
Lanesborough Longford 5 H5
Laragh Wicklow 11 F 3
Larne Antrim 3 G4
Larne L Antrim 3 G4
Laune, R Kerry 12 D2
Lauragh Kerry 12 D4
Lawrencetown Down 7 E 1
Leane, L Kerry 12 D3
Leap Cork 13 F 5
Lecarrow Roscommon 5 H6
Leckaun Leitrim 5 G2
Lee, R Cork 13 G4
Leenane Galway 4 C6
Legionel Antrim 3 F 5
Leighlinbridge Carlow 10 D5
Leinster, Mt Wexford 10 D5
Leitrim Leitrim 5 H3
Leixlip Kildare 11 E 1
Lemybrien Waterford 14 D3
Lenadoon Pt Sligo 5 E 2
Lene, L Westmeath 6 C5
Letterbreen Fermanagh 6 A2
Letterfrack Galway 4 B6
Letterkenny Donegal 1 H4
Lettermacaward Donegal 1 G4
Lettermullan Galway 8 C2
Levally L Mayo 4 D3
Liffey, R Leinster 11 E 1
Lifford Donegal 2 B4
Limavady Derry 2 C3
Limerick Limerick 9 F 5
Lisacul Roscommon 5 F 4
Lisbellaw Fermanagh 6 B2
Lisburn Antrim 3 F 6
Liscannor Clare 8 D3
Liscannor B 8 C4
Liscarney Mayo 4 C5
Liscarroll Cork 13 G2
Lisdoonvarna Clare 8 D3
Lismore Waterford 14 B3
Lisnagary Limerick 9 F 5
Lisnakill Waterford 15 E 3
Lisnaskea Fermanagh 6 B2
Lispole Kerry 12 C2
Lisryan Longford 6 B5
Lissatinning Bridge Kerry 12 C3
Lissycasey Clare 8 D5
Listerlin Kilkenny 15 E 2
Listowel Kerry 8 C6
Lit. Brosna, R Offaly 9 H2
Littleton Tipperary 10 A5
Lixnaw Kerry 8 C6
Loch Garman *see* Wexford
Loch Gowna Cavan 6 B4
Lochglinn Roscommon 5 F 4
Loghill Limerick 8 D5
Londonderry Derry 2 B3
Longford Longford 6 A5
Loop Hd Clare 8 B6
Lough Key Forest Park
Roscommon 5 H3
Loughbrickland Down 7 E 1
Loughermore, mt Derry 2 C3
Loughgall Armagh 7 E 1
Loughlinstown Dublin 11 F 2
Loughrea Galway 9 F 2
Loughros More B Donegal 1 F 4
Loughsalt Mt Donegal 1 H3
Louisburgh Mayo 4 B5
Loup, The Derry 3 E 5
Louth Louth 7 E 4
Lucan Dublin 11 E 1
Lugnaquillia Mt Wicklow 11 E 3
Luimneach *see* Limerick
Lukeswell Kilkenny 15 E 2
Lurgan Armagh 3 E 6
Lusk Dublin 7 F 6
Lyracrompane Kerry 13 E 1

Maam Galway 4 C6
Maam Cross Galway 4 C6
Maas Donegal 1 G4
Macgillicuddy's Reeks, mts
Kerry 12 D3
Macnean Lower, L Fermanagh 6 A2
Macnean Upper, L Ulster 5 H2
Macosquin Derry 2 D3
Macroom Cork 13 F 4
McSwynes B Donegal 1 F 5
Magharee Is *see* Seven Hogs, The
Maghera Derry 2 D4
Magherafelt Derry 2 D5
Magheralin Down 3 F 6
Maghery Armagh 3 E 6
Magilligan Pt Derry 2 C2
Maguiresbridge Fermanagh 6 B2
Mahoonagh Limerick 9 E 6
Maigue, R Limerick 9 E 6
Main, R Antrim 3 E 4
Maine, R Kerry 12 D2
Mal B Clare 8 C4
Mala *see* Mallow
Malahide Dublin 7 F 6
Malin Donegal 2 B2
Malin B Donegal 1 E 5
Malin Hd Donegal 2 B1
Malin More Donegal 1 E 5
Mallow Cork 13 G2
Mangerton Mt Kerry 13 E 3
Mannin B Galway 4 A6
Mannin L Mayo 5 E 4
Manorcunningham Donegal 2 A4
Manorhamilton Leitrim 5 G2
Manulla Mayo 4 D4
Markethill Armagh 7 E 2
Mask, L Galway/Mayo 4 D5
Maumakeagh, mt Mayo 4 C2
Maumtrasna, mt Mayo 4 C5
Maumturk Mountains Galway 4 C6
Maynooth Kildare 11 E 1
Meentullynagarn Donegal 1 F 5
Melvin, L Leit/Ferm 5 G1
Mew I Down 3 H5
Middletown Armagh 6 D2
Midleton Cork 14 B5
Mile House Wexford 11 E 6
Milestone Tipperary 9 H5
Milford Armagh 6 D1
Milford Cork 13 G1
Milford Donegal 2 A3
Millbrook Meath 6 C5
Millisle Down 3 H5
Millstreet Cork 13 F 3
Millstreet Waterford 14 C3
Milltown Cavan 6 B3
Milltown Galway 5 E 5
Milltown Kerry 12 B2
Milltown Kerry 12 D2
Milltown Kildare 10 D2
Miltown Malbay Clare 8 D4
Minane Bridge Cork 14 A6
Mine Hd Waterford 14 D4
Mine Head Waterford 14 D4
Mitchelstown Cork 14 A3
Mizen Hd Cork 12 D6
Mizen Hd Wicklow 11 F 4
Moate Westmeath 10 A1
Moher, Cliffs of Clare 8 C4

Mohil *Leitrim* 5 H4
Mohill *Kilkenny* 10 C5
Moira *Down* 3 F6
Monaghan *Monaghan* 6 C2
Monalty L *Monaghan* 6 D3
Monasterevan *Kildare* 10 C2
Monavullagh Mts *Waterford* 14 C3
Moneygall *Offaly* 9 H4
Moneymore *Derry* 2 D5
Moneyneany *Derry* 2 D4
Moneyrea *Down* 3 G6
Monivea *Galway* 9 F1
Mooncoin *Kilkenny* 15 E3
Moone *Kildare* 10 D3
Moore B *Clare* 8 B5
Moorfields *Antrim* 3 F4
Morley's Bridge *Kerry* 13 E3
Moss-side *Antrim* 3 E2
Mount Bellew *Galway* 5 F6
Mount Hamilton *Tyrone* 2 C4
Mount Nugent *Cavan* 6 C4
Mount Talbot *Roscommon* 5 G6
Mountcharles *Donegal* 1 G5
Mountcollins *Limerick* 13 F1
Mountjoy *Tyrone* 2 B5
Mountmellick *Laois* 10 B3
Mountnorris *Armagh* 7 E2
Mountrath *Laois* 10 B3
Mountshannon *Clare* 9 G4
Mourne, L *Donegal* 1 H5
Mourne Mountains *Down* 7 F2
Mourne, R *Tyrone* 2 B5
Moville *Donegal* 2 C2
Moy *Tyrone* 2 D6
Moy, R *Mayo/Sligo* 5 E3
Moyard *Galway* 4 B6
Moyasta *Clare* 8 C5
Moycullen *Galway* 8 D1
Moyer, mt *Cavan* 6 D4
Moyett *Cavan* 6 C4
Moygawnagh *Mayo* 4 D2
Moylough *Galway* 5 F6
Moynalty *Meath* 6 D4
Moyne *Roscommon* 6 A4
Moyola, R *Derry* 2 D4
Moyrus *Galway* 8 B1
Moyvalley *Kildare* 10 D1
Moyvore *Westmeath* 6 A6
Moyvoughly *Westmeath* 10 A1
Muckish Mt *Donegal* 1 H3
Muckno L *Monaghan* 6 D3
Muckross *Kerry* 13 E3
Muckross H *Donegal* 1 F5
Muff *Donegal* 2 B3
Muine Bheag *Carlow* 10 D5
Muineachán *see* Monaghan
Mullagh *Clare* 8 C4
Mullagh *Galway* 9 G2
Mullaghaboy *Antrim* 3 G4
Mullaghaneany, mt *Derry/Tyrone* 2 C4
Mullaghanish, mt *Kerry/Cork* 13 F3
Mullaghareirk, mt *Cork* 13 F1
Mullaghareirk Mts *Cork* 13 F1
Mullaghbeg, mt *Kerry* 12 C4
Mullaghcarn, mt *Tyrone* 2 C5
Mullaghcleevaun, mt *Wicklow* 11 E3
Mullaghcloga, mt *Tyrone* 2 C4
Mullaghroe *Sligo* 5 G3
Mullaghmore, mt *Derry* 2 D4
Mullan *Fermanagh* 6 A2
Mullany's Cross *Sligo* 5 E3
Mullet, The pen *Mayo* 4 A2
Mullinavat *Kilkenny* 15 E2
Mullingar *Westmeath* 6 B6
Mulrany *Mayo* 4 B4
Mulroy B *Donegal* 1 H2
Mungret *Limerick* 9 F5
Muntervary *see* Sheep's Hd
Murrisk, mts *Mayo* 4 B5
Murroogh *Clare* 8 D2
Musheramore, mt *Cork* 13 F3
Mutton I *Clare* 8 C4
Mweelrea, mt *Mayo* 4 B5
Mweenish I *Galway* 8 B1
Myshall *Carlow* 10 D5

Naas *Kildare* 10 D2
Nacung, L *Donegal* 1 G3
Nagles Mts *Cork* 13 H2
Narin *Donegal* 1 F4
Naul *Dublin* 7 F6
Neagh, L *N Ireland* 3 E5
Neale *Mayo* 4 D6
Nenagh *Tipperary* 9 G4
Nephin Beg, mt *Mayo* 4 C3
Nephin Beg Range *Mayo* 4 C3
Nephin, mt *Mayo* 4 D3
New Birmingham *Tipperary* 10 A5
New Buildings *Derry* 2 B4
New Inn *Cavan* 6 C4
New Inn *Laois* 10 C3
New Inn *Tipperary* 10 A6
New Kildimo *Limerick* 9 E5
New Ross *Wexford* 15 F2
Newbliss *Monaghan* 6 C2
Newbridge *Galway* 5 G6
Newbridge *Limerick* 9 E6
Newcastle *Down* 7 G2
Newcastle *Dublin* 11 E1
Newcastle *Tipperary* 14 C3
Newcastle *Wicklow* 11 F3
Newcastle West *Limerick* 9 E6
Newmarket *Cork* 13 F2
Newmarket *Kilkenny* 10 C6
Newmarket-on-Fergus *Clare* 9 E4
Newport *Mayo* 4 C4
Newport *Tipperary* 9 G5
Newport Trench *Tyrone* 3 E5
Newry *Down* 7 E2
Newry Canal *Down* 7 E1
Newton Crommelin *Antrim* 3 F3
Newtonards *Down* 3 G6
Newtown *Limerick* 13 G1
Newtown *Offaly* 9 H2
Newtown *Tipperary* 9 G6
Newtown Hamilton *Armagh* 7 E2
Newtownabbey *Antrim* 3 G5
Newtownbreda *Down* 3 G6
Newtownbutler *Fermanagh* 6 B2
Newtowncunningham *Donegal* 2 B3
Newtownforbes *Longford* 6 A5
Newtowngore *Leitrim* 6 A3
Newtownmountkennedy *Wicklow* 11 F3
Newtownstewart *Tyrone* 2 B5
Ninemilehouse *Tipperary* 10 B6
Nobber *Meath* 6 D4
Nohoval *Cork* 13 H5
North Ring *Cork* 13 G5
North Sound *Galway* 8 B2
Nowen Hill *Cork* 13 F5
Nurney *Carlow* 10 D5
Nurney *Kildare* 10 D3
Nutt's Corner *Antrim* 3 F5

O'Brien's Bridge *Clare* 9 F5
O'Flyn, L *Roscommon* 5 F5
Oily, R *Donegal* 1 F5
Old Leighlin *Carlow* 10 C5
Oldcastle *Meath* 6 C5
Oldtown *Dublin* 7 F6
Omagh *Tyrone* 2 B6
Omeath *Louth* 7 F3
Omey I *Galway* 4 A6
Oola *Limerick* 9 G6
Oran *Roscommon* 5 G5
Oranmore *Galway* 9 E2
Oristown *Meath* 6 D5
Oughter, L *Cavan* 6 B3
Oughterard *Galway* 4 D6
Oulart *Wexford* 11 E6
Ovens *Cork* 13 G4
Owel, L *Westmeath* 6 B6
Owena, R *Donegal* 1 G4
Owenbeg *Sligo* 5 E2
Owenduff, R *Mayo* 4 B3
Oweniny *Mayo* 4 C2
Owenmore, R *Mayo* 4 C2
Owenreagh, R *Tyrone* 2 B6
Owey I *Donegal* 1 F3
Ox Mountains *see* Slieve Gamph
Oylgate *Wexford* 11 E6

Pallas Green *Limerick* 9 G6
Pallaskenry *Limerick* 9 E5
Paps, The, mts *Kerry* 13 E3
Park *Derry* 2 C4
Parknasilla *Kerry* 12 C4
Partry *Mayo* 4 D5
Partry Mts *Mayo* 4 C5
Passage East *Waterford* 15 E3
Passage West *Cork* 13 H4
Patrickswell *Limerick* 9 F5
Peakeen Mt *Kerry* 12 D3
Pettigo *Fermanagh* 1 H6
Piltown *Kilkenny* 14 D2
Plumbridge *Tyrone* 2 C5
Pocket, The, mt *Kerry* 12 C3
Pomeroy *Tyrone* 2 D6
Pontoon *Mayo* 4 D3
Port Láirge *see* Waterford
Port Laoise *Laois* 10 B3
Portadown *Armagh* 7 E1
Portaferry *Down* 7 H1
Portarlington *Laois* 10 C2
Portavogie *Down* 7 H1
Portglenone *Antrim* 3 E4
Porthallintrae *Antrim* 3 E2
Portland *Tipperary* 9 G3
Portlaw *Waterford* 14 D3
Portmagee *Kerry* 12 B4
Portnoo *Donegal* 1 F4
Portrane *Dublin* 7 F6
Portroe *Tipperary* 9 G4
Portrush *Antrim* 2 D2
Portsalon *Donegal* 2 A2
Portstewart *Derry* 2 D2
Portumna *Galway* 9 G3
Portumna Forest Park *Galway/Tipperary* 9 G3
Porturlin *Mayo* 4 C1
Poulgorm Bridge *Kerry* 13 E3
Power Hd *Cork* 14 B5
Power's Cross *Galway* 9 G3
Poyntzpass *Armagh* 7 E2
Prince William's Seat *Dublin* 11 F2
Prosperous *Kildare* 10 D2
Puckane *Tipperary* 9 G4
Purple Mt *Kerry* 12 D3

Quin *Clare* 9 E4
Quoile, R *Down* 7 G1

Raford, R *Galway* 9 F2
Raghtin More, mt *Donegal* 2 B2
Raharney *Westmeath* 6 C6
Ramor, L *Cavan* 6 C4
Ramsgate *Wexford* 15 F3
Randalstown *Antrim* 3 E5
Rasharkin *Antrim* 3 E3
Rath *Offaly* 10 A2
Ráth Luirc *Cork* 13 G1
Rathangan *Kildare* 10 C2
Rathconrath *Westmeath* 6 B6
Rathcoole *Dublin* 11 E2
Rathcormac *Cork* 14 A4
Rathdangan *Wicklow* 11 E4
Rathdowney *Laois* 10 B4
Rathdrum *Wicklow* 11 F3
Rathfarnham *Dublin* 11 E1
Rathfriland *Down* 7 F2
Rathgormuck *Waterford* 14 D2
Rathkeale *Limerick* 9 E6
Rathkeevin *Tipperary* 14 C2
Rathlackan *Mayo* 4 D2
Rathlee *Sligo* 5 E2
Rathlin I *Antrim* 3 F2
Rathlin O'Birne I. *Donegal* 1 E5
Rathmelton *Donegal* 2 A3
Rathmolyon *Meath* 6 D6
Rathmore *Kerry* 13 F3
Rathmullen *Donegal* 2 B3
Rathnew *Wicklow* 11 F3
Rathnure *Wexford* 10 D6
Rathowen *Westmeath* 6 B5
Rathvilly *Carlow* 10 D4
Ratoath *Meath* 7 E6
Raphoe *Donegal* 2 A4
Rea, L *Galway* 9 F2
Reanagowan *Kerry* 13 E1
Rear Cross *Tipperary* 9 G5
Recess *Galway* 4 C6
Red B *Antrim* 3 F3
Redcross *Wicklow* 11 F4
Redhills *Cavan* 6 B3
Ree, Lough *R'common/Long/W'meath* 5 H6
Rhode *Offaly* 10 C1
Richhill *Armagh* 7 E1
Ring *Waterford* 14 D4
Ringsend *Derry* 2 D3
Rinn L *Leitrim* 6 A4
Riverstown *Sligo* 5 G3
Roaringwater Bay *Cork* 13 E6
Robe, R *Mayo* 4 D5
Rochfort Bridge *Westmeath* 10 B1
Rockchapel *Cork* 13 F1
Rockcorry *Monaghan* 6 C3
Rockhill *Limerick* 9 F6
Roe, R *Derry* 2 C3
Roosky *Roscommon* 5 H4
Rosapenna *Donegal* 1 H2
Rosbeg *Donegal* 1 F4
Rosbercon *Tipperary* 15 F2
Roscommon *Roscommon* 5 G5
Roscrea *Tipperary* 10 A3
Rosegreen *Tipperary* 10 A6
Rosenallis *Laois* 10 B2
Rosroe, L *Clare* 9 E4
Rossan Pt *Donegal* 1 E5
Rosscahill *Galway* 8 D1
Rosscarbery *Cork* 13 F5
Rossduff *Waterford* 15 E3
Rosses B *Donegal* 1 F3
Rosses Point *Sligo* 5 F1
Rosses, The, reg *Donegal* 1 F3
Rossinver *Leitrim* 5 H1
Rosslare *Wexford* 15 G3
Rosslare Harbour *Wexfod* 15 H3
Rosslare Pt *Wexford* 15 H2
Rosslea *Fermanagh* 6 C2
Rossmore Forest Park *Monaghan* 6 C2
Rossnowlagh *Donegal* 1 G6
Rostellan *Cork* 14 A5
Rostrevor *Down* 7 F3
Roughty, R *Kerry* 13 E4
Roundstone *Galway* 8 B1
Roundwood *Wicklow* 11 F3
Royal Canal *Longford* 6 A5
Runabay Hd *Antrim* 3 F2
Rush *Dublin* 7 F6
Saggart *Dublin* 11 E2
Saintfield *Down* 3 G6
St. Finan's B *Kerry* 12 B4
St John's L. *Leitrim* 5 H3
St. John's Pt *Donegal* 1 F6
St. John's Pt *Down* 7 G2
St. Johnston *Donegal* 2 B4
Saliahig *Kerry* 12 C4
Sallins *Kildare* 10 D2
Sallybrook *Cork* 13 H3
Saltee Is *Wexford* 15 G3
Sandyford *Dublin* 11 F2
Sawel, mt *Derry/Tyrone* 2 C4
Scalp Mt *Donegal* 2 B3
Scalp, mt *Galway* 9 F3
Scarriff *Clare* 9 F4
Scariff I *Kerry* 12 B4
Scartaglen *Kerry* 13 E2
Scarva *Down* 7 E1
Scattery I *Clare* 8 C5
Schull *Cork* 12 D6
Scotch Corner *Monaghan* 6 D2
Scotstown *Monaghan* 6 C2
Scramoge *Roscommon* 5 H5
Screeb *Galway* 8 C1
Screggan *Offaly* 10 B2
Seapatrick *Down* 7 F1
Seefin *Cork* 12 D5
Seefin, mt *Cork* 13 F3
Seefin, mt *Kerry* 12 C3
Seefin, mt *Waterford* 14 C3
Seven Heads, pt *Cork* 13 G6
Seven Hogs, The *Kerry* 12 C1
Shanacrane *Cork* 13 F4
Shanagarry *Cork* 14 B5
Shanagolden *Limerick* 8 D6
Shanavogh *Clare* 8 D4
Shannon *Clare* 9 E5
Shannon, Mouth of the *Irish Rep.* 8 B6
Shannon R *Irish Rep* 9 G2
Shannonbridge *Offaly* 9 H2
Shantonagh *Monaghan* 6 D3
Shanvus *Leitrim* 5 G2
Sharavogue *Offaly* 10 A3
Sheddings, The *Antrim* 3 F4
Sheelin, Lough *Cavan/Meath/W'meath* 6 B4
Sheep Haven, B *Donegal* 1 H1
Sheep's Hd *Cork* 12 C6
Shehy Mts *Cork* 13 E4
Shercock *Cavan* 6 D3
Sherkin I *Cork* 13 E6
Shillelagh *Wicklow* 11 E5
Shinrone *Offaly* 9 H3
Shrule *Mayo* 5 E6
Silent Valley Resr. *Down* 7 F2
Sillan L *Cavan* 6 D3
Silver, R *Offaly* 10 A2
Silvermines *Tipperary* 9 G4
Sion Mills *Tyrone* 2 B4
Six Road Ends *Down* 3 H5
Sixmilebridge *Clare* 9 E5
Sixmilecross *Tyrone* 2 C6
Skellig Rock *Kerry* 12 A4
Skerries *Dublin* 7 F6
Skibereen *Cork* 13 E6
Slane *Meath* 7 E5
Slaney, R *Wexford* 11 E6
Slea Hd *Kerry* 12 B2
Slemish Mt *Antrim* 3 F4
Slievanea *Kerry* 12 B2
Slieve Anierin, mt *Leitrim* 5 H3
Slieve Aughty Mts *Galway* 9 F3
Slieve Beagh, mt *Tyrone* 6 C1
Slieve Bernagh, mts *Clare* 9 F5
Slieve Bloom Mountains *Offaly/Laois* 10 A3
Slieve Callan, mt *Clare* 8 D4
Slieve Car, mt *Mayo* 4 C3
Slieve Croob, mt *Down* 7 F1
Slieve Donard, mt *Down* 7 G2
Slieve Elva, mt *Clare* 8 D3
Slieve Gallion, mt *Derry* 2 D5
Slieve Gamph, mts *Mayo/Sligo* 5 E3
Slieve Gullion, mt *Armagh* 7 E3
Slieve League, mt *Donegal* 1 E5
Slieve Meelbeg, mt *Down* 7 F2
Slieve Mish Mountains *Kerry* 12 C2
Slieve Miskish Mts *Cork* 12 C5
Slieve More, mt *Mayo* 4 B3
Slieve na Calliagh, mt *Meath* 6 C5
Slieve Rushen, mt Fermanagh 6 A2
Slieve Snacht, mt *Donegal* 1 G3
Slieve Snaght, mt *Donegal* 2 B2
Slieveanarra, mt *Antrim* 3 F3
Slieveardagh Hills *Tipperary* 10 B5
Slievefelim Mts *Limerick* 9 G5
Slievekimalta *Tipperary* 9 G5
Slievekirk, mt *Derry* 2 B4
Slievenakilla, mt *Cavan* 5 H2
Slievenamuck, mt *Tipperary* 9 G6
Slievetooey, mt *Donegal* 1 F5
Sligeach see Sligo
Sligo *Sligo* 5 G2
Sligo B *Sligo* 5 F2
Slyne Hd *Galway* 8 A1
Smerwick Harbour *Kerry* 12 B2

Smithborough	Monaghan	6 C2
Snave Bridge	Cork	13 E5
Sneem	Kerry	12 C4
South Sound	Galway	8 C3
Spa	Kerry	12 D1
Sperrin Mountains		
	Derry/Tyrone	2 C5
Spiddle	Galway	8 D2
Spink	Laois	10 C4
Srah	Mayo	4 D5
Stacks Mts	Kerry	12 D1
Stewartstown	Tyrone	2 D6
Stoneyford	Kilkenny	10 C6
Strabane	Tyrone	2 B4
Stradbally	Kerry	12 C2
Stradbally	Laois	10 C3
Stradbally	Waterford	14 D3
Stradone	Cavan	6 C3
Strandhill	Sligo	5 F2
Strangford	Down	7 H1
Strangford L	Down	3 H6
Stranocum	Antrim	3 E3
Stranorlar	Donegal	1 H4
Stratford	Wicklow	10 D3
Strokestown	Roscommon	5 H5
Strule, R	Tyrone	2 B5
Suck, R	Galway/R'common	5 G6
Sugarloaf Mt	Cork	12 D5
Suir, R	Munster	15 E3
Sullane, R	Cork	13 F4
Summerhill	Meath	6 D6
Swan	Laois	10 C4
Swanlinbar	Cavan	6 A2
Swatragh	Derry	2 D4
Swilly, Lough	Donegal	2 B2
Swilly, R	Donegal	2 B3
Swinford	Mayo	5 E4
Swords	Dublin	7 F6
Sybil Pt	Kerry	12 A2
Table Mt	Wicklow	11 E3
Taghmon	Wexford	15 G2
Tall, R	Armagh	7 E1
Tallaght	Dublin	11 E2

Tallow	Waterford	14 B4
Tallowbridge	Waterford	14 B4
Talt, L	Sligo	5 E3
Tamlaght	Fermanagh	6 B1
Tamney	Donegal	2 A2
Tandragee	Armagh	7 E1
Tang	Westmeath	6 A6
Tar, R	Tipperary	14 C3
Tara, Hill of	Meath	7 E6
Tarbert	Kerry	8 D6
Tassagh	Armagh	6 D2
Taur, mt	Cork	13 F2
Tawin I	Galway	9 E2
Tearaght I	Kerry	12 A3
Templeboy	Sligo	5 F2
Templehouse, L	Sligo	5 F3
Templenoe	Kerry	12 D4
Templepatrick	Antrim	3 F5
Templetouhy	Tipperary	10 A4
Tempo	Fermanagh	6 B1
Termonfeckin	Louth	7 F5
Terryglass	Tipperary	9 G3
Thomastown	Kilkenny	10 C6
Three Castle Hd	Cork	12 C6
Thurles	Tipperary	10 A5
Tiltibane, mt	Cavan	6 A2
Timahoe	Kildare	10 D1
Timahoe	Laois	10 C3
Timoleague	Cork	13 G5
Timolin	Kildare	10 D3
Tinahely	Wicklow	11 E4
Tipperary	Tipperary	9 G6
Tober	Offaly	10 A1
Tobercurry	Sligo	5 F3
Tobermore	Derry	2 D4
Toberscanavan	Sligo	5 G2
Toe Head	Cork	13 E6
Togher	Cork	13 F4
Togher	Louth	7 F5
Togher	Offaly	10 A1
Tollymore Forest Park	Down	7 G2
Tomgraney	Clare	9 F4
Tonelagee, mt	Wicklow	11 E3
Toombeola	Galway	4 B6
Toomebridge	Antrim	3 E5

Toomyvara	Tipperary	9 H4
Toormore	Cork	12 D6
Tore Mt	Kerry	13 E3
Torr Hd	Antrim	3 F2
Tory I	Donegal	1 G2
Tory Sd	Donegal	1 G2
Trá Lí see Tralee		
Tralee	Kerry	12 D1
Tralee B	Kerry	12 C1
Tramore	Waterford	15 E3
Tramore Bay	Waterford	15 E4
Trawmore Bay	Mayo	4 B2
Trillick	Tyrone	2 B6
Trim	Meath	6 D6
Trostan, R	Antrim	3 F3
Truskmore, mt	Sligo	5 G1
Tuam	Galway	5 E6
Tulach Mhór see Tullamore		
Tulla	Clare	9 F4
Tullamore	Offaly	10 B2
Tullaroan	Kilkenny	10 B5
Tullow	Carlow	10 D4
Tullyallen	Louth	7 E5
Tullybrack	Fermanagh	6 A1
Tullycanna	Wexford	15 F3
Tullyhogue	Tyrone	2 D5
Tullynagrow	Monaghan	6 D2
Tulsk	Roscommon	5 G4
Tuskar Rock	Wexford	15 H3
Twelve Pins, The mts	Galway	4 B6
Two Rock Mt	Dublin	11 F2
Twomileborris	Tipperary	10 A5
Tydavnet	Monaghan	6 C2
Tyholland	Monaghan	6 D2
Tyrella	Down	7 G2
Ulster Canal		
	Armagh/Monaghan	6 B2
Union Hall	Cork	13 F6
Upperchurch	Tipperary	9 H5
Upperlands	Derry	2 D4
Urlaur L	Mayo	5 F4
Urlingford	Kilkenny	10 B5

Valencia I	Kerry	12 B3
Valleymount	Wicklow	11 E2
Varty Res.	Wicklow	11 F3
Ventry	Kerry	12 B2
Vicarstown	Laois	10 C3
Villierstown	Waterford	14 C4
Virginia	Cavan	6 C4
Waringstown	Down	3 E6
Warrenpoint	Down	7 F3
Waterford	Waterford	15 E3
Waterford Harbour		
	Waterford/Wexford	15 F3
Watergrasshill	Cork	14 A4
Waterside	Derry	2 B3
Waterville	Kerry	12 B4
Wattlebridge	Fermanagh	6 B3
Wellington Bridge		
	Wexford	15 F3
Westport	Mayo	4 C4
Westport Quay	Galway	4 C4
Wexford	Wexford	15 G2
Wexford B	Wexford	15 H2
Wexford Harbour	Wexford	15 G2
Whiddy I	Cork	12 D5
Whiteabbey	Antrim	3 G5
Whitegate	Cork	14 A5
Whitehall	Kilkenny	10 C5
Whitehead	Antrim	3 G5
Whitehouse	Antrim	3 G5
Wicklow	Wicklow	11 F3
Wicklow Hd	Wicklow	11 G3
Wicklow Mountains	Wicklow	11 E4
Wilkinstown	Meath	6 D5
Windgap	Kilkenny	10 B6
Woodenbridge	Wicklow	11 F4
Woodford	Galway	9 G3
Woodtown	Meath	6 D4
Youghal	Cork	14 C5
Youghal Bay	Cork/W'ford	14 C5

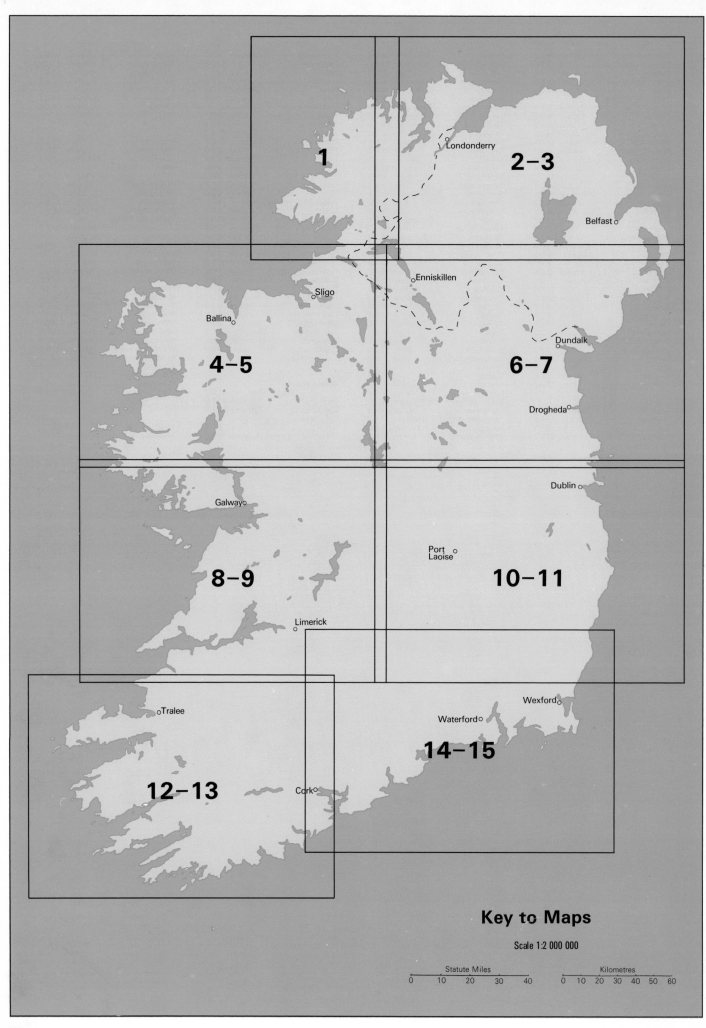

1

2–3

Londonderry

Belfast

Enniskillen

4–5

Sligo

Ballina

6–7

Dundalk

Drogheda

Dublin

Galway

8–9

Port
Laoise

10–11

Limerick

Tralee

Wexford

Waterford

14–15

12–13

Cork

Key to Maps

Scale 1:2 000 000

Statute Miles

0   10   20   30   40

Kilometres

0   10   20   30   40   50   60

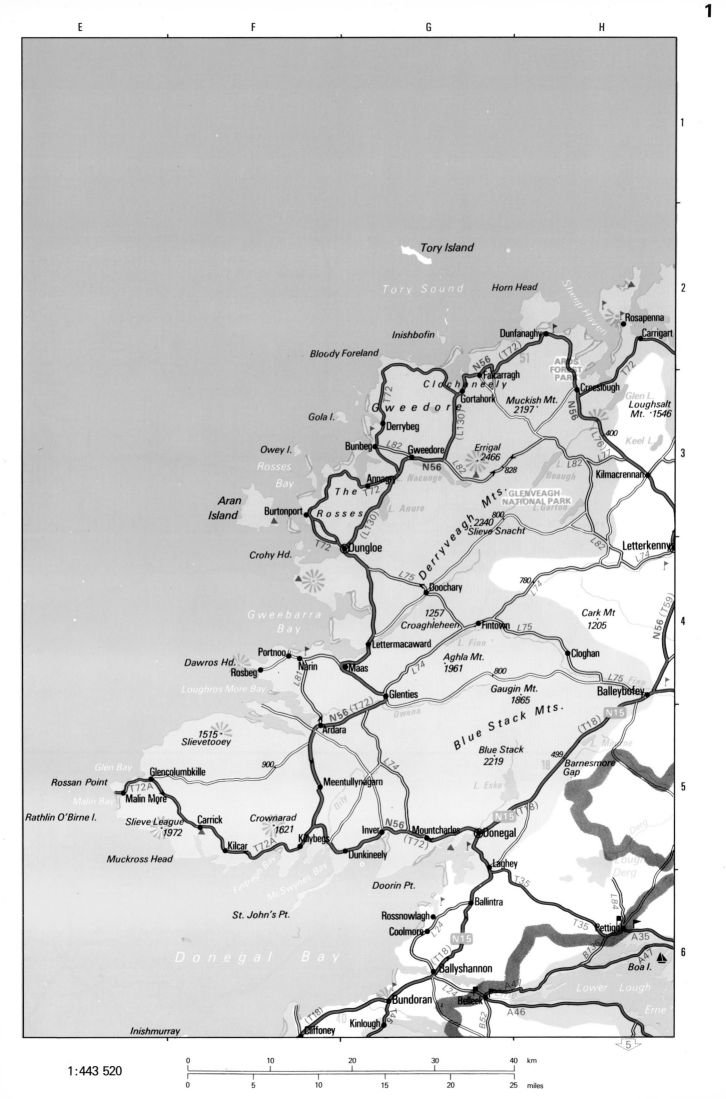

1 : 443 520

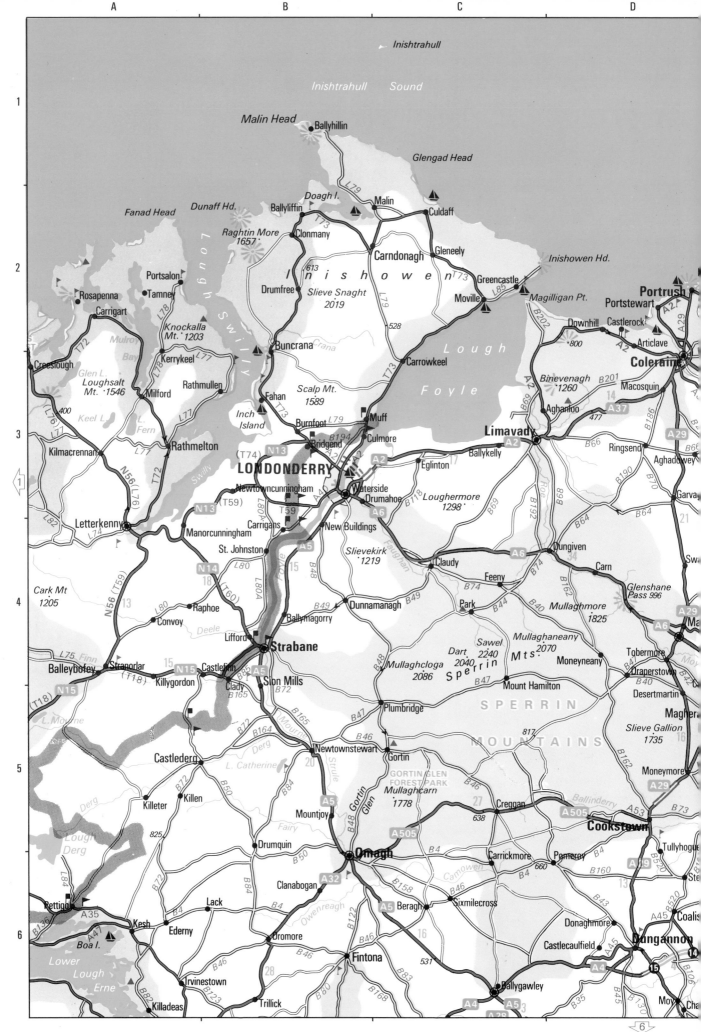

Inishtrahull

Inishtrahull Sound

Malin Head ● Ballyhillin

Glengad Head

Fanad Head

Dunaff Hd. Ballyliffin *Doagh I.* Malin ● Culdaff

Raghtin More 1657 Clonmany

Portsalon Carndonagh Gleneely *Inishowen Hd.*

Rosapenna Tamney *I n i s h o w e n* 613 Greencastle **Portrush**
Carrigart Drumfree *T73* Moville Portstewart
Slieve Snaght 2019 528 *Magilligan Pt.* Castlerock
Knockalla Mt. 1203 *L79* Downhill ●800 Articlave **Coleraine**
Kerrykeel Buncrana Carrowkeel Binevenagh 1260 Macosquin
Glen L. Loughsalt Mt. 1546 Milford *Crana* Aghanloo
Creeslough Rathmullan Rathmillen *Scalp Mt. 1589* *Lough Foyle* 477 Limavady B66 Ringsend
Kilmacrennan *Inch Island* Fahan Muff **Limavady** Aghadowey
Rathmelton Burnfoot Culmore Ballykelly Garva
L. Fern Bridgend Eglinton
Londonderry Waterside Loughermore 1298 Dungiven
Letterkenny Newtowncunningham Drumahoe A6 Carn
Manorcunningham New Buildings Claudy Glenshane Pass 996
Carrigans *Slievekirk 1219* Feeny Mullaghmore 1825
St. Johnston Dunnamanagh Park
Cark Mt. 1205 Raphoe Sawel 2240 Mullaghaneany 2070 Tobermore
Convoy Ballymagorry Dart 2040 Moneyneany Draperstown
Lifford **Strabane** Mullaghcloga 2086 *Sperrin Mts* Desertmartin
Balleybofey Castlefinn Mount Hamilton Magher
Straporlar Killygordon Clady *SPERRIN* Slieve Gallion 1735
Sion Mills 817 Moneymore
L. Mourne *MOUNTAINS*
Castlederg Newtownstewart Gortin
Killeter Killen *GORTIN GLEN FOREST PARK* Creggan Cookstown
Mullaghcarn 1778 Tullyhogu
825 Mountjoy
Drumquin **Omagh** Carrickmore Pomeroy
Pettigo Clanabogan Donaghmore **Dungannon**
Kesh Lack Beragh Sixmilecross Castlecaulfield
Ederny Dromore Coalis
Boa I. Fintona 531 Ballygawley Moy
Lower Lough Erne Irvinestown
Killadeas Trillick

1 : 443 520

E   F   G   H

Kilchenzie
Campbeltown
Machrihanish
Davarr I.
B843
B842
Southend

1

Bull Pt.
Rathlin Island
N O R T H
Mull of Kintyre
Sanda

bane Hd.
B146
t's
way
A2
Bushmills
B17
Moss-side
B67
ykeighan
Dervock
B62
B66
oney
B16
Rasharkin
B62
Portglenone
Cullybackey
Ballymena
Ahoghill
ellaghy
Toomebridge
Randalstown
Ballyronan
Loup
Newport Trench
Maghery
Lurgan
Craigavon
Waringstown

Ballintoy
B15
Ballycastle
A2
Ballyvoy
Fair Head
Torr Head
Runabay Head
Armoy
Stranocum
Knocklayd 1695
Cushendun
B92
1141 1676. Slieveanarra
Cushendall
Red Bay
Glenariff
1817 Trostan
B14
1364
Garron Pt.
GLENARIFF FOREST PARK
Clogh Mills
Newtown Crommelin
Collin Top 1426
Carnlough
Carnlough Bay
Clogh
Glenarm
623
The Sheddings
Broughshane
Slemish Mt. 1437
Ballygalley
Ballygalley Hd.
Carncastle
Drains Bay
B148
Larne
Glynn
Mullaghaboy Island
Magee
Moorfields
1025
Glenoe
Kells
Connor
928
Ballycarry
Black Hd.
Ballynure
Whitehead
Doagh
899
Ballyclare
Eden
Carrickfergus
Antrim
Templepatrick
Newtownabbey
Whiteabbey
Grey Pt.
Groomsport
Glengormley
Whitehouse
Crawfordsburn
Bangor
Donaghadee
Aldergrove
Nutt's Corner
985
Holywood
Six Road Ends
Millisle
Crumlin
Legoniel
Conlig
Glenavy
Divis 1574
Belfast
Dundonald
Newtownards
704
Newtownbreda
Comber
Ards
Dunmurry
Moneyrea
Ballywalter
Aghalee
Lisburn
Carryduff
Greyabbey
Peninsula
Moira
Ballygowan
Ballyhalbert
Magheralin
Kircubbin
Maghery
Hillsborough
Saintfield
Ardkeen
Portavogie
Cloughey

To Stranraer & Cairnryan

To Douglas & Liverpool

Mew I.
Copeland I.

Strangford Lough

Lough Neagh

2

3

4

5

6

7

| 0 | | 10 | | 20 | | 30 | | 40 km |

| 0 | 5 | 10 | 15 | 20 | 25 miles |

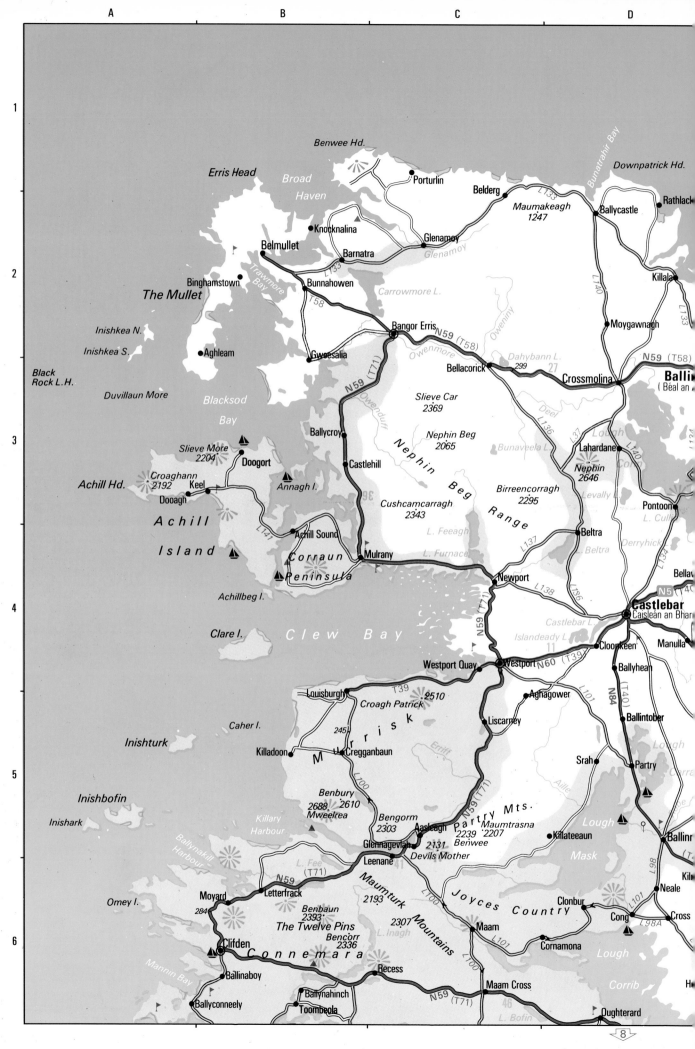

A B C D

1

2

3

4

5

6

Benwee Hd.

Erris Head

Broad
Haven

Porturlin
Belderg
L133
Downpatrick Hd.
Ballycastle
Rathlack
Maumakeagh
1247

Knocknalina
Glenamoy
Killala
Belmullet
Barnatra
L133
L140
Moygawnagh
L133
The Mullet
Bunnahowen
Carrowmore L.
Glenamoy

Binghamstown
T58
Owenmore

Inishkea N.
Bangor Erris
N59 (T58)
Dahybann L.
299
27
N59 (T58)
Inishkea S.
Aghleam
Gweesalia
Bellacorick
Crossmolina
Balli
Black
Rock L.H.
N59 (T71)
Owenmore
(Béal an

Duvillaun More
Blacksod
Bay
Owenduff
Slieve Car
2369
Deel
L137
Lough
Ballycroy
Nephin Beg
2065
Bunaveela L.
Lahardane
L140
Slieve More
2204
Doogort
L136
Nephin
2646
Croaghann
2192
Keel
Castlehill
Nephin Beg
Birreencorragh
2295
Pontoon
L. Cull
Achill Hd.
Dooagh
Annagh I.
Cushcamcarragh
2343
Range
Beltra
Derryhick
Achill
L141
36
L137
Achill Sound
L. Feeagh
Beltra
Island
Corraun
Mulrany
L. Furnace
Newport
L138
Bellav
Achillbeg I.
Peninsula
L386
N5 (T40)
N59 (T71)
Castlebar
Caisleán an Bhar
Clare I.
Clew Bay
Castlebar L.
Islandeady L.
11
Cloonkeen
Manulla
Westport Quay
Westport
N60 (T39)
Ballyhean
Louisburgh
T39
2510
Aghagower
L101
N84
Croagh Patrick
Liscarney
Ballintober
Caher I.
245
M *r* *r* *i* *s* *k*
Srah
Partry
Inishturk
Killadoon
Cregganbaun
L100
Erriff
Aille
L98
Inishbofin
Benbury
2688
2610
Mweelrea
Bengorm
2303
Partry Mts.
Maumtrasna
2239 2207
Lough
Killateeaun
Ballin
Inishark
Aasleagh
Benwee
Glennagevlah
2131
Mask
Kil
Killary
Harbour
Leenane
Devils Mother
Joyces
Neale
Ballynakill
L. Fee
(T71)
Maumturk
2193
L100
Country
Clonbur
L101
Cross
Omey I.
Moyard
Letterfrack
N59
Benbaun
2393
Mountains
2307
Maam
Cong
L98A
284
The Twelve Pins
Bencorr
2336
L. Inagh
L107
Cornamona
Lough
Clifden
Connemara
Recess
Maam Cross
Corrib
Ballinaboy
Ballynahinch
N59 (T71)
46
Oughterard
Ballyconneely
Toombeola
L. Bofin

8

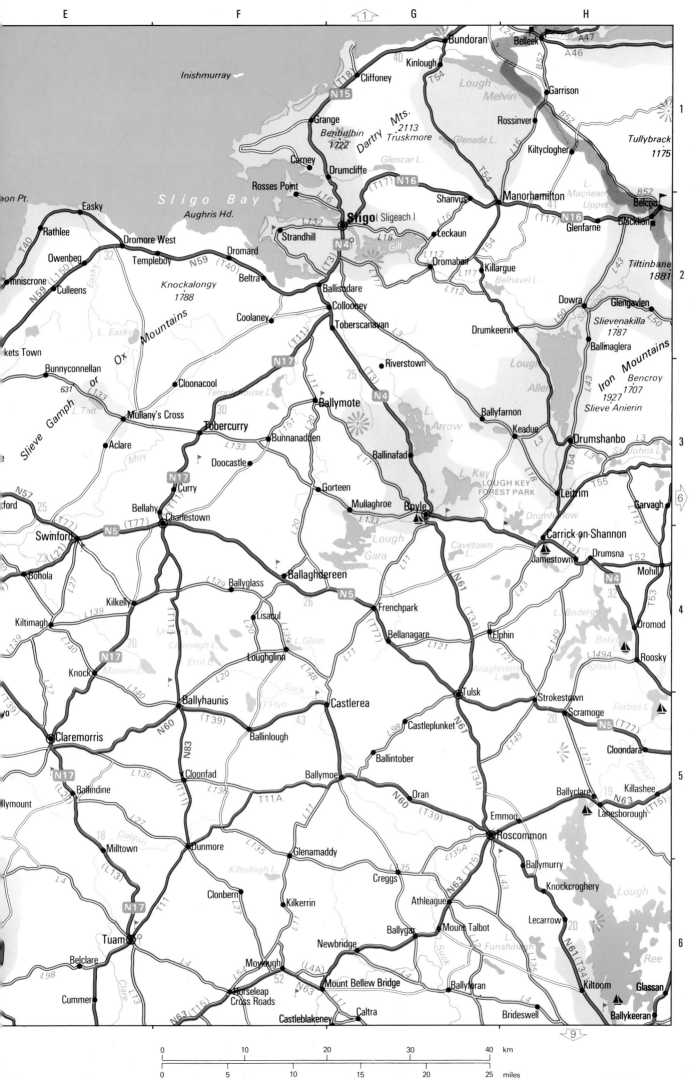

0   10   20   30   40   km

0   5   10   15   20   25   miles

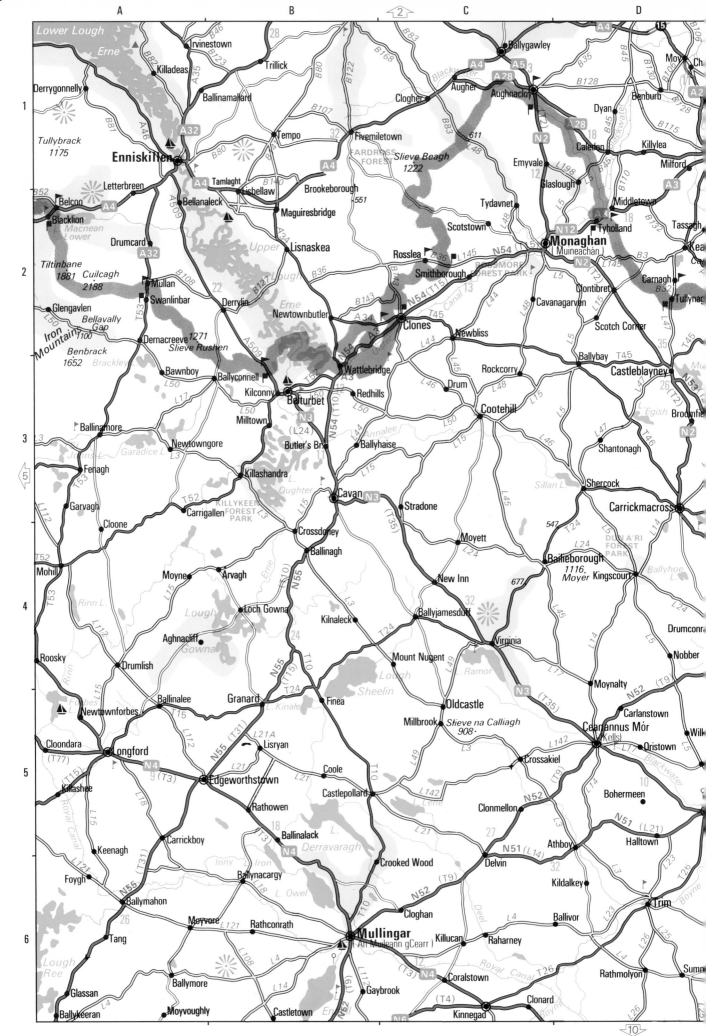

1:443 520

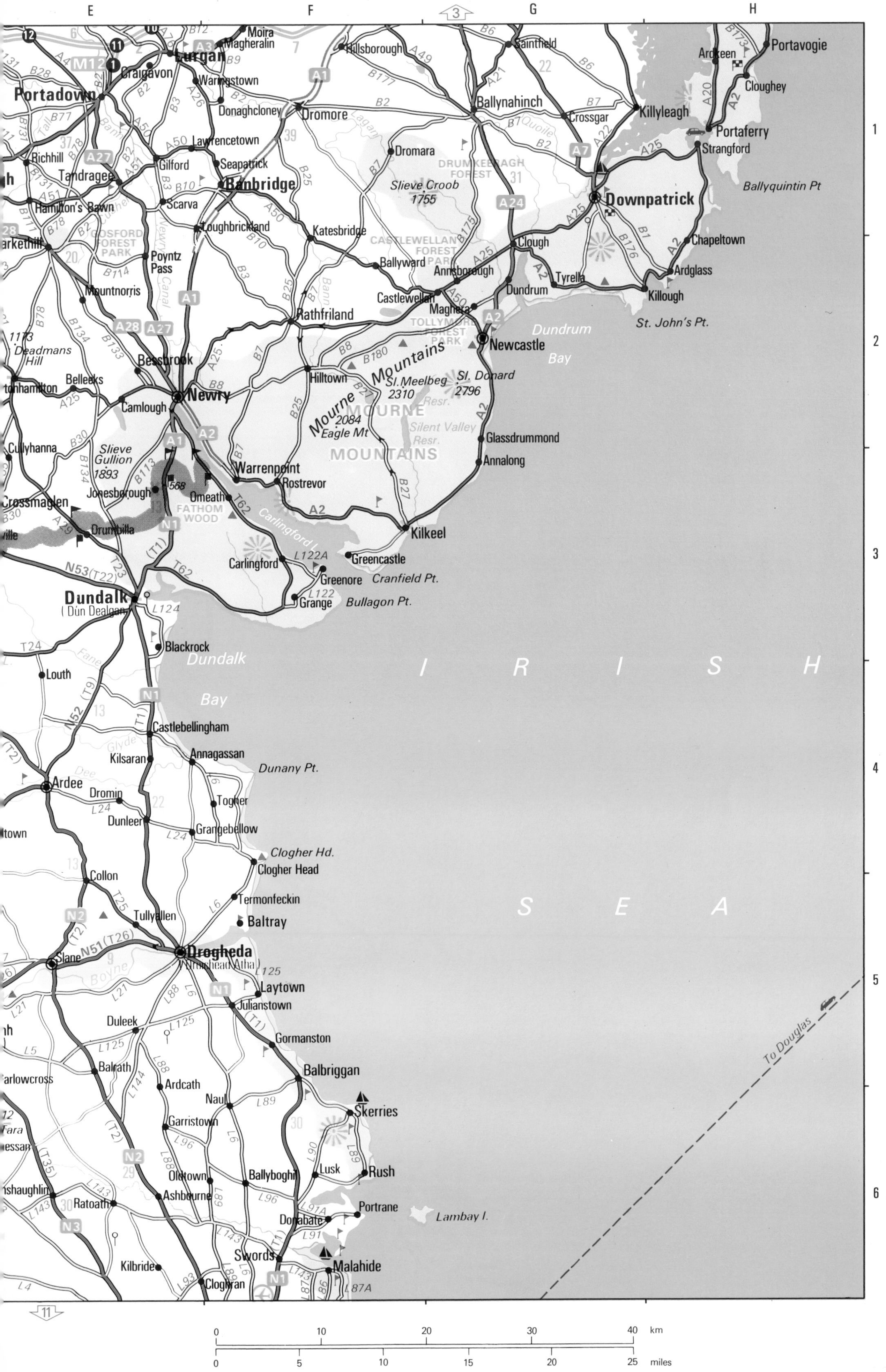

E F G H

12
11 M12
1
Portadown

Moira
Magheralin
Lurgan
Craigavon
Warringstown
Donaghcloney
Dromore
Hillsborough

Saintfield
Ballynahinch
Crossgar
Killyleagh

Ardkeen
Portavogie
Cloughey

Portaferry
Strangford

Richhill
Tandragee
Hamilton's Bawn
rkethill
Gilford
Seapatrick
Banbridge
Scarva
Loughbrickland
Katesbridge

Dromara
Slieve Croob
1755

DRUMKEERAGH FOREST

Downpatrick

Ballyquintin Pt.

Chapeltown

GOSFORD FOREST PARK
Poyntz Pass
Mountnorris

Rathfriland
Ballyward
Annsborough
Castlewellan
Maghera

CASTLEWELLAN FOREST PARK
Clough
Tyrella
Dundrum

Ardglass
Killough
St. John's Pt.

1173
Deadmans Hill
nhamilton
Belleeks
Bessbrook
Camlough
Newry

Hilltown

Mourne Mountains
Sl. Meelbeg 2310
Sl. Donard 2796

TOLLYMORE FOREST PARK
Newcastle

Dundrum Bay

Cullyhanna
Slieve Gullion 1893
Jonesborough
Omeath

Warrenpoint
Rostrevor

2084
Eagle Mt

MOURNE MOUNTAINS

Silent Valley Resr.

Glassdrummond
Annalong

Crossmaglen
ville
Drumbilla
FATHOM WOOD

Carlingford L.
Kilkeel

Dundalk
(Dún Dealgan)

Carlingford
Greenore
Grange

Greencastle
Cranfield Pt.
Bullagon Pt.

I R I S H

Blackrock

Louth
Dundalk Bay

Castlebellingham

Kilsaran
Annagassan
Dunany Pt.

Ardee
Dromin
Togher
Dunleer
Grangebellow

Collon
Clogher Hd.
Clogher Head

Termonfeckin

Tullyallen
Baltray

Slane
Drogheda
(Droichead Átha)

Laytown
Julianstown

Duleek
Gormanston

Balrath
Ardcath
Naul
Garristown

Balbriggan

Skerries

S E A

Oldtown
Ballyboghil
Ashbourne
Lusk
Rush

Ratoath
Portrane
Donabate
Lambay I.

Kilbride
Swords
Cloghran
Malahide

To Douglas

0 10 20 30 40 km
0 5 10 15 20 25 miles

Slyne Hd.

Ballyconneely
Ballynahinch
Toombeola
N59 (T71)
Maam Cross
L. Bofin
Oughterard

Ballyconneely Bay
L102
Roundstone
Rosscahill
Derryrush
Screeb
L102
N59

Bertraghboy Bay
Glinsk
L100
Iar Connaght
Moyrus
Glennemurrin L.
Moy
Carna
L102
Kilkieran
(T71)

Mweenish I.
Costelloe

Gorumna
Carraroe
Galway Bay

Lettermullan
Island
Inverin
Spiddle
L100
Bar
Golam Hd.

North Sound

Black Hd.
Murrough

Kitmurvy
Inishmore
Ballyvaghan

Aran
Kilronan
Sl. Elva
1109
728
Bu
N67 (T69)

Islands
Inishmaan

Inisheer
South
Sound
Lisdoonvarna
L53

Doolin Pt.
(L54)
L53A
Inchquin L.
Kilfenora
L. Bu

Cliffs of
Moher
N67
T69
L69

Hags Head
Liscannor
T69
Ennistymon

Liscannor
Bay
Lahinch
Cullenagh
T70

Inagh
L55

Miltown Malbay
L. Bur
N67 (T69)
Slieve Callan
1282
756
L52
L31

Mal Bay
Shanavogh
K

Mutton I.
38
Mullagh
Doo L.
644

Doonbeg Bay
L31
L195
Lissycasey

Donegal Pt.
Doonbeg
Creegh
Ball

Doonbeg
Cooraclare
Kilmihill
34
L54

Moore Bay
Kilkee
N68 (T41)

L51
N67 (T41)
Moyasta
L51
Kilmurry McMahon
Killadyser

Kilrush
Knock
Labasheeda

Carrigaholt
Killimer
Clonderalaw Bay
N67

Scattery I.
Loghill

Loop Head
Kilbaha
Carrig I.
Tarbert (T68)
Glin
Ballyhahill

Mouth of the Shannon
L105
L105
N69
L37
L10

Ballylongford
L9

Ballybunion
Ahafona
L106
Galey
11

Cashen
L704
L10
Athea
L10

Ballyduff
Listowel
Newcastl

Kerry Hd.
Causeway
Finuge
Feale
L37

Lixnaw
L105
Duagh
T36
20

N21

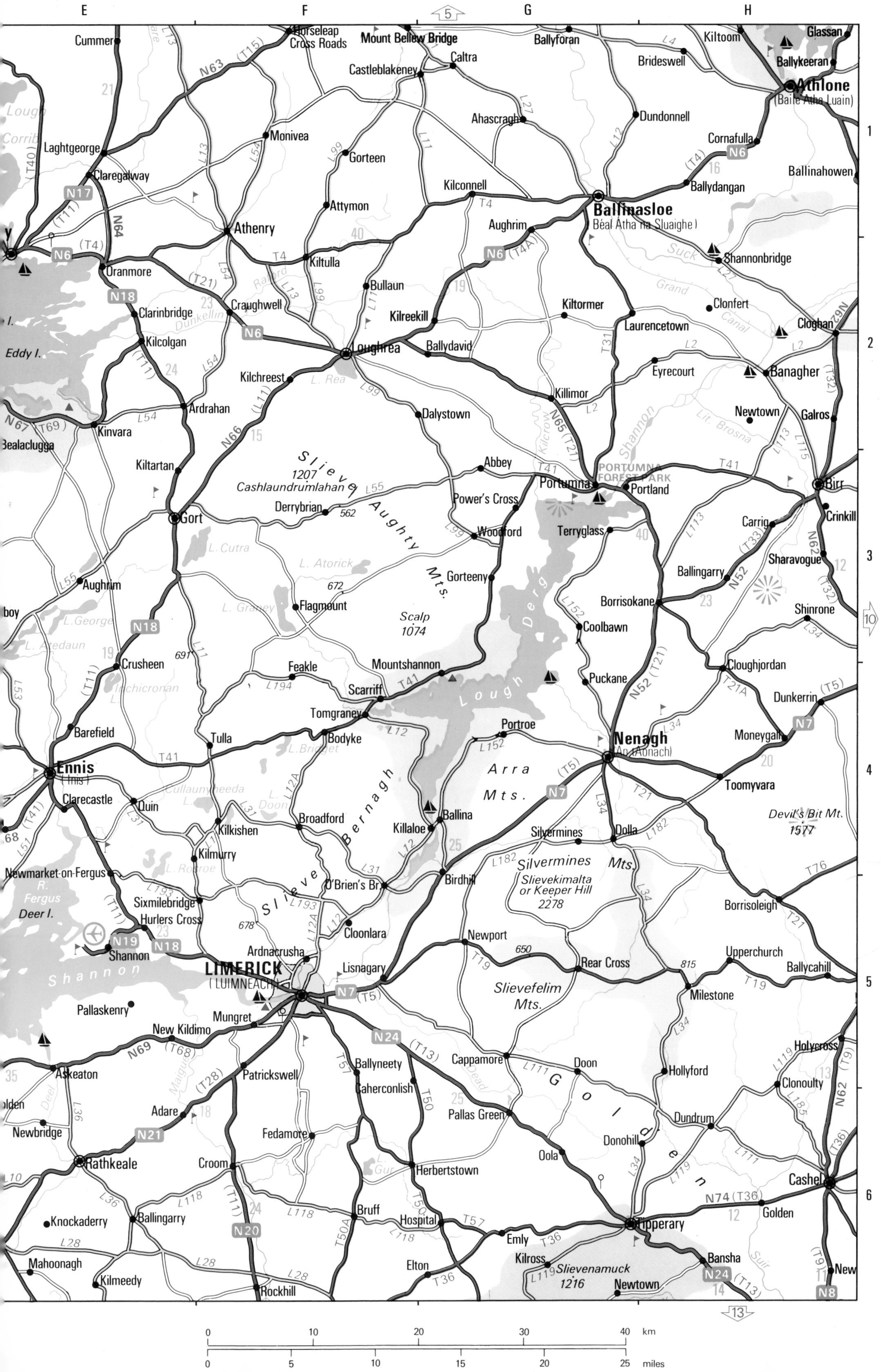

E   F   5   G   H

Cummer
Horseleap Cross Roads
Mount Bellew Bridge
Ballyforan
Kiltoom
Glassan
L4
Ballykeeran
N63 (T15)
Castleblakeney
Caltra
Brideswell
Athlone (Baile Átha Luain)
21
Monivea
Ahascragh
Dundonnell
Cornafulla (T4)
N6
Laghtgeorge
L13
Gorteen
L27
16
Ballinahowen
Claregalway
L99
L11
Kilconnell
Ballydangan
N17 (T11)
Attymon
T4
Ballinasloe (Béal Átha na Sluaighe)
N64
Athenry
40
Aughrim
Shannonbridge
N6 (T4)
Suck
N6
Oranmore
T4
Kiltulla
N6 (T4A)
Grand
Canal
L32
N18
Craughwell
Bullaun
L17
19
Kiltormer
Clonfert
Cloghan
L'n9
Clarinbridge
L13
Kilreekill
Laurencetown
Eddy I.
Kilcolgan
N6
Ballydavid
L31
L2
Cloghan
L54
Loughrea
Killimor
Eyrecourt
Banagher
(T32)
Kilchreest
L99
Kiltartan
Dalystown
Kilcron
Newtown
Galros
Ardrahan
L54
L66
15
Sli eve
Abbey
Portumna FOREST PARK
T41
L113
L115
Birr
Kinvara
1207
Cashlaundrumlahan
L55
Power's Cross
Portland
T41
L113
Crinkill
Bealaclugga
562
Derrybrian
Woodford
Terryglass
Carrig
N62
12
Gort
A ughty
Gorteeny
40
Ballingarry
N52
(T33)
Sharavogue
(T32)
L. Cutra
672
Mts.
Derg
Borrisokane
23
Shinrone
Aughrim
L. Atorick
Scalp
Coolbawn
L34
N18
Flagmount
1074
Lough
Puckane
Cloughjordan
L. Graney
Feakle
Mountshannon
T41
N52 (T21)
T21A
Dunkerrin (T5)
Crusheen
691
L194
Scarriff
Moneygall
L53
Inchicronan
Tomgraney
L12
Portroe
N7
Barefield
Tulla
Bodyke
L152
Nenagh (An tAonach)
L34
20
Ennis (Inis)
T41
L. Bridget
Arra
T5
Toomyvara
Clarecastle
L31
Broadford
Killaloe
Mts.
N7
Devil's Bit Mt.
1577
Quin
L. Doon
Ballina
Silvermines
Dolla
L182
Kilkishen
Bernagh
Birdhill
25
Silvermines
T76
Kilmurry
L31
O'Brien's Br.
L182
Slievekimalta or Keeper Hill 2278
Mts.
Borrisoleigh
Newmarket-on-Fergus
678
Cloonlara
Newport
Upperchurch
T21
R. Fergus
Deer I.
Sli eve
L193
L12A
Newport
650
Rear Cross
815
Ballycahill
T19
Shannon
N19
Ardnacrusha
N7 (T5)
Slievefelim
Milestone
N18
23
Limerick (Luimneach)
Lisnagary
Mts.
L34
Holycross
Pallaskenry
N7
Mungret
Holyford
L119
Clonoulty
New Kildimo
N24 (T13)
Cappamore
Doon
Dundrum
L185
N69 (T68)
Patrickswell
L111
Golden
L171
Askeaton
Adare
18
Caherconlish
T50
Pallas Green
Donohill
L36
N21
Fedamore
25
Oola
Cashel
Newbridge
Croom
Herbertstown
Donohill
N74 (T36)
Golden
Rathkeale
L118
Bruff
Hospital
T57
Tipperary
12
Knockaderry
Ballingarry
N20
L118
T50A
L718
Emly
T36
Bansha
N24 (T13)
Mahoonagh
L28
Elton
T36
Slievenamuck 1216
N8
Kilmeedy
Rockhill
Kilross
Newtown
14

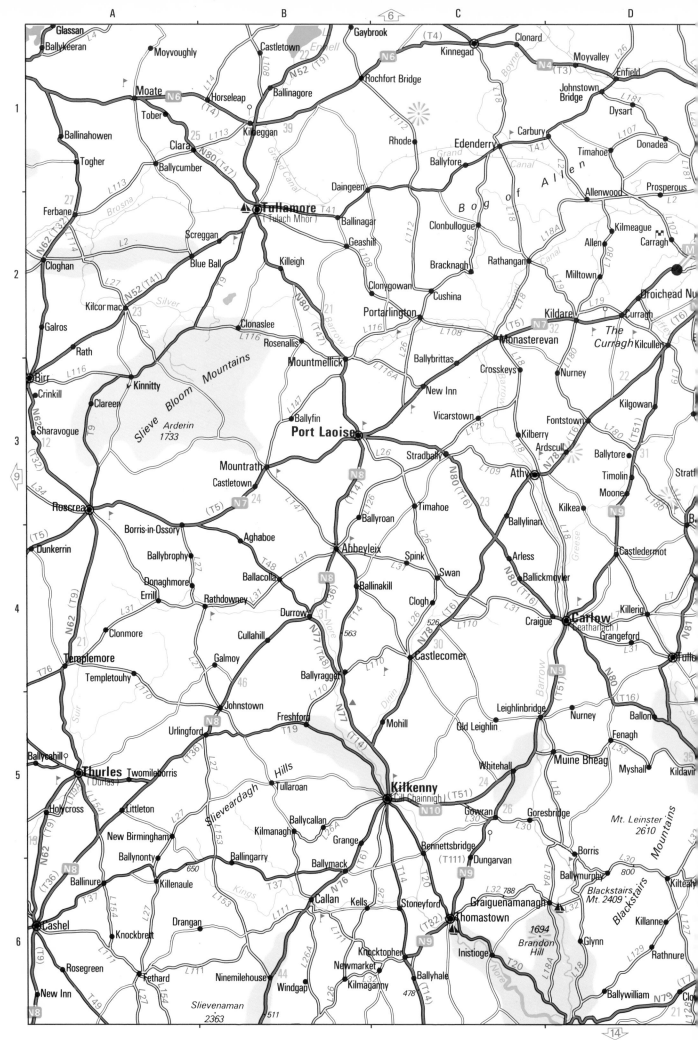

1:443 520

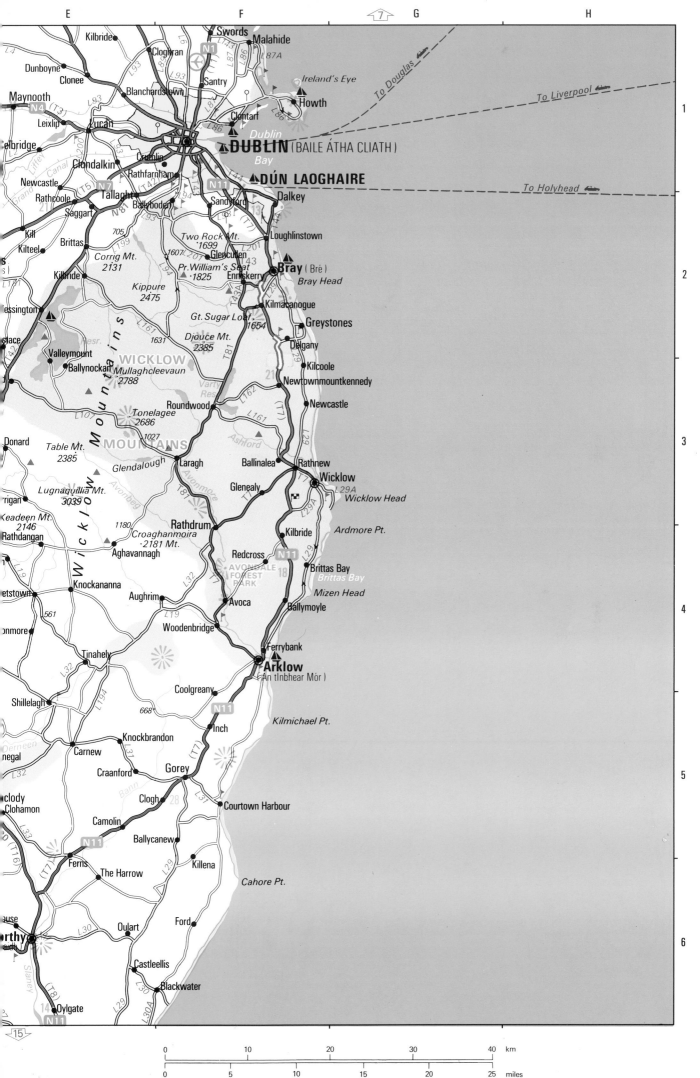

E F G H

Kilbride
Swords
Malahide
Cloghran
L87A
Dunboyne
Clonee
Santry
Ireland's Eye
To Douglas
To Liverpool
Maynooth
N4 (T3)
Blanchardstown
Howth
Leixlip
Lucan
Clontarf
Dublin
Bay
DUBLIN (BAILE ÁTHA CLIATH)
Newcastle
Clondalkin
Crumlin
Rathfarnham
DÚN LAOGHAIRE
To Holyhead
Rathcoole
Tallaght
N7 (T4)
Ballyboden
Sandyford
Dalkey
Saggart
N81
Kill
Brittas
705
Two Rock Mt.
1699
Loughlinstown
Kilteel
Kilbride
Corrig Mt.
2131
1607
Glencullen
L43
Bray (Bré)
essington
Kippure
2475
Pr. William's Seat
1825
Enniskerry
Bray Head
1631
Gt. Sugar Loaf
1654
Kilmacanogue
Valleymount
WICKLOW
Djouce Mt.
2385
Greystones
Ballynockan
Mullaghcleevaun
2788
Delgany
MOUNTAINS
Kilcoole
Tonelagee
2686
Roundwood
Newtownmountkennedy
1027
Newcastle
Donard
Table Mt.
2385
Ashford
trigan
Glendalough
Laragh
Ballinalea
Rathnew
Lugnaquillia Mt.
3039
Glenealy
Wicklow
Wicklow Head
1180
Rathdrum
Keadeen Mt.
2146
Croaghanmoira
2181 Mt.
Kilbride
Ardmore Pt.
Rathdangan
Aghavannagh
Redcross
N11
Brittas Bay
Knockananna
AVONDALE
FOREST
PARK
18
Brittas Bay
Aughrim
Avoca
Mizen Head
561
Woodenbridge
Ballymoyle
onmore
Tinahely
Ferrybank
Arklow
(An tInbhear Mór)
Coolgreany
668
N11
Kilmichael Pt.
Shillelagh
Inch
Knockbrandon
Carnew
Courtown Harbour
clody
Clohamon
Craanford
Gorey
Clogh
28
Camolin
Ballycanew
N11
Killena
Ferns
The Harrow
Cahore Pt.
Oulart
Ford
orthy
Castleellis
Blackwater
14
Oylgate
N11

0 10 20 30 40 km

0 5 10 15 20 25 miles

A B C D

1

Kerry Hd.
Causeway
Lixnaw
Ballyheige
L105
L104
Brick
Ballyheige
Bay
Kilflynn
The Seven Hogs or
Magharee Islands
Rough Pt.
Ardfert
N69 (T68)
Stack
Bay
1170
Tralee
Fenit
Spa
Tralee
N21

2

Brandon Hd.
·2509
Brandon
Brandon
Bay
Castlegregory
Castleregory
Tralee
Bay
Fenit
N21
Ballydavid Hd.
Brandon Mt.
3127
·2764
Cloghane
Stradbally
Blennerville
Smerwick
Harbour
Glashabeg
Brandon Pk.
Beenoskee
2713
Camp
T68
Derrymore
Sybil Pt.
Ballysitterach
2050
Slievanea
2026
DINGLE
Caherconree
2713
Baurtregaum
2796
Slieve Mish Mountains
N70 (T66)
Ballyferriter
Milltown
Dingle T68
Annascaul
Inch
Castlemaine
Maine
L103
Inishtooskert
Dunquin
Mt.Eagle
1695
Ventry
Lispole
Castlemaine
Harbour
Milltown
L103

3

Gt. Blasket I.
Slea Hd.
Blasket Sound
Killorglin
T67
Tearaght I.
Cromane
Laune
Inishvickillane
Dingle Bay
Glenbeigh
1621
Seefin
Caragh
L.
42
Beaufort
Darby's Br.
Beenmore
·2199
Gap of
Dunloe
Knocknadober
2267
N70 (T66)
Coomacarrea
2541
Carrauntoohil
3414
795
Purple M
2739
Doulus Hd.
404
Colly
2258
Macgillicuddy's Reeks
Cahersiveen
IVERAGH
Lissatinning Br.
667
Ballaghbeama
Gap
852
Boughil
2065
Peakeen
1825
N71
Valencia I.
Knightstown
Foilclogh
1639
Derriana
L.
The Pocket
2468
306
Bray Hd.
Aghnager Br.
Inny
Cloonaghlin
L.
Knocknagullion
1360
Templenoe
Portmagee
Saliahig
N70 (T66)

4

St. Finan's
Bay
Ballinskelligs
Waterville
Ballybrack
L.Currane
Sneem
50
Parknasilla
Cloonee
Loughs
N71
Bolus Hd.
Mullaghbeg
1678
1785
Eagles Hill
Kenmare
River
Caha
2003
993
Ballinskelligs Bay
·814
Caherdaniel
Lauragh
Caha Mts.
BEARA
Glengarriff
DERRYNANE
NAT.
HIST. PK.
Collorus
Glenmore
L.
Scariff I.
Lamb's
Hd.
Ardgroom
L62
Glenbeg
L.
Hungry Hill
2251
Sugarloaf Mt.
1887
Adrigole
L61
Wh
Skellig Rock
Cod's Hd.
Eyeries
Slieve Mish Mts.
Castletown Bere
Bantry

5

Allihies
L61
Bear I.
Bay
Gera
Ballydonegan
L61A
Dursey Island
Dursey Hd.
Seefin
1136
Ahakista
L
Muntervary or
Sheep's Head
Kilcrohane
Dunmanus
Bay
Mt.
1.
Schu
Toormore
L57
·1034
Knocknamaddree
Goleen
L56
Three Castle Hd.
Crookhaven

6

Mizen Hd.
Cape Cle
Fastnet Rock

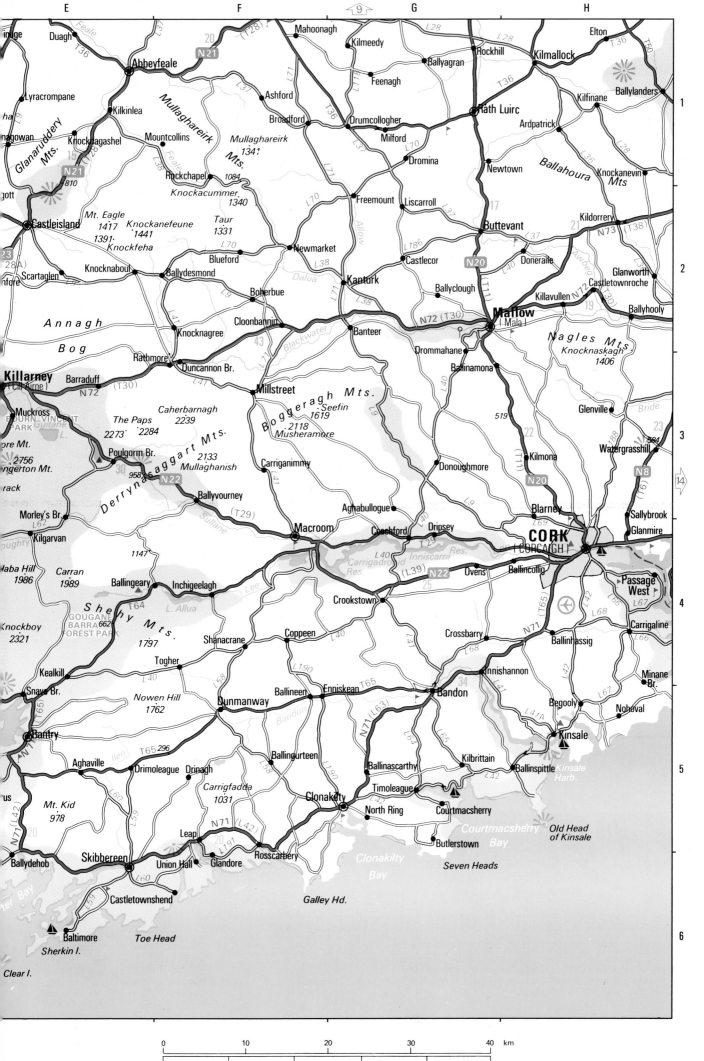

Duagh
Mahoonagh
Kilmeedy
Elton
Lyracrompane
Kilmallock
Abbeyfeale
Rockhill
Ballylanders
Mullaghareirk
Ballyagran
Kilinlea
Ashford
Feenagh
Kilfinane
Mountcollins
Broadford
Ráth Luirc
Knocknagashel
Drumcollogher
Ardpatrick
Mullaghareirk
Mts.
1341
Milford
Newtown
Knockanevin
Rockchapel
1084
Dromina
Ballahoura
Mts
Knockacummer
1340
Freemount
Liscarroll
Kildorrery
Mt. Eagle
1417
1391
Knockanefeune
1441
Taur
1331
Buttevant
N73 (T38)
Castleisland
Newmarket
Castlecor
Doneraile
Glanworth
Knockfeha
N20
Castletownroche
Blueford
Dalua
Killavullen
Scartaglen
Knocknaboul
Ballydesmond
Kanturk
Ballyhooly
Annagh
Bog
Boherbue
Ballyclough
Mallow
Killarney
Knocknagree
Cloonbannin
Banteer
(Mala)
Nagles Mts
Barraduff
Rathmore
Duncannon Br.
Drommahane
Knocknaskagh
1406
Muckross
Millstreet
Ballinamona
Glenville
The Paps
Caherbarnagh
2239
Boggeragh Mts.
Seefin
1619
Poulgorm Br.
2133
Mullaghanish
Musheramore
2118
Kilmona
Watergrasshill
N8
Ballyvourney
Carriganimmy
Donoughmore
Morley's Br.
Aghabullogue
Blarney
Sallybrook
Macroom
Coachford
Dripsey
Glanmire
Kilgarvan
Carran
1989
Ballingeary
Inchigeelagh
Ovens
Ballincollig
CORK
(CORCAIGH)
Passage
West
Knockboy
2321
Shehy Mts.
Crookstown
Crossbarry
Carrigaline
Shanacrane
Coppeen
Togher
Ballineen
Enniskean
Bandon
Ballinhassig
Minane
Br.
Snave Br.
Nowen Hill
1762
Dunmanway
Begooly
Nohoval
Bantry
Aghaville
Kinsale
Kilbrittain
Drimoleague
Drinagh
Ballingurteen
Ballinascarthy
Ballinspittle
Carrigfadda
1031
Clonakilty
Timoleague
Kinsale
Harb.
Mt. Kid
978
North Ring
Courtmacsherry
Old Head
of Kinsale
Leap
Butlerstown
Skibbereen
Union Hall
Glandore
Rosscarbery
Courtmacsherry
Bay
Castletownshend
Galley Hd.
Clonakilty
Bay
Seven Heads
Baltimore
Toe Head
Sherkin I.
Clear I.

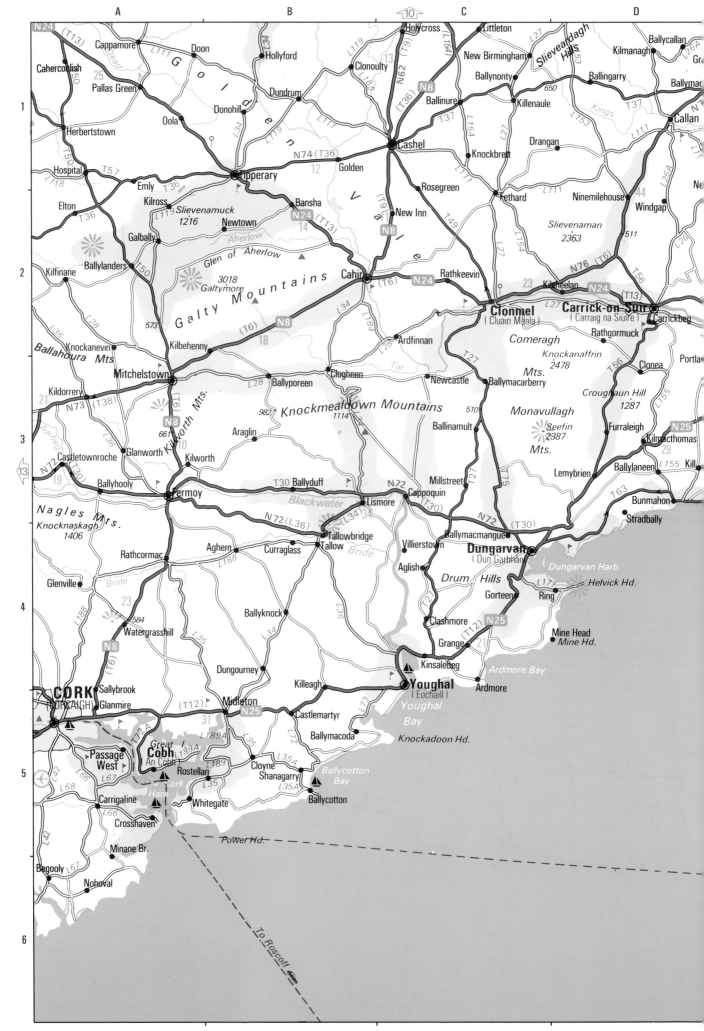

1:443 520

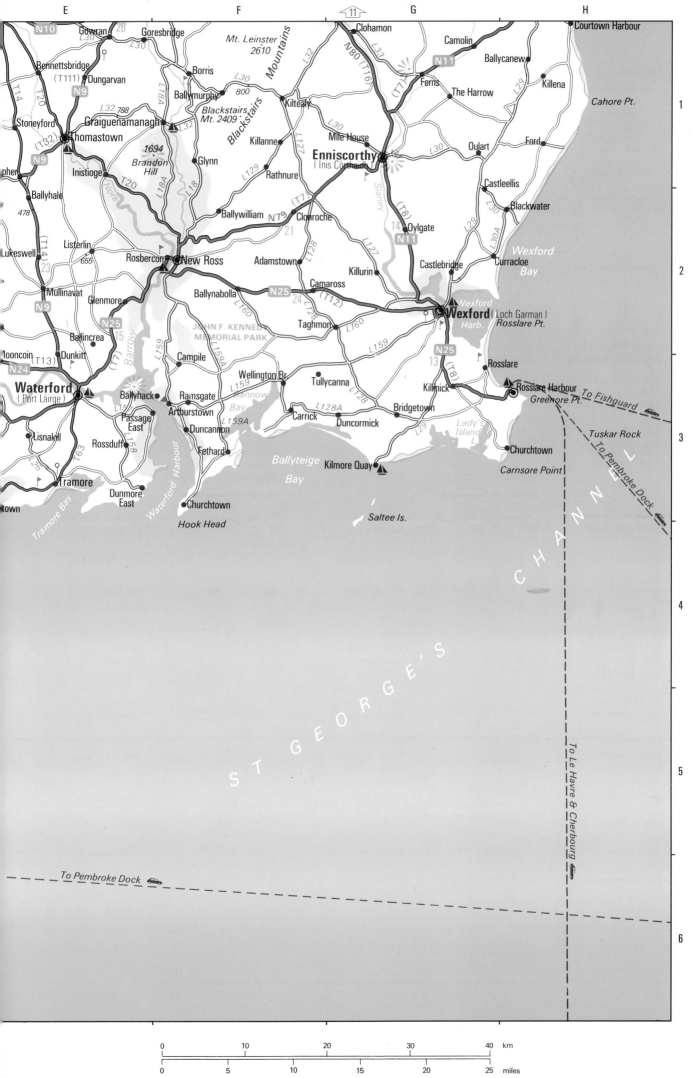

N10
Gowran
Goresbridge
Clohamon
Camolin
Courtown Harbour
L30
Mt. Leinster 2610
N80 (T16)
Ballycanew
N11
Bennettsbridge
(T111)
Dungarvan
Borris
Ferns
The Harrow
Killena
L29
Cahore Pt.
N9
Ballymurphy
800
Kiltealy
L30
Stoneyford
Graiguenamanagh
Blackstairs Mt. 2409
Killanne
Mile House
Oulart
Ford
Thomastown
L32
Glynn
L127
Enniscorthy
(Inis Córthaidh)
L30
Castleellis
1694 Brandon Hill
Rathnure
L129
Blackwater
Inistioge
Oylgate
L30A
N9
Ballyhale
Ballywilliam
N79
Clonroche
14
N11
Wexford Bay
478
Slaney
Curracloe
Lukeswell
Listerlin
Rosbercon
New Ross
Adamstown
Killurin
Castlebridge
Curracloe
655
Camaross
Wexford
(Loch Garman)
Rosslare Pt.
Glenmore
Ballynabolla
24 (T12)
L128
Wexford
Harb.
Ballincrea
JOHN F. KENNEDY MEMORIAL PARK
Taghmon
L160
N25
Rosslare
looncoin
(T13)
Dunkitt
Campile
L159
Wellington Br
Tullycanna
L128
Killinick
13 (T8)
Rosslare Harbour
Greenore Pt.
To Fishguard
Waterford
(Port Láirge)
Ballyhack
Ramsgate
Carrick
L128A
Duncormick
Bridgetown
Tuskar Rock
Lisnakill
Arthurstown
Duncannon
Lady's Island L.
Churchtown
To Pembroke Dock
Rossduff
Fethard
Carnsore Point
Tramore
Dunmore East
Churchtown
Ballyteige Bay
Kilmore Quay
Saltee Is.
Hook Head

ST GEORGE'S CHANNEL

To Le Havre & Cherbourg

To Pembroke Dock

| 0 | 10 | 20 | 30 | 40 | km |

| 0 | 5 | 10 | 15 | 20 | 25 | miles |

NORTHERN IRELAND

Roads		Routes		Straßen
motorway with interchange and service area		autoroute avec accès, et aire de service		Autobahn mit Anschlußstelle und Versorgungsstätte
motorway under construction		autoroute en construction		Autobahn im Bau
primary route	A10	grand itinéraire	A10	Fernstraße
dual carriageway		chaussées séparées		Getrennte Fahrbahnen
main 'A' road	A21	route principale "A"	A21	Hauptstraße 'A'
'B' road	B125	route "B"	B125	Straße 'B'
unclassified road		autre route		Sonstige Straße

REPUBLIC OF IRELAND

Roads		Routes		Straßen
national primary route	N9 (T5)	grand itinéraire	N9 (T5)	Fernstraße
national secondary route	N19 (T7)	nationale ordinaire	N19 (T7)	Verbindungsstraße
trunk road	T14	autre route importante	T14	Fernverkehrstaße
link road	L107	route secondaire	L107	Nebenstraße
unclassified road		autre route		Sonstige Straße
distance in miles	20 ② ③ ④	distance (miles)	20 ② ③ ④	Entfernung (miles)
gradient; viewpoint road height (feet)	31 1543	rampe; point de vue; altitude (feet)	31 1543	Steigung; Aussichtspunkt; Höhe (feet)
frontier crossing point		passage frontalier		Grenzübergang
car ferry		bac pour autos		Autofähre
airport		aéroport		Flughafen
golf course; race course; motor racing circuit		terrain de golf; hippodrome; autodrome		Golfplatz Rennbahn Rennstrecke
sailing centre; sandy beach		centre de voile; plage sablonneuse		Segelhafen Strand
scenic area; place of popular interest		beau paysage; centre d'intérêt touristique		Schöne Landschaft Sehenswürdigkeit
spot height (feet)	Errigal · 2466	altitude (feet)	Errigal · 2466	Höhe (feet)
built-up area		terrain bâti		Bebaute Fläche
youth hostel	▲	auberge de jeunesse	▲	Jugendherberge
international boundary		frontière		Staatsgrenze

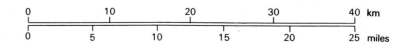